CERES™
Celestial Legend
Volume 13: Ten'nyo

STORY & ART BY YUU WATASE

Editor's Note: At the author's request, the spelling of Ms. Watase's first name has been changed from "Yû," as it has appeared on previous VIZ publications, to "Yuu."

English Adaptation/Gary Leach

Translation/Lillian Olsen
Touch–Up Art & Lettering/Melanie Lewis
Cover & Graphic Design/Hidemi Sahara
Editor/Shaenon K. Garrity
Supervising Editor/Frances E. Wall

Managing Editor/Annette Roman
Director of Production/Noboru Watanabe
Vice President of Publishing/Alvin Lu
Sr. Director of Acquisitions/Rika Inouye
Vice President of Sales & Marketing/Liza Coppola
Publisher/Hyoe Narita

Printed in Canada

Published by VIZ Media, LLC
P.O. Box 77010 • San Francisco CA 94107

Shôjo Edition

10 9 8 7 6 5 4 3 2 1

First printing, October 2005

www.viz.com
store.viz.com

VIZ GRAPHIC NOVEL

Ceres

Celestial Legend

Vol. 13: Ten'nyo

Story and Art by
Yuu Watase

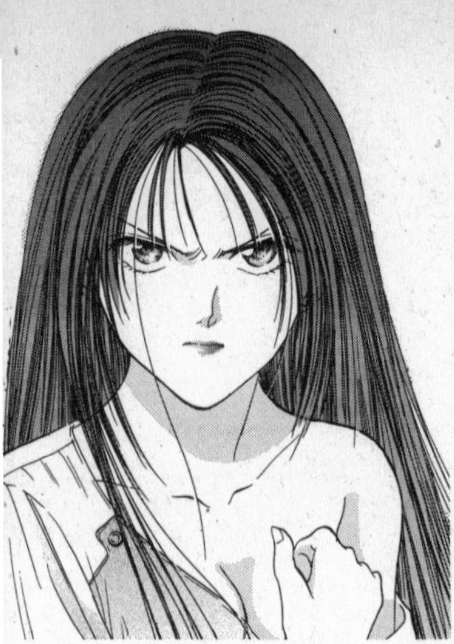

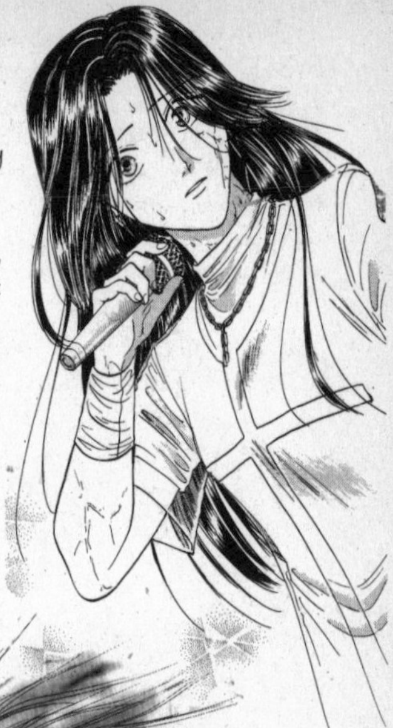

SHURO: A woman who once passed as a man (as part of the wildly popular Japanese pop duo GeSANG), Shuro is yet another conflicted celestial, ambiguous not only about her powers, but also her sexuality.

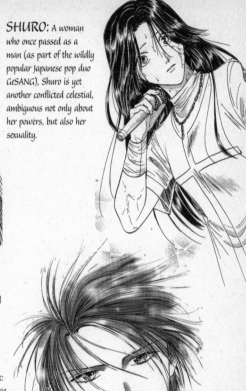

CERES: A *ten'nyo* or "celestial being" prevented from returning to the heavens after her *hagoromo* or "celestial robes" were stolen, Ceres bears little love for the descendants born of her union with a mortal male—the being known as "the Progenitor."

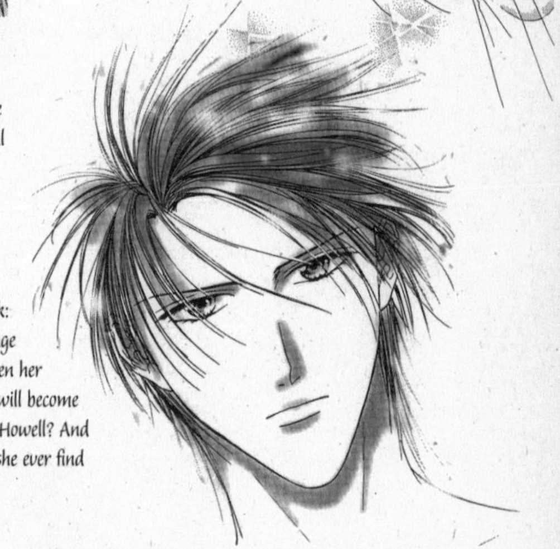

TÔYA: Tôya had finally recovered his memory and found happiness with Aya when tragedy struck: he was killed during a rescue mission into the Mikage compound. Now Aya's grief over his death has driven her to the most desperate measures imaginable. What will become of Tôya's body, thrown into the sea by a repentant Howell? And now that Aya knows of Tôya's strange origin, will she ever find out what it *means*?

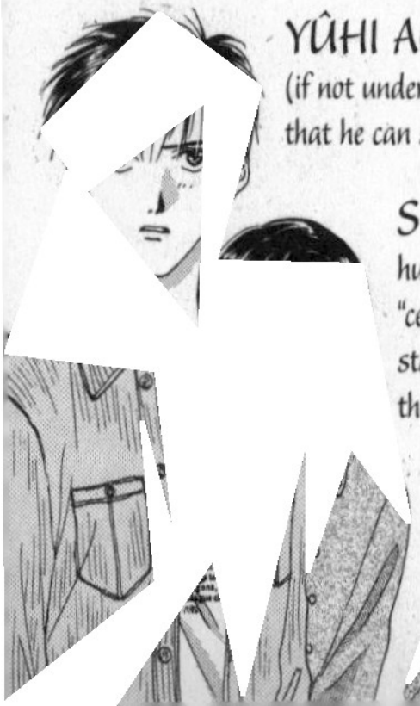

YÛHI AOGIRI: Once it hurt just to look at her, but gradually Yûhi is learning to accept (if not understand) the love Aya bears for his rival, Tôya. Another benefit? The knowledge that he can still care for and love—without necessarily being *in* love with—someone.

SUZUMI AOGIRI: Current head of the Aogiri household (after her husband, Yûhi's half-brother, passed away) and possessor of some *ten'nyo* or "celestial" blood herself. A "big sister" figure to both Yûhi and to Aya, from the start Suzumi's protection and support has meant a great deal...maybe even the difference between Aya's life and death.

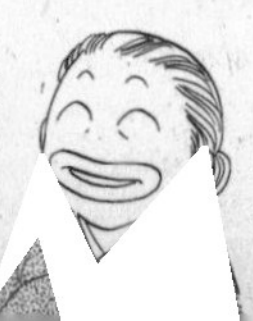

MRS. Q (ODA-KYÛ): Eccentric yet loyal-to-a-fault servant (?) to the Aogiri household...and not without a few secret powers of her own.

AYA MIKAGE: A direct descendant of Ceres, Aya is the human vessel of the celestial maiden, able to communicate with Ceres and call her forth...but unable, it seems, to use her celestial powers to protect those she loves. Pregnant and consumed with grief over the loss of Tôya and Chidori, Aya has decided to stop the slaughter and cruelty of the Mikages in the only way she knows: by surrendering and joining the mysterious C-Project.

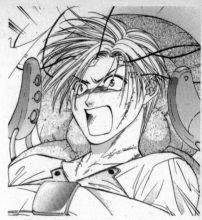

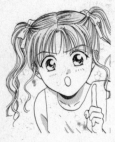

AKI MIKAGE: Aya's twin brother and host to (or hostage of, more like) the angry, Ceres-obsessed "Progenitor." Although Aya still believes that, somewhere deep inside, her brother still exists, the longer he is exposed to the insane love of the Progenitor for Ceres (who of course inhabits Aya), the less the real Aki remains.

CHIDORI KURUMA: A childlike teenager with a hopeless crush on Yûhi, Chidori possessed celestial DNA, which gave her some degree of celestial power...and made her a target of the Mikages. Kidnapped and imprisoned in the C-Project laboratories, Chidori was surgically harvested for her genetic material...then killed while trying to escape.

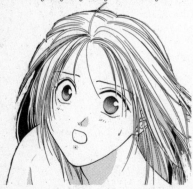

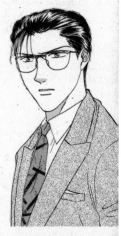

HOWELL: A brilliant research scientist working in the Mikage labs and directly accountable to Kagami himself, Alexander Howell ("Alec") spends what little time he doesn't spend in the lab watching anime, playing video games, collecting action figures...a real *otaku*, in other words.

KAGAMI MIKAGE: Scion of the family empire and founder of the nefarious "C-Project." His passion mistaken by Aki/The Progenitor as lust for Ceres, Kagami's true motive for searching for Ceres' *hagoromo* is slowly being revealed.

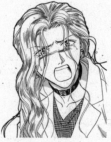

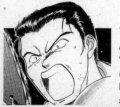

DR. KUROZUKA: A gruff-talking country doctor who's also endlessly kind, "Kurozuka-*sensei*" is there with open arms to welcome both Tôya and Aya into their new lives as a self-supporting couple...or *mostly* self-supporting, anyway.

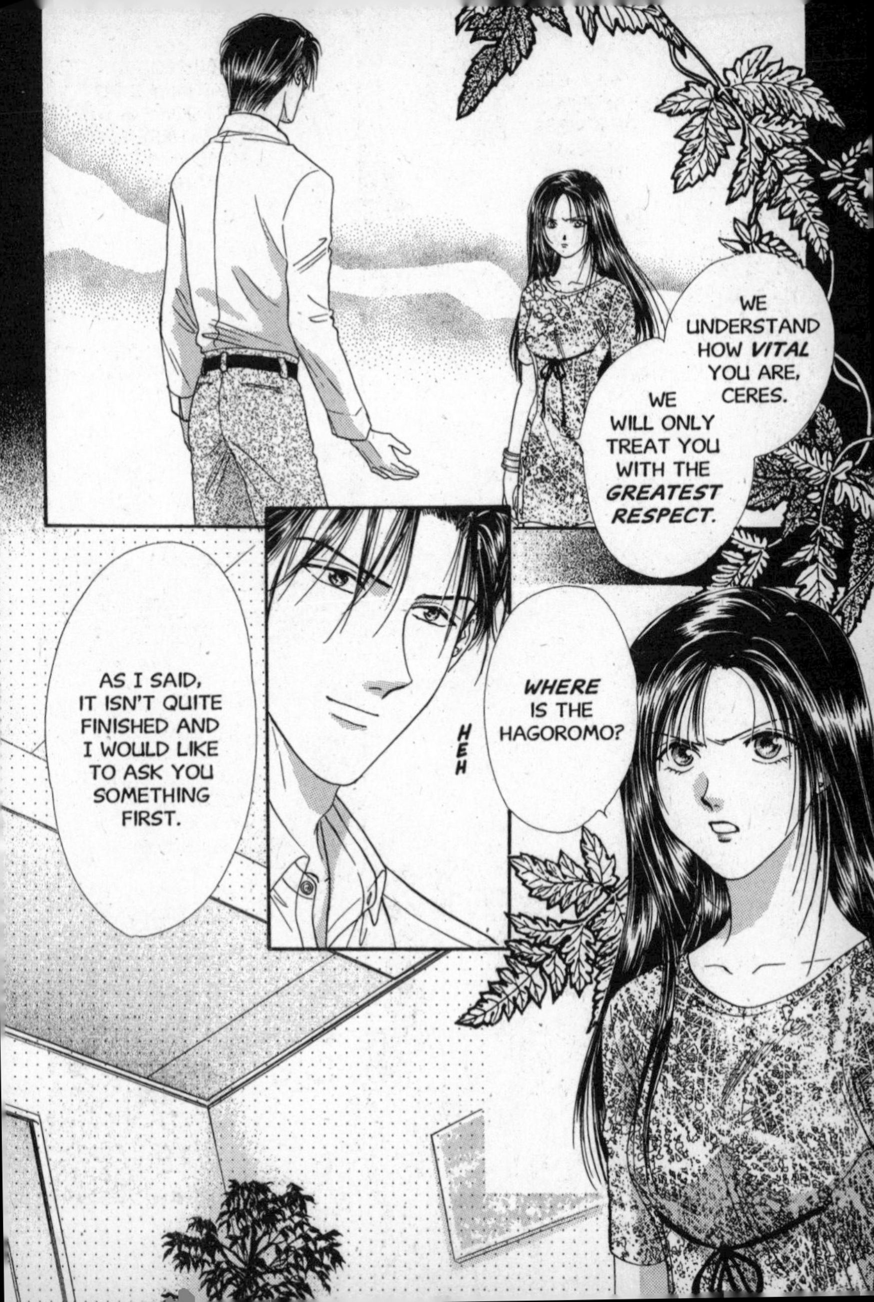
WE UNDERSTAND HOW *VITAL* YOU ARE, CERES.
WE WILL ONLY TREAT YOU WITH THE *GREATEST RESPECT.*
WHERE IS THE HAGOROMO?
HEH
AS I SAID, IT ISN'T QUITE FINISHED AND I WOULD LIKE TO ASK YOU SOMETHING FIRST.

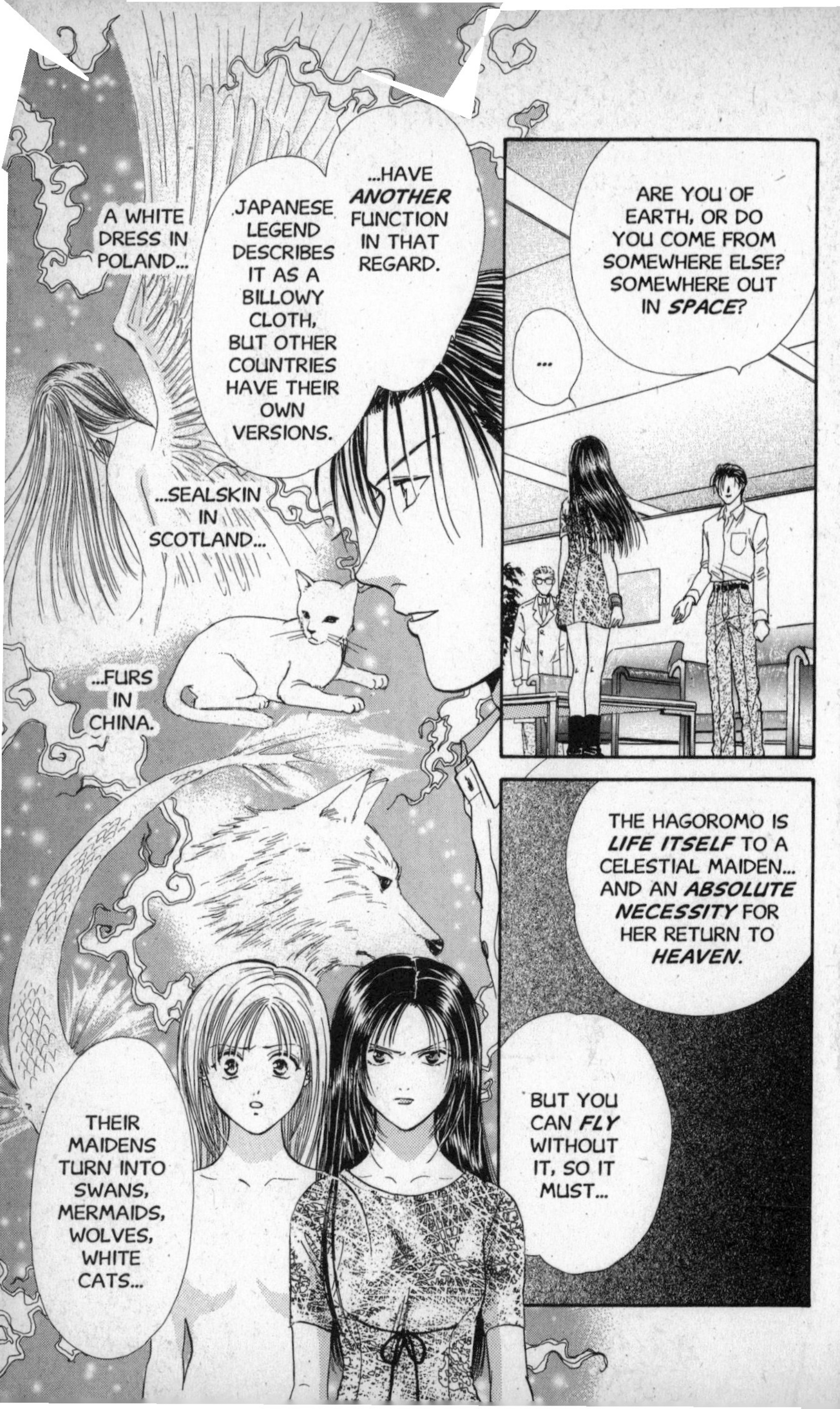
ARE YOU OF EARTH, OR DO YOU COME FROM SOMEWHERE ELSE? SOMEWHERE OUT IN *SPACE*?
...
THE HAGOROMO IS *LIFE ITSELF* TO A CELESTIAL MAIDEN... AND AN *ABSOLUTE NECESSITY* FOR HER RETURN TO *HEAVEN*.
BUT YOU CAN *FLY* WITHOUT IT, SO IT MUST...
...HAVE *ANOTHER* FUNCTION IN THAT REGARD.
JAPANESE LEGEND DESCRIBES IT AS A BILLOWY CLOTH, BUT OTHER COUNTRIES HAVE THEIR OWN VERSIONS.
A WHITE DRESS IN POLAND...
...SEALSKIN IN SCOTLAND...
...FURS IN CHINA.
THEIR MAIDENS TURN INTO SWANS, MERMAIDS, WOLVES, WHITE CATS...

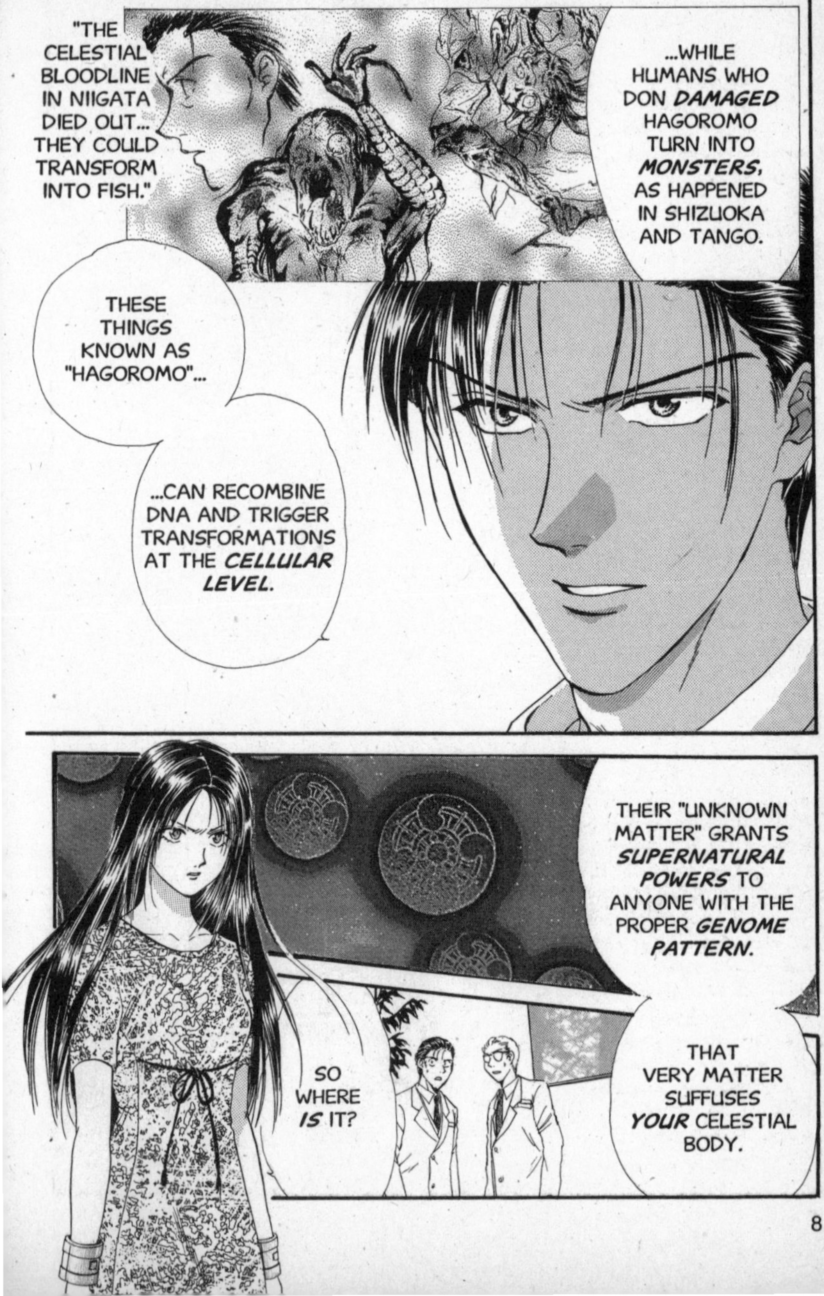
...WHILE HUMANS WHO DON *DAMAGED* HAGOROMO TURN INTO *MONSTERS,* AS HAPPENED IN SHIZUOKA AND TANGO.
"THE CELESTIAL BLOODLINE IN NIIGATA DIED OUT... THEY COULD TRANSFORM INTO FISH."
THESE THINGS KNOWN AS "HAGOROMO"...
...CAN RECOMBINE DNA AND TRIGGER TRANSFORMATIONS AT THE *CELLULAR LEVEL.*
THEIR "UNKNOWN MATTER" GRANTS *SUPERNATURAL POWERS* TO ANYONE WITH THE PROPER *GENOME PATTERN.*
THAT VERY MATTER SUFFUSES *YOUR* CELESTIAL BODY.
SO WHERE *IS* IT?

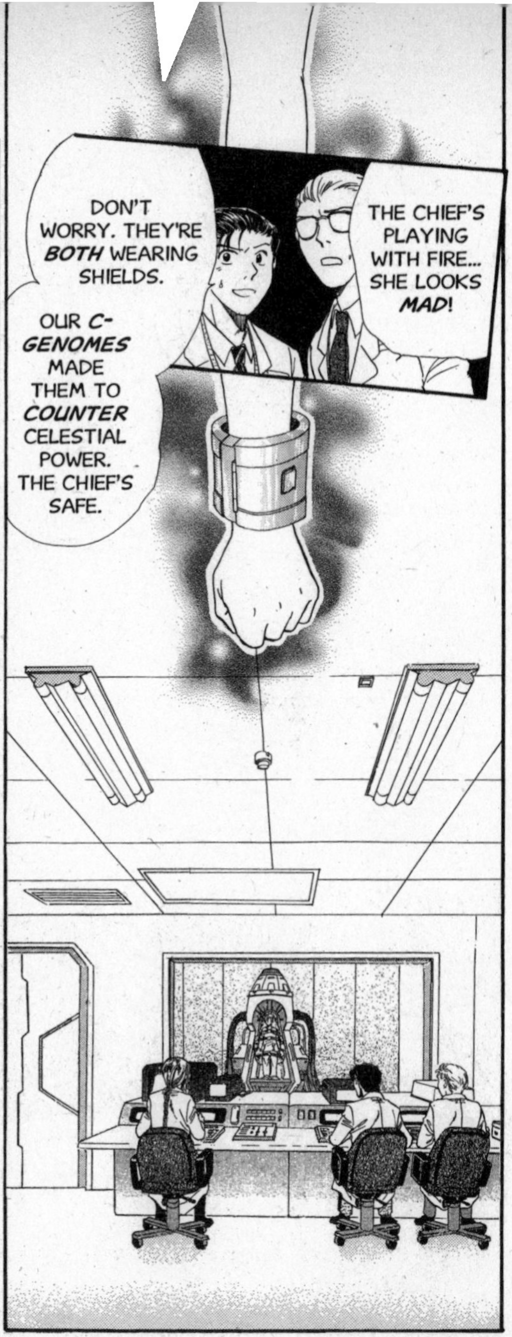
THE CHIEF'S PLAYING WITH FIRE... SHE LOOKS *MAD*!
DON'T WORRY. THEY'RE *BOTH* WEARING SHIELDS.
OUR *C-GENOMES* MADE THEM TO *COUNTER* CELESTIAL POWER. THE CHIEF'S SAFE.

Hello, hello, hello, hello x100! Watase here!

We're approaching the climax of **Ceres**!! I'm amazed I've come this far. ◡̈ I hope you can stick around a little longer.

The story is getting a bit difficult (with all the biological stuff)...though I guess it's always been pretty complicated. Sorry about that. Some of my friends have told me the plot reads like a manga for adults. Well, the idea was to approach that type of material from a shojo manga perspective...but I guess it didn't necessarily have to run in the anthology "Shojo Comics." ◡̈

One editor pointed out that my readers tend to be very smart (this includes kids who can express mature opinions). ◡̈ So I'm sure the readers who have come this far will be able to keep up! (Hopefully...) I'm amazed that kids in grade school read this...

Okay, I'd planned the cover art for this volume long ago, so I was all smiles when I got to draw it. ♡ Speaking of wings, I'm finally playing Final Fantasy VIII right now. ◡̈ I'd bought it when it came out and left it unopened, but my assistants and readers kept telling me that the relationship between Squall and Rinoa develops like Aya's relationship with Tōya. That convinced me to start it, six months later. I named Squall "Tōya," of course, and Rinoa was "Aya." I kept laughing my head off. ◡̈

This is hard to write... I'll get a different pen.

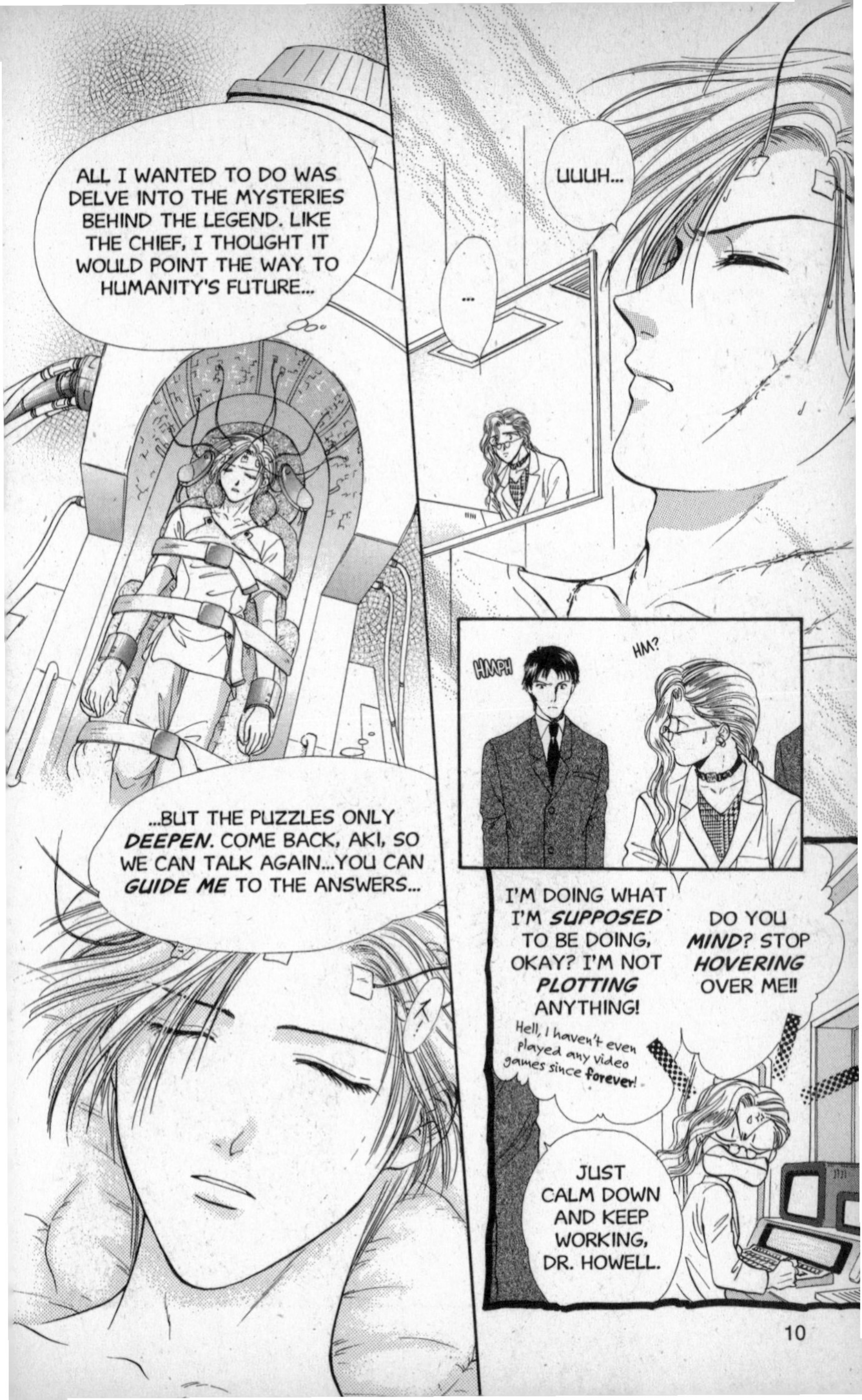
UUUH...
...
HM?
HMPH
DO YOU *MIND*? STOP *HOVERING* OVER ME!!
I'M DOING WHAT I'M *SUPPOSED* TO BE DOING, OKAY? I'M NOT *PLOTTING* ANYTHING!
Hell, I haven't even played any video games since **forever**!
JUST CALM DOWN AND KEEP WORKING, DR. HOWELL.
ALL I WANTED TO DO WAS DELVE INTO THE MYSTERIES BEHIND THE LEGEND. LIKE THE CHIEF, I THOUGHT IT WOULD POINT THE WAY TO HUMANITY'S FUTURE...
...BUT THE PUZZLES ONLY *DEEPEN*. COME BACK, AKI, SO WE CAN TALK AGAIN...YOU CAN *GUIDE ME* TO THE ANSWERS...

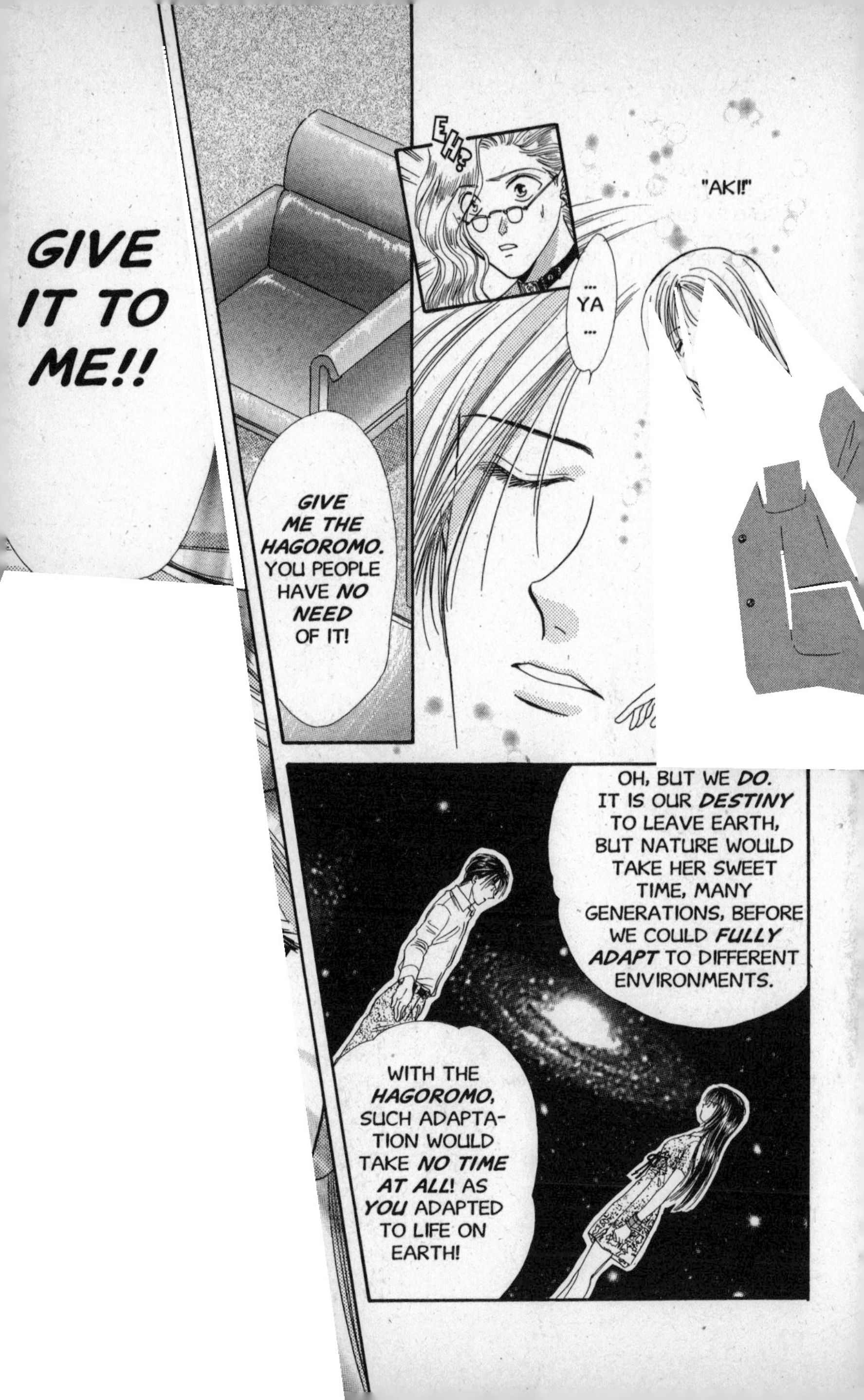
"AKI!"
EH?
... YA ...
GIVE ME THE HAGOROMO. YOU PEOPLE HAVE NO NEED OF IT!
OH, BUT WE DO. IT IS OUR DESTINY TO LEAVE EARTH, BUT NATURE WOULD TAKE HER SWEET TIME, MANY GENERATIONS, BEFORE WE COULD FULLY ADAPT TO DIFFERENT ENVIRONMENTS.
WITH THE HAGOROMO, SUCH ADAPTATION WOULD TAKE NO TIME AT ALL! AS YOU ADAPTED TO LIFE ON EARTH!
GIVE IT TO ME!!

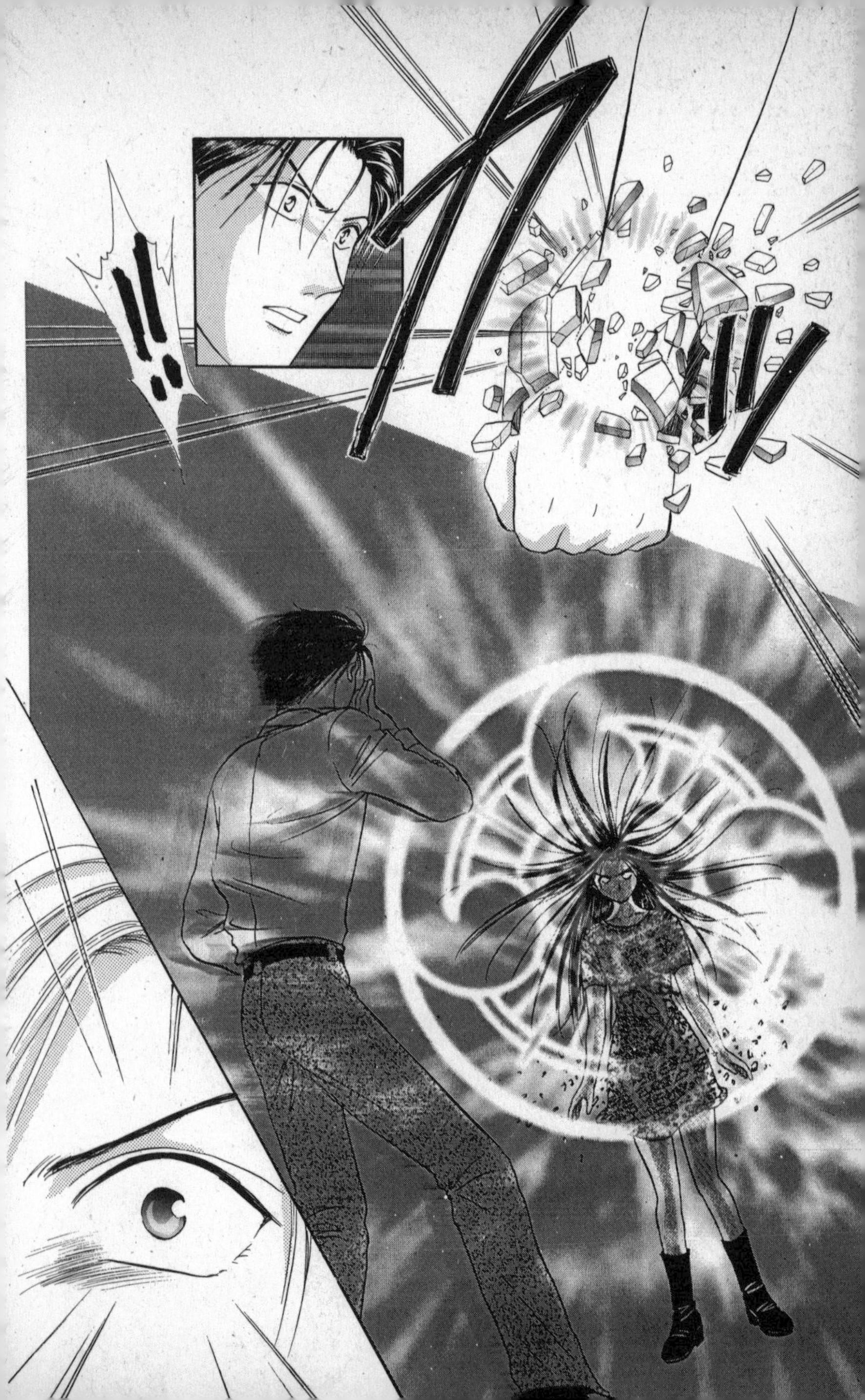
!!

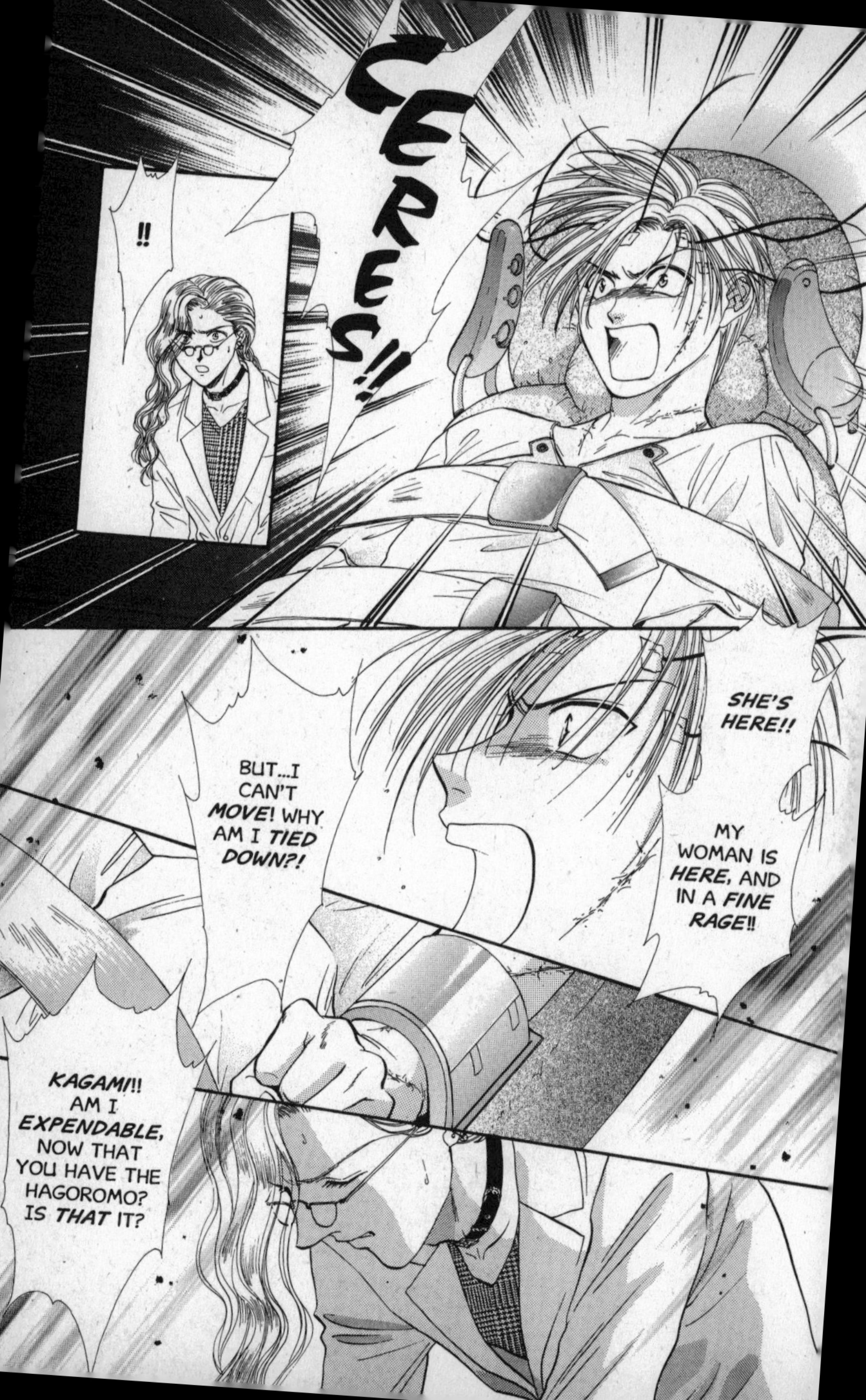
CERES!!
!!
SHE'S HERE!!
MY WOMAN IS HERE, AND IN A FINE RAGE!!
BUT...I CAN'T MOVE! WHY AM I TIED DOWN?!
KAGAMI!! AM I EXPENDABLE, NOW THAT YOU HAVE THE HAGOROMO? IS THAT IT?

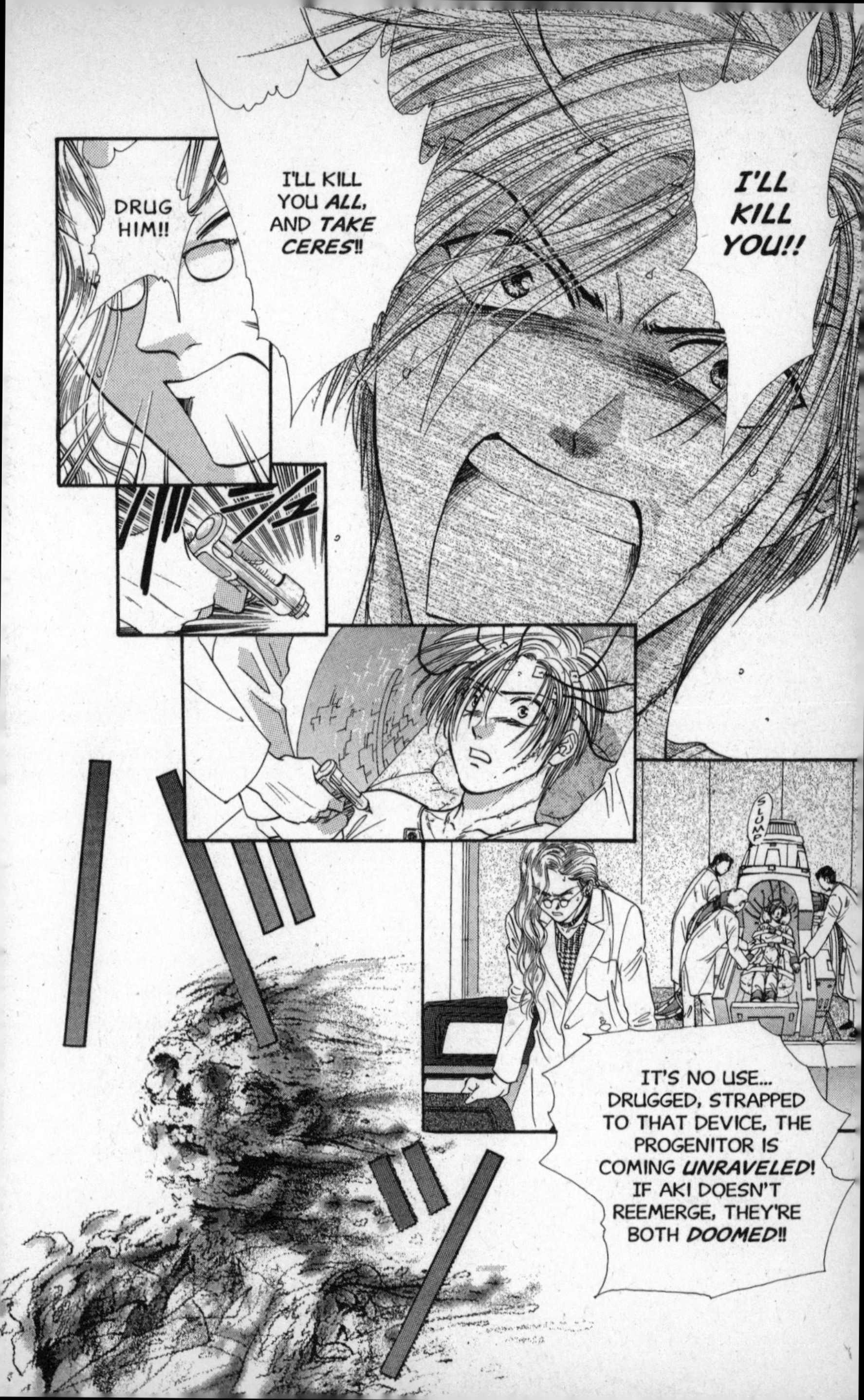
I'LL KILL YOU!!
I'LL KILL YOU ALL, AND TAKE CERES!!
DRUG HIM!!
SLUMP
IT'S NO USE... DRUGGED, STRAPPED TO THAT DEVICE, THE PROGENITOR IS COMING UNRAVELED! IF AKI DOESN'T REEMERGE, THEY'RE BOTH DOOMED!!

Ceres: 13

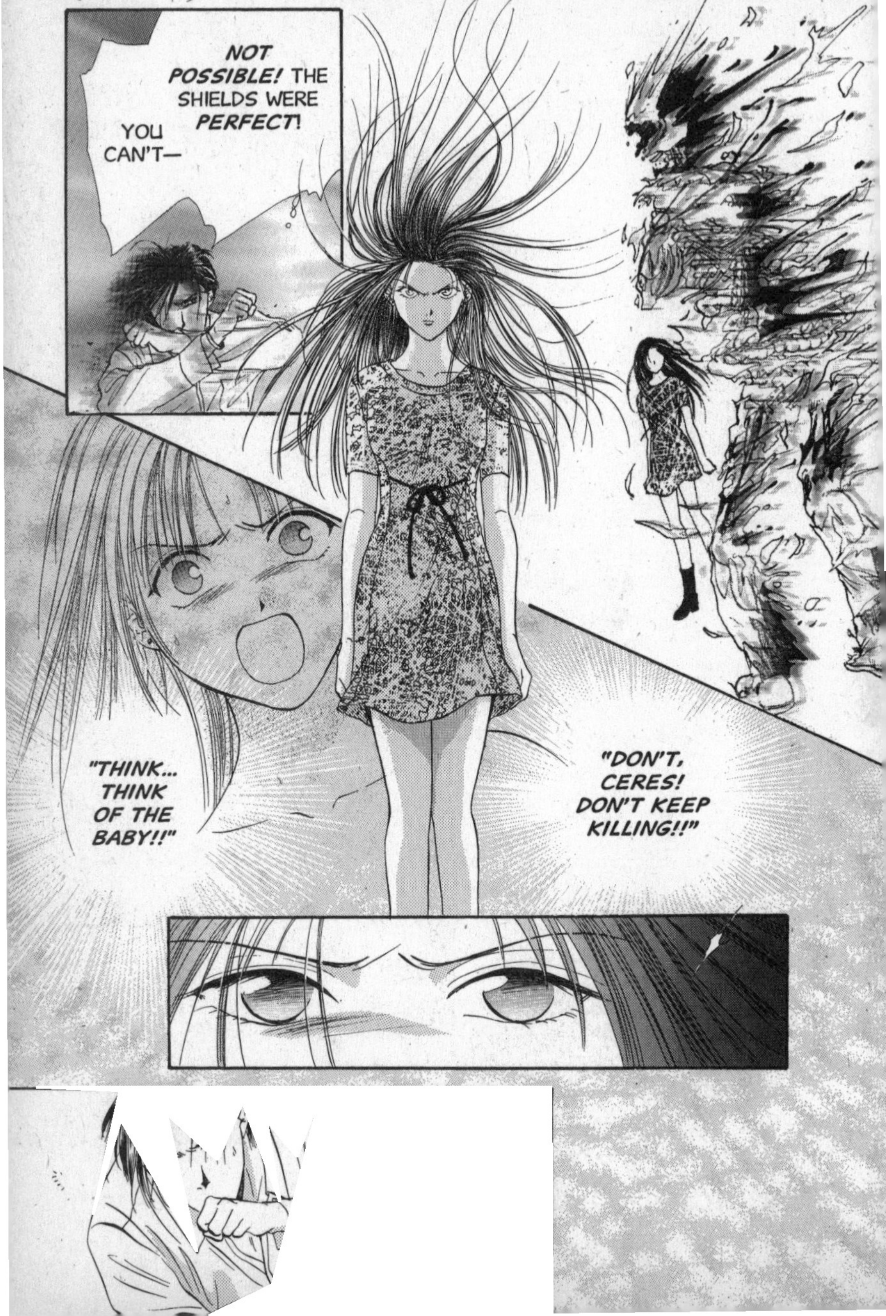
NOT POSSIBLE! THE SHIELDS WERE PERFECT!
YOU CAN'T—
"DON'T, CERES! DON'T KEEP KILLING!!"
"THINK... THINK OF THE BABY!!"

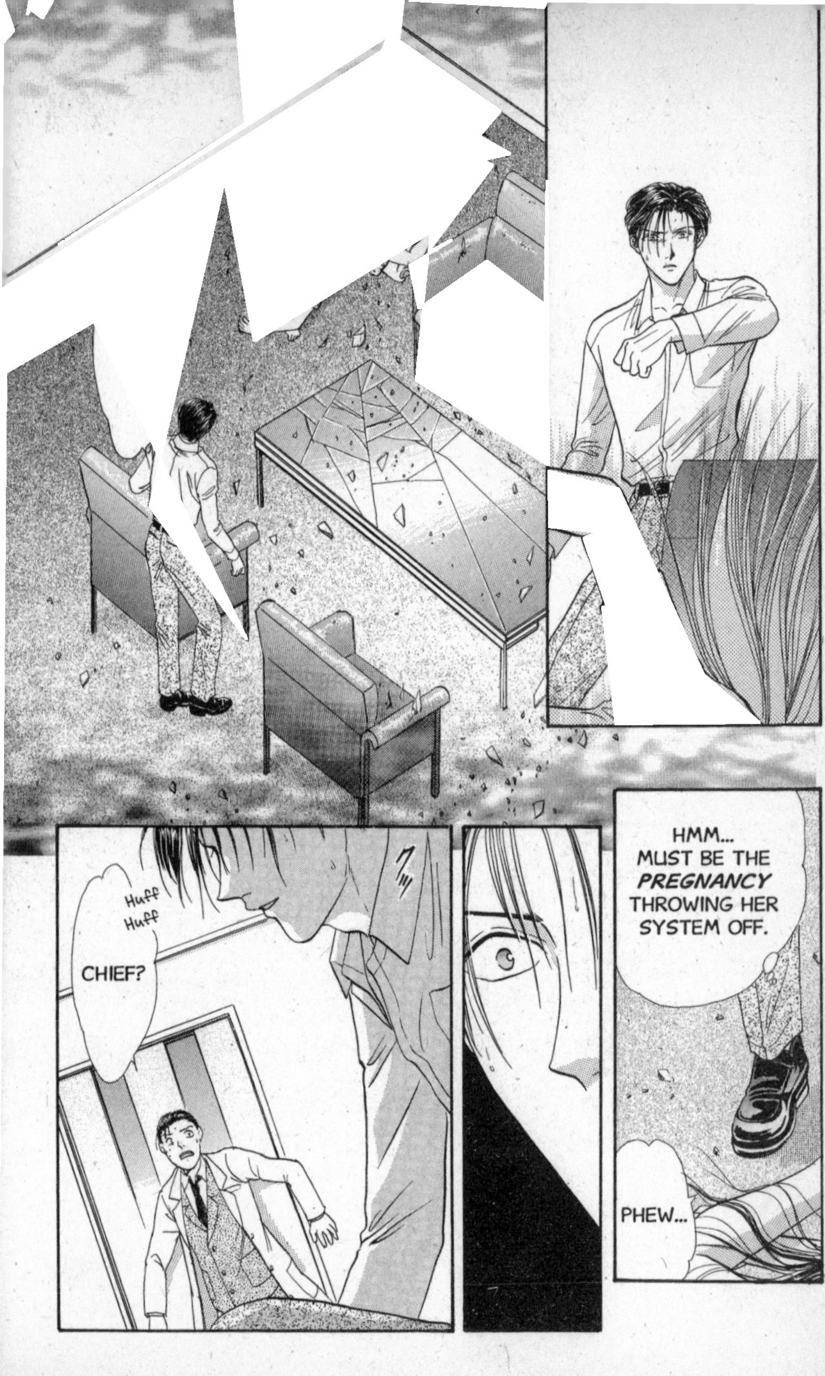
HMM... MUST BE THE *PREGNANCY* THROWING HER SYSTEM OFF.
PHEW...
Huff Huff
CHIEF?

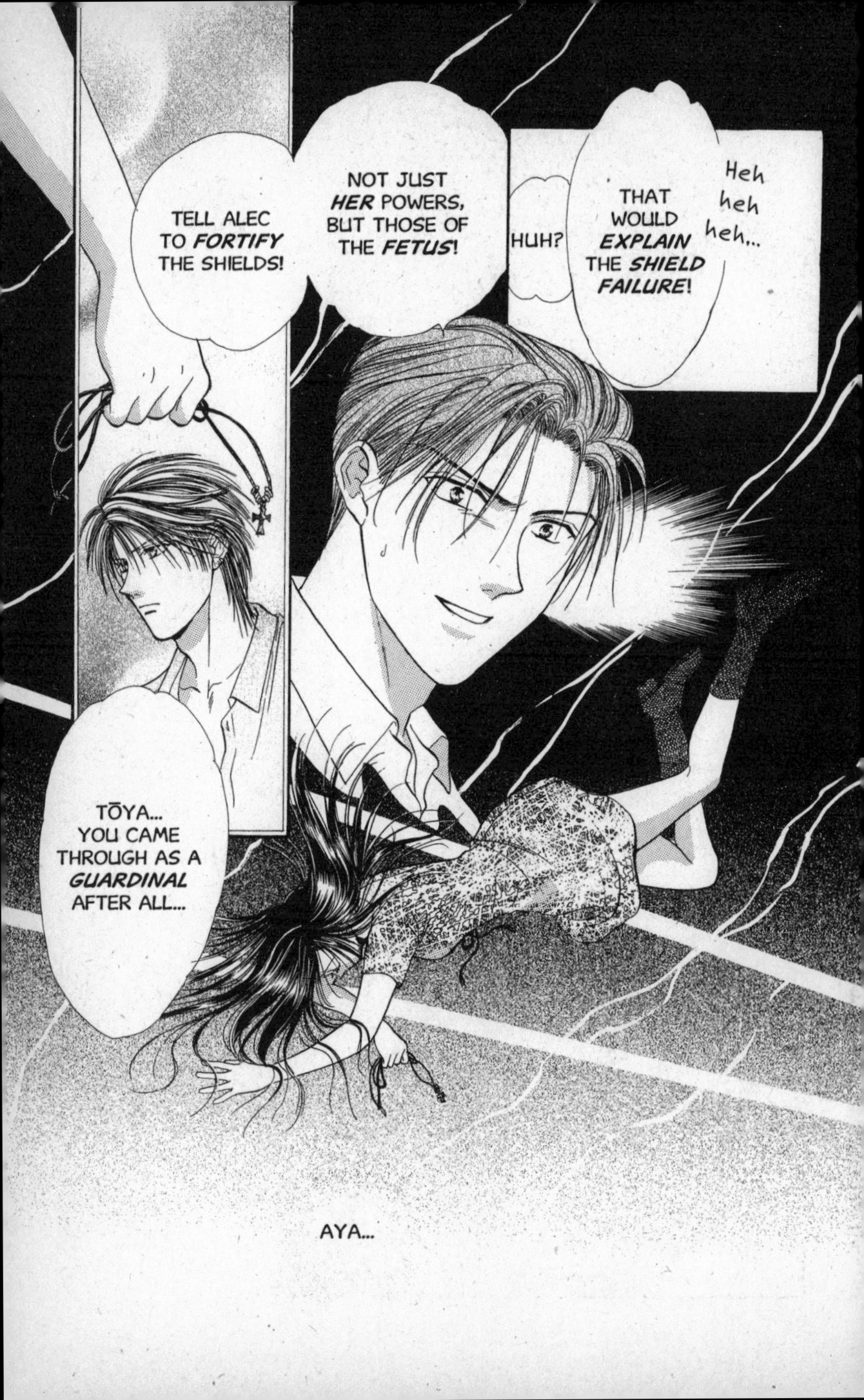
Heh heh heh...
THAT WOULD EXPLAIN THE SHIELD FAILURE!
HUH?
NOT JUST HER POWERS, BUT THOSE OF THE FETUS!
TELL ALEC TO FORTIFY THE SHIELDS!
TŌYA... YOU CAME THROUGH AS A GUARDINAL AFTER ALL...
AYA...

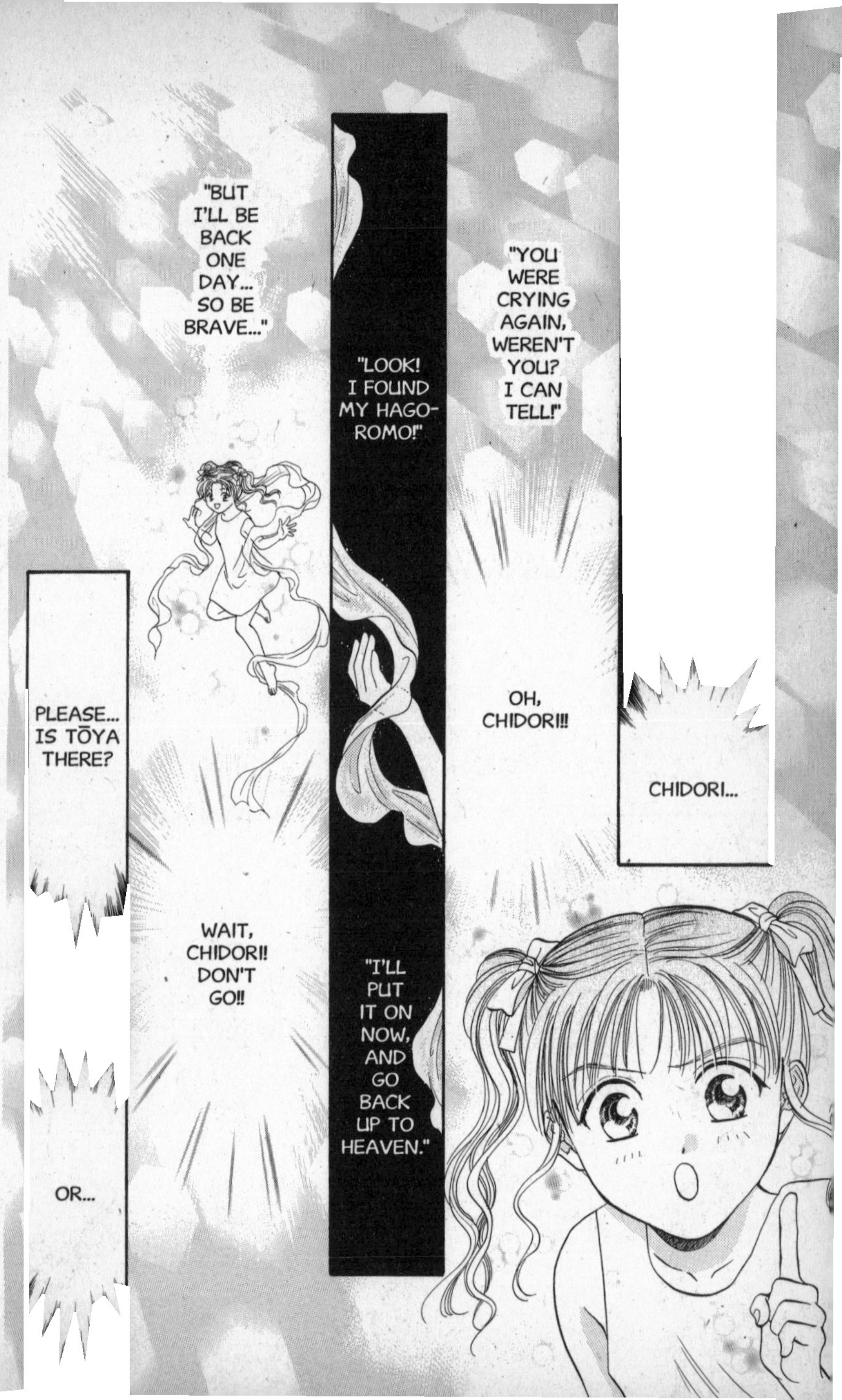
"YOU WERE CRYING AGAIN, WEREN'T YOU? I CAN TELL!"
"LOOK! I FOUND MY HAGO-ROMO!"
"BUT I'LL BE BACK ONE DAY... SO BE BRAVE..."
CHIDORI...
OH, CHIDORI!!
"I'LL PUT IT ON NOW, AND GO BACK UP TO HEAVEN."
WAIT, CHIDORI! DON'T GO!!
PLEASE... IS TŌYA THERE?
OR...

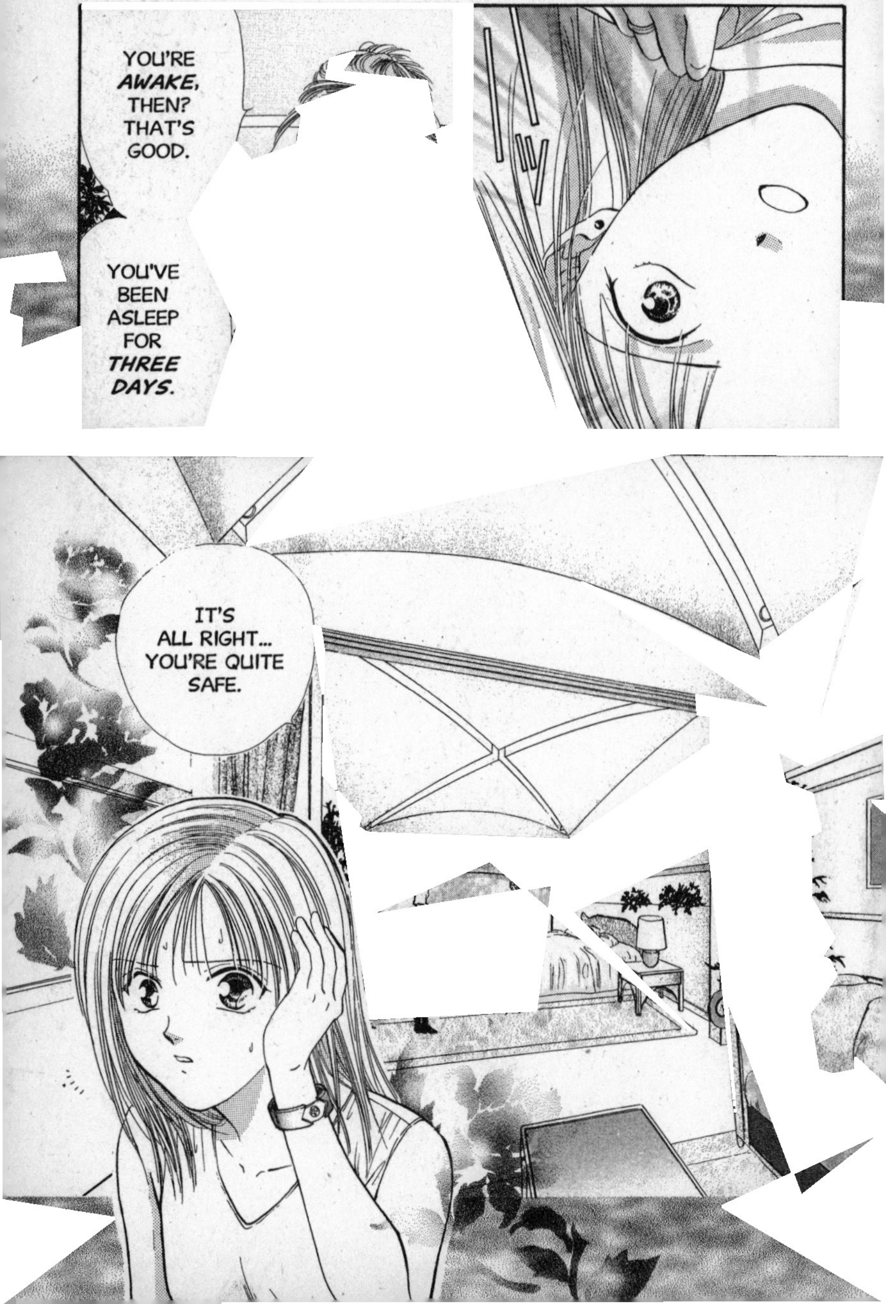
YOU'RE AWAKE, THEN? THAT'S GOOD.
YOU'VE BEEN ASLEEP FOR THREE DAYS.
IT'S ALL RIGHT... YOU'RE QUITE SAFE.

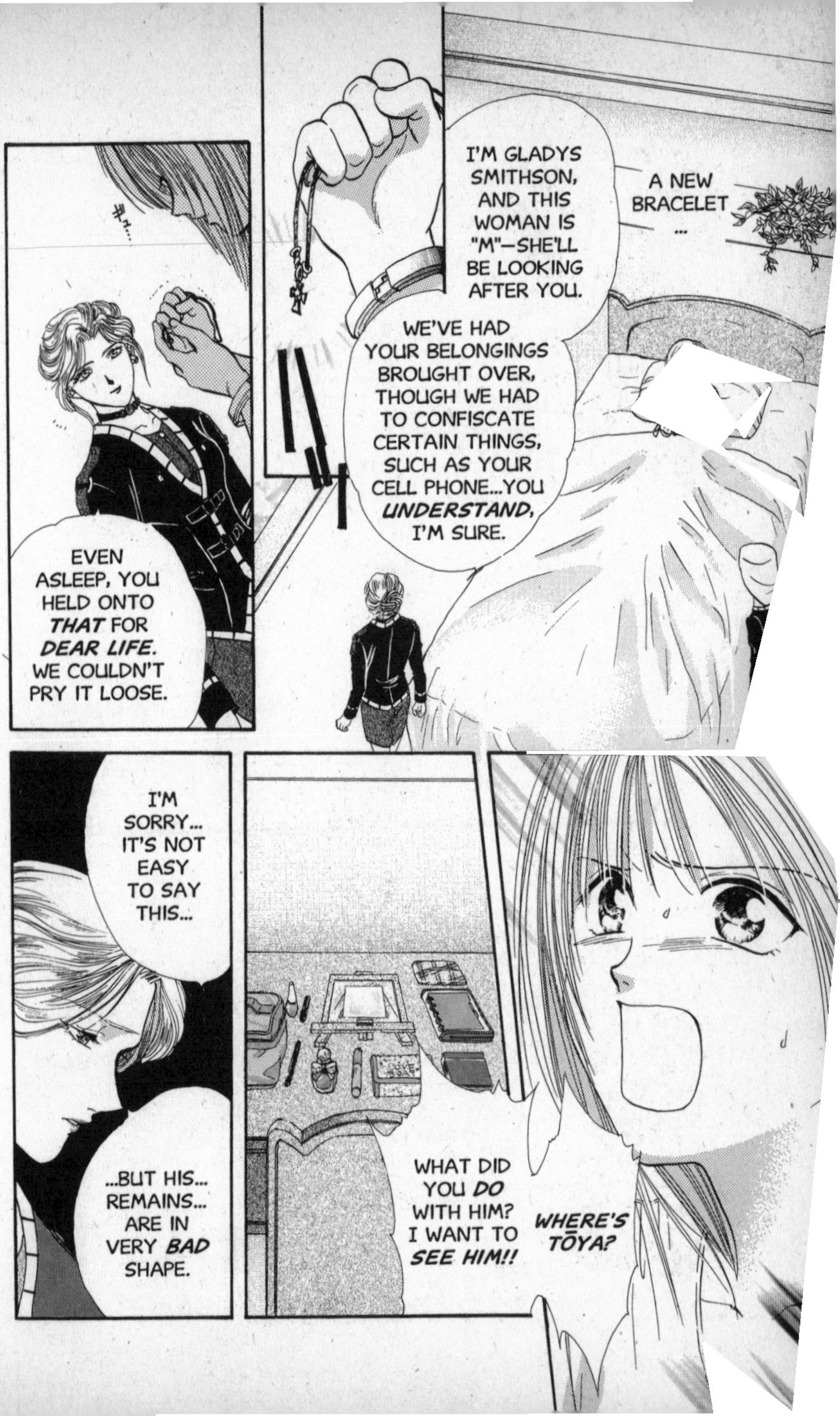
A NEW BRACELET ...
I'M GLADYS SMITHSON, AND THIS WOMAN IS "M"—SHE'LL BE LOOKING AFTER YOU.
WE'VE HAD YOUR BELONGINGS BROUGHT OVER, THOUGH WE HAD TO CONFISCATE CERTAIN THINGS, SUCH AS YOUR CELL PHONE...YOU *UNDERSTAND*, I'M SURE.
EVEN ASLEEP, YOU HELD ONTO *THAT* FOR *DEAR LIFE*. WE COULDN'T PRY IT LOOSE.
WHERE'S TŌYA?
WHAT DID YOU *DO* WITH HIM? I WANT TO *SEE HIM!!*
I'M SORRY... IT'S NOT EASY TO SAY THIS...
...BUT HIS... REMAINS... ARE IN VERY *BAD* SHAPE.

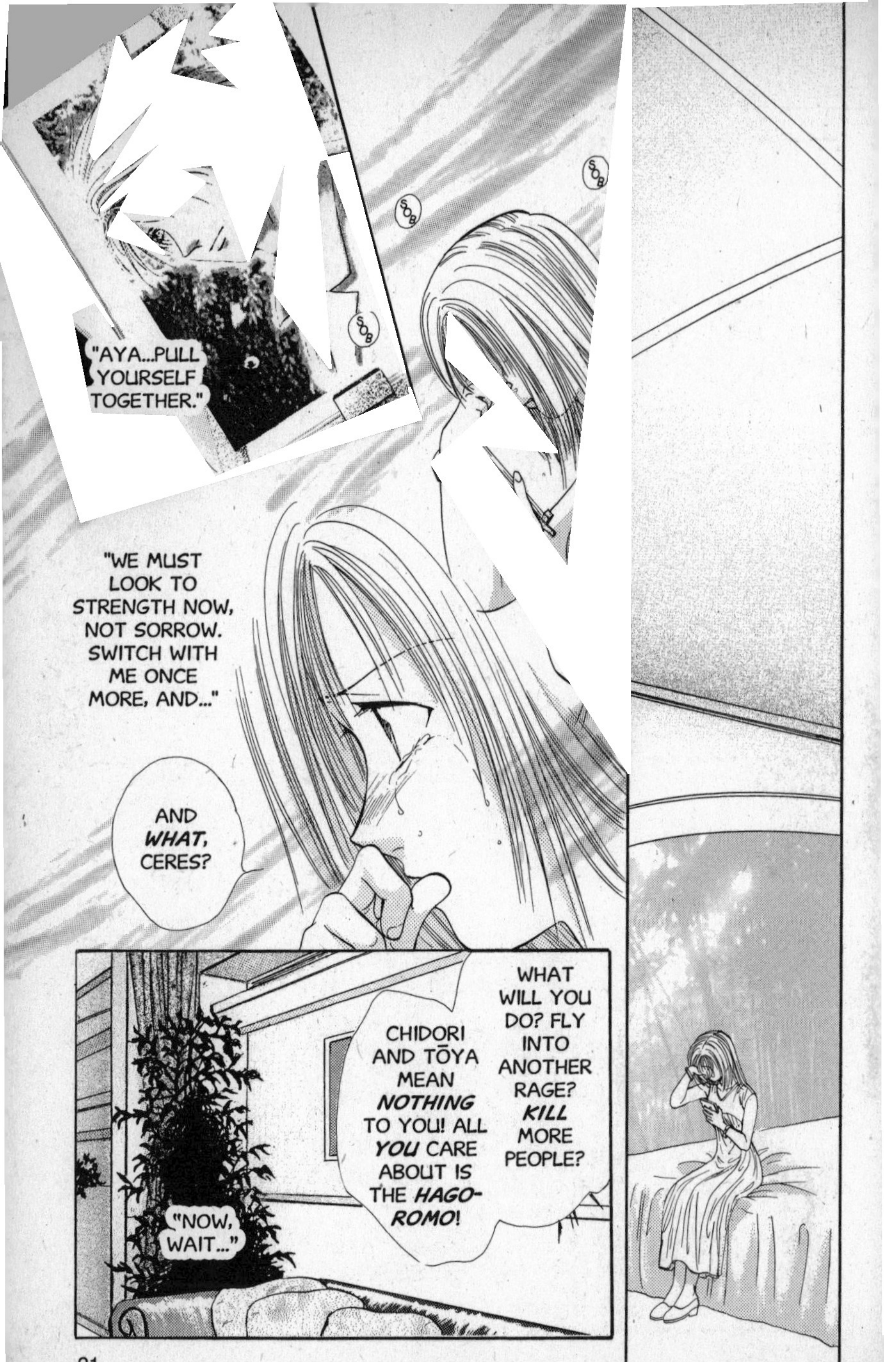
SOB
SOB
SOB
"AYA...PULL YOURSELF TOGETHER."
"WE MUST LOOK TO STRENGTH NOW, NOT SORROW. SWITCH WITH ME ONCE MORE, AND..."
AND *WHAT*, CERES?
WHAT WILL YOU DO? FLY INTO ANOTHER RAGE? *KILL* MORE PEOPLE?
CHIDORI AND TŌYA MEAN *NOTHING* TO YOU! ALL *YOU* CARE ABOUT IS THE *HAGO-ROMO*!
"NOW, WAIT..."

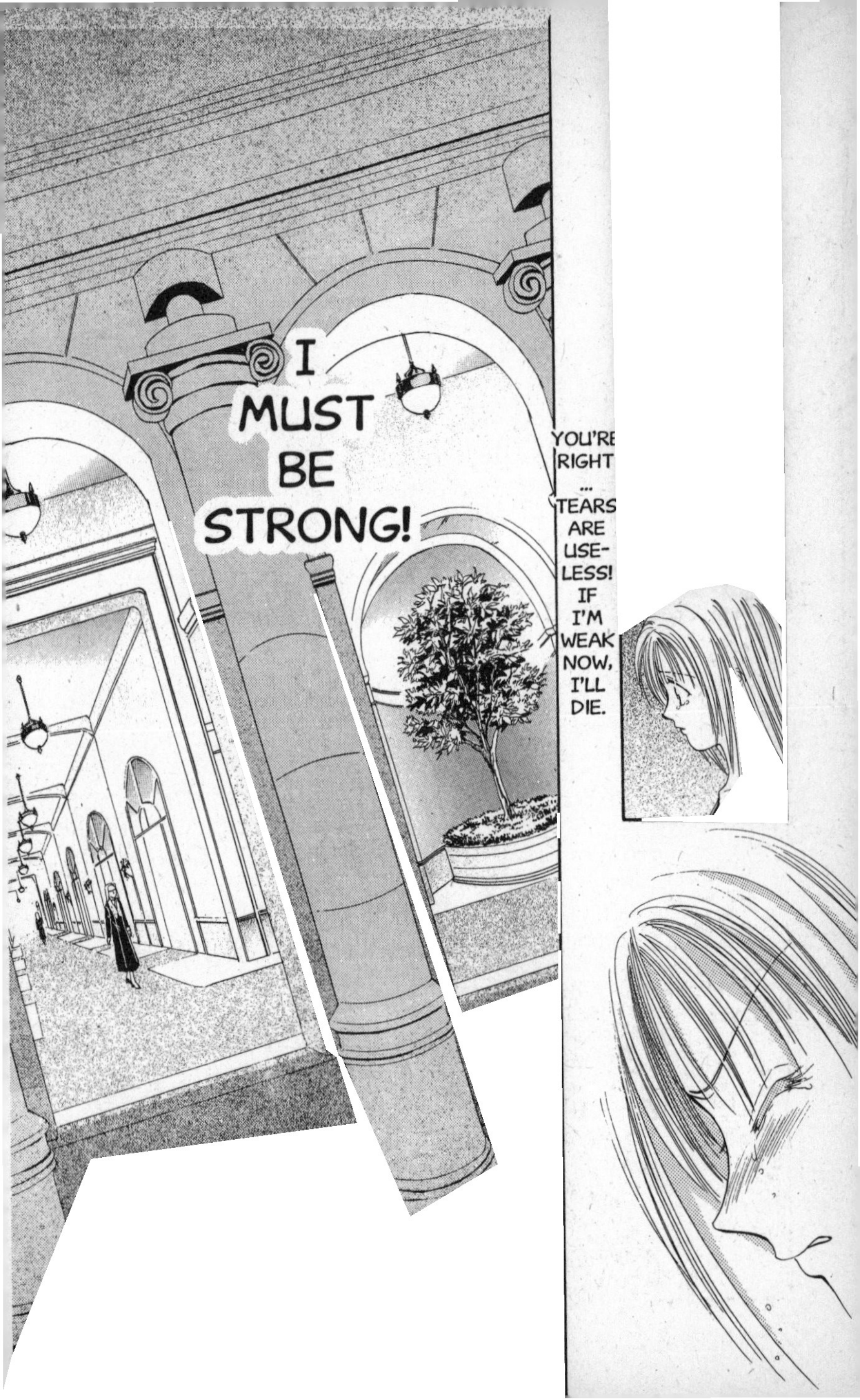
YOU'RE RIGHT... TEARS ARE USELESS! IF I'M WEAK NOW, I'LL DIE.
I MUST BE STRONG!

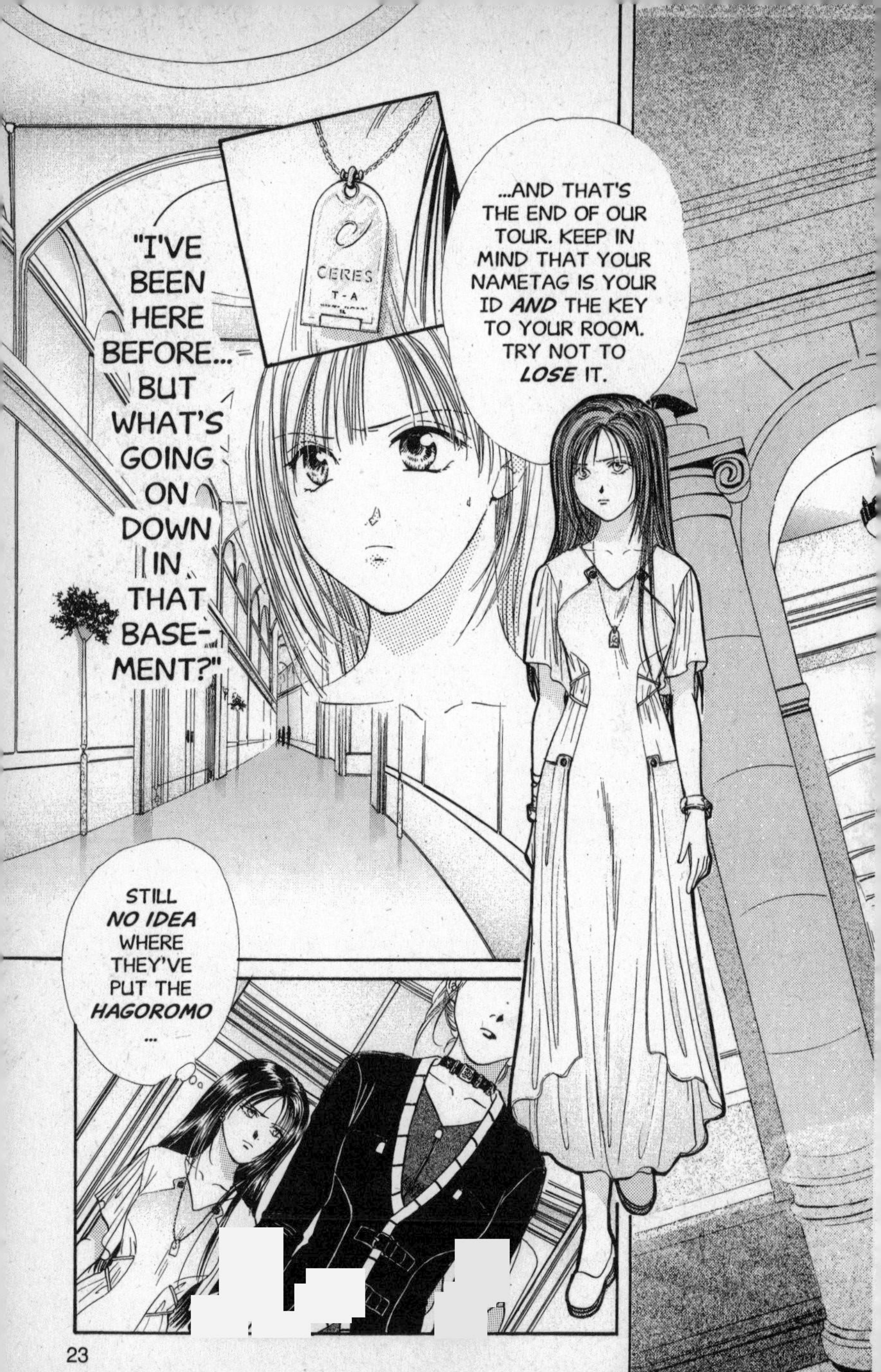
...AND THAT'S THE END OF OUR TOUR. KEEP IN MIND THAT YOUR NAMETAG IS YOUR ID *AND* THE KEY TO YOUR ROOM. TRY NOT TO *LOSE* IT.
CERES
T - A
"I'VE BEEN HERE BEFORE... BUT WHAT'S GOING ON DOWN IN THAT BASE-MENT?"
STILL *NO IDEA* WHERE THEY'VE PUT THE *HAGOROMO* ...

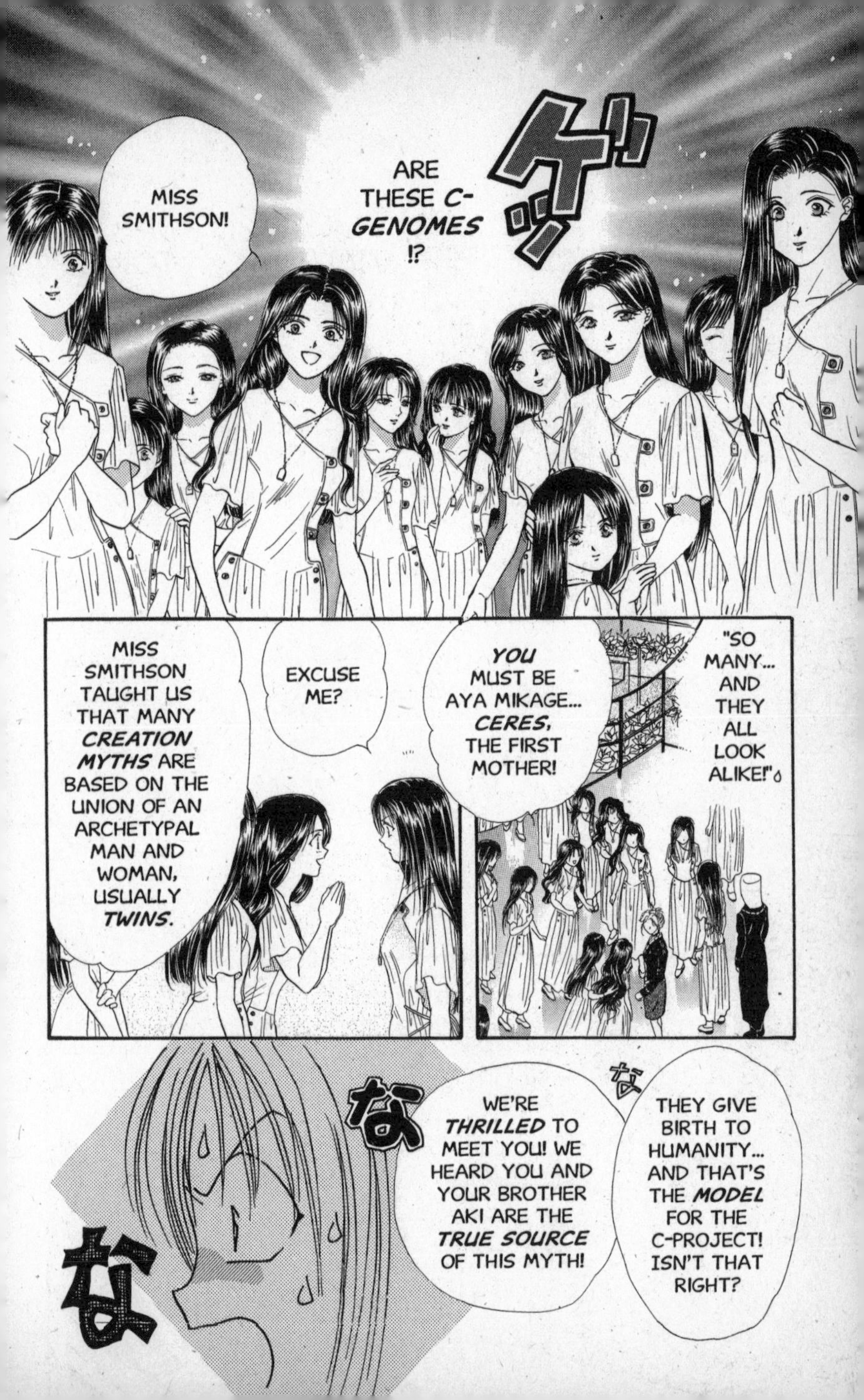
ゲッ
ARE THESE C-GENOMES !?
MISS SMITHSON!
"SO MANY... AND THEY ALL LOOK ALIKE!"
YOU MUST BE AYA MIKAGE... CERES, THE FIRST MOTHER!
EXCUSE ME?
MISS SMITHSON TAUGHT US THAT MANY CREATION MYTHS ARE BASED ON THE UNION OF AN ARCHETYPAL MAN AND WOMAN, USUALLY TWINS.
な
THEY GIVE BIRTH TO HUMANITY... AND THAT'S THE MODEL FOR THE C-PROJECT! ISN'T THAT RIGHT?
WE'RE THRILLED TO MEET YOU! WE HEARD YOU AND YOUR BROTHER AKI ARE THE TRUE SOURCE OF THIS MYTH!
な
な

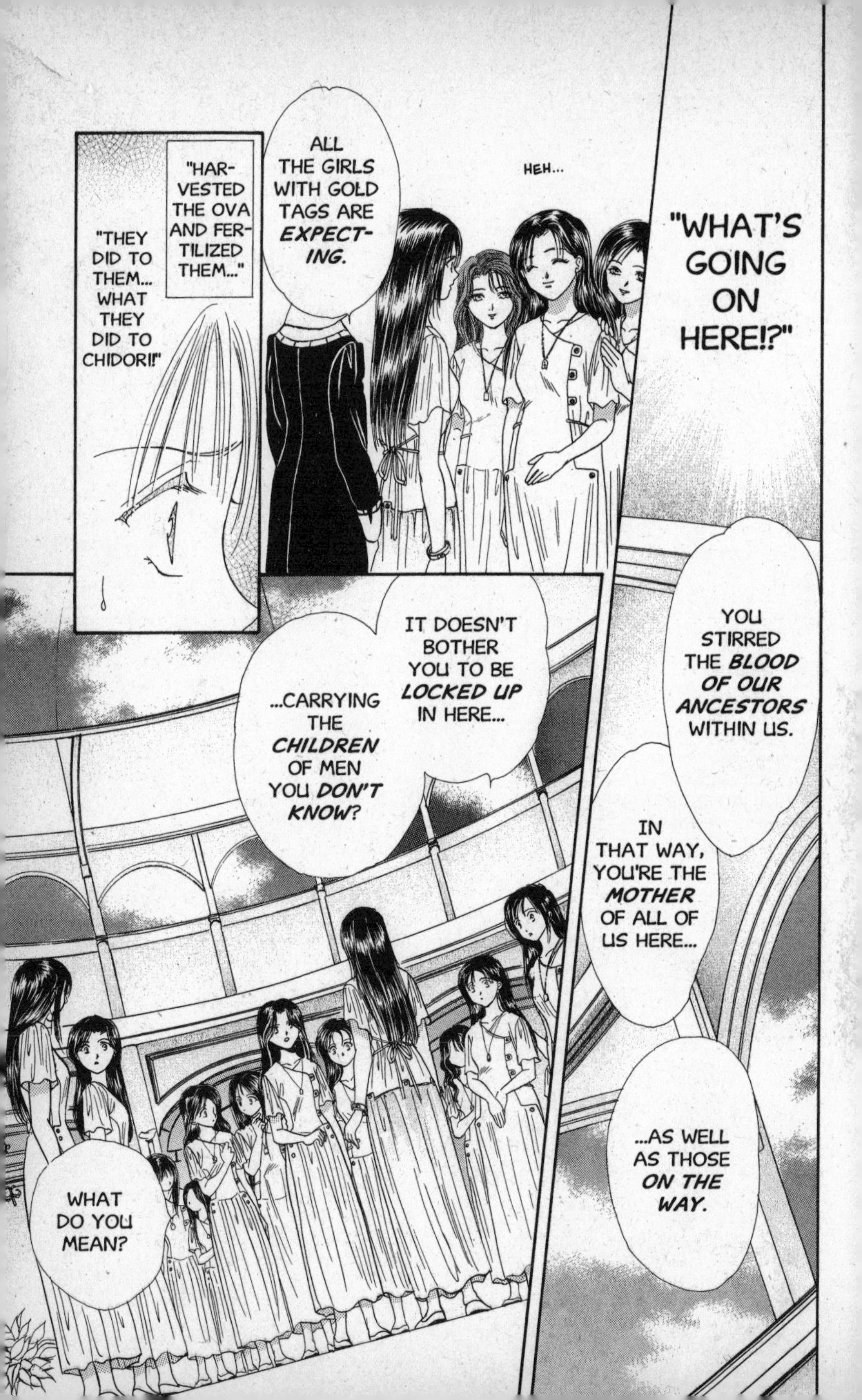
"WHAT'S GOING ON HERE!?"
YOU STIRRED THE BLOOD OF OUR ANCESTORS WITHIN US.
IN THAT WAY, YOU'RE THE MOTHER OF ALL OF US HERE...
...AS WELL AS THOSE ON THE WAY.
HEH...
ALL THE GIRLS WITH GOLD TAGS ARE EXPECTING.
"HARVESTED THE OVA AND FERTILIZED THEM..."
"THEY DID TO THEM... WHAT THEY DID TO CHIDORI!"
IT DOESN'T BOTHER YOU TO BE LOCKED UP IN HERE...
...CARRYING THE CHILDREN OF MEN YOU DON'T KNOW?
WHAT DO YOU MEAN?

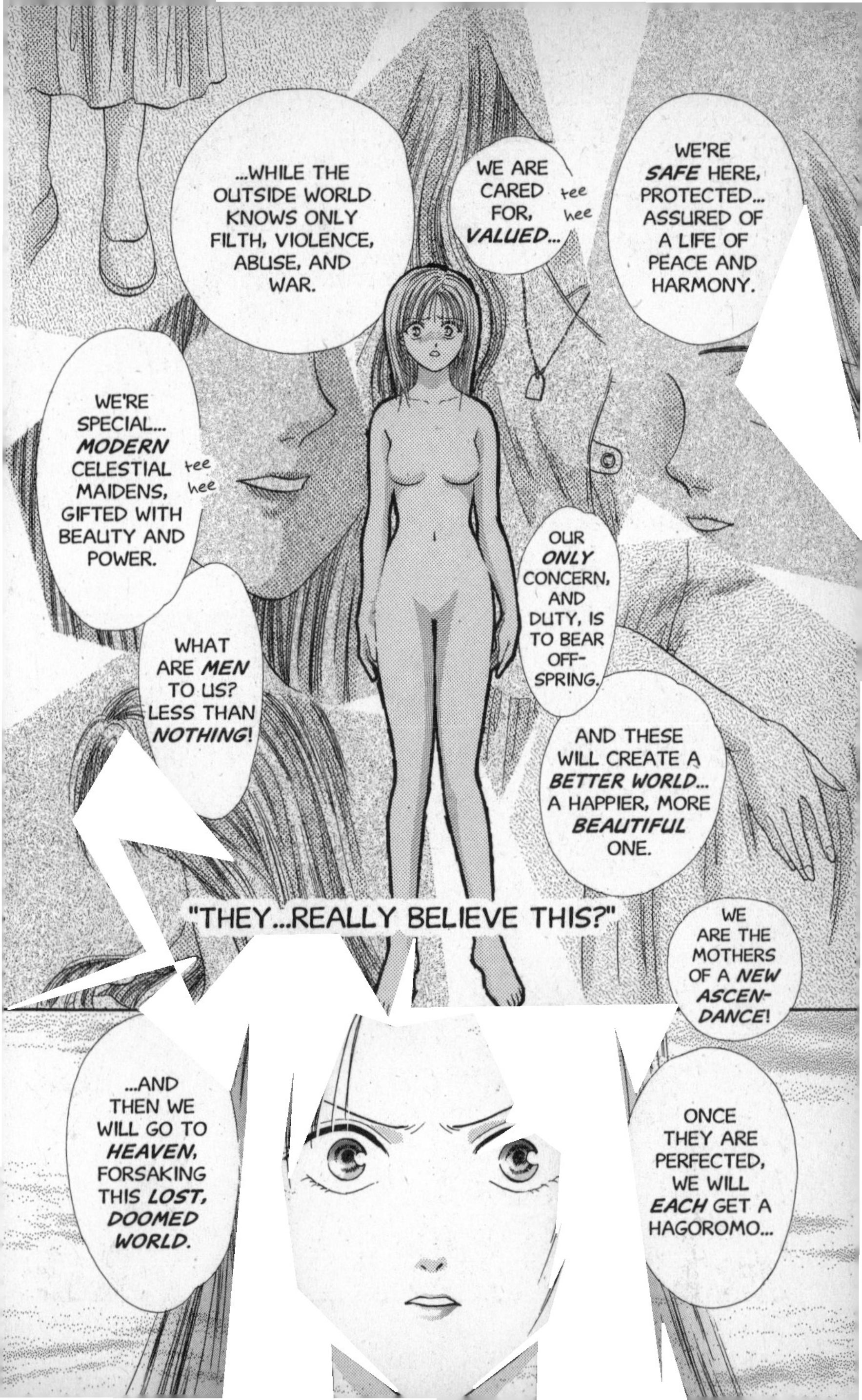
WE'RE SAFE HERE, PROTECTED... ASSURED OF A LIFE OF PEACE AND HARMONY.
WE ARE CARED FOR, VALUED...
tee hee
...WHILE THE OUTSIDE WORLD KNOWS ONLY FILTH, VIOLENCE, ABUSE, AND WAR.
WE'RE SPECIAL... MODERN CELESTIAL MAIDENS, GIFTED WITH BEAUTY AND POWER.
tee hee
WHAT ARE MEN TO US? LESS THAN NOTHING!
OUR ONLY CONCERN, AND DUTY, IS TO BEAR OFF-SPRING.
AND THESE WILL CREATE A BETTER WORLD... A HAPPIER, MORE BEAUTIFUL ONE.
WE ARE THE MOTHERS OF A NEW ASCEN-DANCE!
"THEY...REALLY BELIEVE THIS?"
ONCE THEY ARE PERFECTED, WE WILL EACH GET A HAGOROMO...
...AND THEN WE WILL GO TO HEAVEN, FORSAKING THIS LOST, DOOMED WORLD.

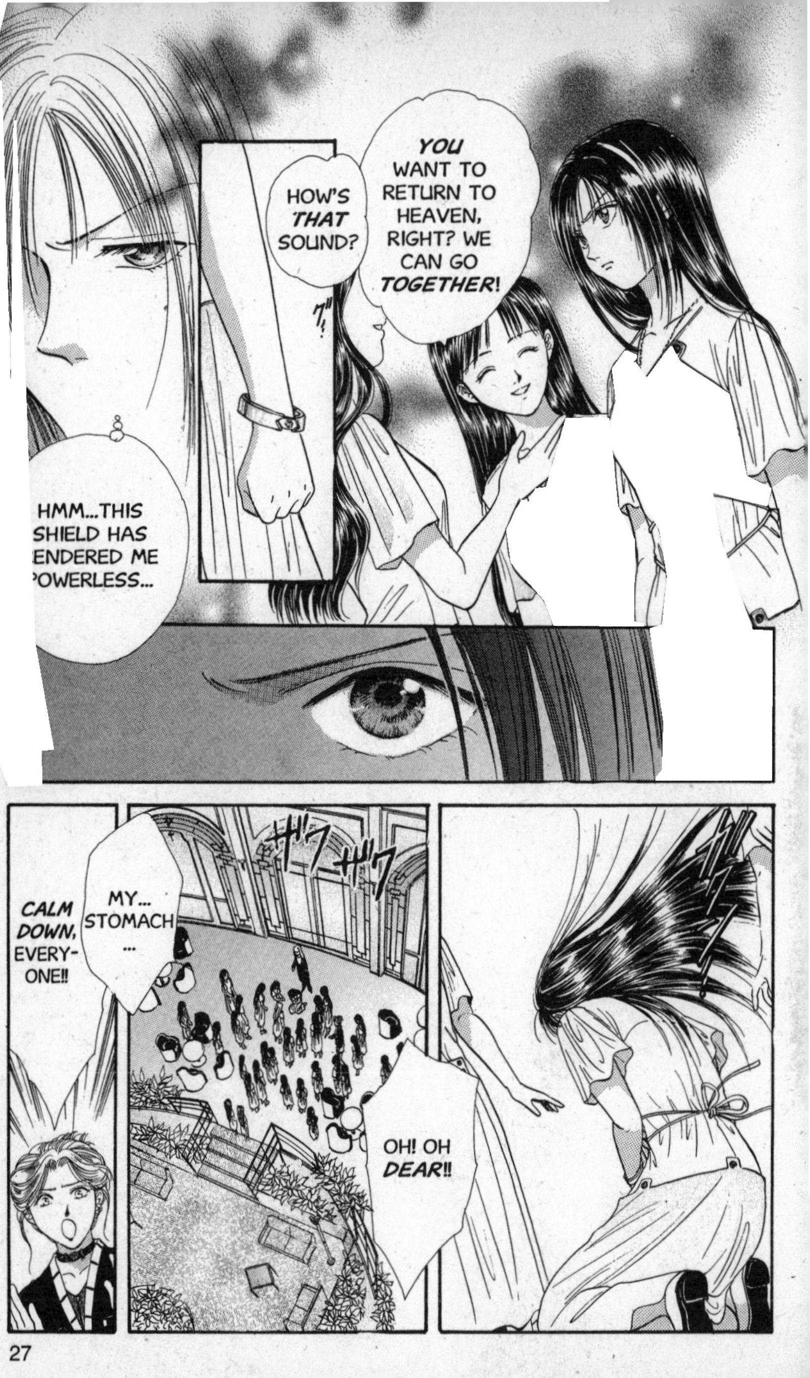
YOU WANT TO RETURN TO HEAVEN, RIGHT? WE CAN GO TOGETHER!
HOW'S THAT SOUND?
HMM...THIS SHIELD HAS ENDERED ME POWERLESS...
OH! OH DEAR!!
ザワ ザワ
MY... STOMACH ...
CALM DOWN, EVERY- ONE!!

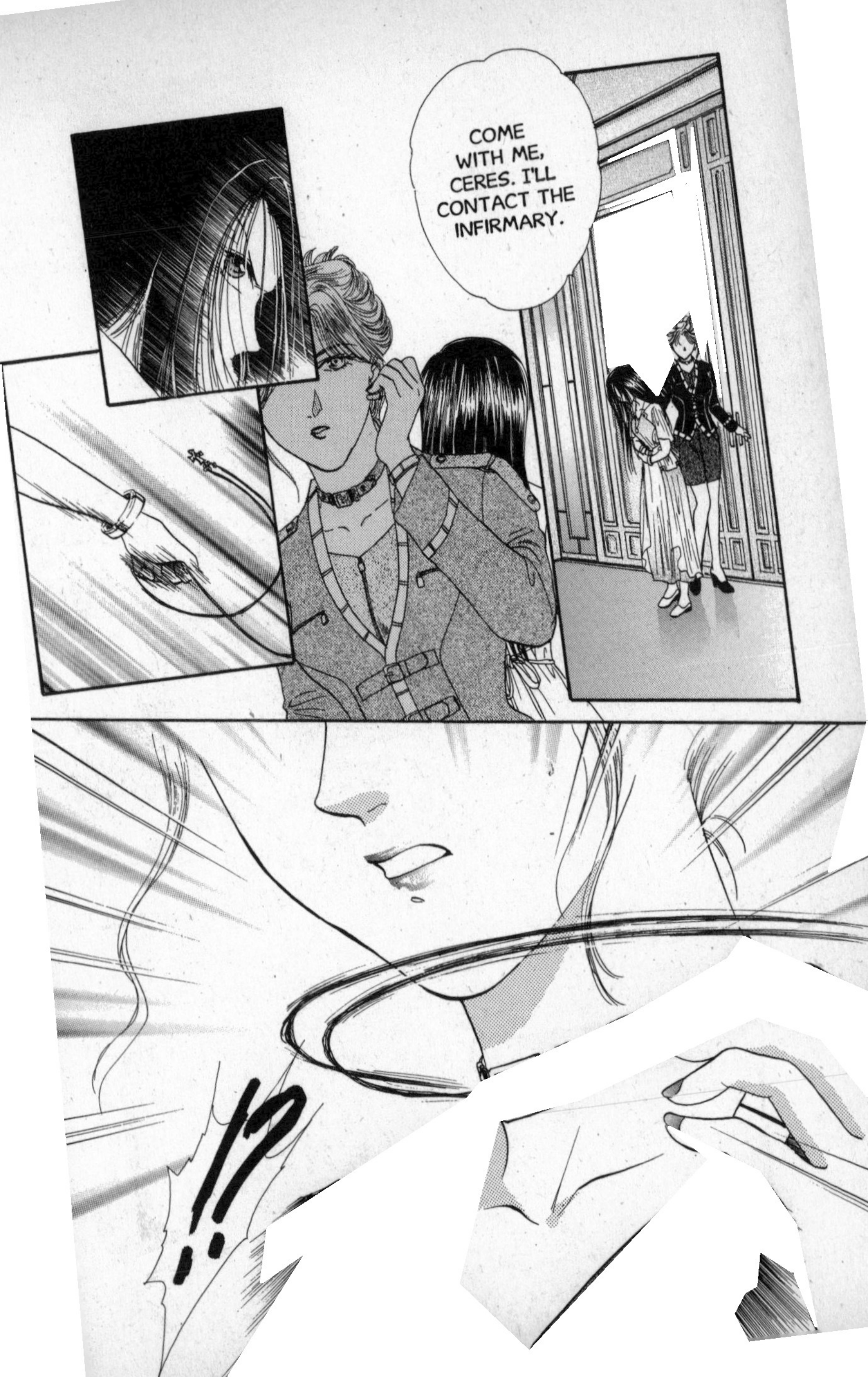
COME WITH ME, CERES. I'LL CONTACT THE INFIRMARY.
!?

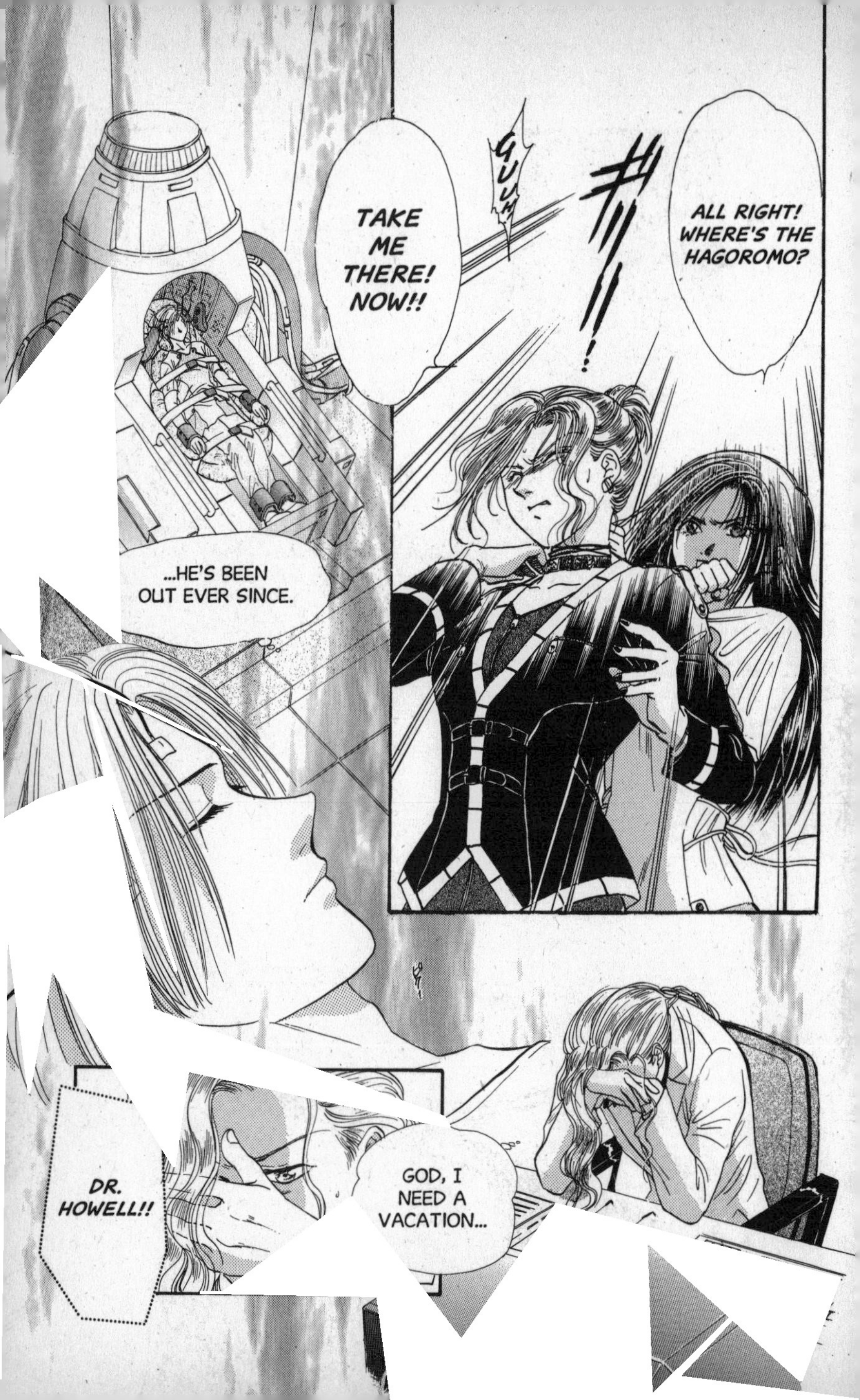
ALL RIGHT! WHERE'S THE HAGOROMO?
GUUH
TAKE ME THERE! NOW!!
...HE'S BEEN OUT EVER SINCE.
GOD, I NEED A VACATION...
DR. HOWELL!!

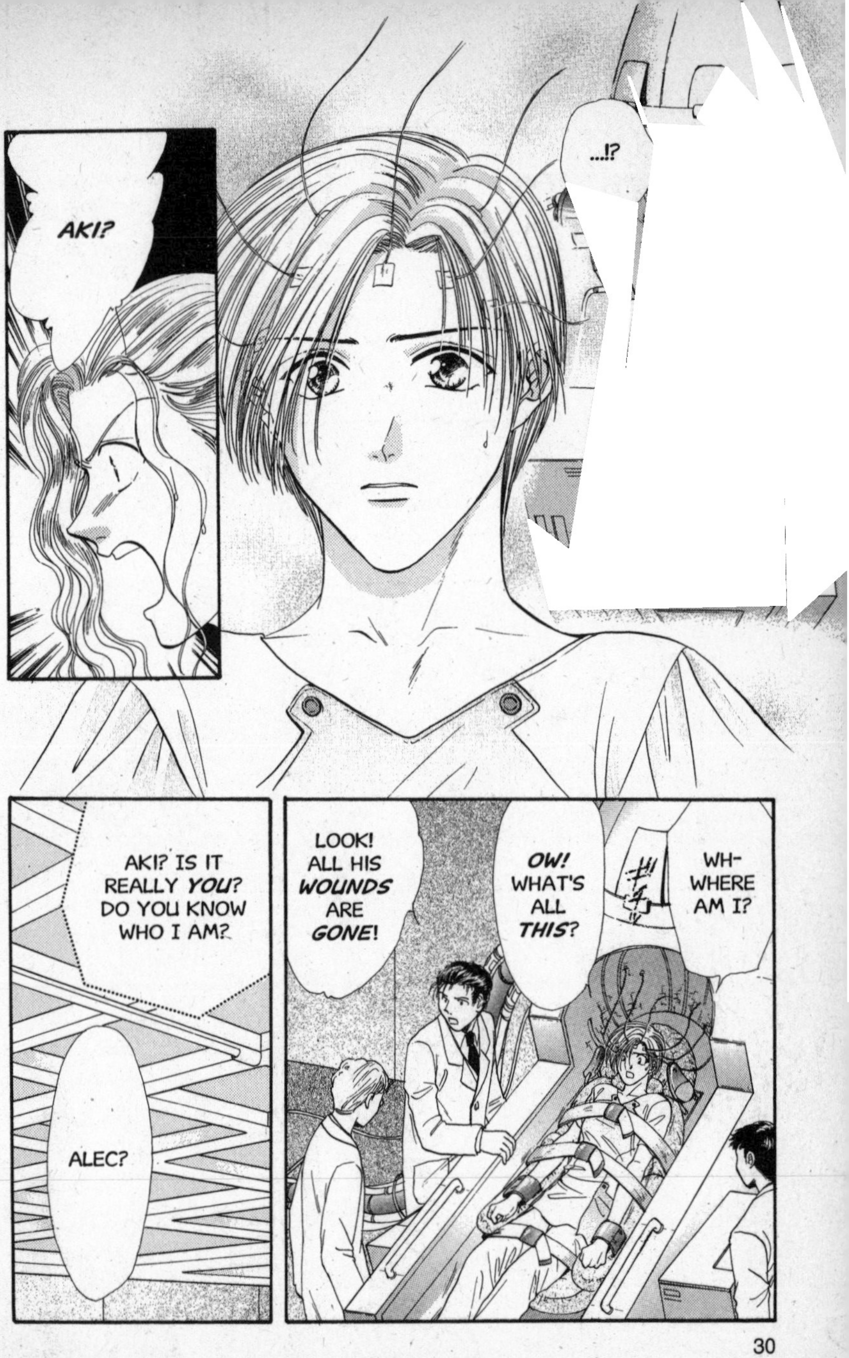
...!?
AKI?
WH- WHERE AM I?
OW! WHAT'S ALL THIS?
LOOK! ALL HIS WOUNDS ARE GONE!
AKI? IS IT REALLY YOU? DO YOU KNOW WHO I AM?
ALEC?

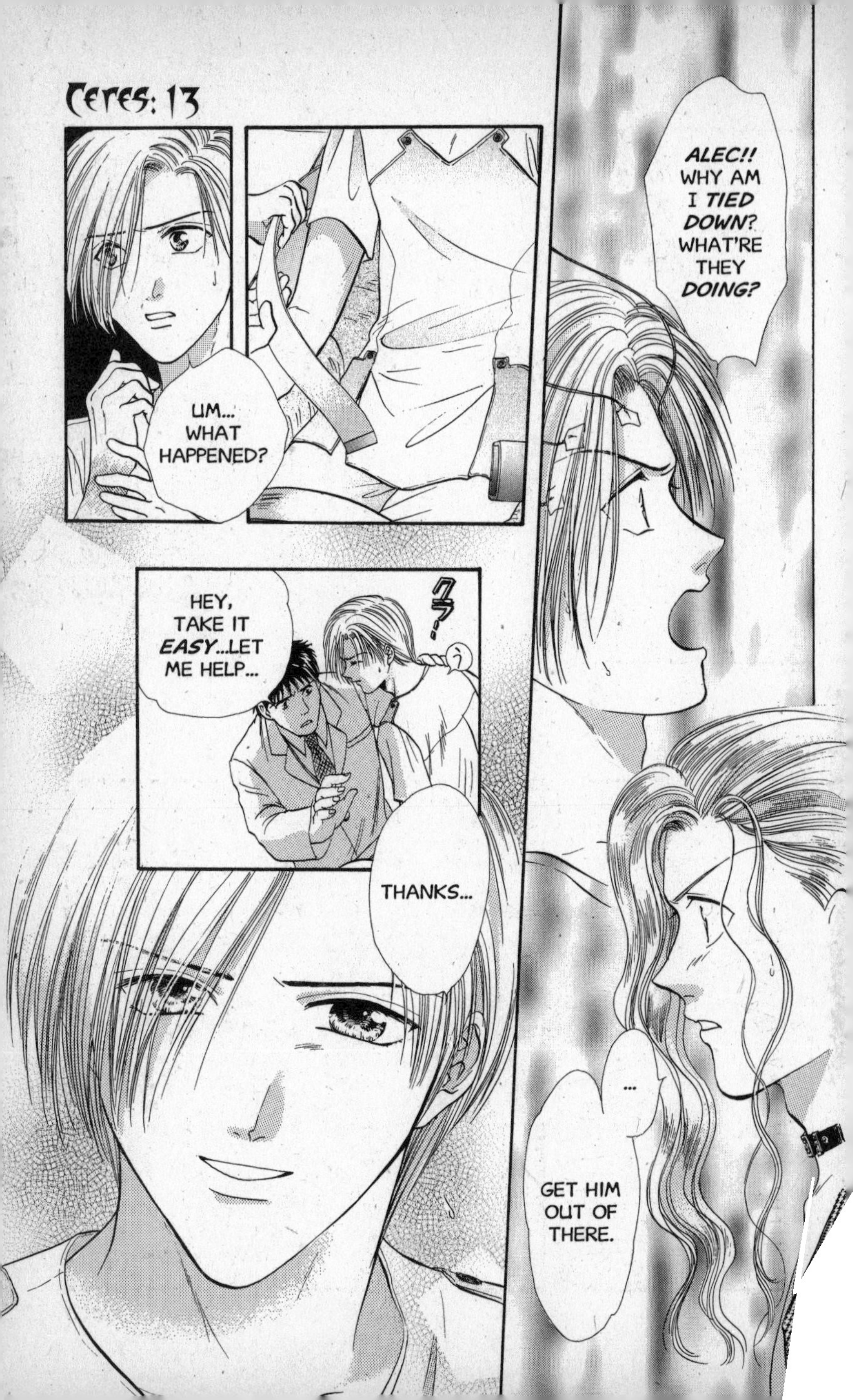
ALEC!! WHY AM I TIED DOWN? WHAT'RE THEY DOING?
UM... WHAT HAPPENED?
HEY, TAKE IT EASY...LET ME HELP...
クラ‥
THANKS...
...
GET HIM OUT OF THERE.

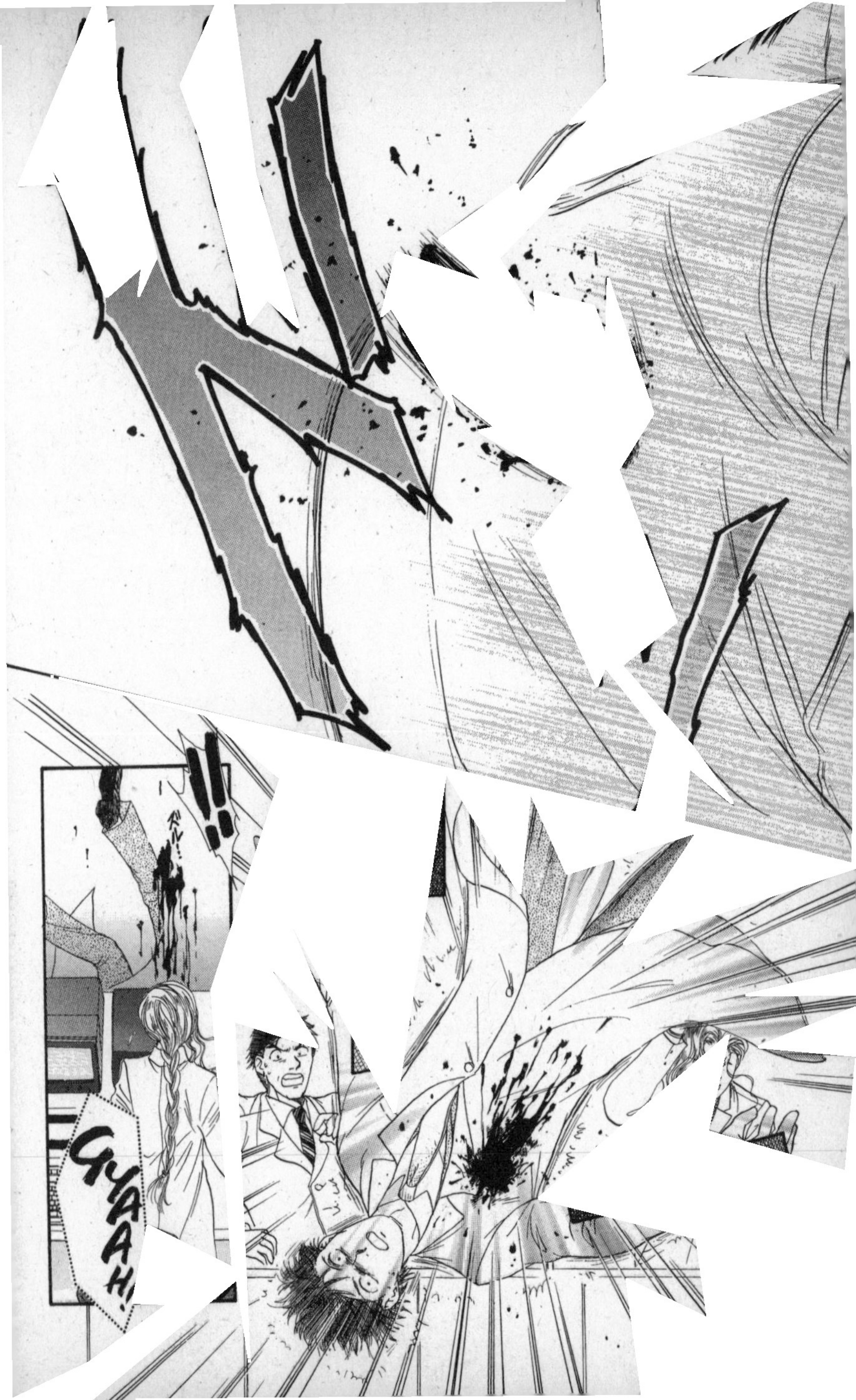
!!
ズル…
GYAAAH!

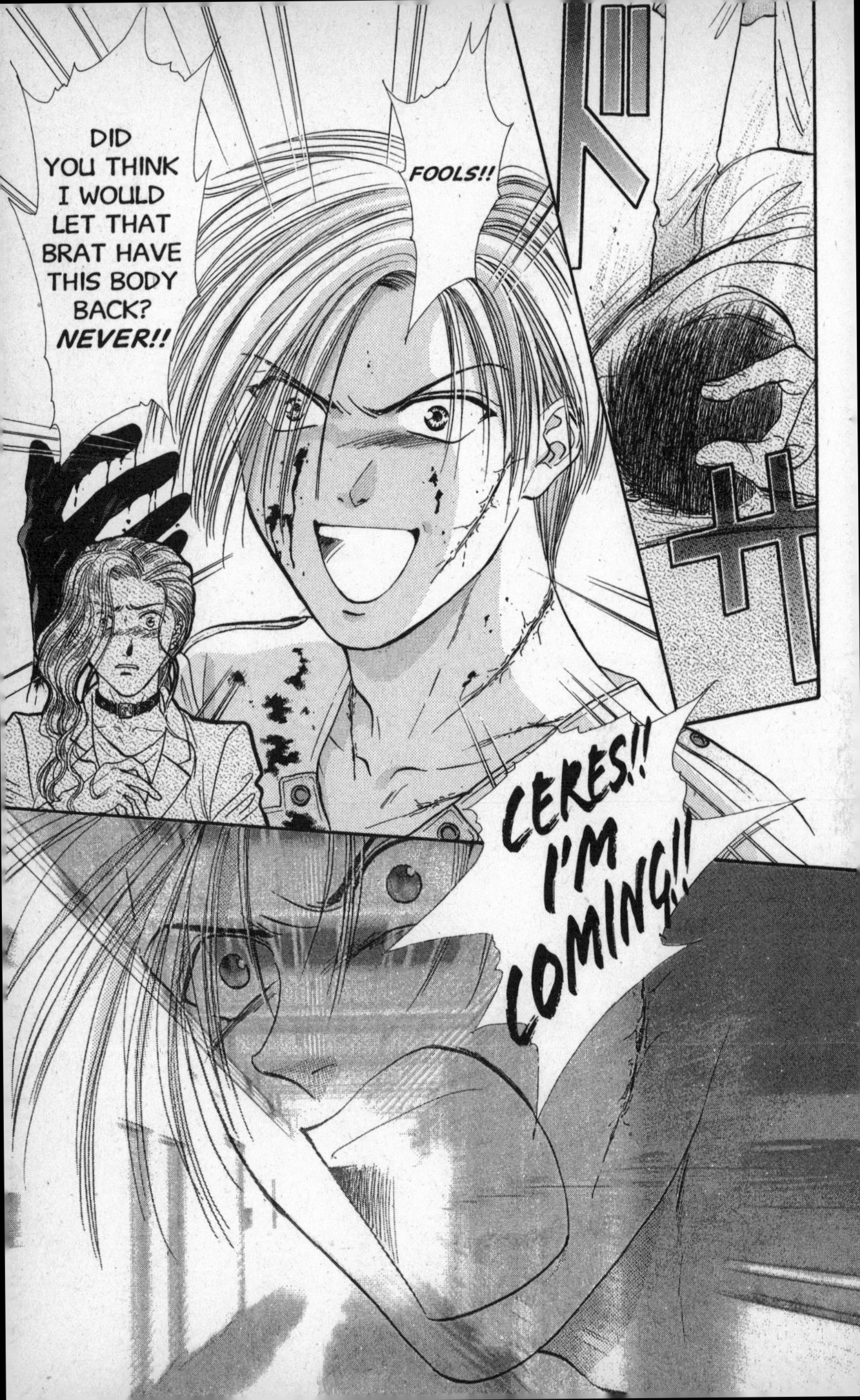
FOOLS!!
DID YOU THINK I WOULD LET THAT BRAT HAVE THIS BODY BACK? NEVER!!
CERES!! I'M COMING!!

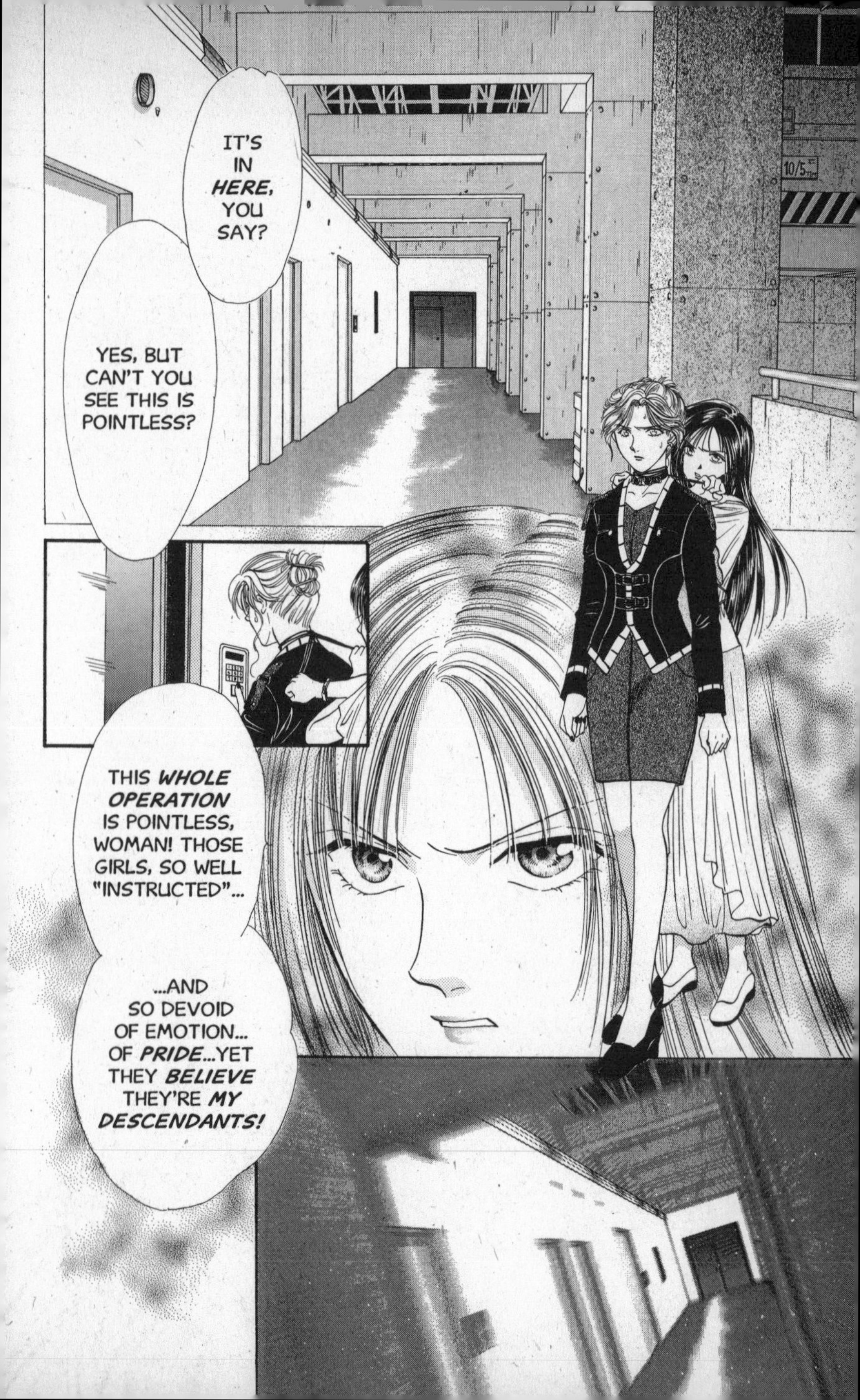
IT'S IN *HERE*, YOU SAY?
YES, BUT CAN'T YOU SEE THIS IS POINTLESS?
THIS *WHOLE OPERATION* IS POINTLESS, WOMAN! THOSE GIRLS, SO WELL "INSTRUCTED"...
...AND SO DEVOID OF EMOTION... OF *PRIDE*...YET THEY *BELIEVE* THEY'RE *MY DESCENDANTS!*

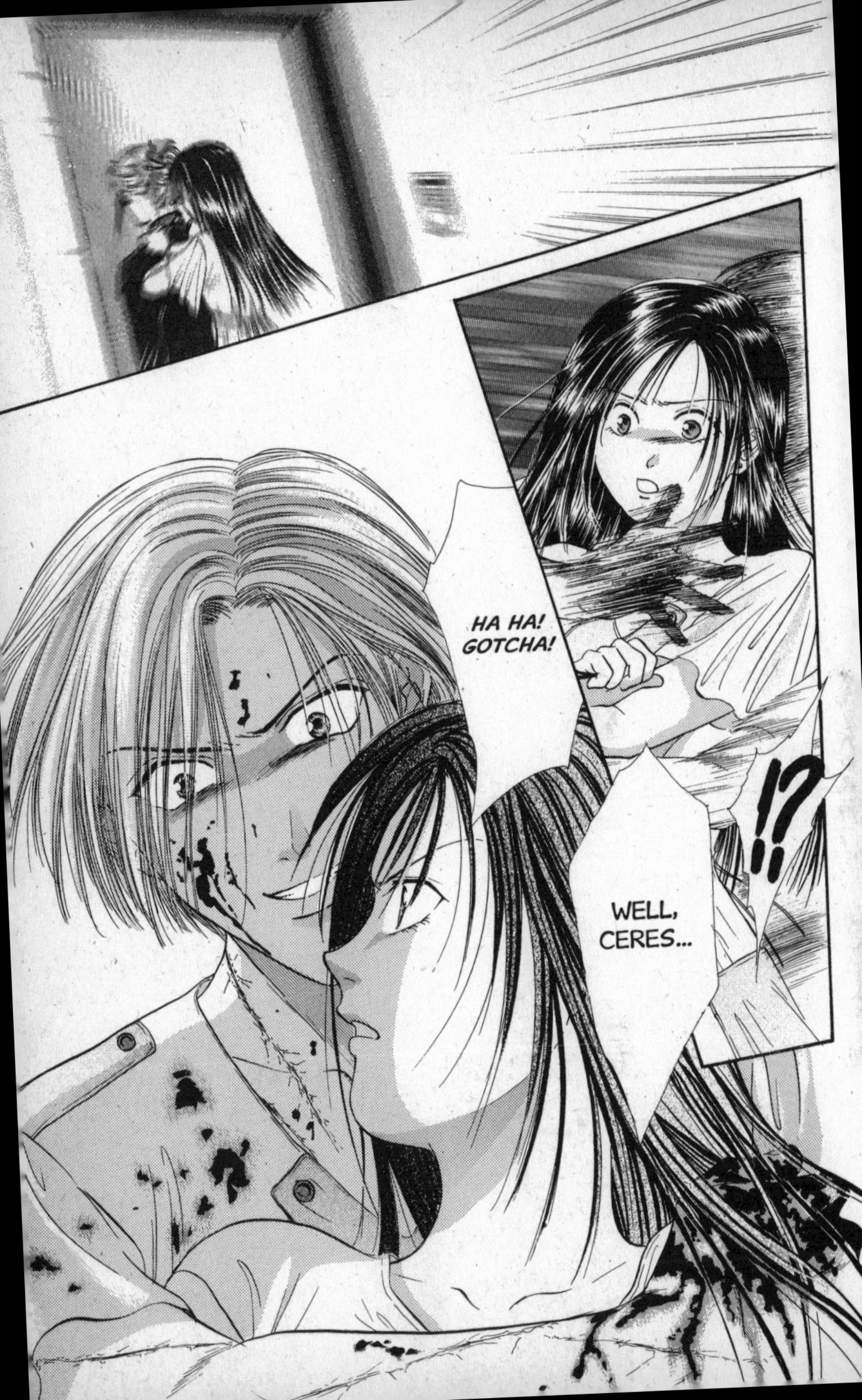
!?
HA HA! GOTCHA!
WELL, CERES...

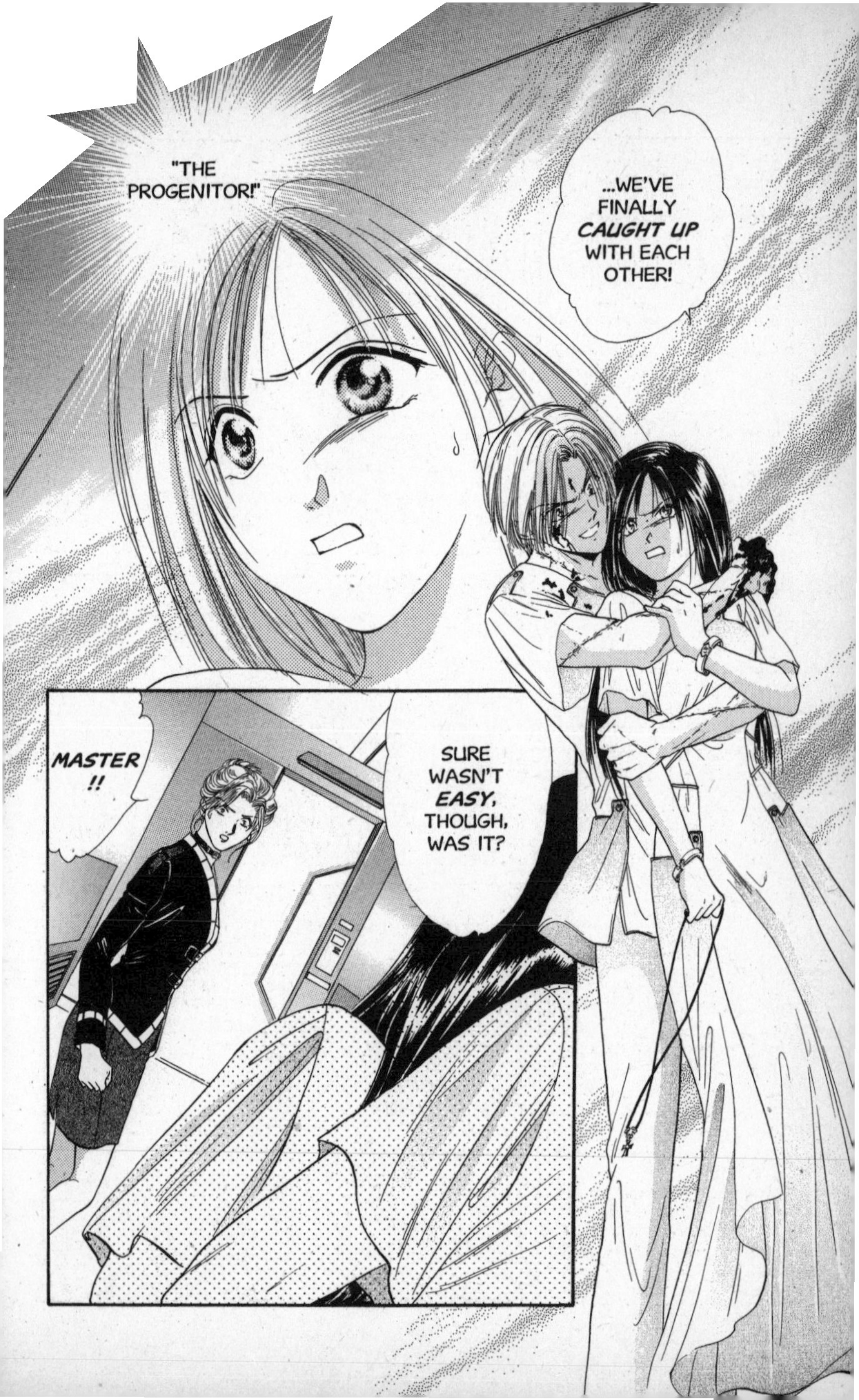
...WE'VE FINALLY CAUGHT UP WITH EACH OTHER!
"THE PROGENITOR!"
SURE WASN'T EASY, THOUGH, WAS IT?
MASTER !!

WHAT'S THIS *ABOUT?*
BE QUIET AND *OPEN THIS DOOR!* WE'RE LEAVING, MY WIFE AND I...*AFTER I KILL KAGAMI!*
HE THOUGHT HE COULD *GET RID* OF ME!!
BASTARD'S EVEN TRYING TO *RECREATE* THE HAGOROMO! RIGHT BEHIND *HERE,* I BET!!

By the way, I heard that Squall was modeled after Gackt, a former member of the band Malice Mizer. Takako Matsu was supposedly the model for Rinoa... I don't see it.

And I heard Ami Suzuki was modeled on Selphie. But then my editor, Mr. Y, insisted that it was Ryoko Hirosue.

Anyway...it's true that they're a lot like Aya and Tōya, at least as they were in the beginning, so I decided to name the other characters after the ones in Ceres! (Though some of them ended up getting totally unrelated names.) So Shiva is "Ceres," Ifrit is "Mikagi" (why?), Diablos is "Kagami." ◡̈ Alexander is simply "Alec," and Carbuncle is "Aki," etc. If I had taken their powers into account, then Quetzacotl, who uses thunder, would be "Pallas," and Siren, since her gift is her voice, would've been "Shuro." But I couldn't very well name Ifrit "Yuki" just because he uses fire. Cerberus was "Mamoru" the dog, by the way...

I just found out that I forgot to get two Guardian Forces, and I'm trying to decide whether I should go back for them or not. And I just made it to Disc Three, too. But what's up with the abrupt mushiness? ◡̈ Nobody's convincing! Squall must've hit his head or gotten food poisoning between Discs Two and Three. I had to yell at the TV, "What's come over you, Tōya!?" The funniest thing is, I named Rinoa's pet dog, Angelo, "Yūhi." Whenever Aya gets in danger, it's "Yūhi Rush" or "Yūhi Cannon!" ◡̈ My assistants howl, "Yūhi, Aya's dog!" Poor thing. He gets treated so differently from Tōya... ◡̈ Zell was more like Yūhi, but you can't rename him. Then again, we call Selphie "Chidori" among ourselves. Quistis looks like Gladys, too. My assistant J, a big Aki fan, named her Chocobo "Aki." But Shiva = Ceres was a good idea.

She's Junctioned onto Aya, of course.

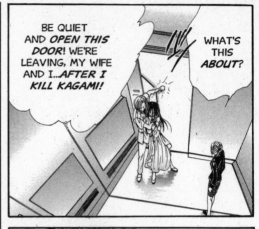

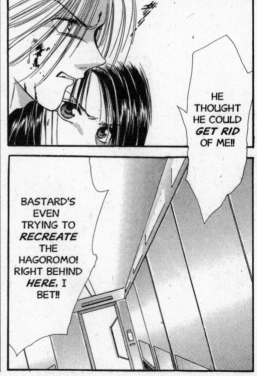

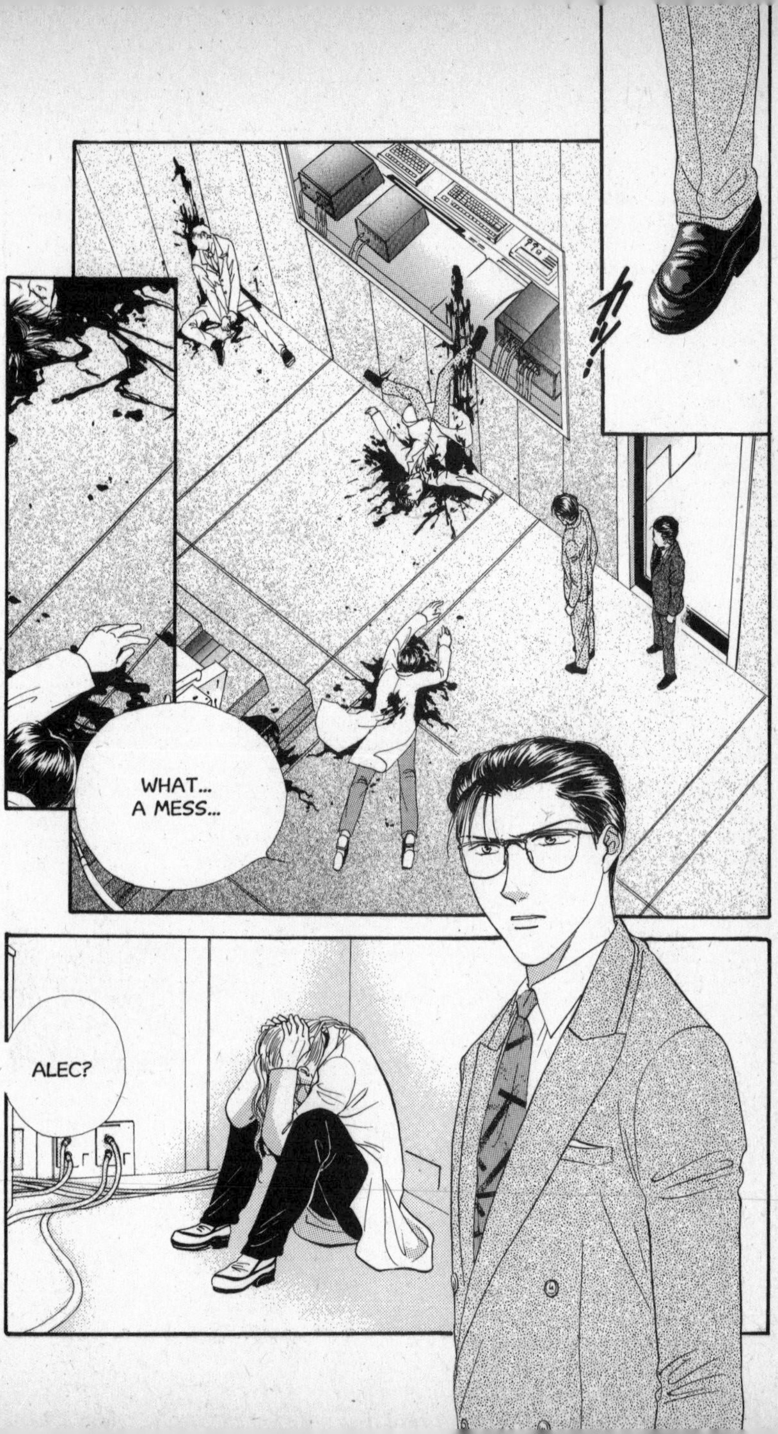
カッ!
WHAT... A MESS...
ALEC?

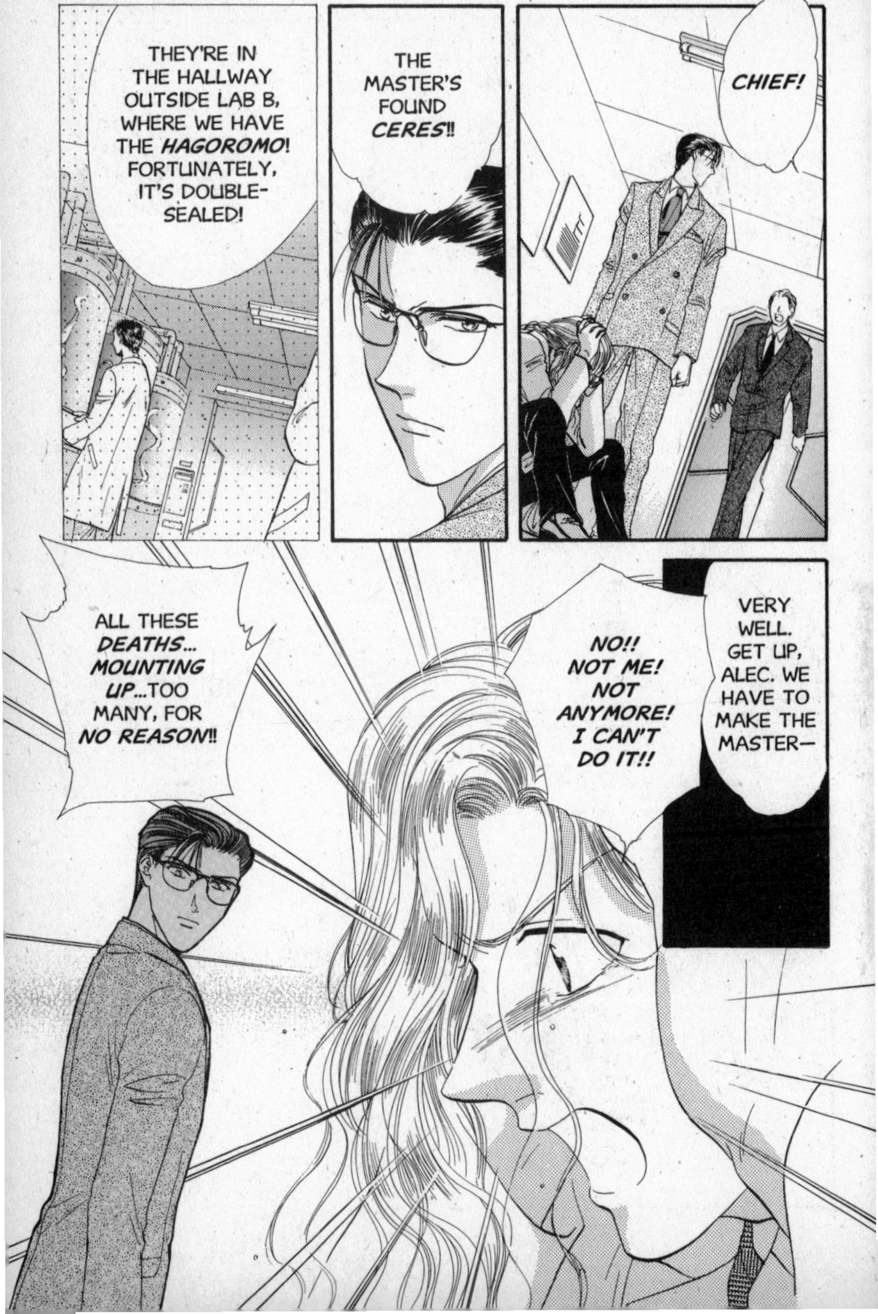
CHIEF!
THE MASTER'S FOUND *CERES*!!
THEY'RE IN THE HALLWAY OUTSIDE LAB B, WHERE WE HAVE THE *HAGOROMO*! FORTUNATELY, IT'S DOUBLE-SEALED!
VERY WELL. GET UP, ALEC. WE HAVE TO MAKE THE MASTER—
NO!! NOT ME! NOT ANYMORE! I CAN'T DO IT!!
ALL THESE *DEATHS... MOUNTING UP*...TOO MANY, FOR *NO REASON*!!

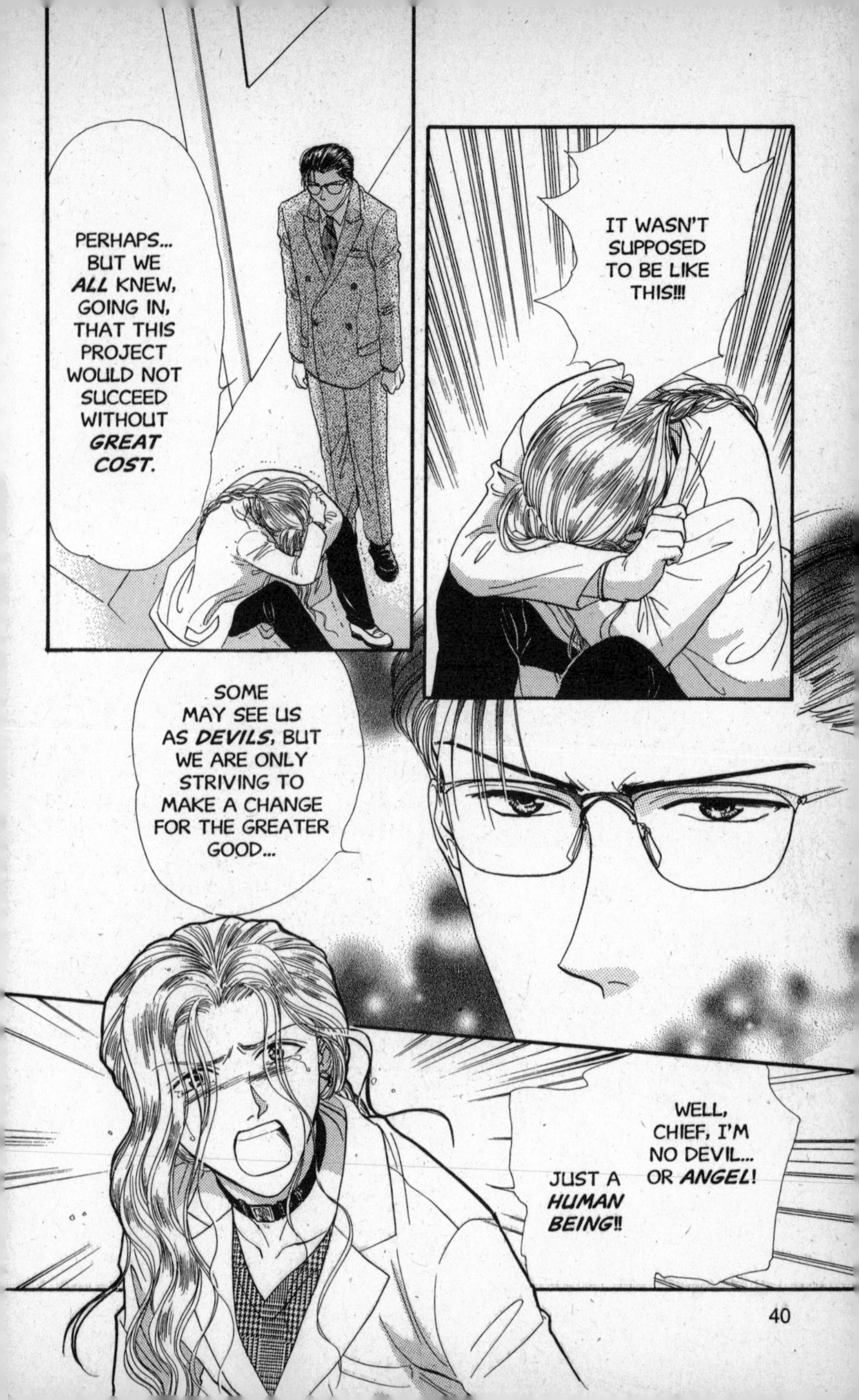
IT WASN'T SUPPOSED TO BE LIKE THIS!!!
PERHAPS... BUT WE *ALL* KNEW, GOING IN, THAT THIS PROJECT WOULD NOT SUCCEED WITHOUT ***GREAT COST.***
SOME MAY SEE US AS ***DEVILS***, BUT WE ARE ONLY STRIVING TO MAKE A CHANGE FOR THE GREATER GOOD...
WELL, CHIEF, I'M NO DEVIL... OR ***ANGEL***!
JUST A ***HUMAN BEING***!!

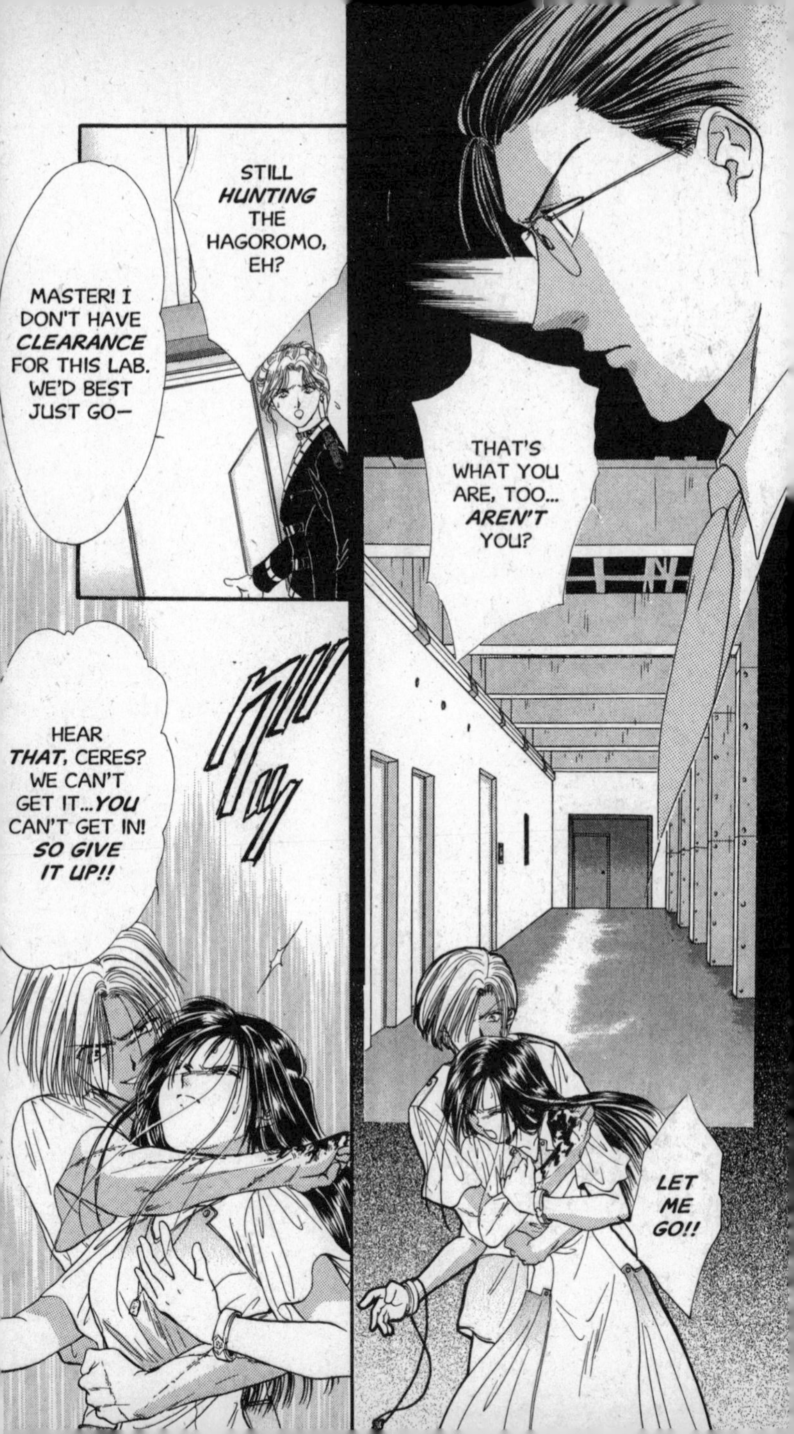
THAT'S WHAT YOU ARE, TOO... *AREN'T* YOU?
STILL *HUNTING* THE HAGOROMO, EH?
MASTER! I DON'T HAVE *CLEARANCE* FOR THIS LAB. WE'D BEST JUST GO—
LET ME GO!!
HEAR *THAT,* CERES? WE CAN'T GET IT...*YOU* CAN'T GET IN! *SO GIVE IT UP!!*

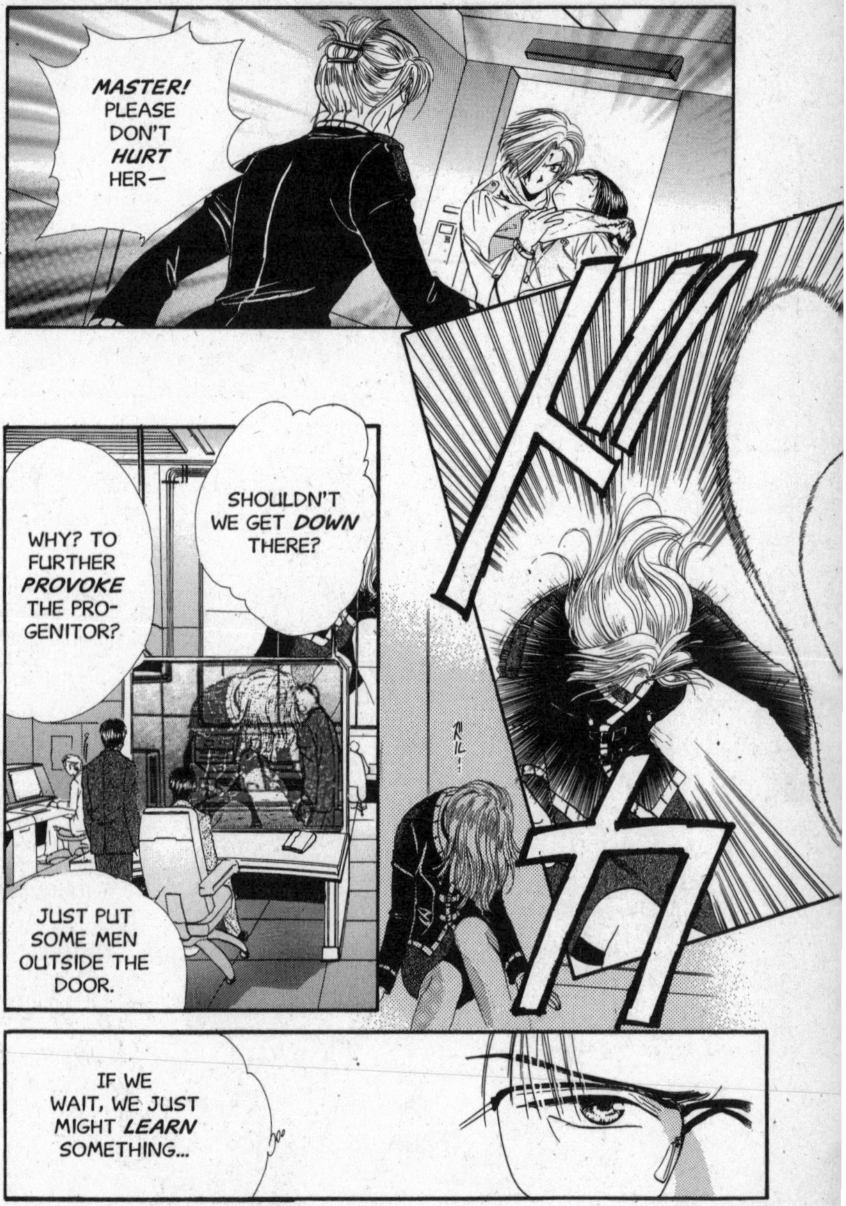
MASTER! PLEASE DON'T HURT HER—
SHOULDN'T WE GET DOWN THERE?
WHY? TO FURTHER PROVOKE THE PRO-GENITOR?
JUST PUT SOME MEN OUTSIDE THE DOOR.
IF WE WAIT, WE JUST MIGHT LEARN SOMETHING...

Ceres: 13

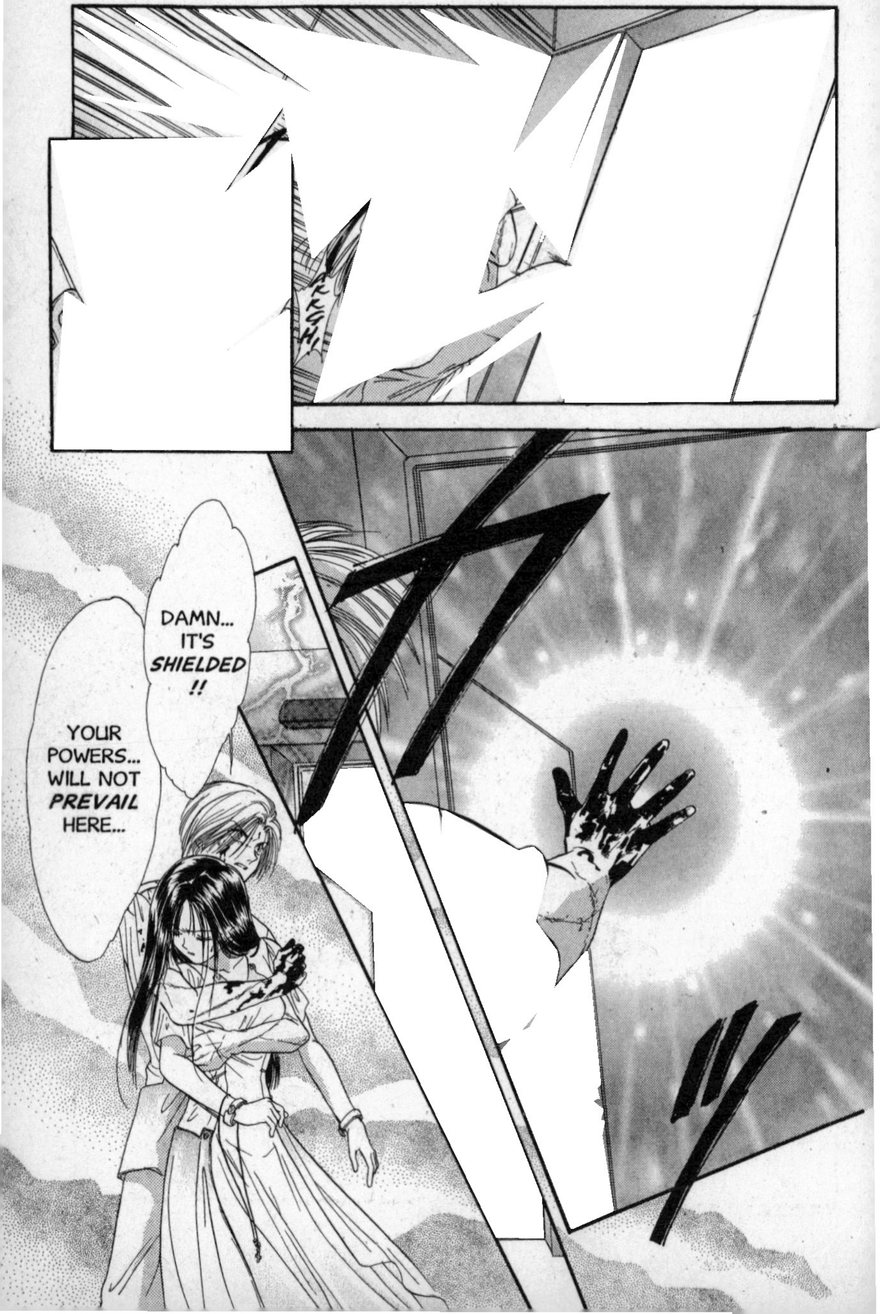
ARRGH!
DAMN... IT'S *SHIELDED* !!
YOUR POWERS... WILL NOT *PREVAIL* HERE...

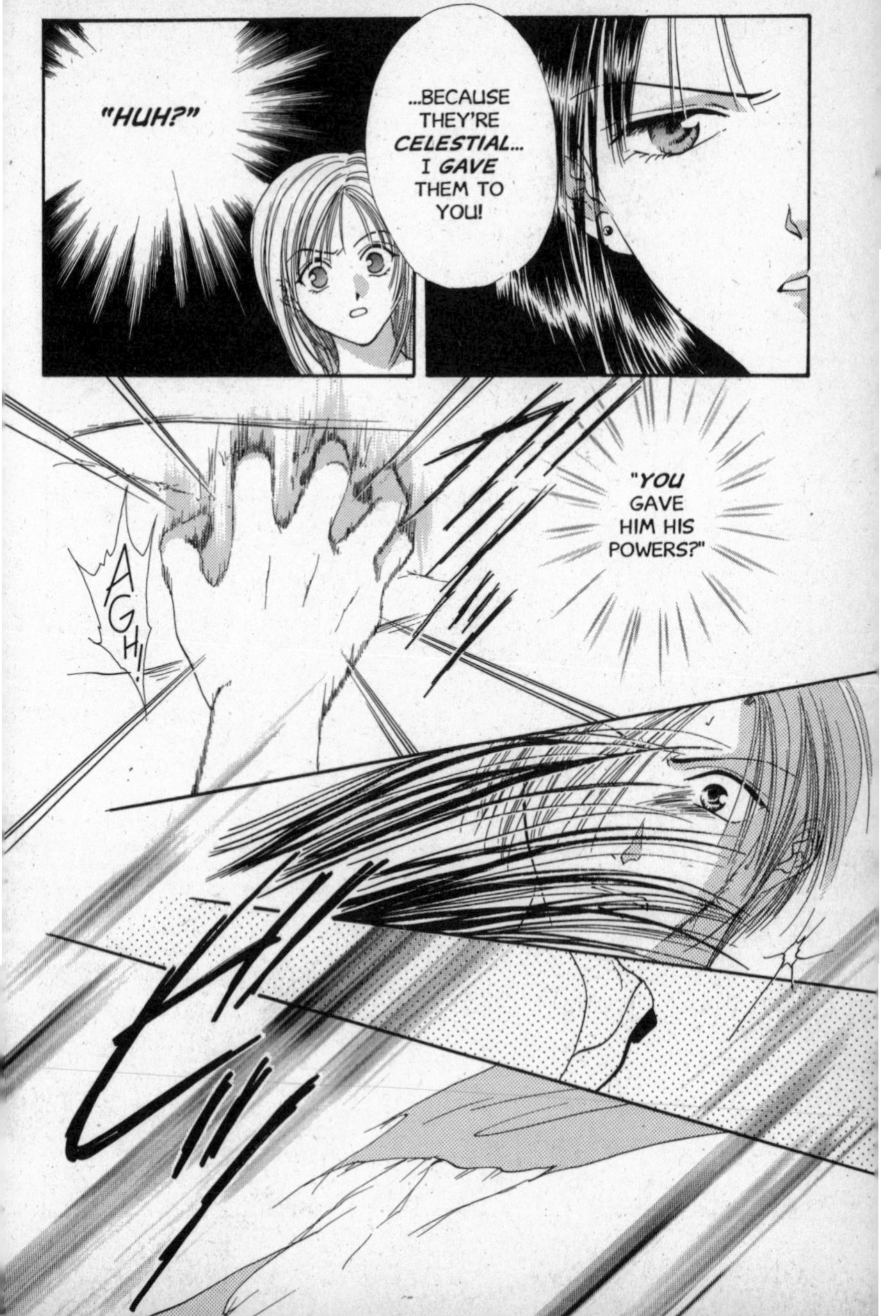
...BECAUSE THEY'RE CELESTIAL... I GAVE THEM TO YOU!
"HUH?"
"YOU GAVE HIM HIS POWERS?"
AGH!

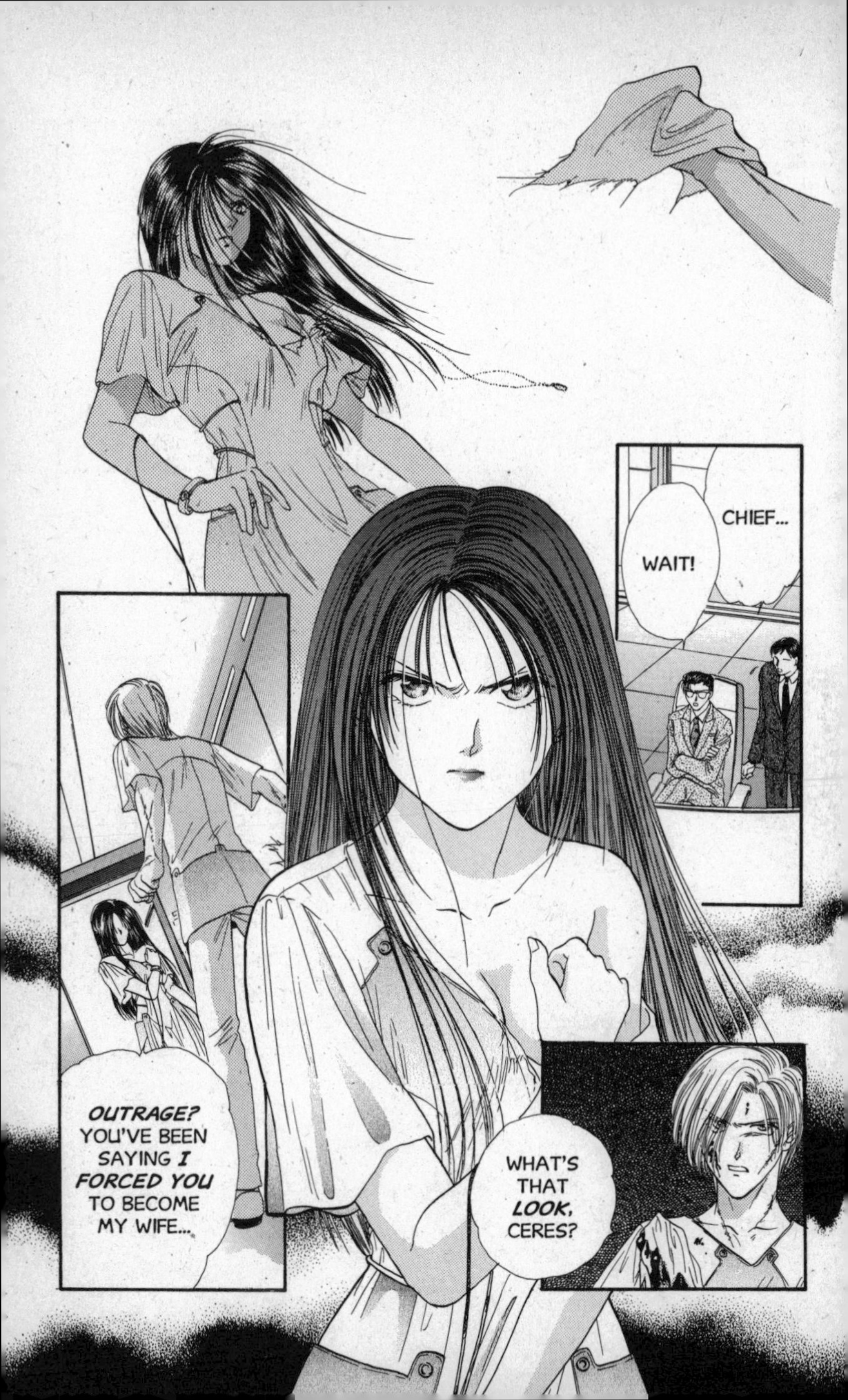
CHIEF...
WAIT!
WHAT'S THAT *LOOK,* CERES?
OUTRAGE? YOU'VE BEEN SAYING *I FORCED YOU* TO BECOME MY WIFE...

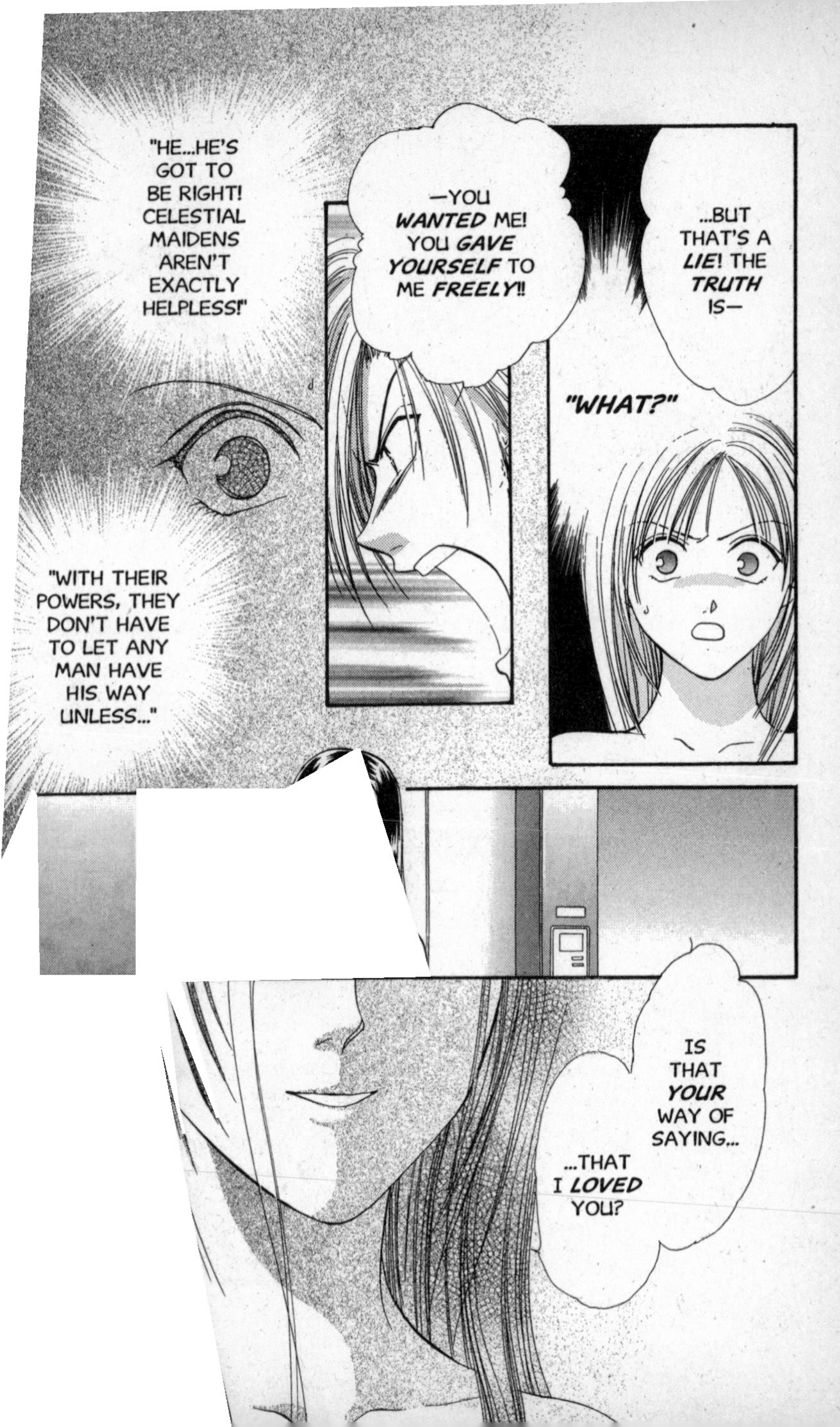
...BUT THAT'S A LIE! THE TRUTH IS—
"WHAT?"
—YOU WANTED ME! YOU GAVE YOURSELF TO ME FREELY!!
"HE...HE'S GOT TO BE RIGHT! CELESTIAL MAIDENS AREN'T EXACTLY HELPLESS!"
"WITH THEIR POWERS, THEY DON'T HAVE TO LET ANY MAN HAVE HIS WAY UNLESS..."
IS THAT YOUR WAY OF SAYING...
...THAT I LOVED YOU?

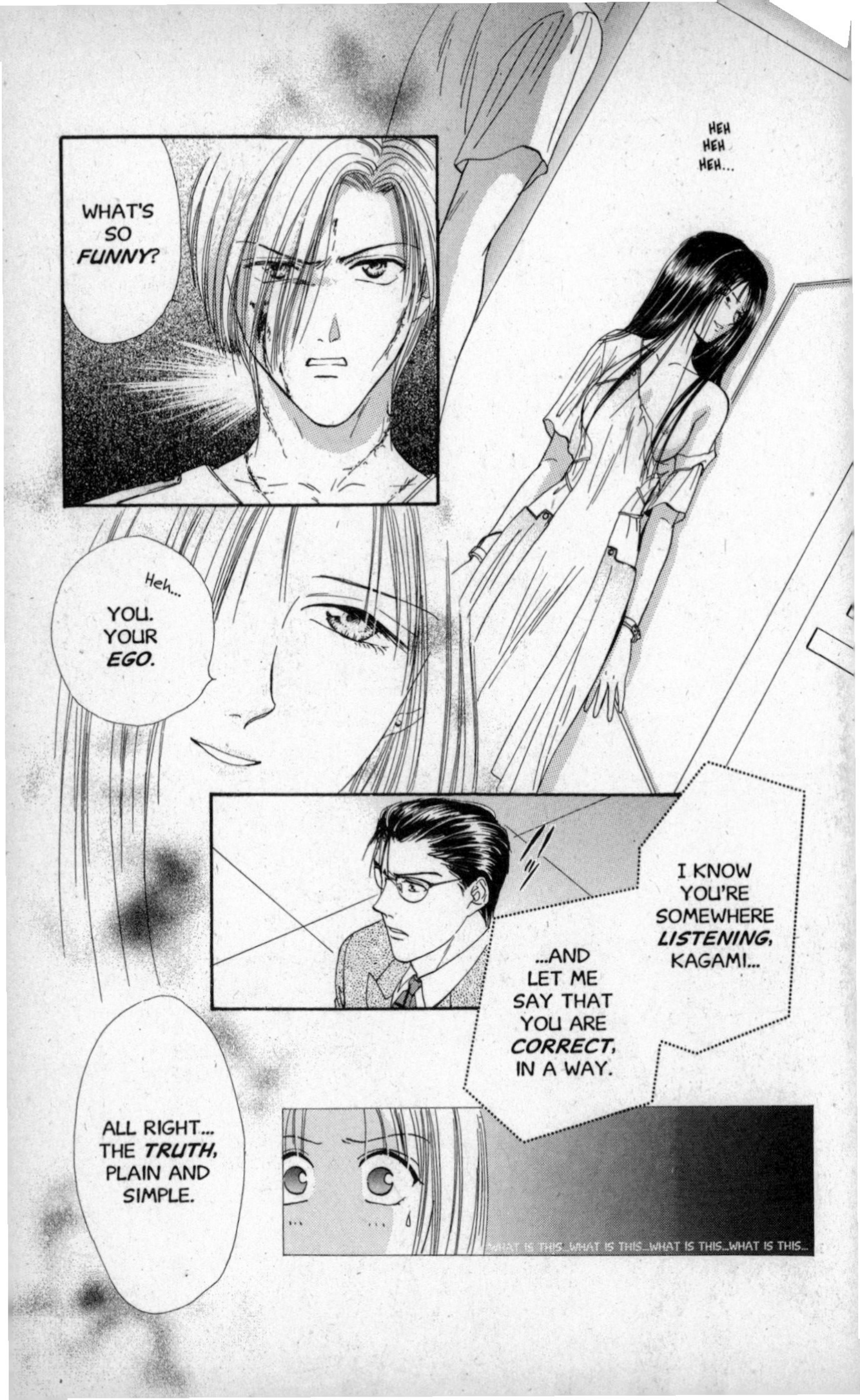
HEH HEH HEH...
WHAT'S SO *FUNNY*?
Heh...
YOU. YOUR *EGO*.
I KNOW YOU'RE SOMEWHERE *LISTENING*, KAGAMI...
...AND LET ME SAY THAT YOU ARE *CORRECT*, IN A WAY.
WHAT IS THIS...WHAT IS THIS...WHAT IS THIS...WHAT IS THIS...
ALL RIGHT... THE *TRUTH*, PLAIN AND SIMPLE.

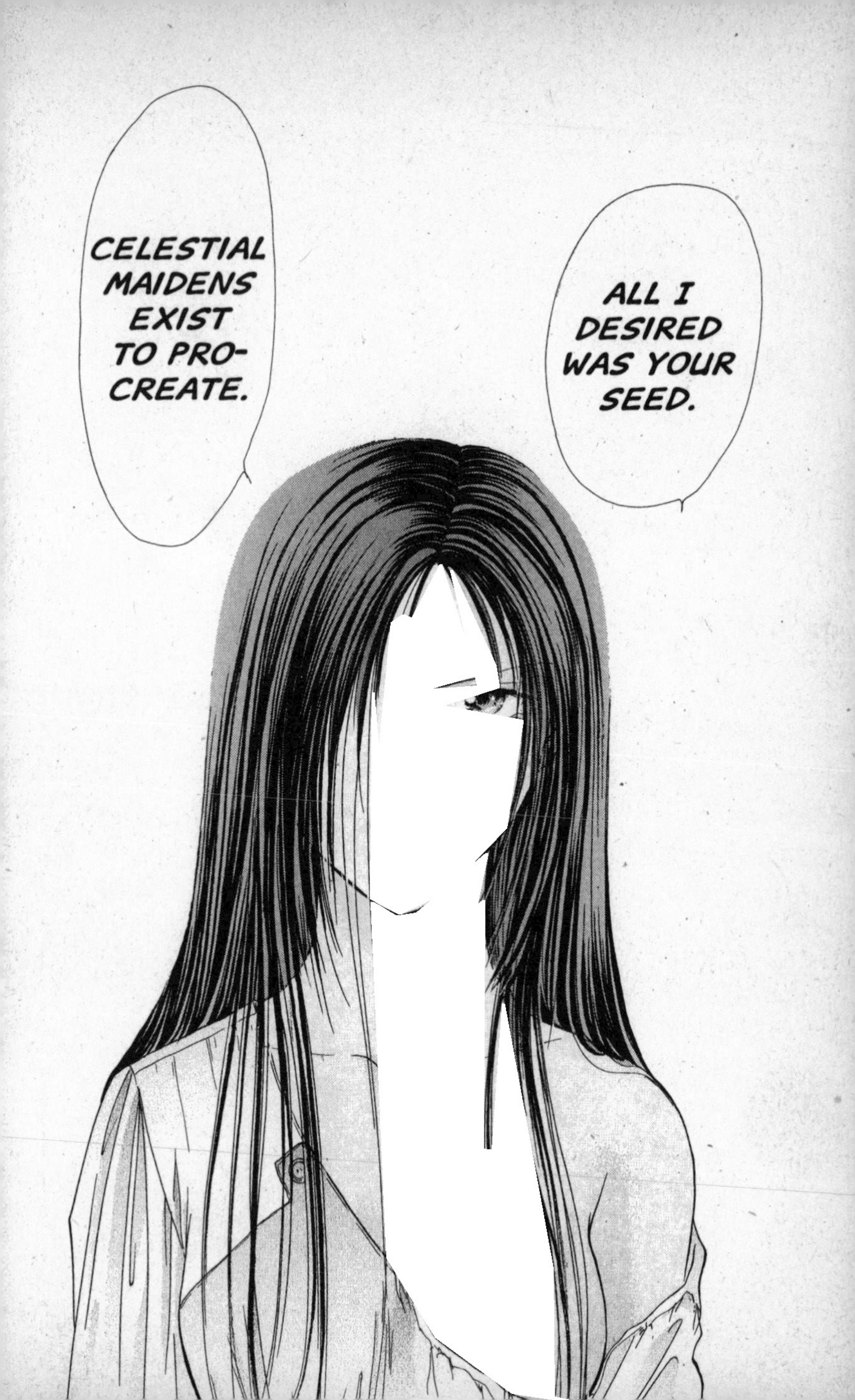
ALL I DESIRED WAS YOUR SEED.
CELESTIAL MAIDENS EXIST TO PRO-CREATE.

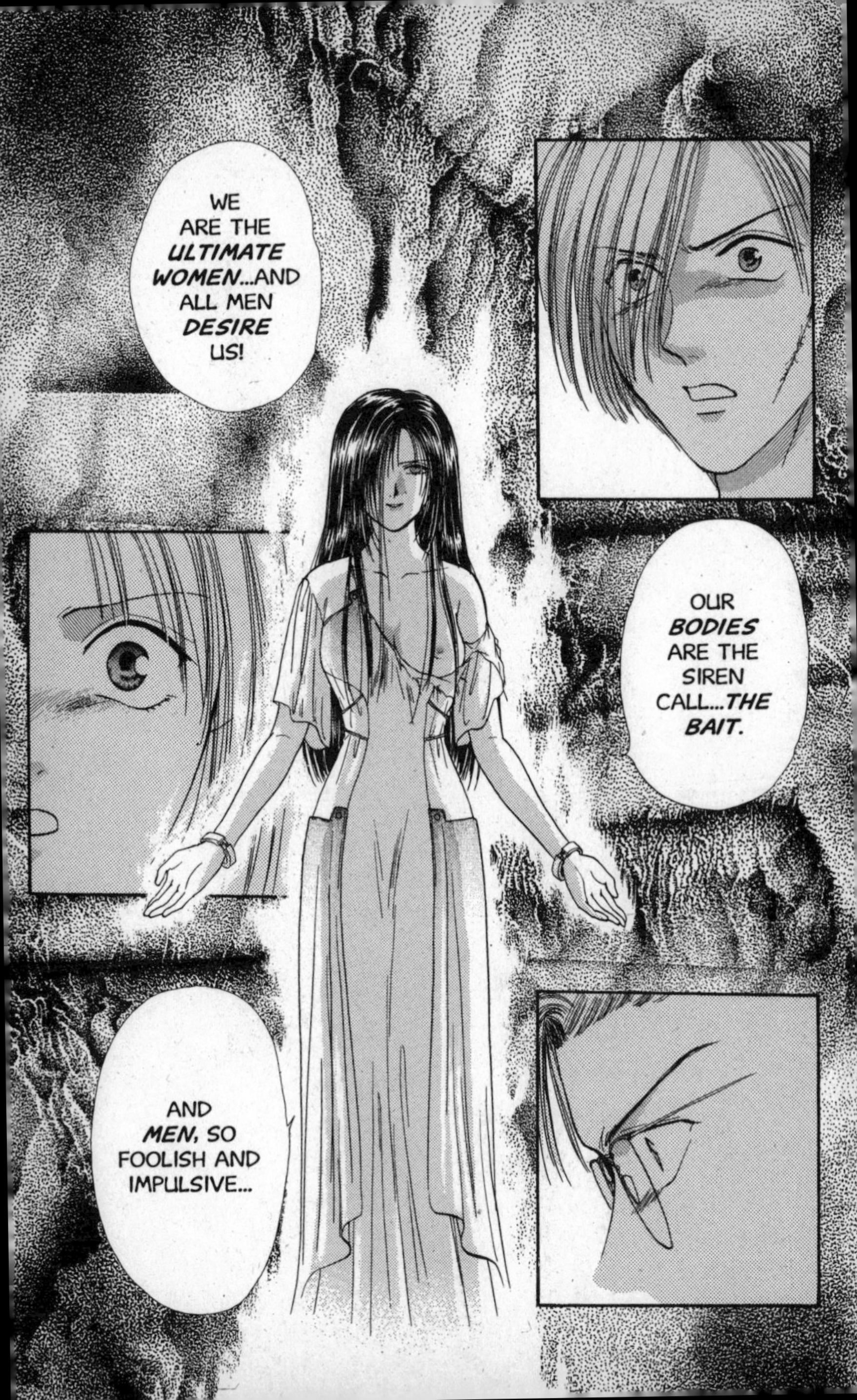
WE ARE THE ULTIMATE WOMEN...AND ALL MEN DESIRE US!
OUR BODIES ARE THE SIREN CALL...THE BAIT.
AND MEN, SO FOOLISH AND IMPULSIVE...

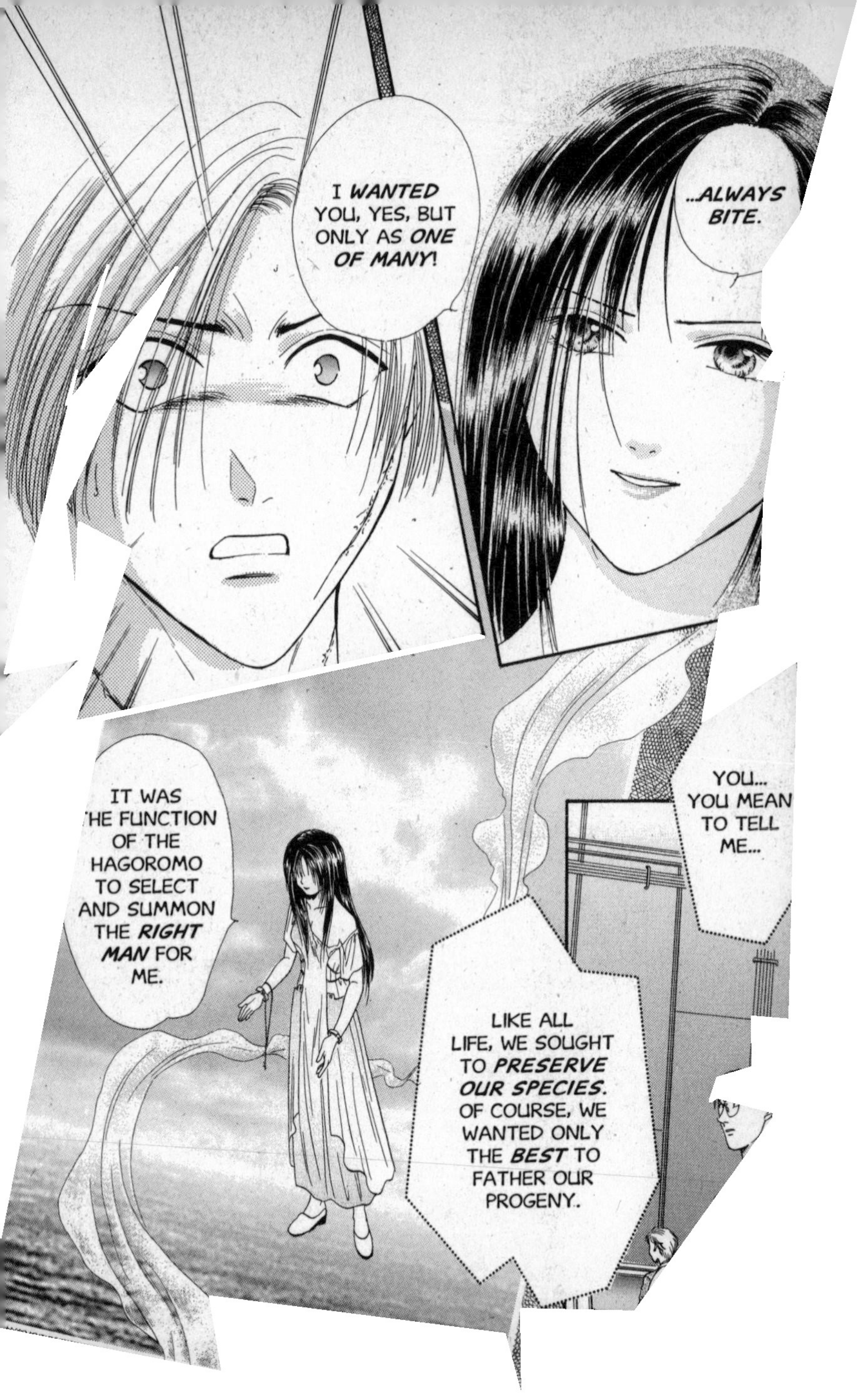

...ALWAYS BITE.
I WANTED YOU, YES, BUT ONLY AS ONE OF MANY!
YOU... YOU MEAN TO TELL ME...
IT WAS THE FUNCTION OF THE HAGOROMO TO SELECT AND SUMMON THE RIGHT MAN FOR ME.
LIKE ALL LIFE, WE SOUGHT TO PRESERVE OUR SPECIES. OF COURSE, WE WANTED ONLY THE BEST TO FATHER OUR PROGENY.

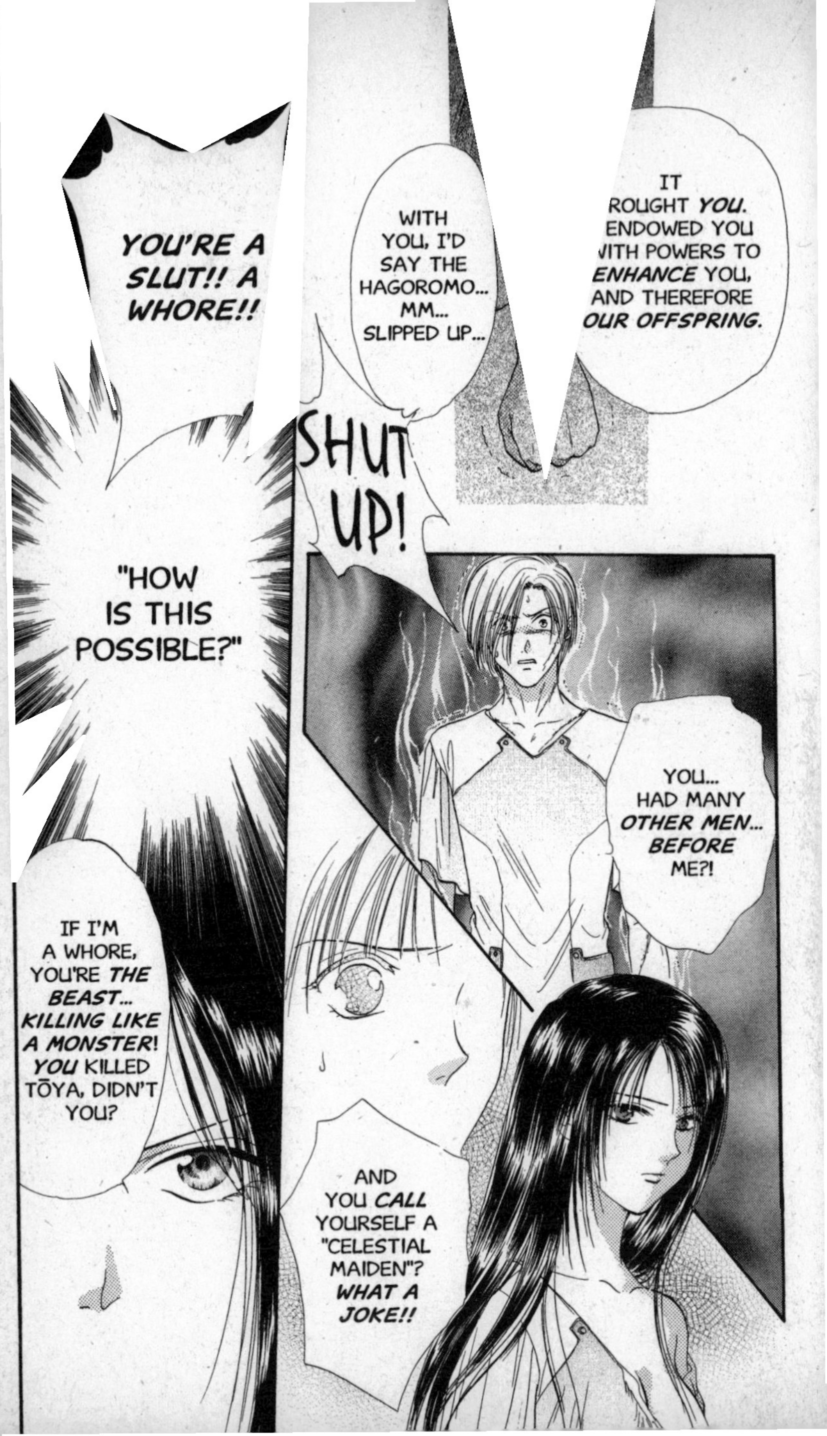
IT ROUGHT *YOU.* ENDOWED YOU ITH POWERS TO *ENHANCE* YOU, AND THEREFORE *OUR OFFSPRING.*
WITH YOU, I'D SAY THE HAGOROMO... MM... SLIPPED UP...
SHUT UP!
YOU'RE A SLUT!! A WHORE!!
"HOW IS THIS POSSIBLE?"
YOU... HAD MANY *OTHER MEN... BEFORE* ME?!
AND YOU *CALL* YOURSELF A "CELESTIAL MAIDEN"? *WHAT A JOKE!!*
IF I'M A WHORE, YOU'RE *THE BEAST... KILLING LIKE A MONSTER! YOU* KILLED TŌYA, DIDN'T YOU?

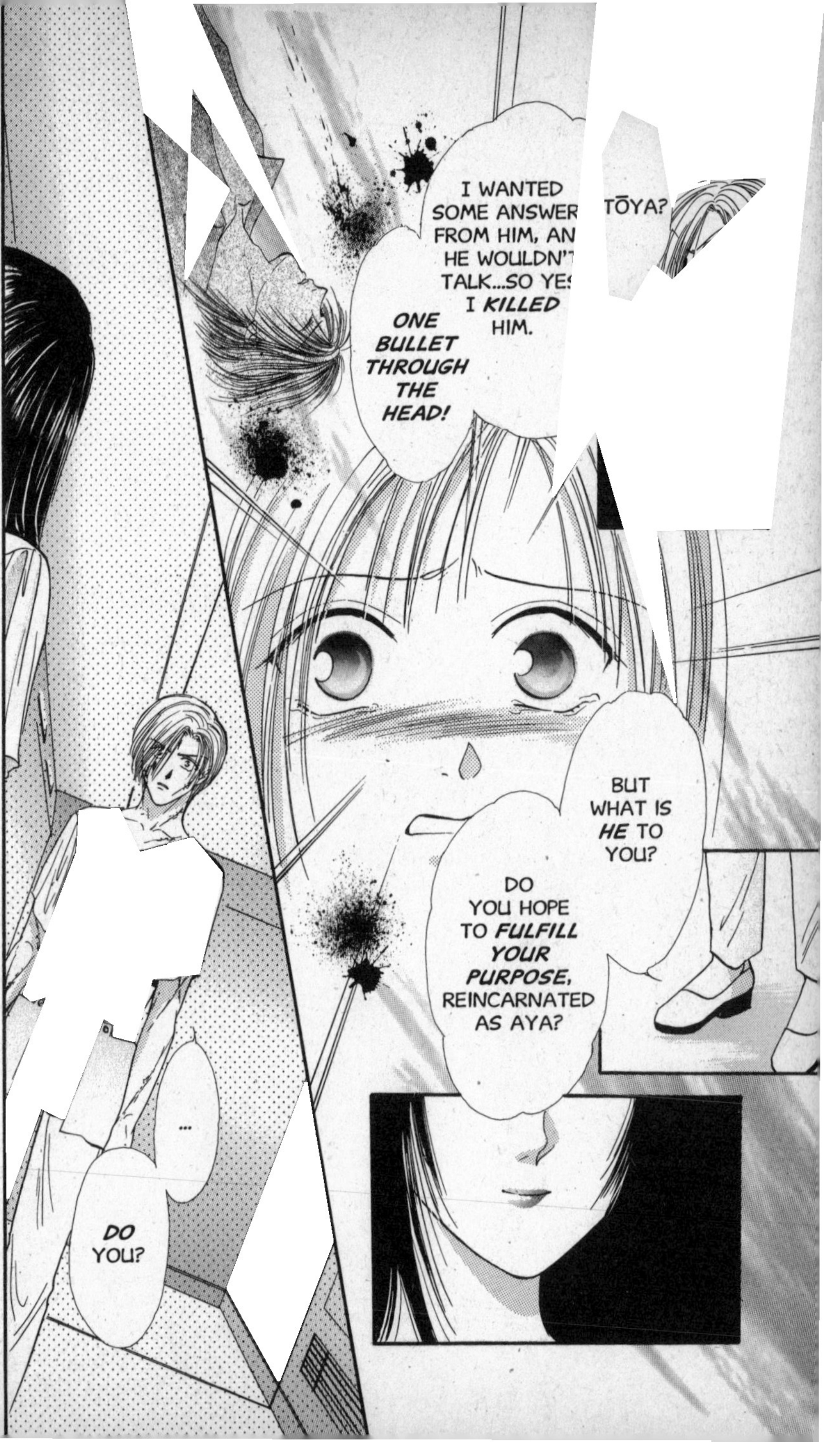
TŌYA?
I WANTED SOME ANSWER FROM HIM, AN HE WOULDN'T TALK...SO YES I KILLED HIM.
ONE BULLET THROUGH THE HEAD!
BUT WHAT IS HE TO YOU?
DO YOU HOPE TO FULFILL YOUR PURPOSE, REINCARNATED AS AYA?
...
DO YOU?

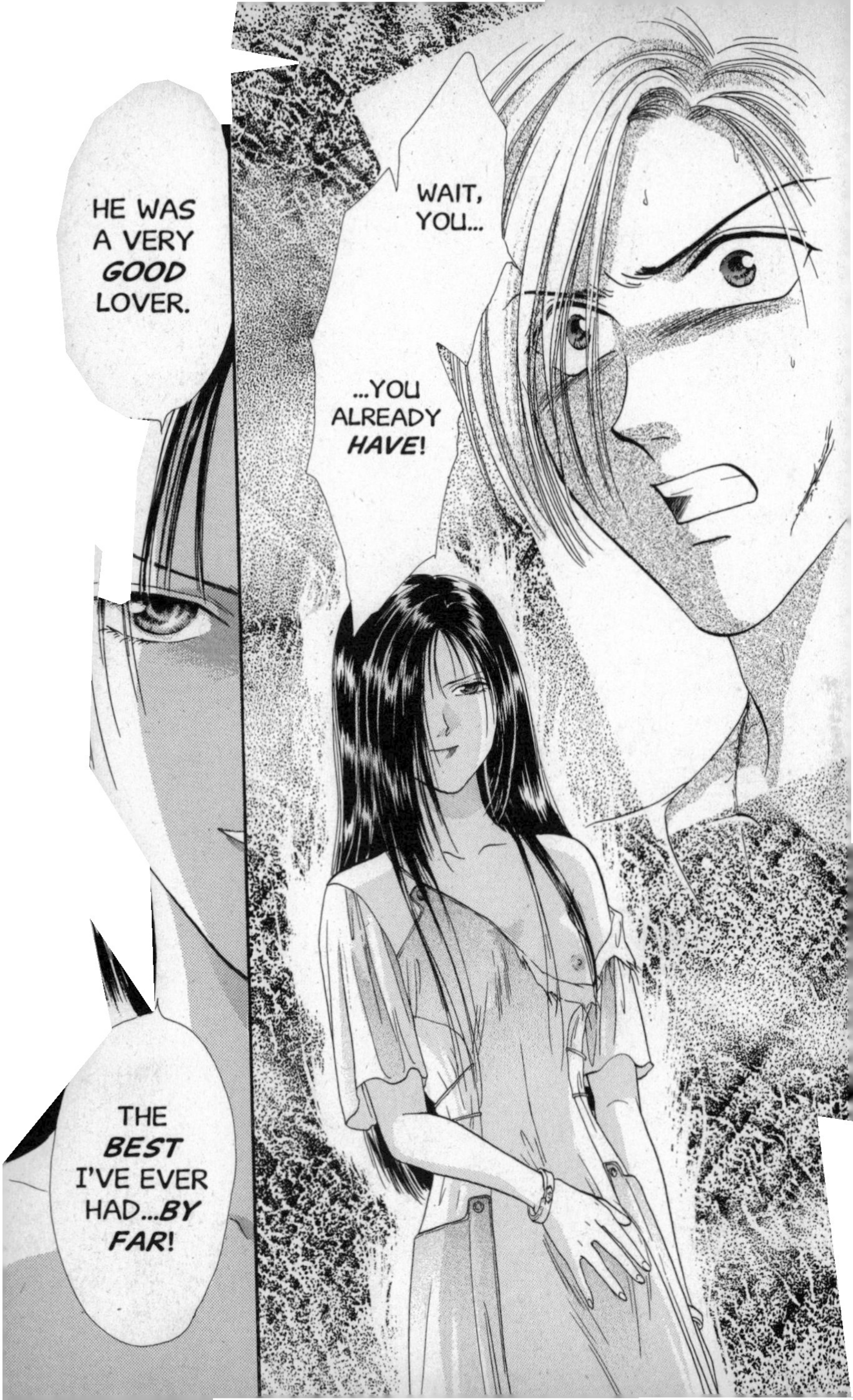
WAIT, YOU...
...YOU ALREADY HAVE!
HE WAS A VERY GOOD LOVER.
THE BEST I'VE EVER HAD...BY FAR!

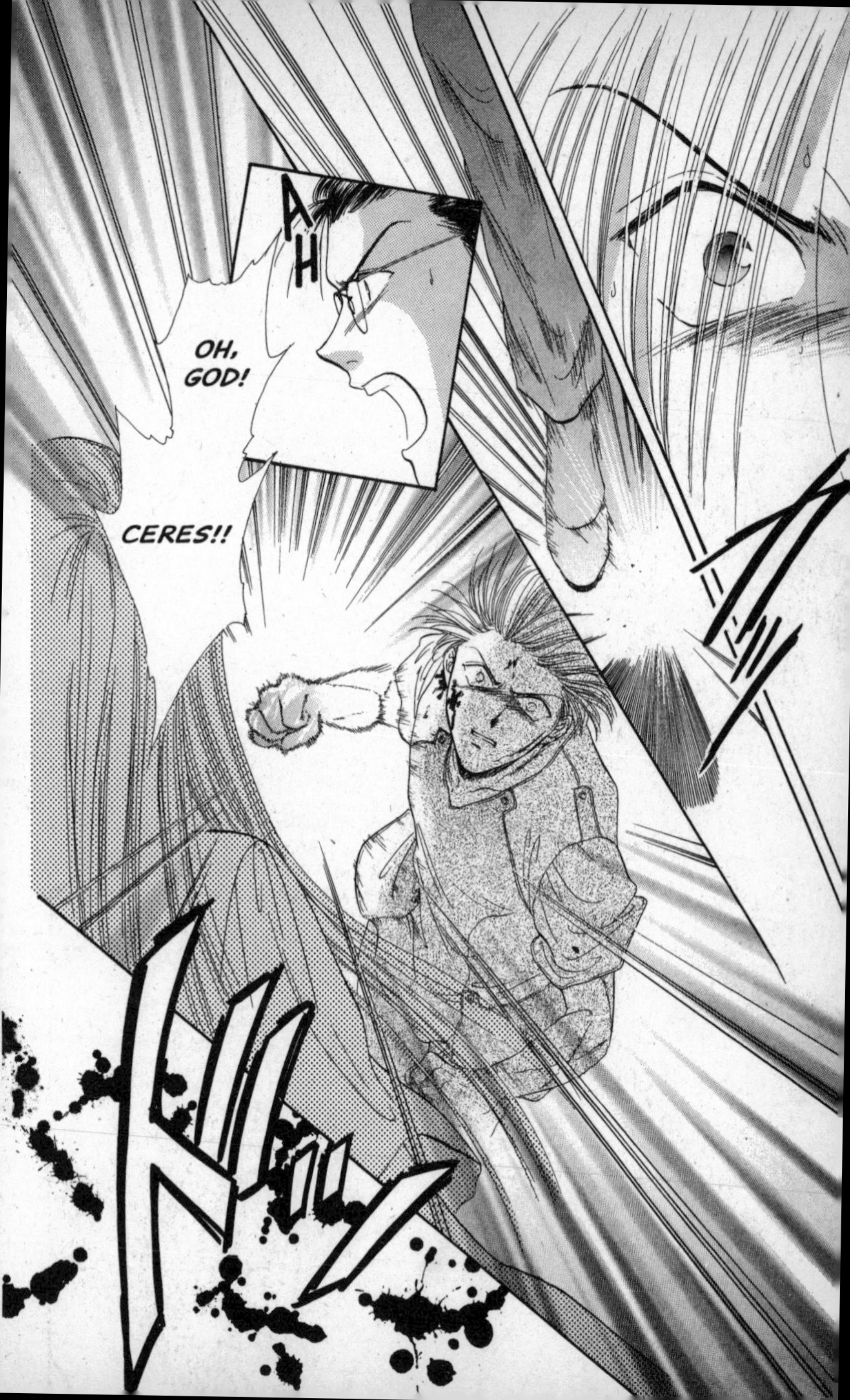
AH
OH, GOD!
CERES!!

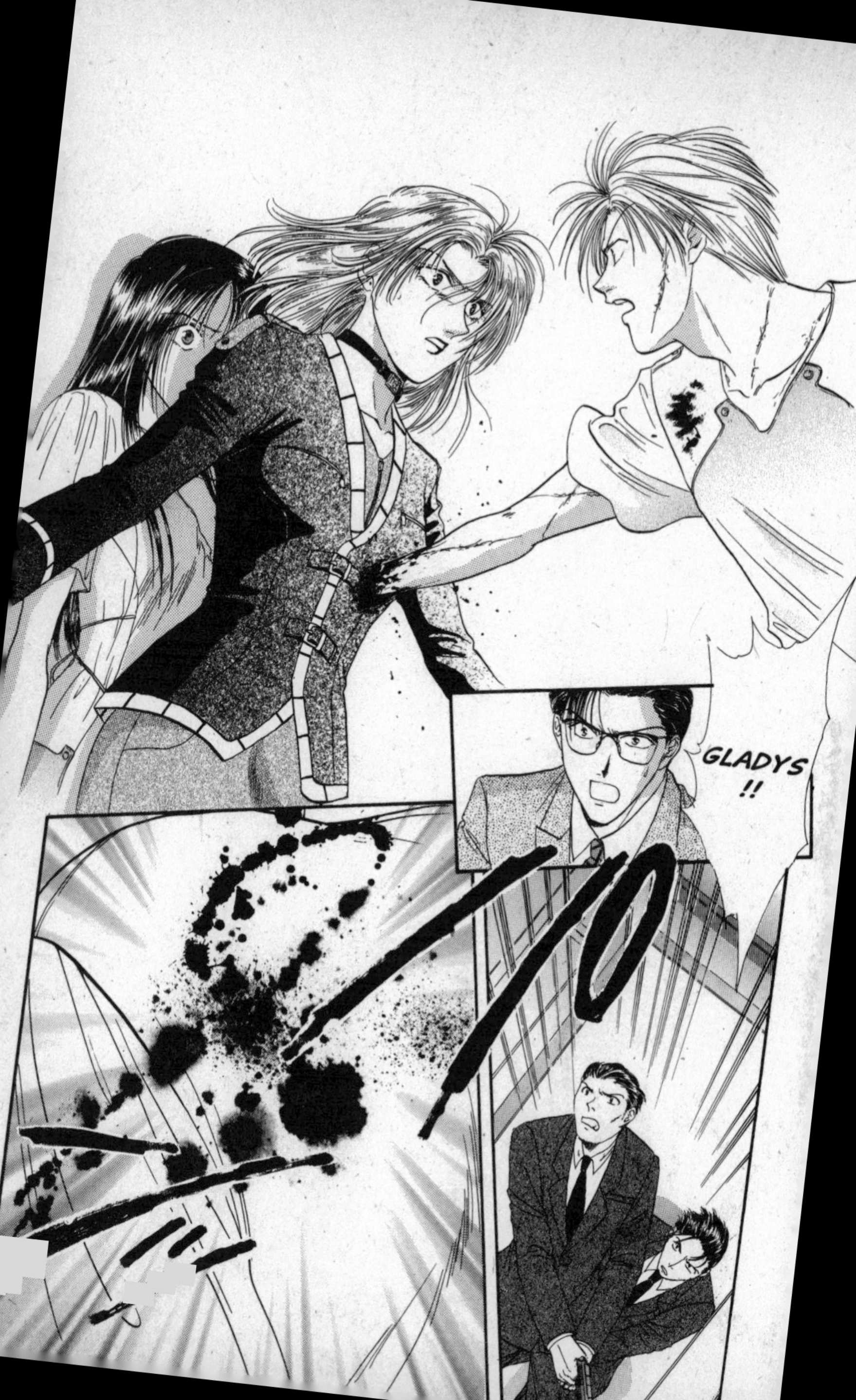
GLADYS !!

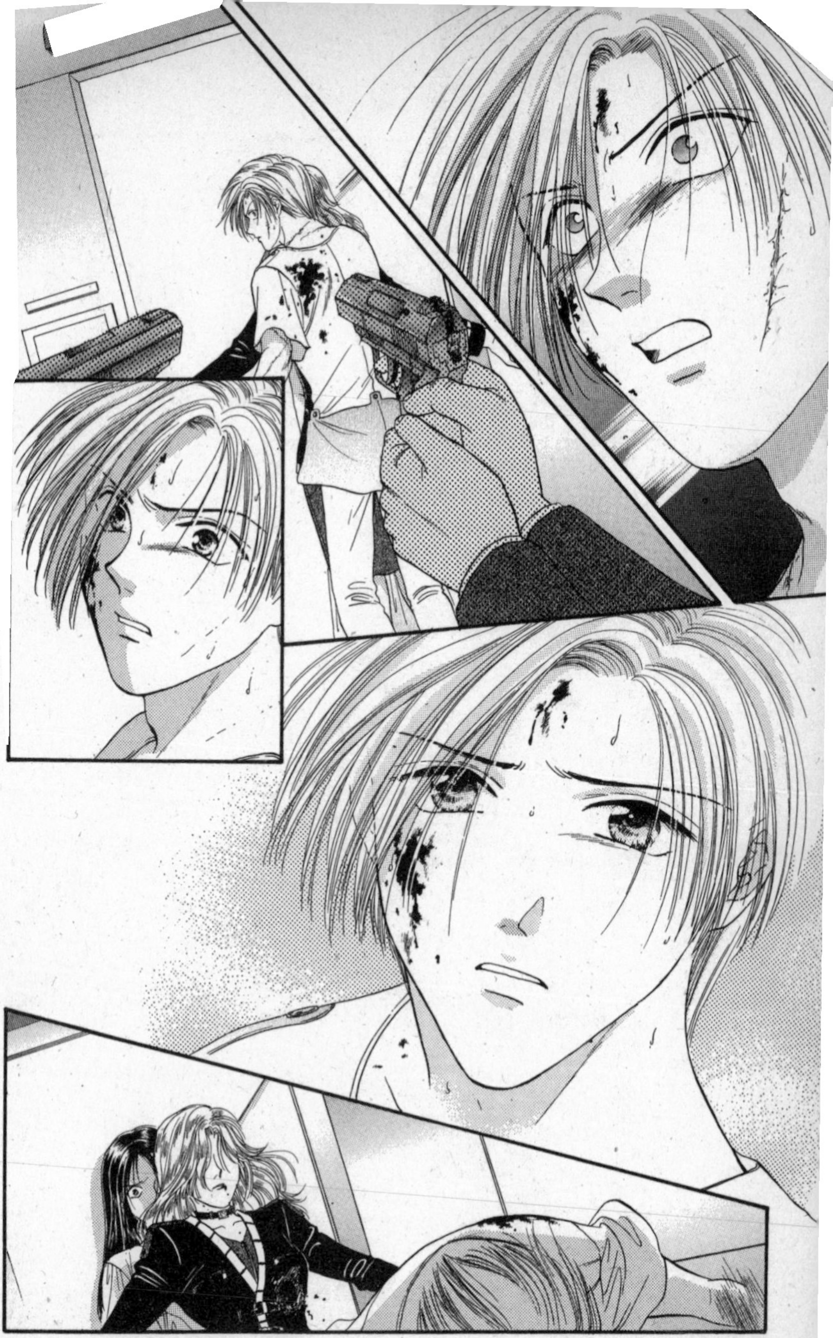

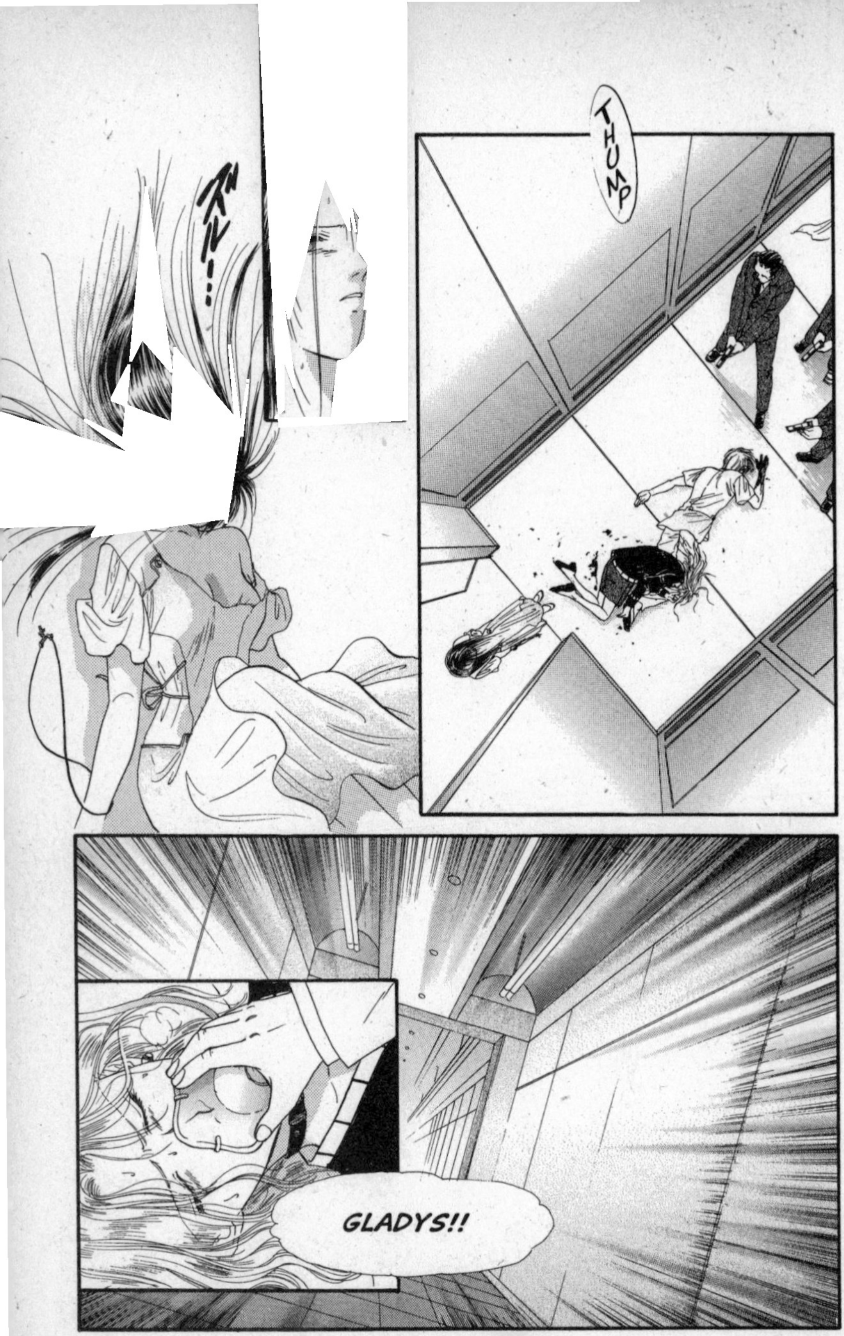
THUMP
ズルー…
GLADYS!!

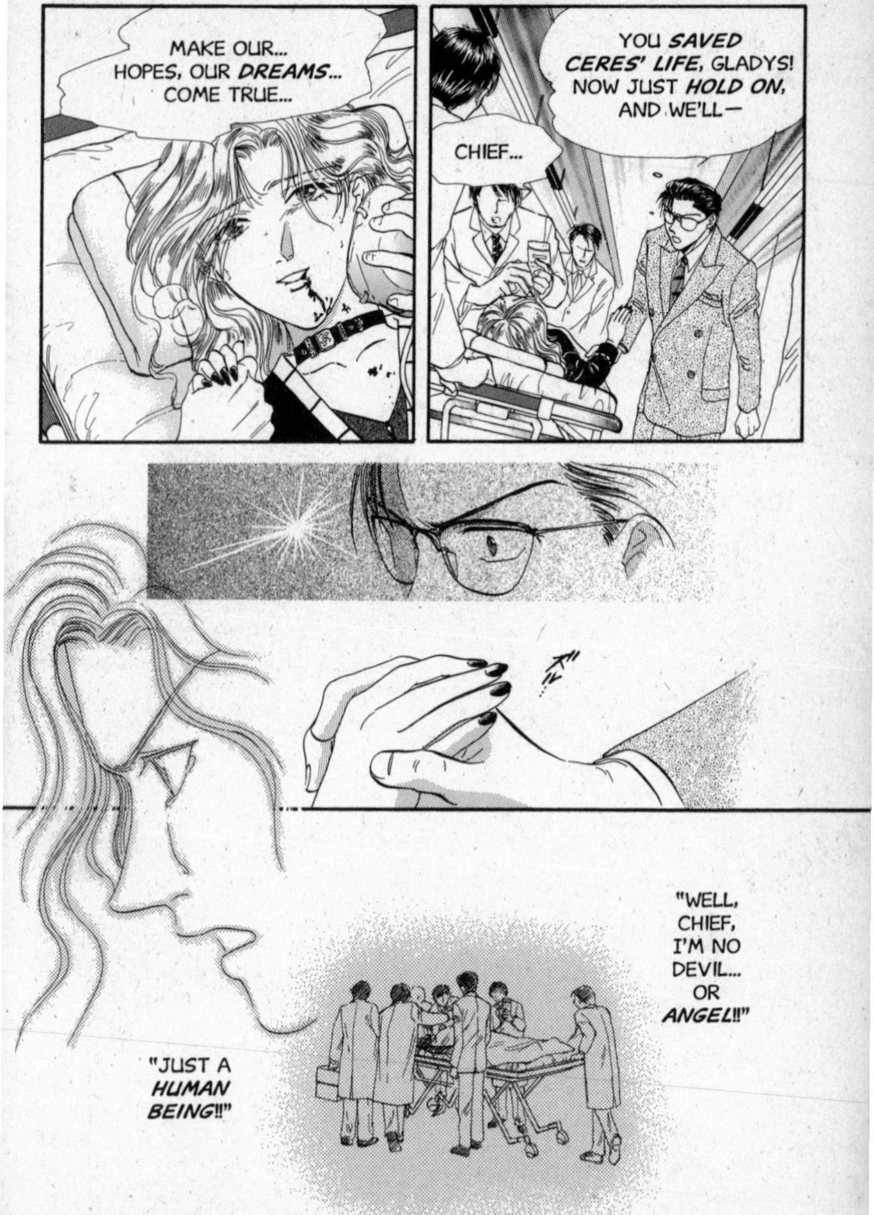
MAKE OUR... HOPES, OUR DREAMS... COME TRUE...
CHIEF...
YOU SAVED CERES' LIFE, GLADYS! NOW JUST HOLD ON, AND WE'LL—
"WELL, CHIEF, I'M NO DEVIL... OR ANGEL!!"
"JUST A HUMAN BEING!!"

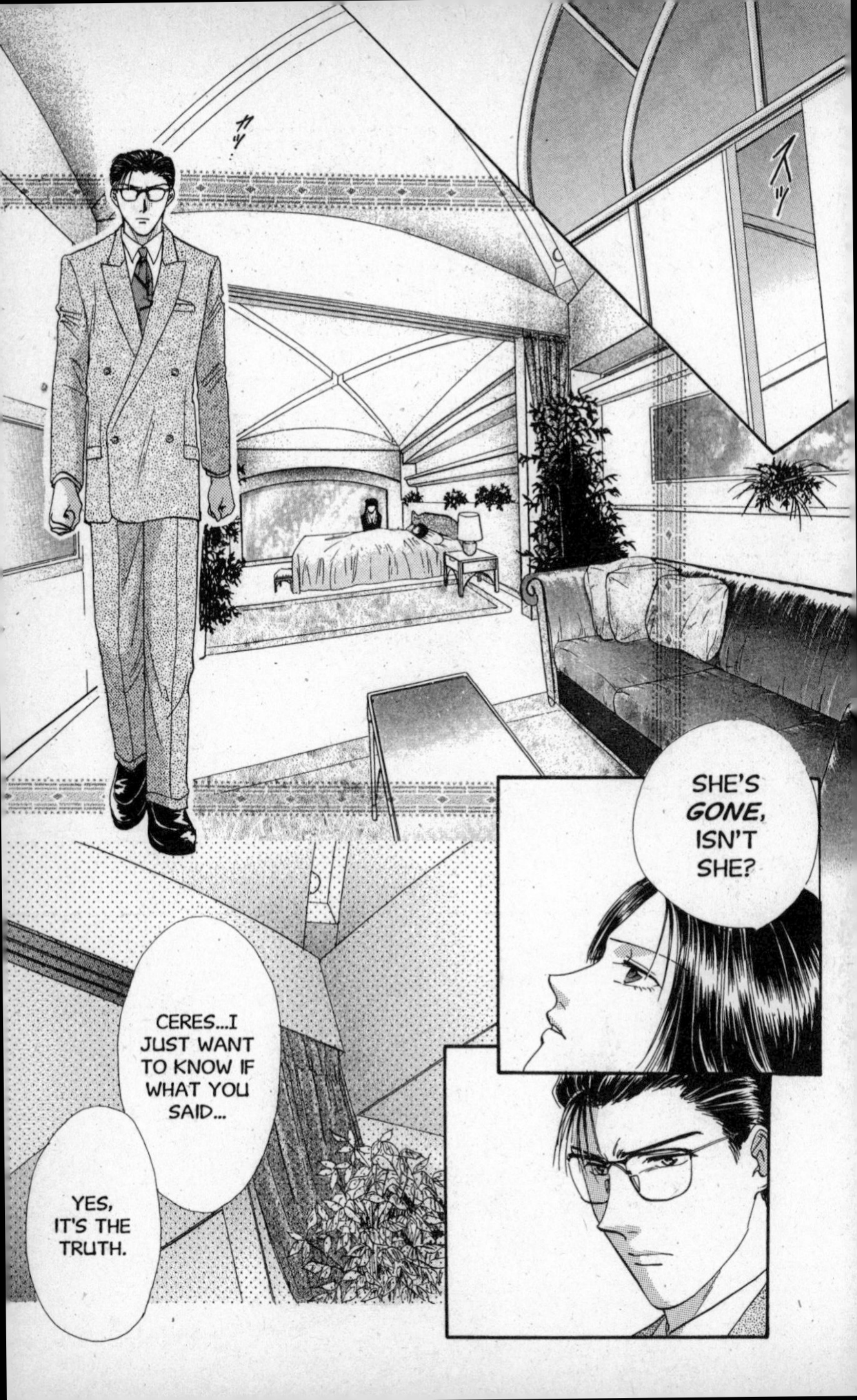
スッ
カッ
SHE'S *GONE,* ISN'T SHE?
CERES...I JUST WANT TO KNOW IF WHAT YOU SAID...
YES, IT'S THE TRUTH.

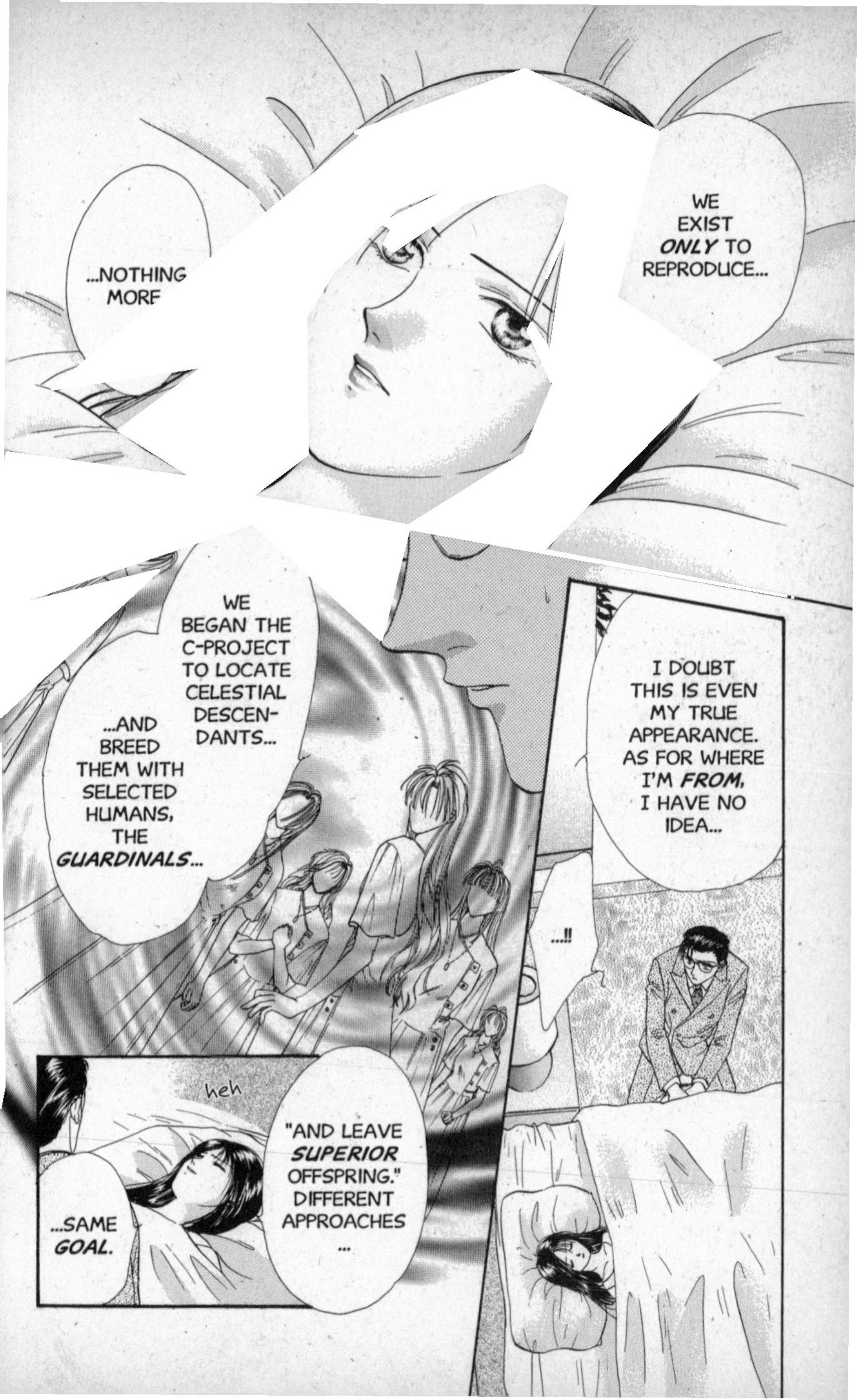
WE EXIST ONLY TO REPRODUCE...
...NOTHING MORE
I DOUBT THIS IS EVEN MY TRUE APPEARANCE. AS FOR WHERE I'M FROM, I HAVE NO IDEA...
...!!
WE BEGAN THE C-PROJECT TO LOCATE CELESTIAL DESCENDANTS...
...AND BREED THEM WITH SELECTED HUMANS, THE GUARDINALS...
heh
"AND LEAVE SUPERIOR OFFSPRING." DIFFERENT APPROACHES ...
...SAME GOAL.

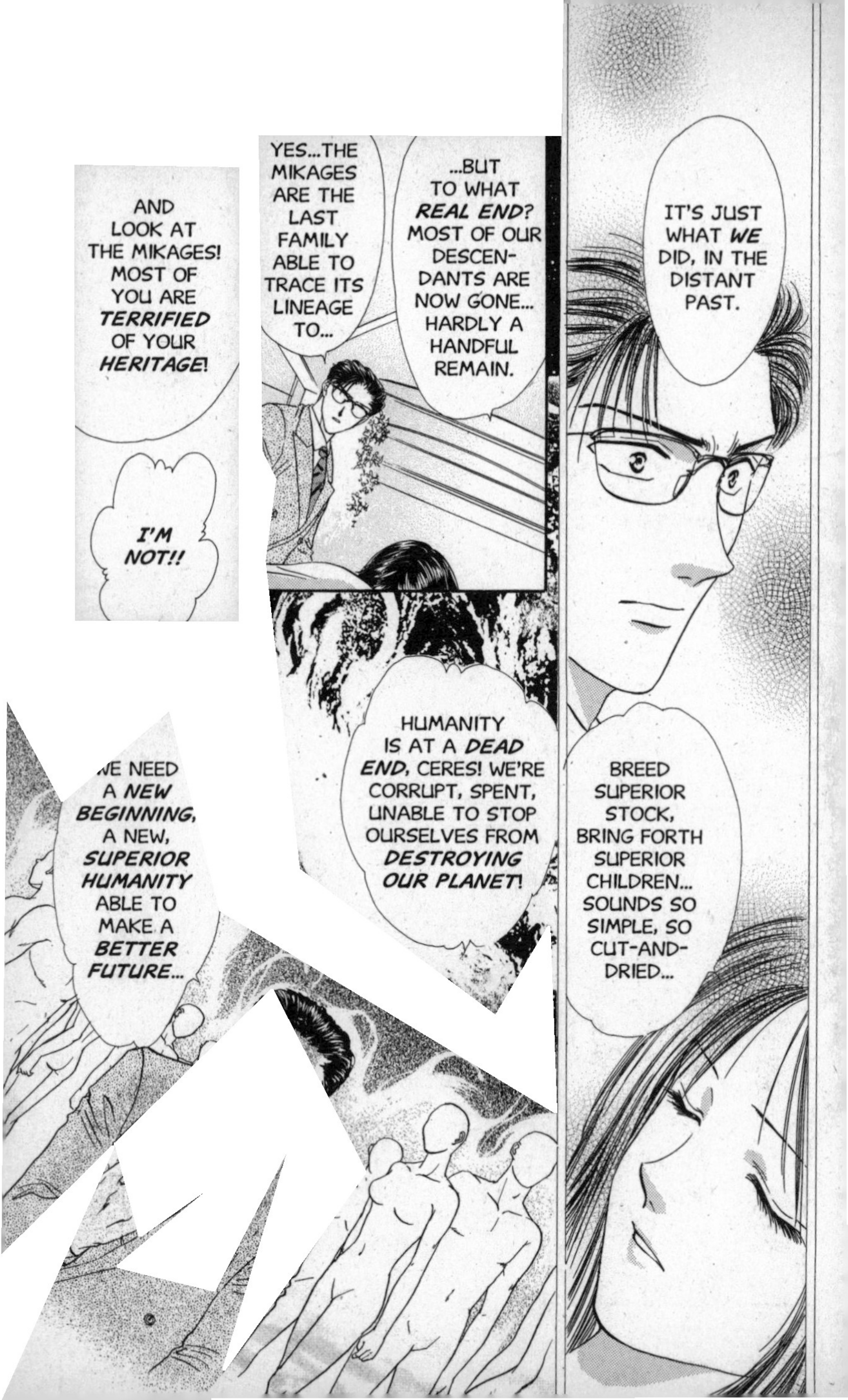
IT'S JUST WHAT WE DID, IN THE DISTANT PAST.
BREED SUPERIOR STOCK, BRING FORTH SUPERIOR CHILDREN... SOUNDS SO SIMPLE, SO CUT-AND-DRIED...
YES...THE MIKAGES ARE THE LAST FAMILY ABLE TO TRACE ITS LINEAGE TO...
...BUT TO WHAT REAL END? MOST OF OUR DESCEN-DANTS ARE NOW GONE... HARDLY A HANDFUL REMAIN.
HUMANITY IS AT A DEAD END, CERES! WE'RE CORRUPT, SPENT, UNABLE TO STOP OURSELVES FROM DESTROYING OUR PLANET!
AND LOOK AT THE MIKAGES! MOST OF YOU ARE TERRIFIED OF YOUR HERITAGE!
I'M NOT!!
WE NEED A NEW BEGINNING, A NEW, SUPERIOR HUMANITY ABLE TO MAKE A BETTER FUTURE...

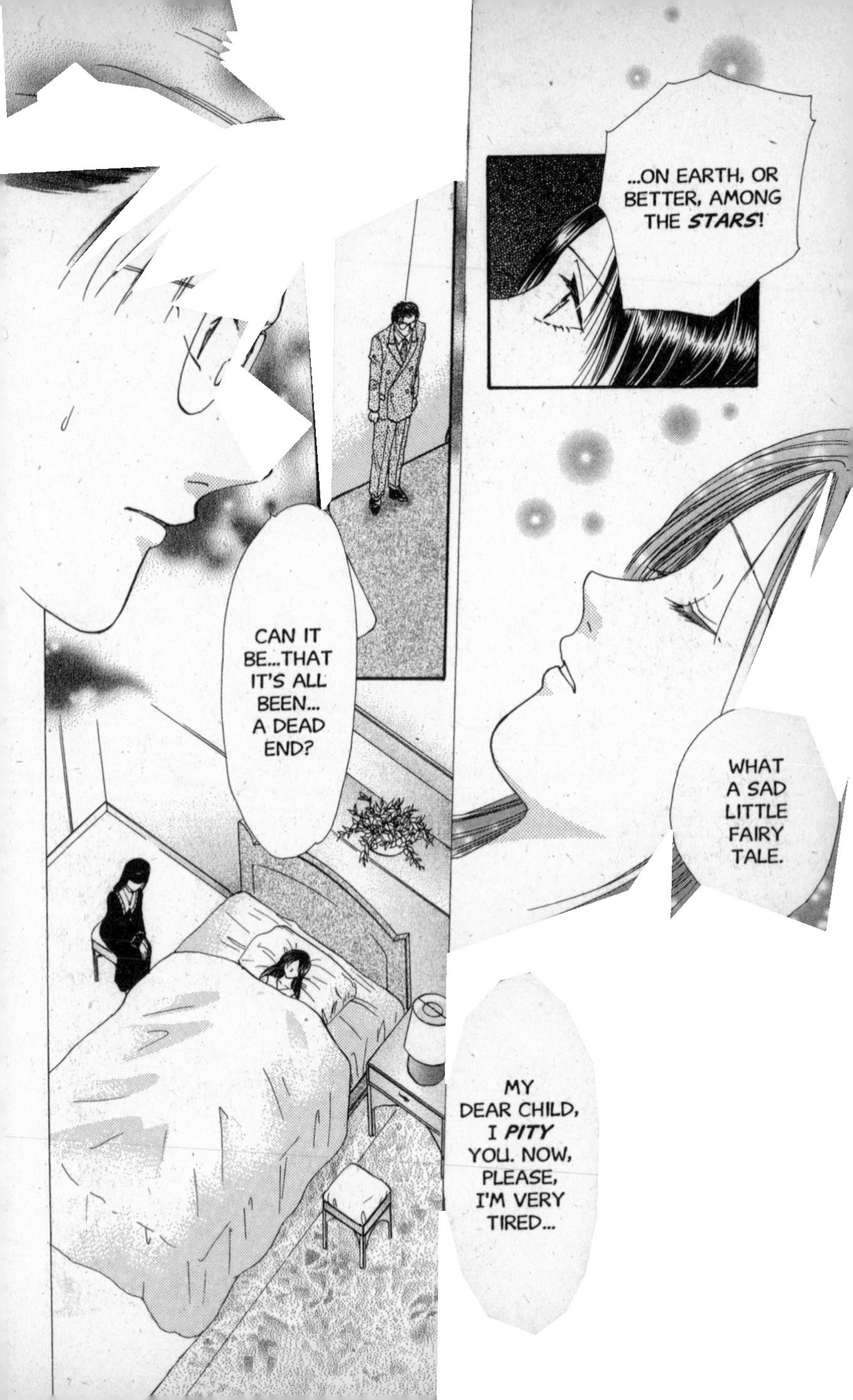
...ON EARTH, OR BETTER, AMONG THE *STARS*!
WHAT A SAD LITTLE FAIRY TALE.
MY DEAR CHILD, I *PITY* YOU. NOW, PLEASE, I'M VERY TIRED...
CAN IT BE...THAT IT'S ALL BEEN... A DEAD END?

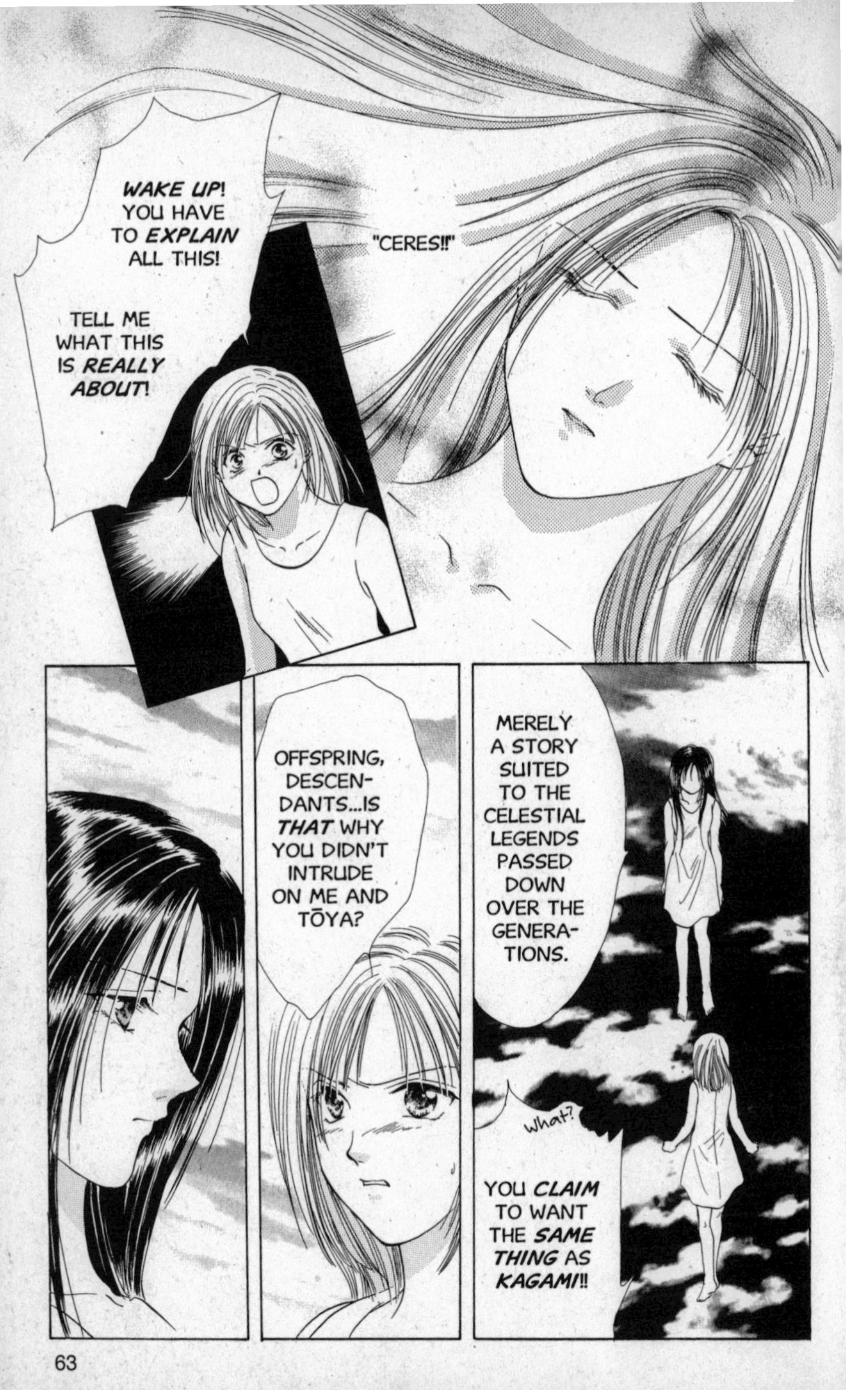
WAKE UP! YOU HAVE TO EXPLAIN ALL THIS!
TELL ME WHAT THIS IS REALLY ABOUT!
"CERES!!"
MERELY A STORY SUITED TO THE CELESTIAL LEGENDS PASSED DOWN OVER THE GENERATIONS.
what?
YOU CLAIM TO WANT THE SAME THING AS KAGAMI!!
OFFSPRING, DESCENDANTS...IS THAT WHY YOU DIDN'T INTRUDE ON ME AND TŌYA?

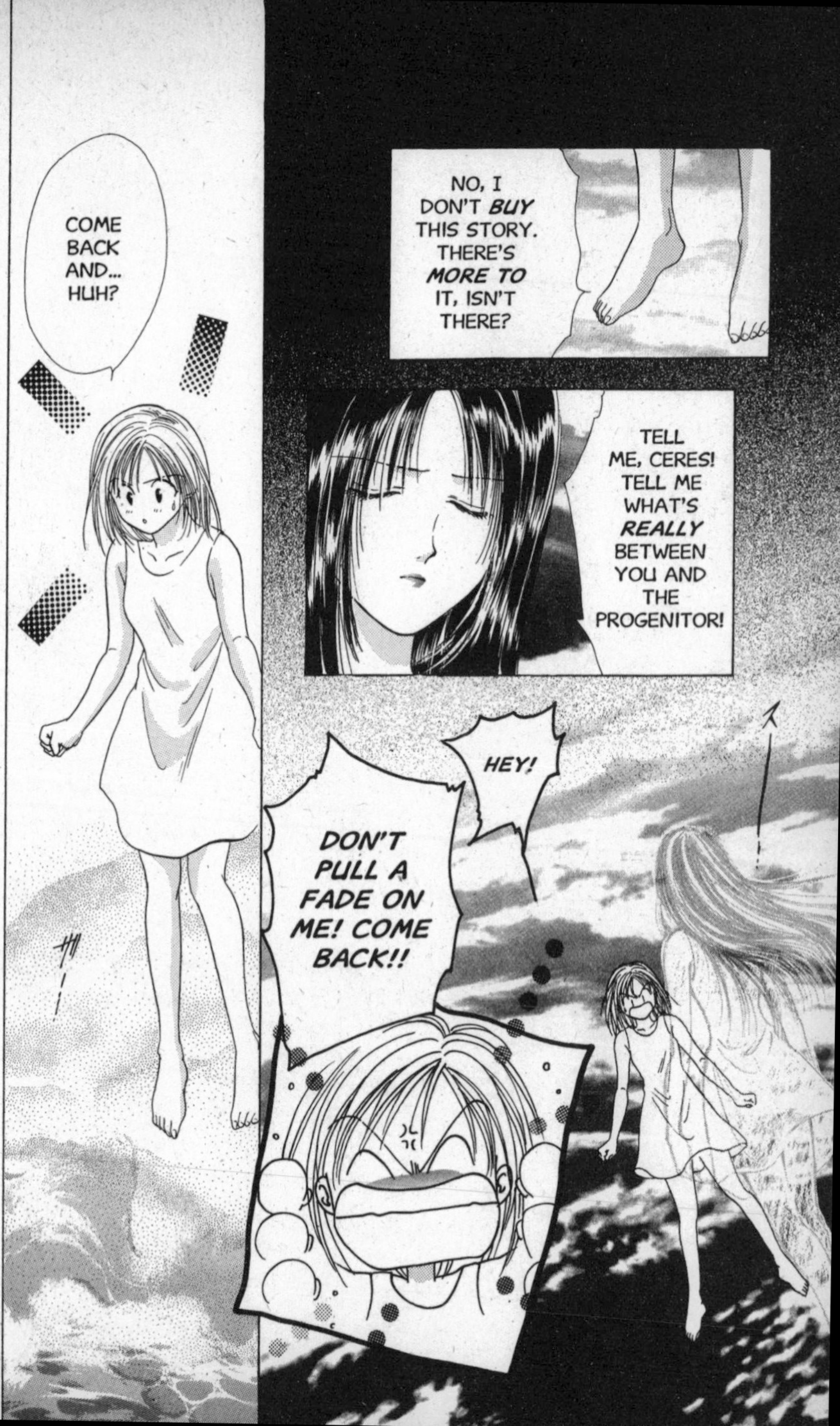
NO, I DON'T *BUY* THIS STORY. THERE'S *MORE TO* IT, ISN'T THERE?
TELL ME, CERES! TELL ME WHAT'S *REALLY* BETWEEN YOU AND THE PROGENITOR!
HEY!
DON'T PULL A FADE ON ME! COME BACK!!
COME BACK AND... HUH?

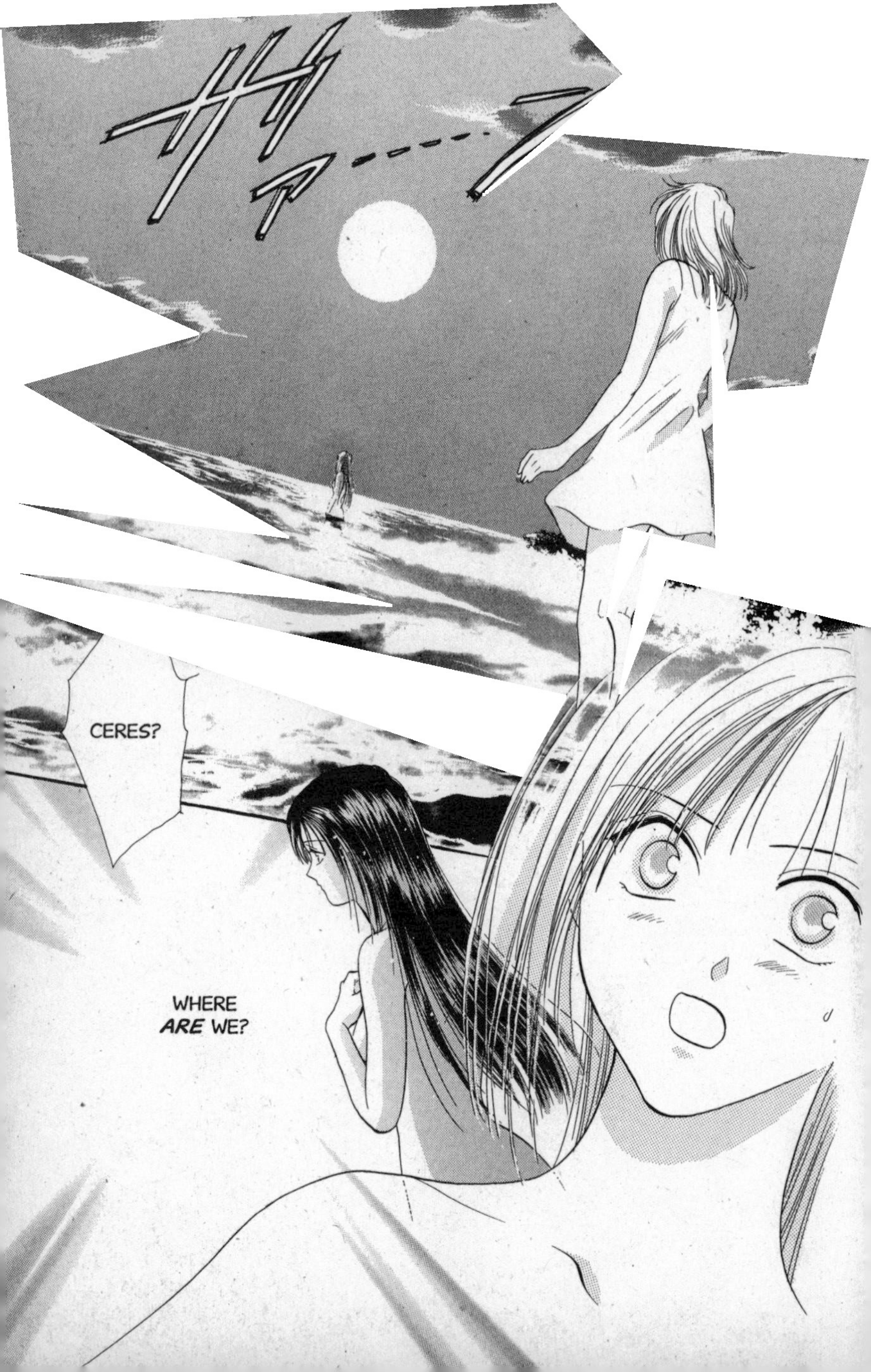
ザァーーーー
CERES?
WHERE *ARE* WE?

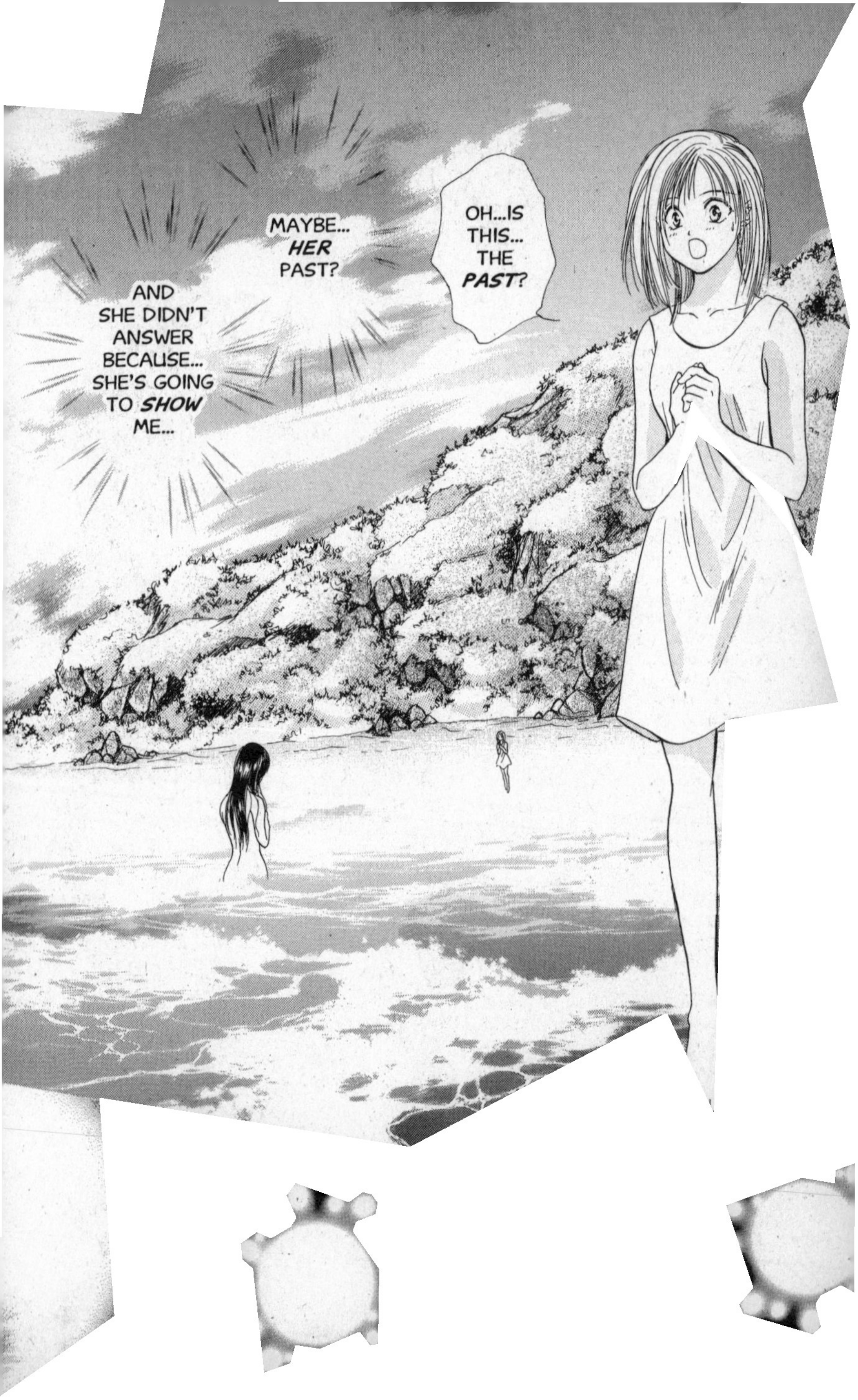
OH...IS THIS... THE PAST?
MAYBE... HER PAST?
AND SHE DIDN'T ANSWER BECAUSE... SHE'S GOING TO SHOW ME...

And I loved the soundtrack! ♡ (I bought the limited edition.) I especially loved the opening song! (The ending song is cool, too! I'm actually listening to the CD right now.) I spotted a Taiwanese poster at the anime convention I went to in North Carolina this March. Sue, one of the staff, got it for me, which was very nice of her. But I still have it rolled up because I don't want to ruin it by putting it up on the wall...

Oh, speaking of Taiwan...I don't know when the Taiwanese version of Volume 13 is coming out, but I want to tell the victims of the recent earthquake to hang in there!! They've been very good to me when I've visited for autograph sessions, and I know a lot of people read my books. FY is their top shōjo manga, and they're sometimes even more passionate than my readers in Japan. I always get a steady stream of fan mail from Taiwan (and Hong Kong)! I'm really worried about them...donated what little I could to the relief effort, but did it really help? I hope they'll be able to rebuild, so I can see their city vibrant again. It reminds me of Osaka, at least a little. It's a wonderful place. Japan has suffered with that big earthquake in Kobe, too. And Cairo, before that... There have been so many earthquakes...it's scary.

Yet here I am writing about serious stuff while I'm listening to the goofy music from the card mini-game in FFVIII... Oh wait, now it's changed over to the waltz. The CG was so awesome in this game...

Hmm, people who haven't played the game won't understand what I'm talking about. Anyway, good luck to the people of Taiwan!!

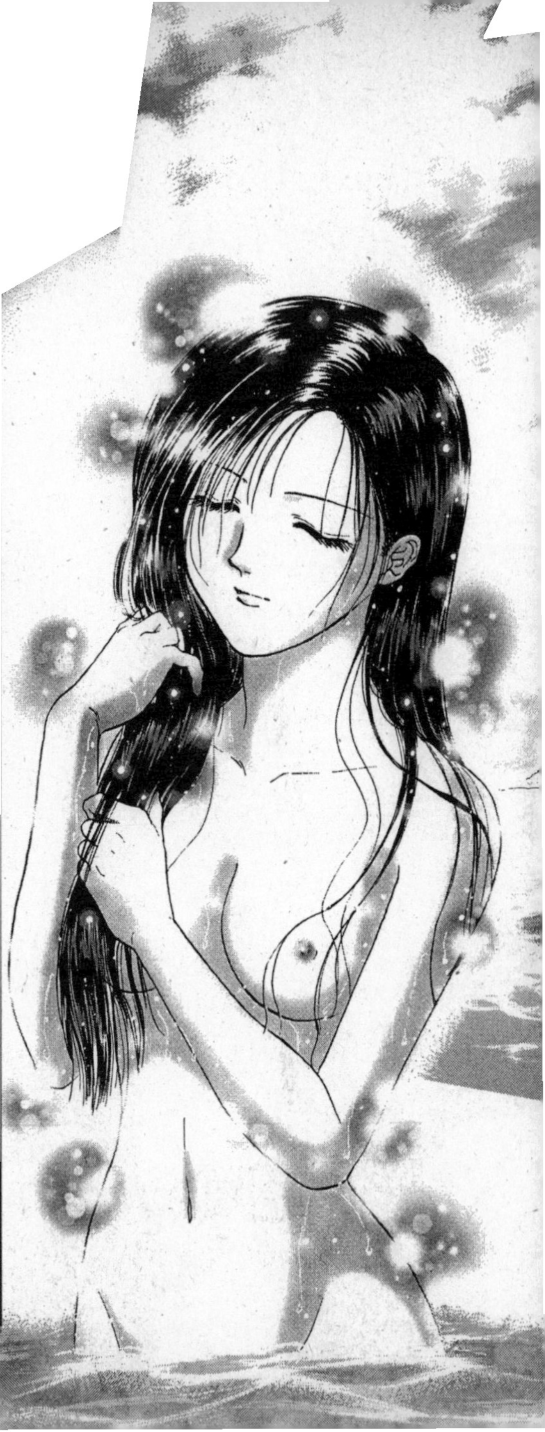

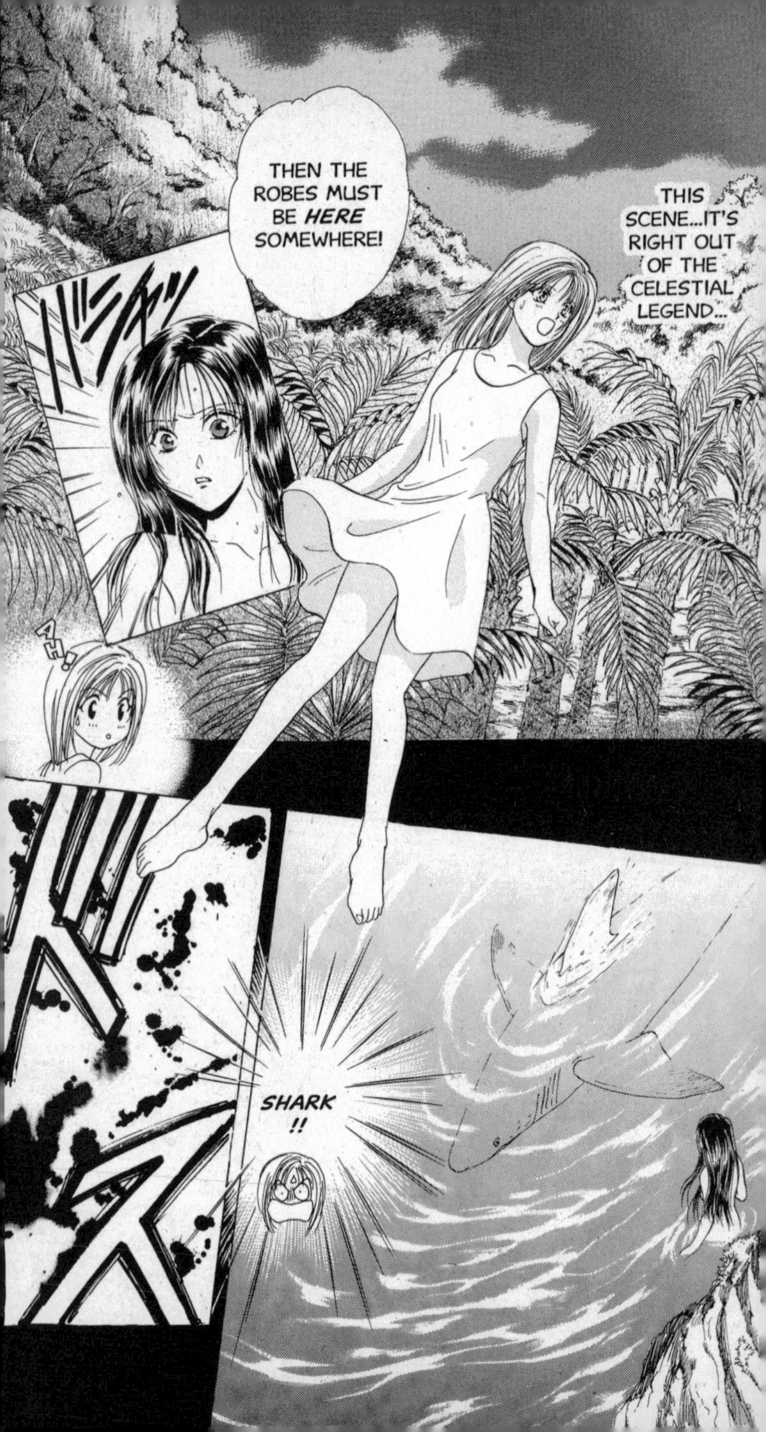
THIS SCENE...IT'S RIGHT OUT OF THE CELESTIAL LEGEND...
THEN THE ROBES MUST BE *HERE* SOMEWHERE!
AH!
SHARK !!

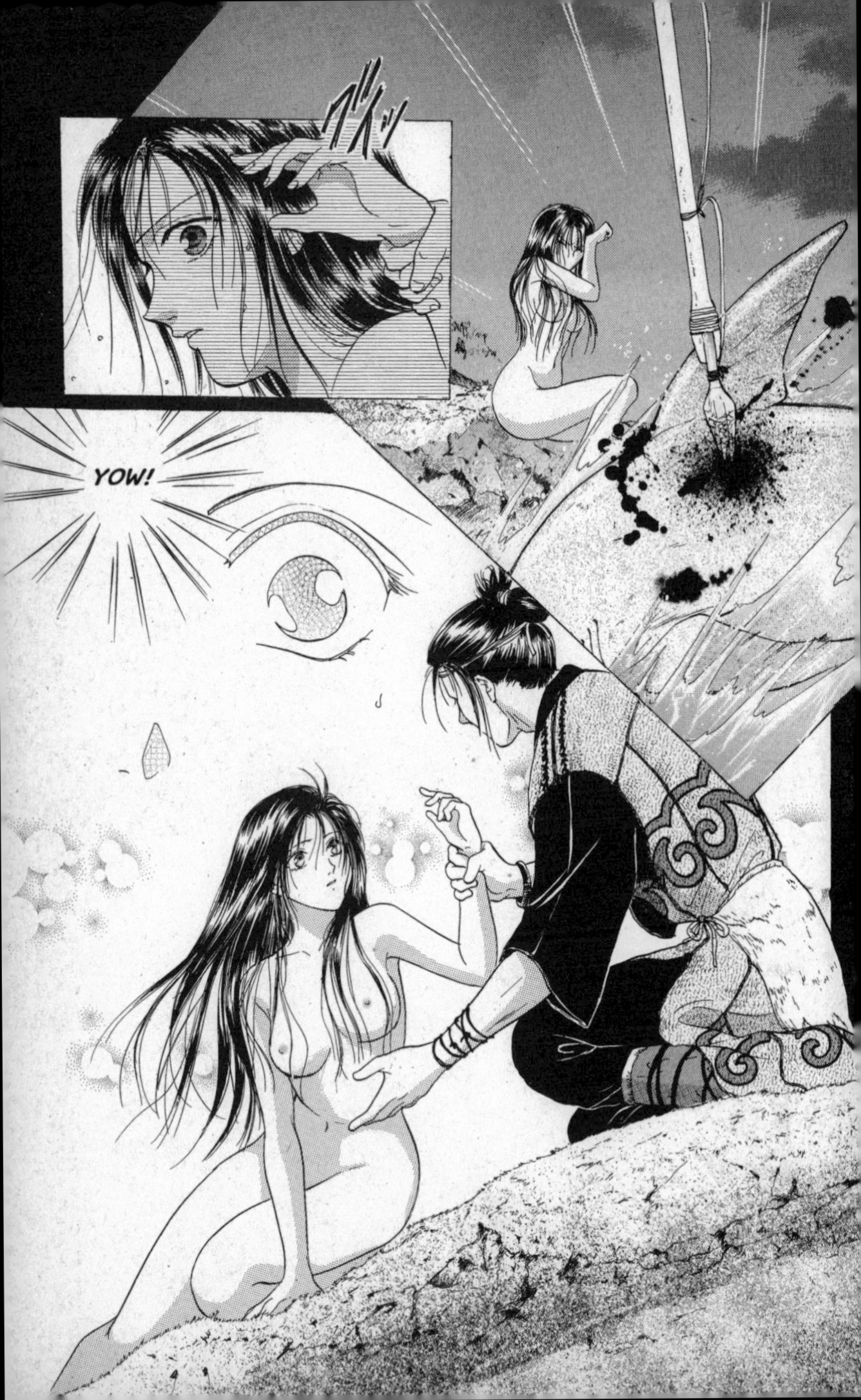
YOW!

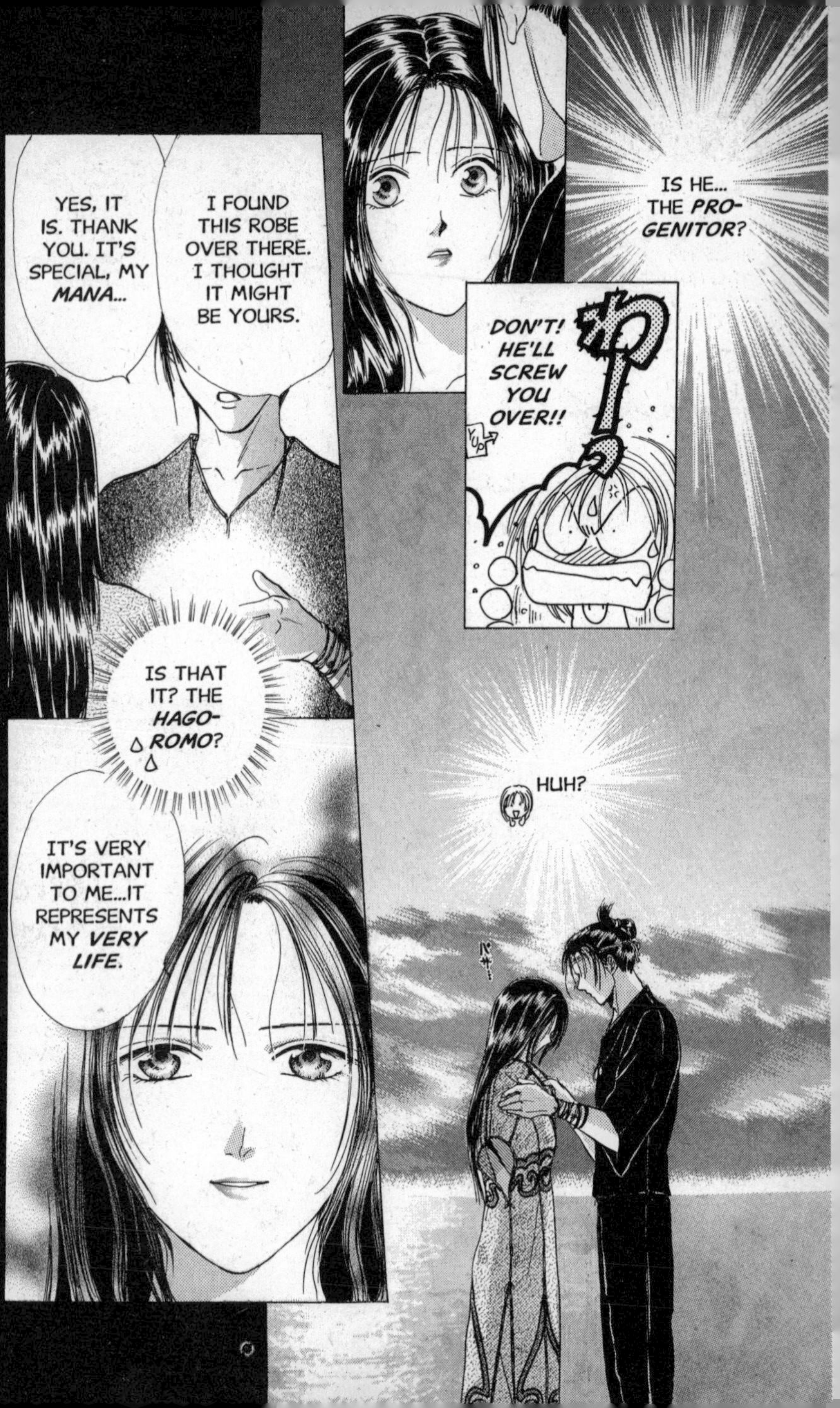
IS HE... THE PROGENITOR?
DON'T! HE'LL SCREW YOU OVER!!
YUP
HUH?
I FOUND THIS ROBE OVER THERE. I THOUGHT IT MIGHT BE YOURS.
YES, IT IS. THANK YOU. IT'S SPECIAL, MY MANA...
IS THAT IT? THE HAGOROMO?
IT'S VERY IMPORTANT TO ME...IT REPRESENTS MY VERY LIFE.

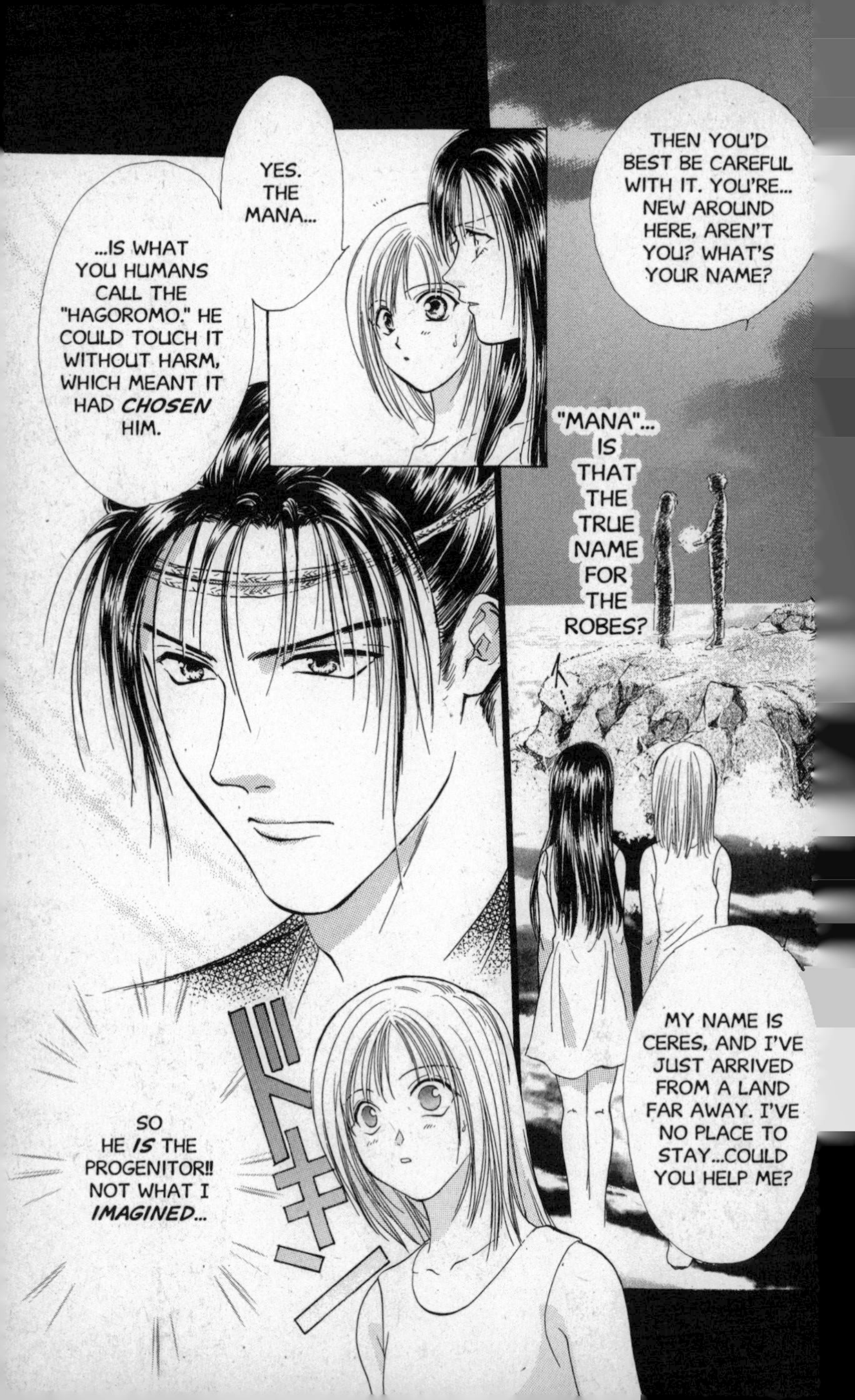
THEN YOU'D BEST BE CAREFUL WITH IT. YOU'RE... NEW AROUND HERE, AREN'T YOU? WHAT'S YOUR NAME?
"MANA"... IS THAT THE TRUE NAME FOR THE ROBES?
MY NAME IS CERES, AND I'VE JUST ARRIVED FROM A LAND FAR AWAY. I'VE NO PLACE TO STAY...COULD YOU HELP ME?
YES. THE MANA...
...IS WHAT YOU HUMANS CALL THE "HAGOROMO." HE COULD TOUCH IT WITHOUT HARM, WHICH MEANT IT HAD *CHOSEN* HIM.
SO HE *IS* THE PROGENITOR!! NOT WHAT I *IMAGINED*...

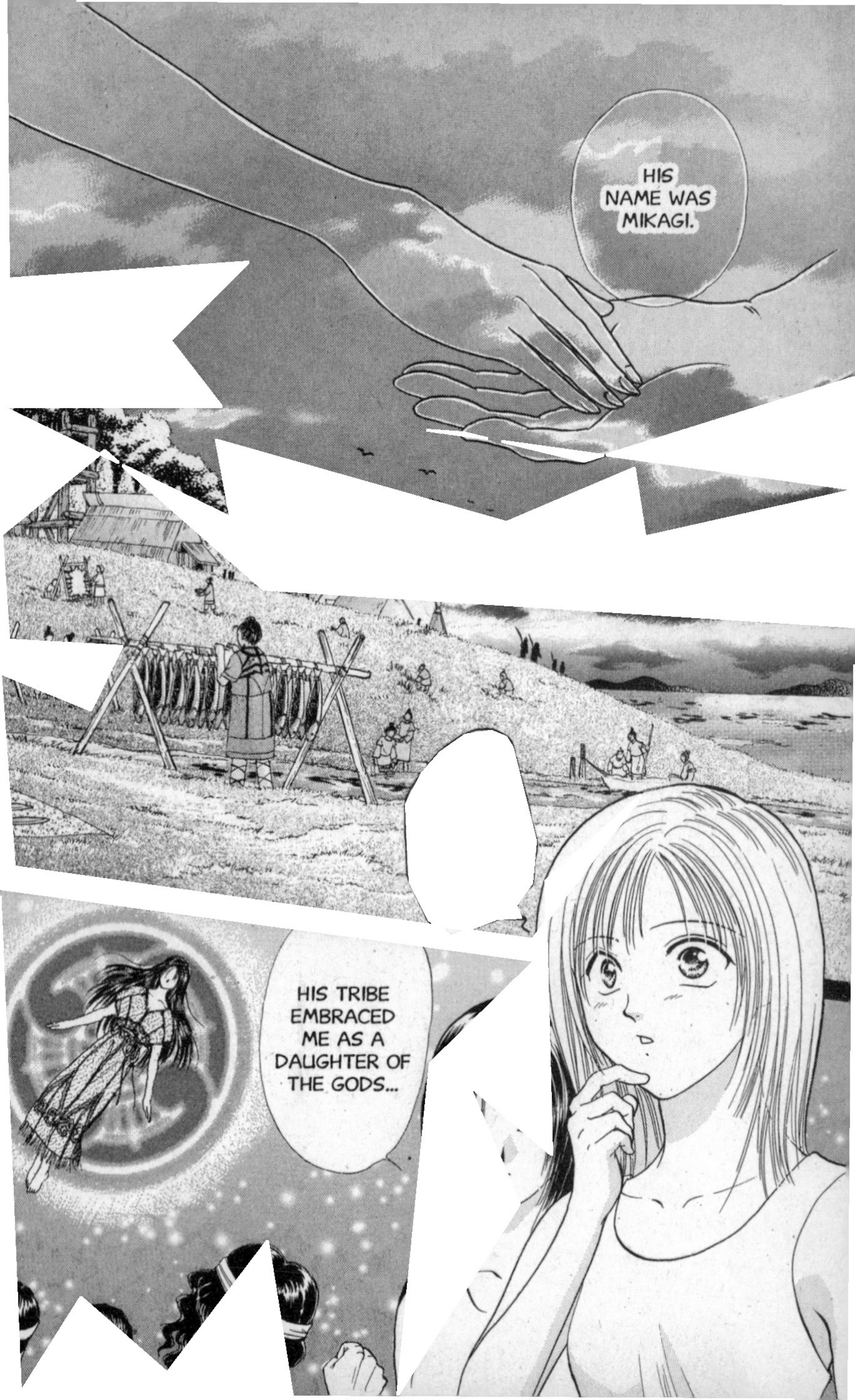
HIS NAME WAS MIKAGI.
HIS TRIBE EMBRACED ME AS A DAUGHTER OF THE GODS...

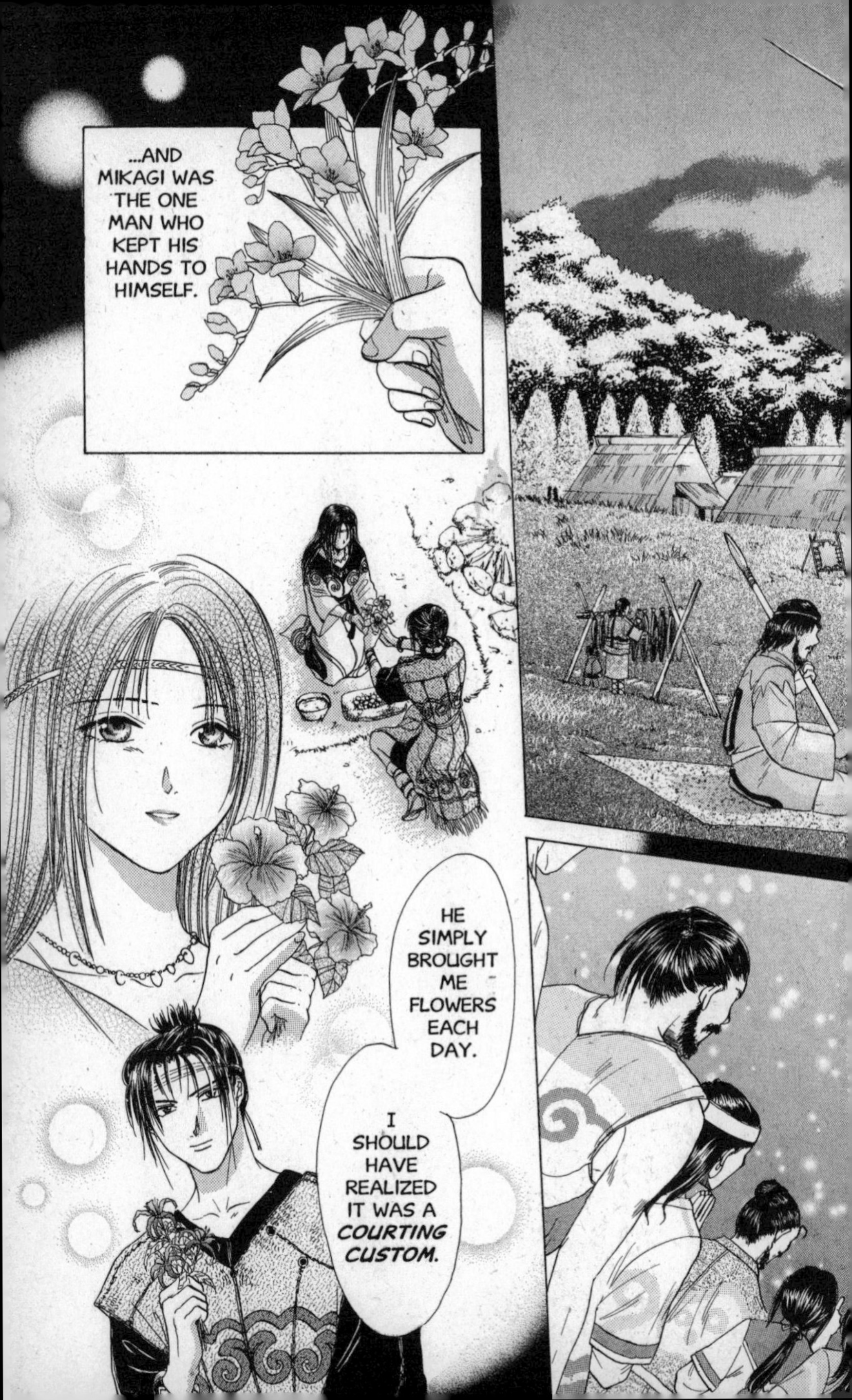
...AND MIKAGI WAS THE ONE MAN WHO KEPT HIS HANDS TO HIMSELF.
HE SIMPLY BROUGHT ME FLOWERS EACH DAY.
I SHOULD HAVE REALIZED IT WAS A *COURTING CUSTOM.*

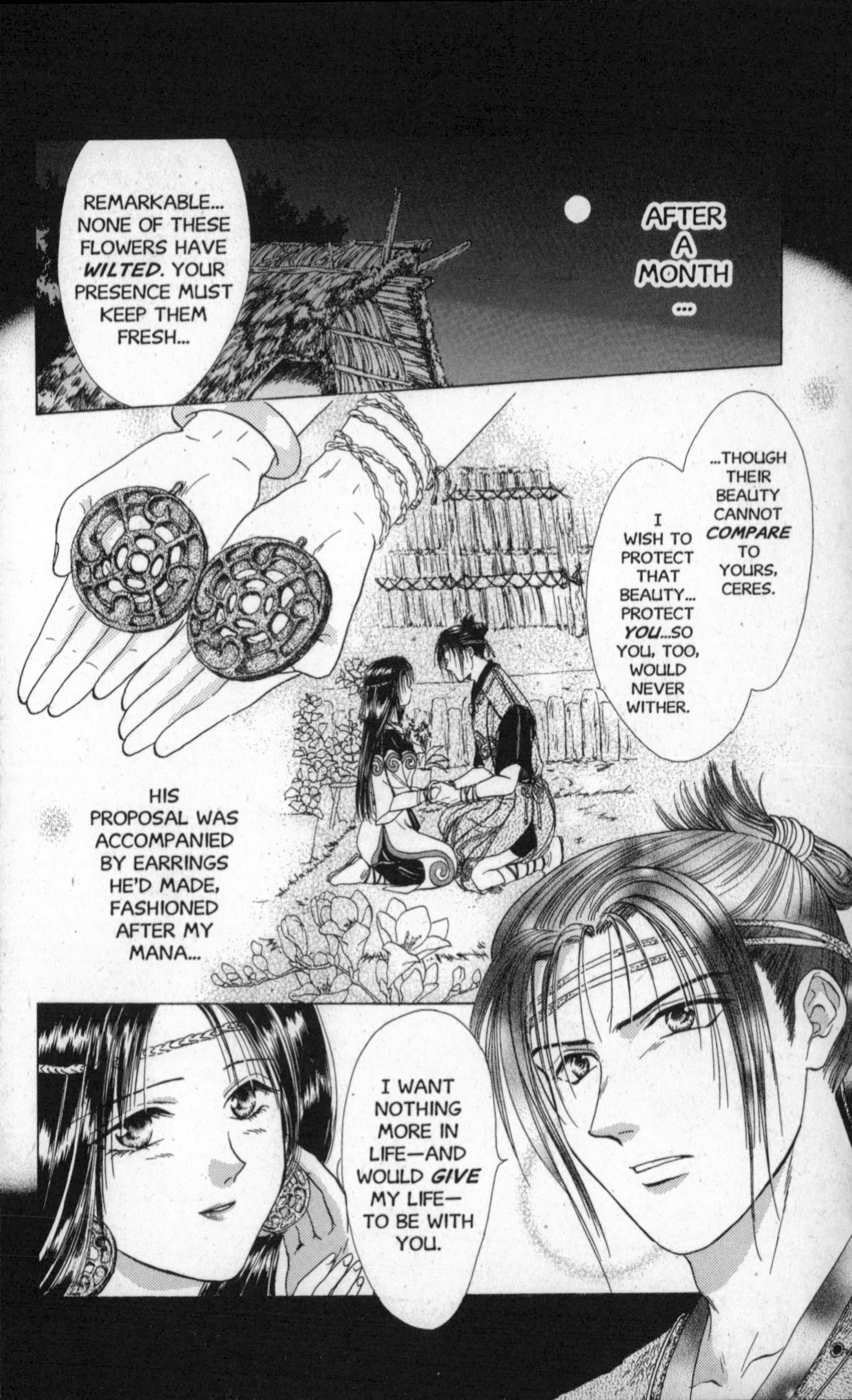
AFTER A MONTH...
REMARKABLE... NONE OF THESE FLOWERS HAVE WILTED. YOUR PRESENCE MUST KEEP THEM FRESH...
...THOUGH THEIR BEAUTY CANNOT COMPARE TO YOURS, CERES.
I WISH TO PROTECT THAT BEAUTY... PROTECT YOU...SO YOU, TOO, WOULD NEVER WITHER.
HIS PROPOSAL WAS ACCOMPANIED BY EARRINGS HE'D MADE, FASHIONED AFTER MY MANA...
I WANT NOTHING MORE IN LIFE—AND WOULD GIVE MY LIFE—TO BE WITH YOU.

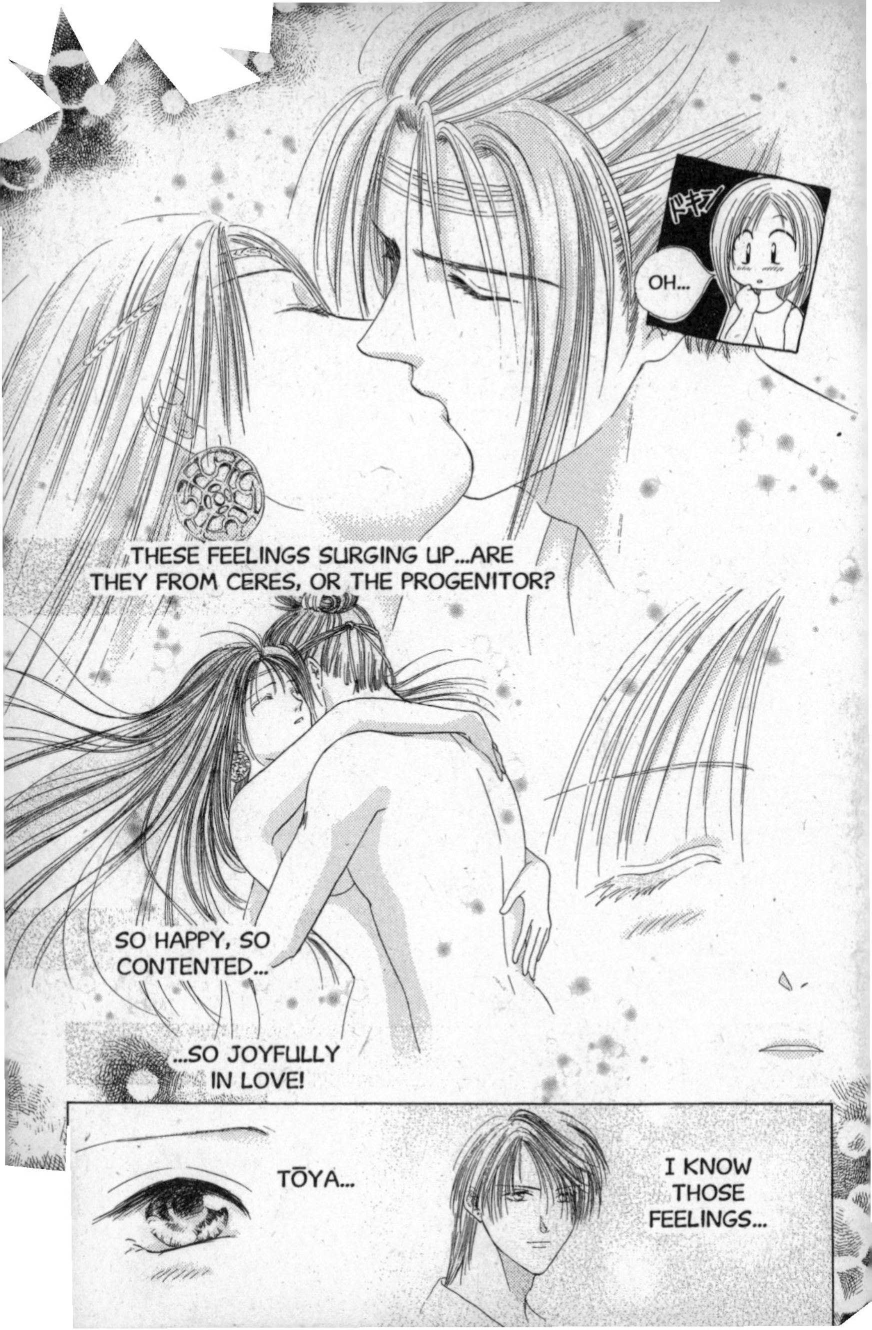
OH...
THESE FEELINGS SURGING UP...ARE THEY FROM CERES, OR THE PROGENITOR?
SO HAPPY, SO CONTENTED...
...SO JOYFULLY IN LOVE!
I KNOW THOSE FEELINGS...
TŌYA...

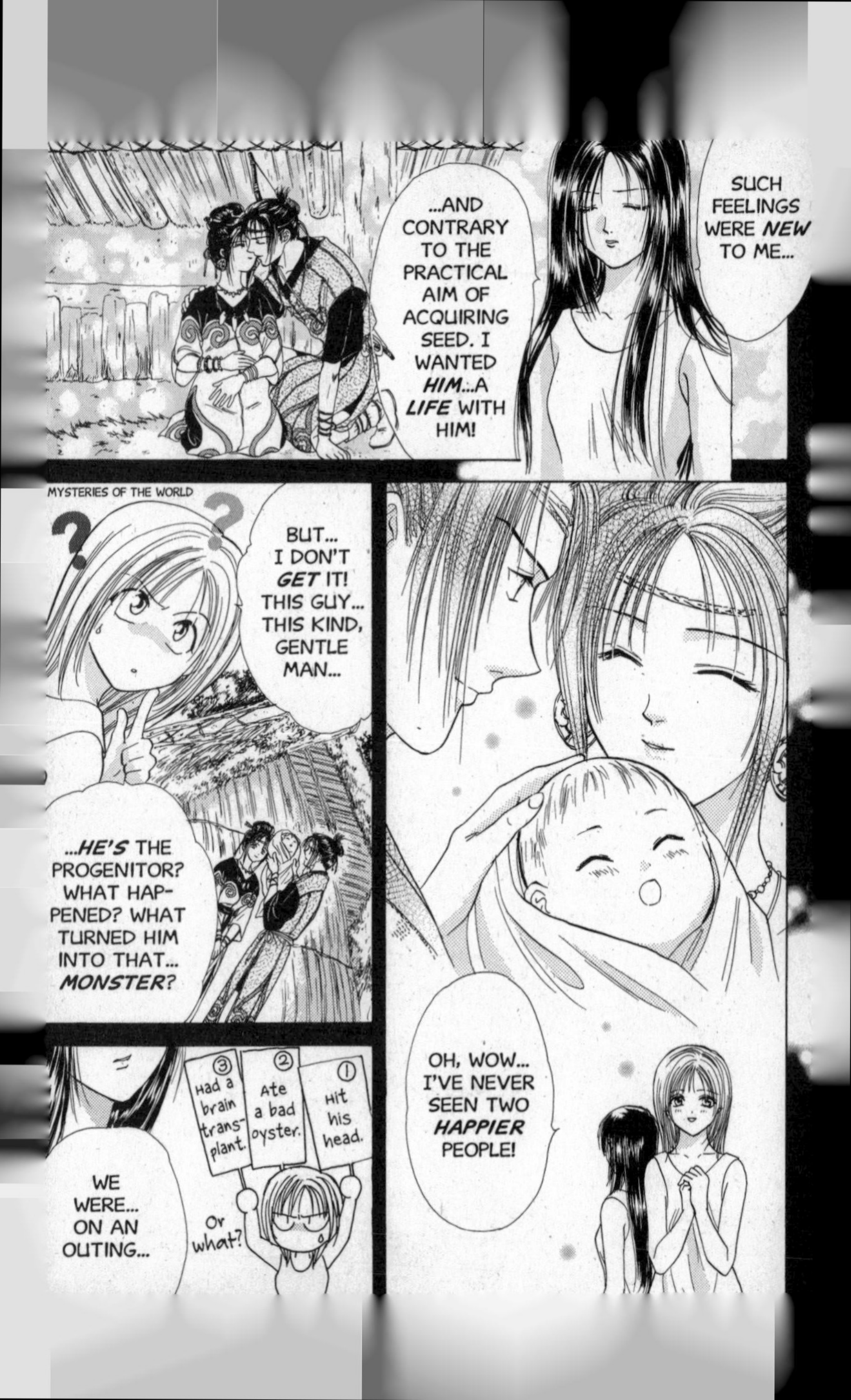
SUCH FEELINGS WERE NEW TO ME...
...AND CONTRARY TO THE PRACTICAL AIM OF ACQUIRING SEED. I WANTED HIM...A LIFE WITH HIM!
OH, WOW... I'VE NEVER SEEN TWO HAPPIER PEOPLE!
MYSTERIES OF THE WORLD
BUT... I DON'T GET IT! THIS GUY... THIS KIND, GENTLE MAN...
...HE'S THE PROGENITOR? WHAT HAPPENED? WHAT TURNED HIM INTO THAT... MONSTER?
① Hit his head.
② Ate a bad oyster.
③ Had a brain transplant.
Or what?
WE WERE... ON AN OUTING...

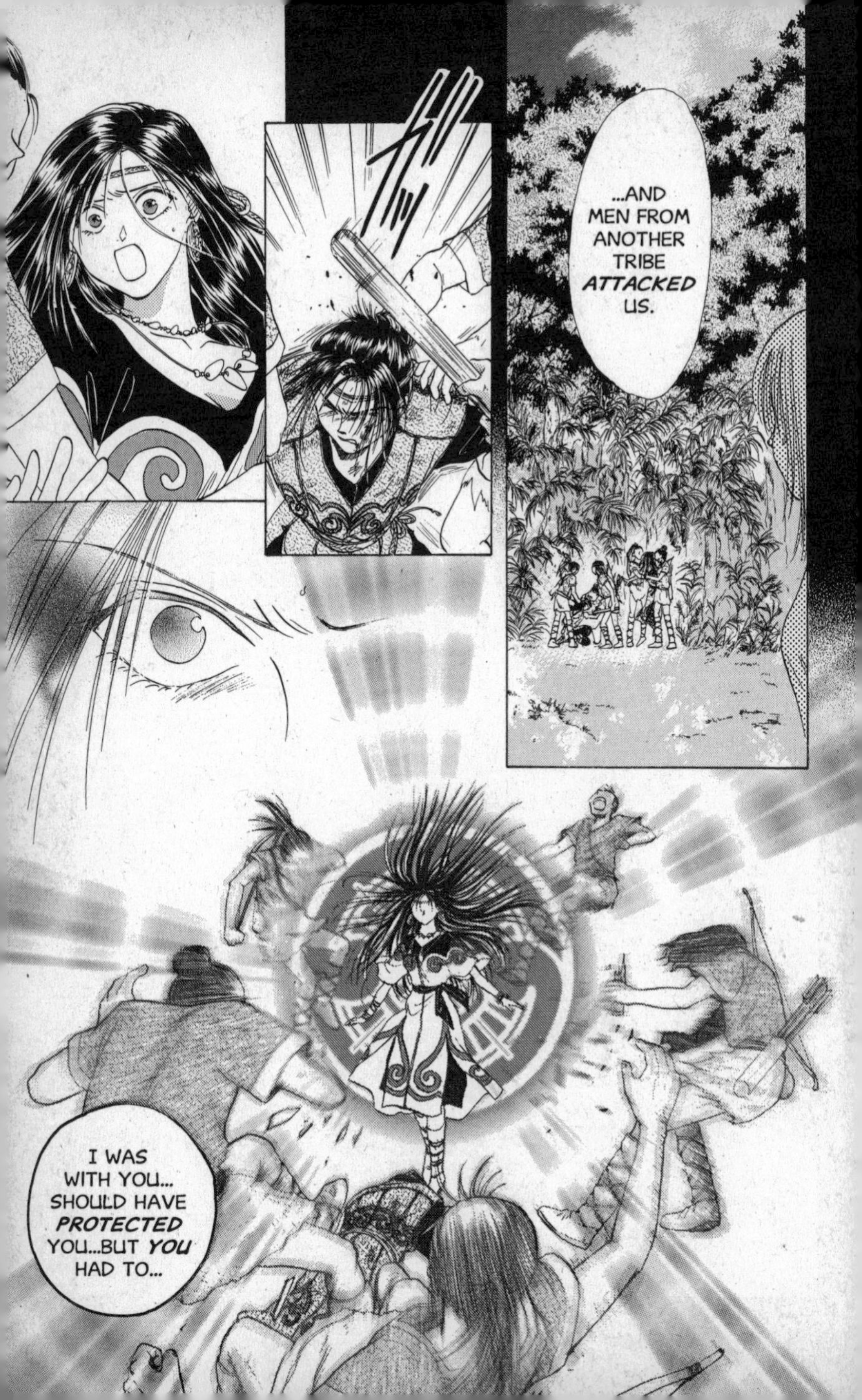
...AND MEN FROM ANOTHER TRIBE ATTACKED US.
I WAS WITH YOU... SHOULD HAVE PROTECTED YOU...BUT YOU HAD TO...

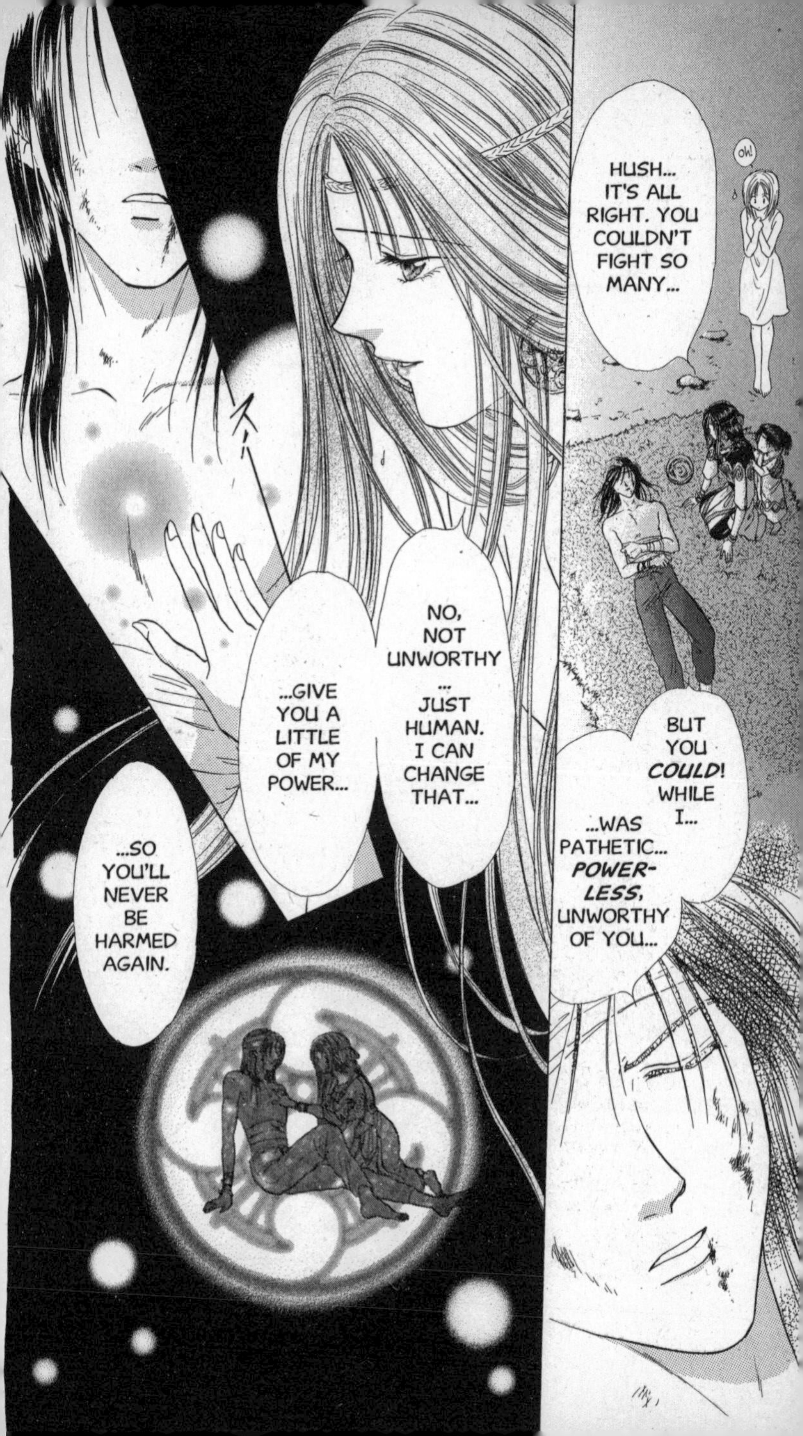
OH!
HUSH... IT'S ALL RIGHT. YOU COULDN'T FIGHT SO MANY...
BUT YOU COULD! WHILE I...
...WAS PATHETIC... POWER-LESS, UNWORTHY OF YOU...
NO, NOT UNWORTHY ... JUST HUMAN. I CAN CHANGE THAT...
...GIVE YOU A LITTLE OF MY POWER...
...SO YOU'LL NEVER BE HARMED AGAIN.

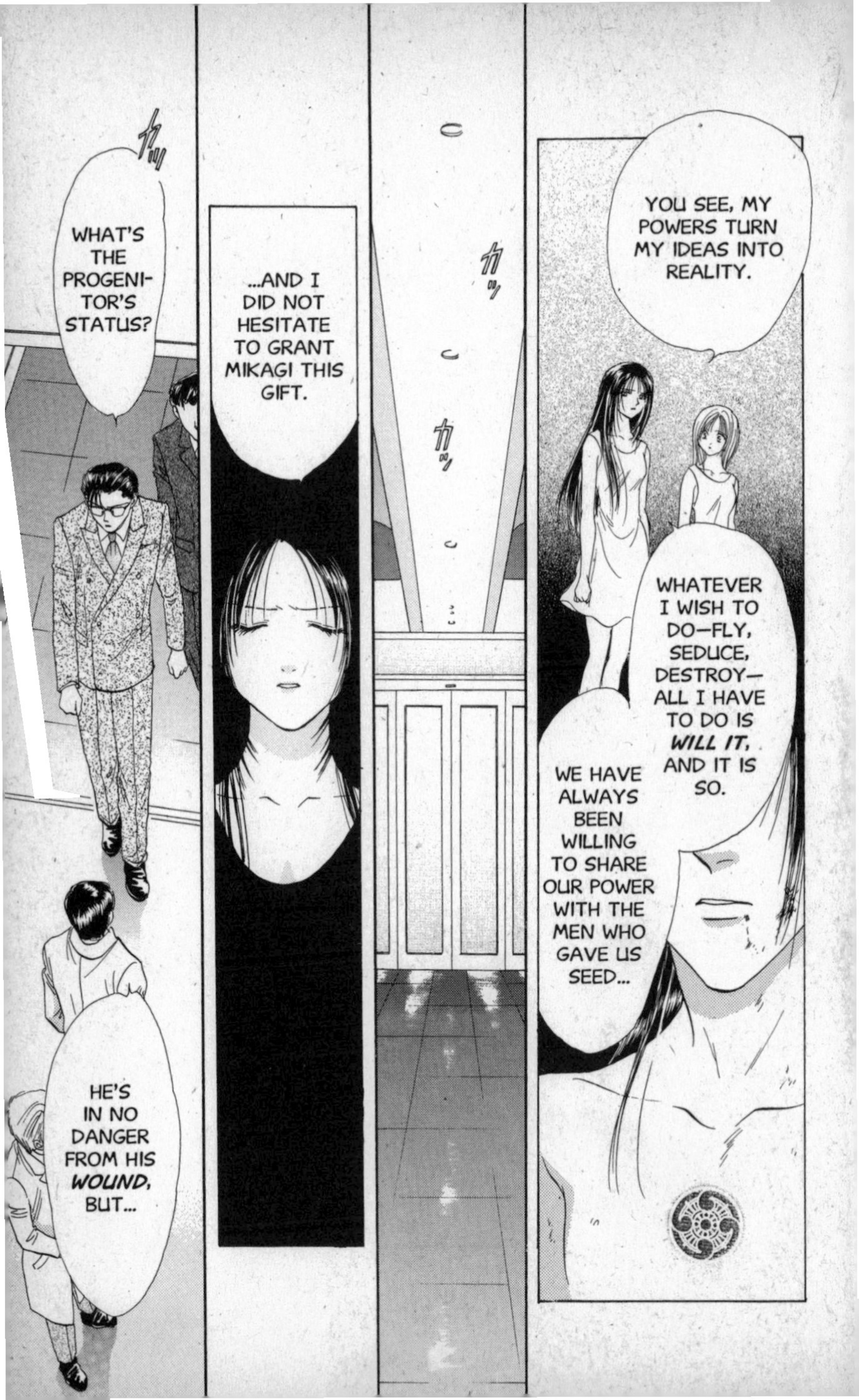
YOU SEE, MY POWERS TURN MY IDEAS INTO REALITY.
WHATEVER I WISH TO DO—FLY, SEDUCE, DESTROY—ALL I HAVE TO DO IS *WILL IT*, AND IT IS SO.
WE HAVE ALWAYS BEEN WILLING TO SHARE OUR POWER WITH THE MEN WHO GAVE US SEED...
...AND I DID NOT HESITATE TO GRANT MIKAGI THIS GIFT.
WHAT'S THE PROGENITOR'S STATUS?
HE'S IN NO DANGER FROM HIS *WOUND*, BUT...

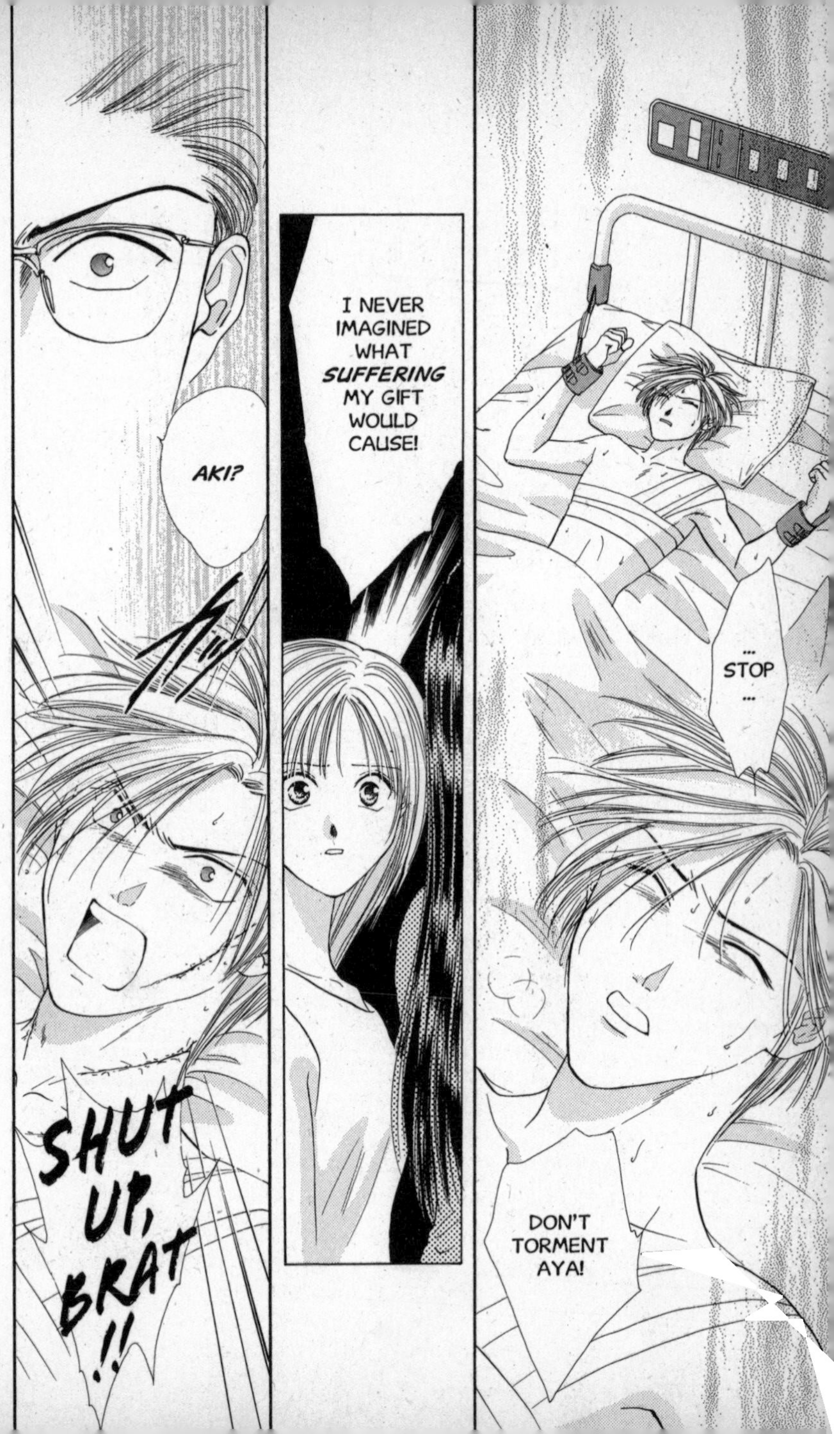
...STOP...
DON'T TORMENT AYA!
I NEVER IMAGINED WHAT SUFFERING MY GIFT WOULD CAUSE!
AKI?
SHUT UP, BRAT!!

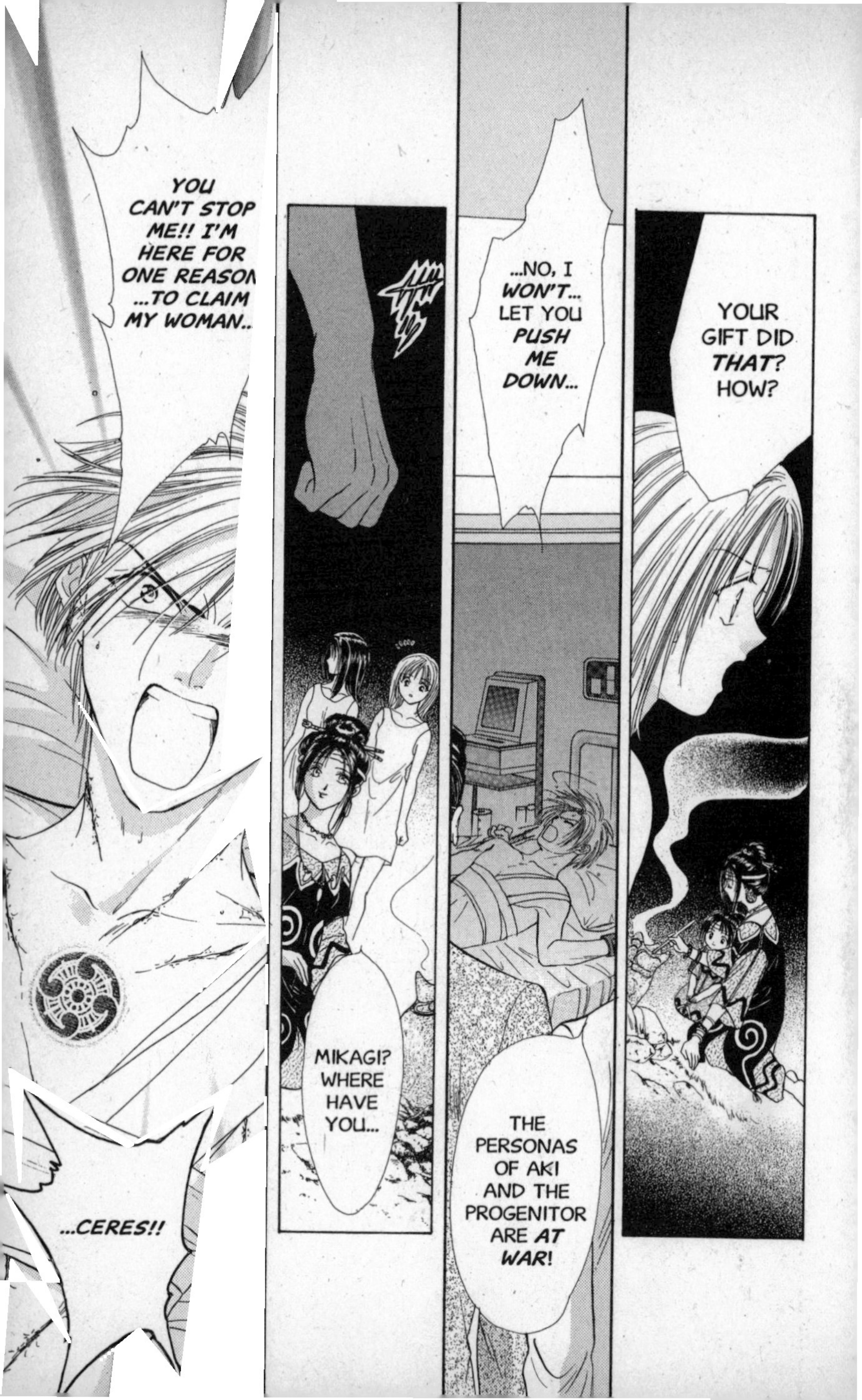
YOUR GIFT DID THAT? HOW?
...NO, I WON'T... LET YOU PUSH ME DOWN...
THE PERSONAS OF AKI AND THE PROGENITOR ARE AT WAR!
MIKAGI? WHERE HAVE YOU...
YOU CAN'T STOP ME!! I'M HERE FOR ONE REASON ...TO CLAIM MY WOMAN...
...CERES!!

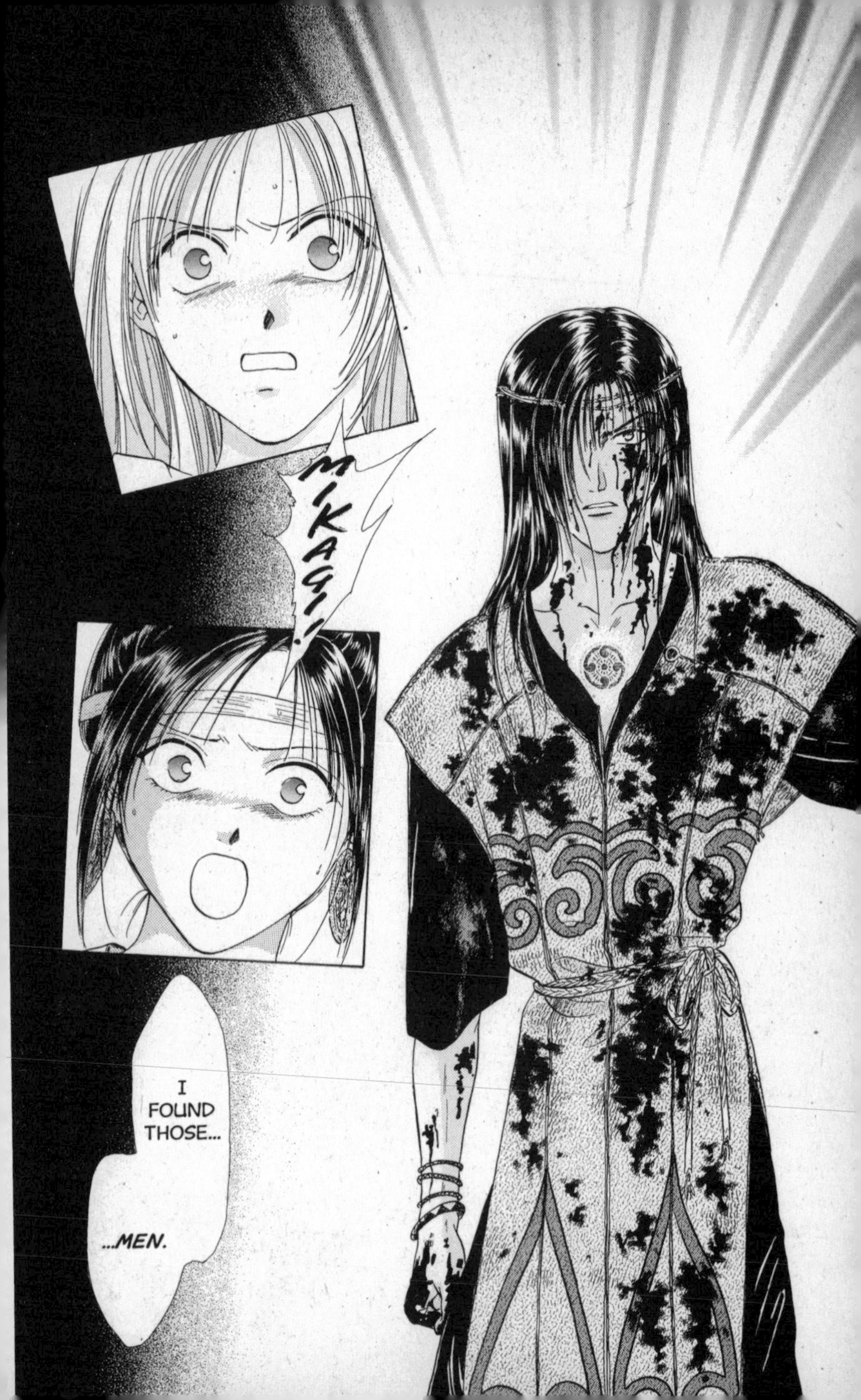
MIKAGI!
I FOUND THOSE...
...MEN.

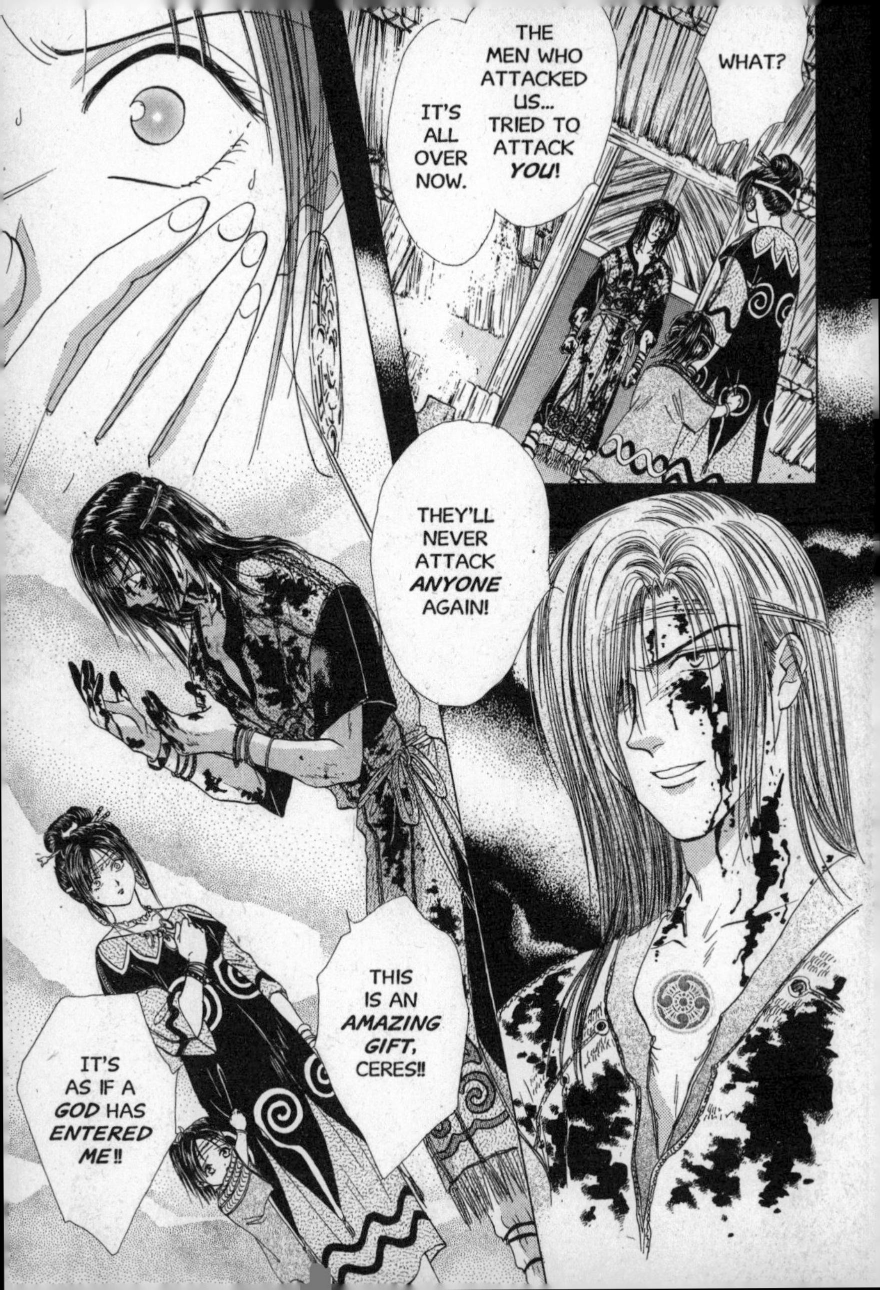
WHAT?
THE MEN WHO ATTACKED US... TRIED TO ATTACK YOU!
IT'S ALL OVER NOW.
THEY'LL NEVER ATTACK ANYONE AGAIN!
THIS IS AN AMAZING GIFT, CERES!!
IT'S AS IF A GOD HAS ENTERED ME!!

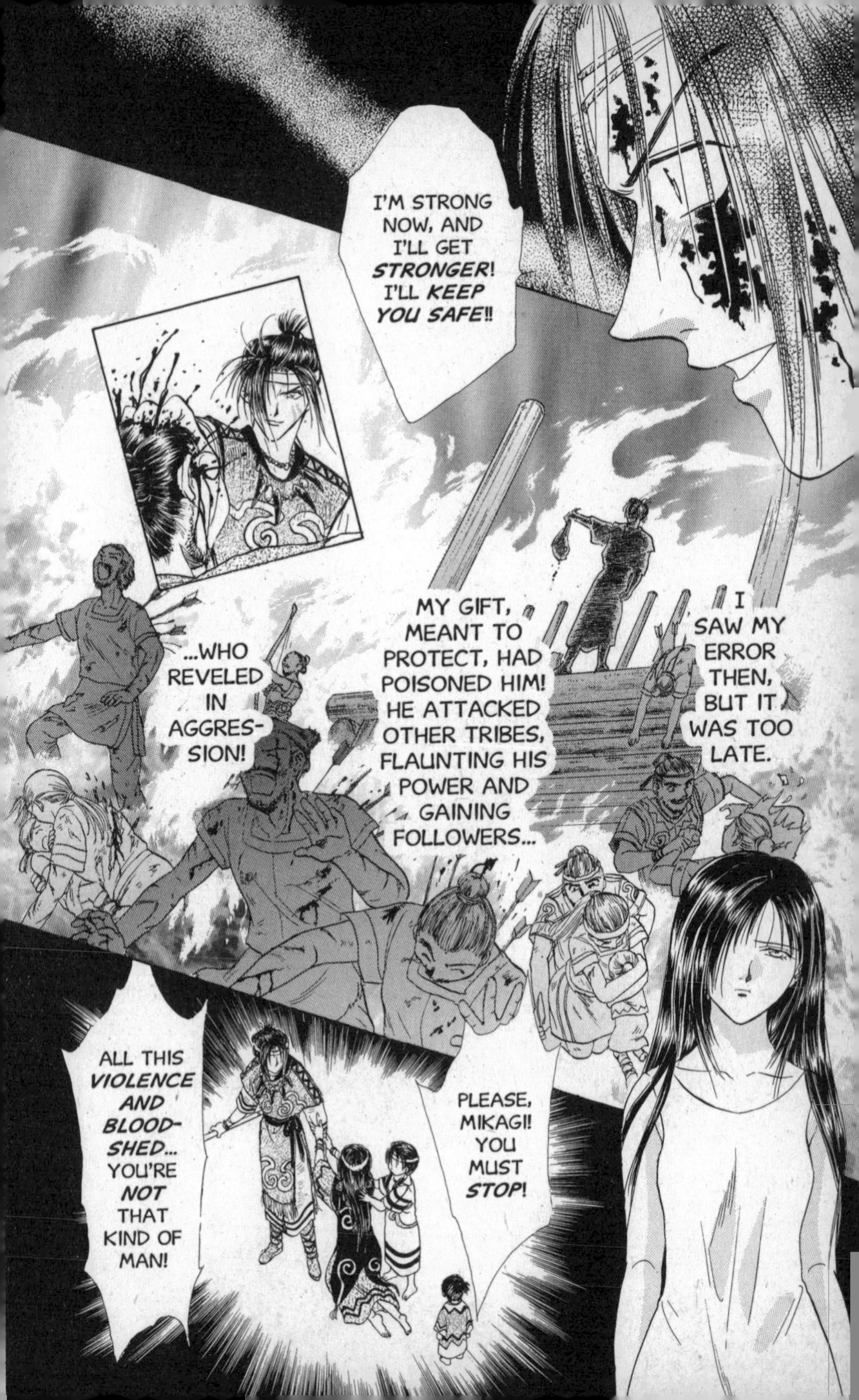
I'M STRONG NOW, AND I'LL GET *STRONGER*! I'LL *KEEP YOU SAFE*!!
I SAW MY ERROR THEN, BUT IT WAS TOO LATE.
MY GIFT, MEANT TO PROTECT, HAD POISONED HIM! HE ATTACKED OTHER TRIBES, FLAUNTING HIS POWER AND GAINING FOLLOWERS...
...WHO REVELED IN AGGRES-SION!
PLEASE, MIKAGI! YOU MUST *STOP*!
ALL THIS *VIOLENCE AND BLOOD-SHED*... YOU'RE *NOT* THAT KIND OF MAN!

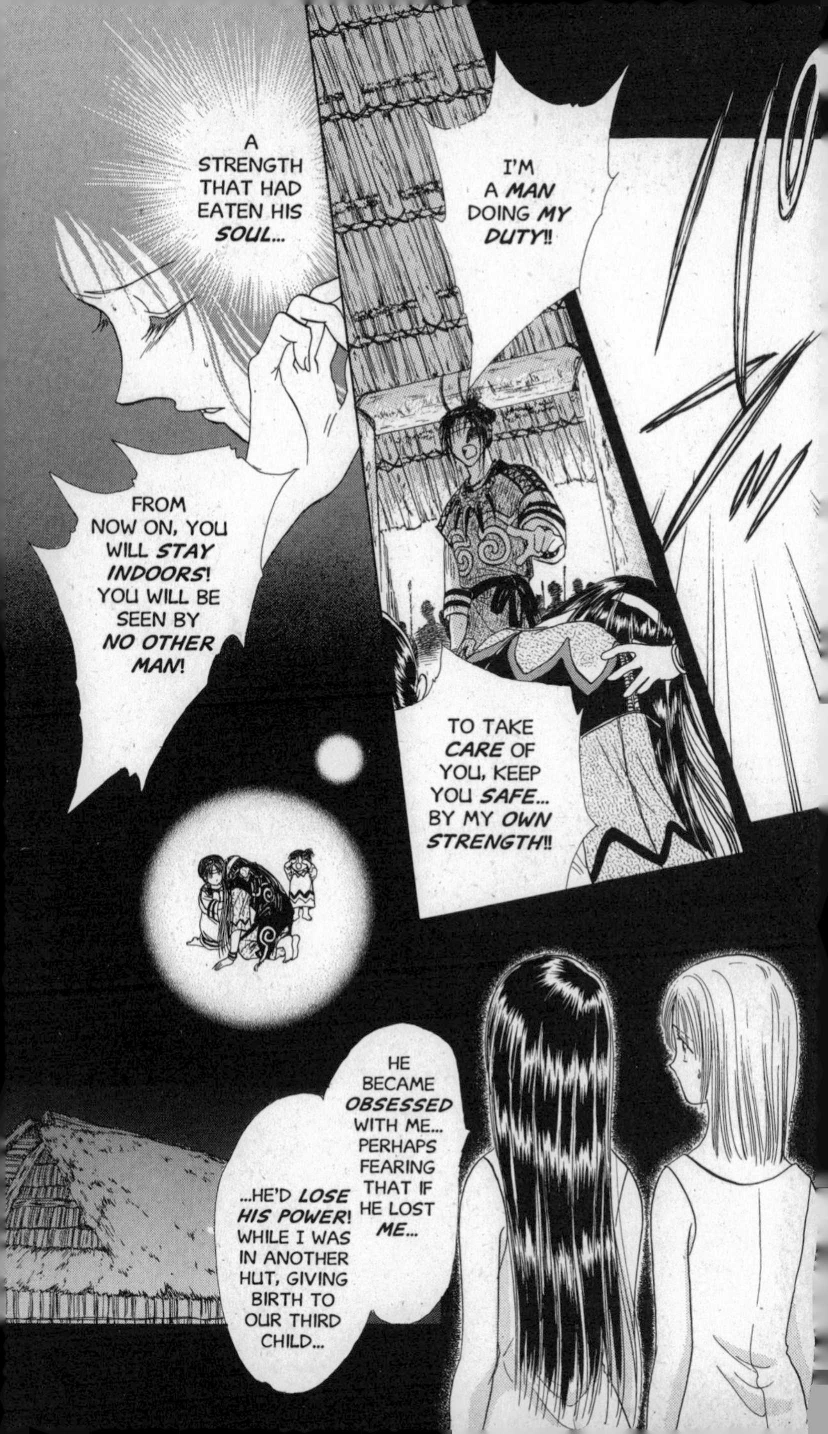

I'M A MAN DOING MY DUTY!!
TO TAKE CARE OF YOU, KEEP YOU SAFE... BY MY OWN STRENGTH!!
A STRENGTH THAT HAD EATEN HIS SOUL...
FROM NOW ON, YOU WILL STAY INDOORS! YOU WILL BE SEEN BY NO OTHER MAN!
HE BECAME OBSESSED WITH ME... PERHAPS FEARING THAT IF HE LOST ME...
...HE'D LOSE HIS POWER! WHILE I WAS IN ANOTHER HUT, GIVING BIRTH TO OUR THIRD CHILD...

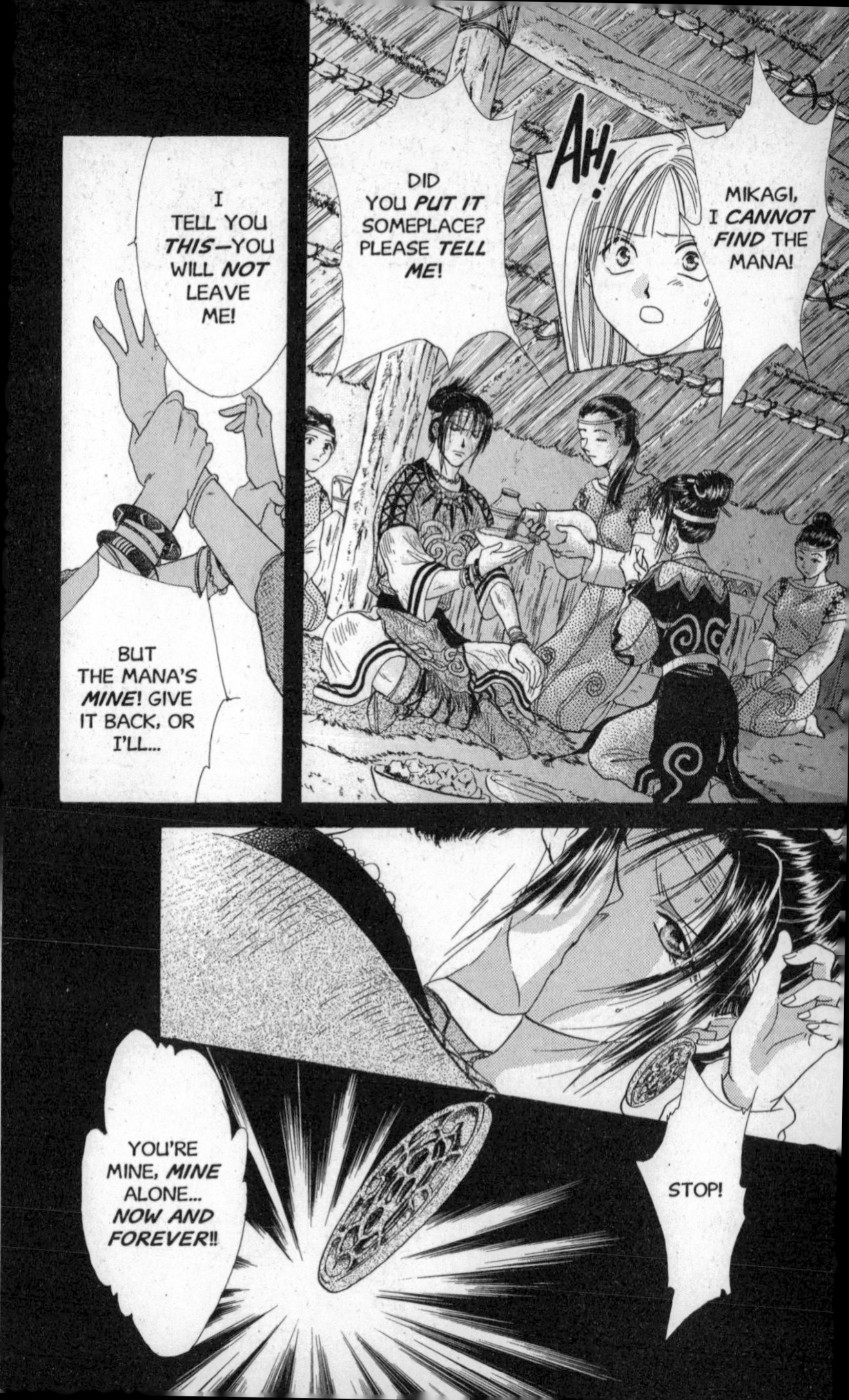
AH!
MIKAGI, I *CANNOT FIND* THE MANA!
DID YOU *PUT IT* SOMEPLACE? PLEASE *TELL ME*!
I TELL YOU *THIS*—YOU WILL *NOT* LEAVE ME!
BUT THE MANA'S *MINE*! GIVE IT BACK, OR I'LL...
STOP!
YOU'RE MINE, *MINE* ALONE... ***NOW AND FOREVER***!!

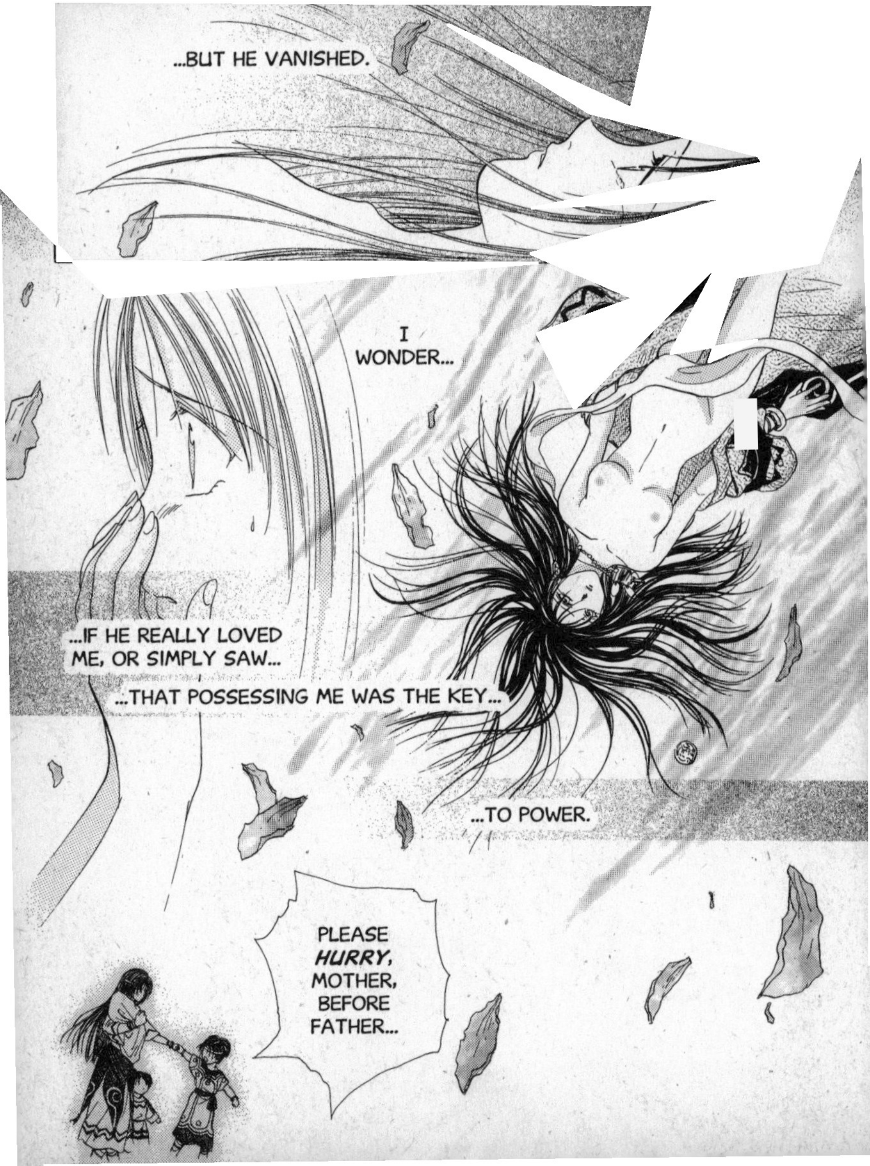
...BUT HE VANISHED.
I WONDER...
...IF HE REALLY LOVED ME, OR SIMPLY SAW...
...THAT POSSESSING ME WAS THE KEY...
...TO POWER.
PLEASE *HURRY*, MOTHER, BEFORE FATHER...

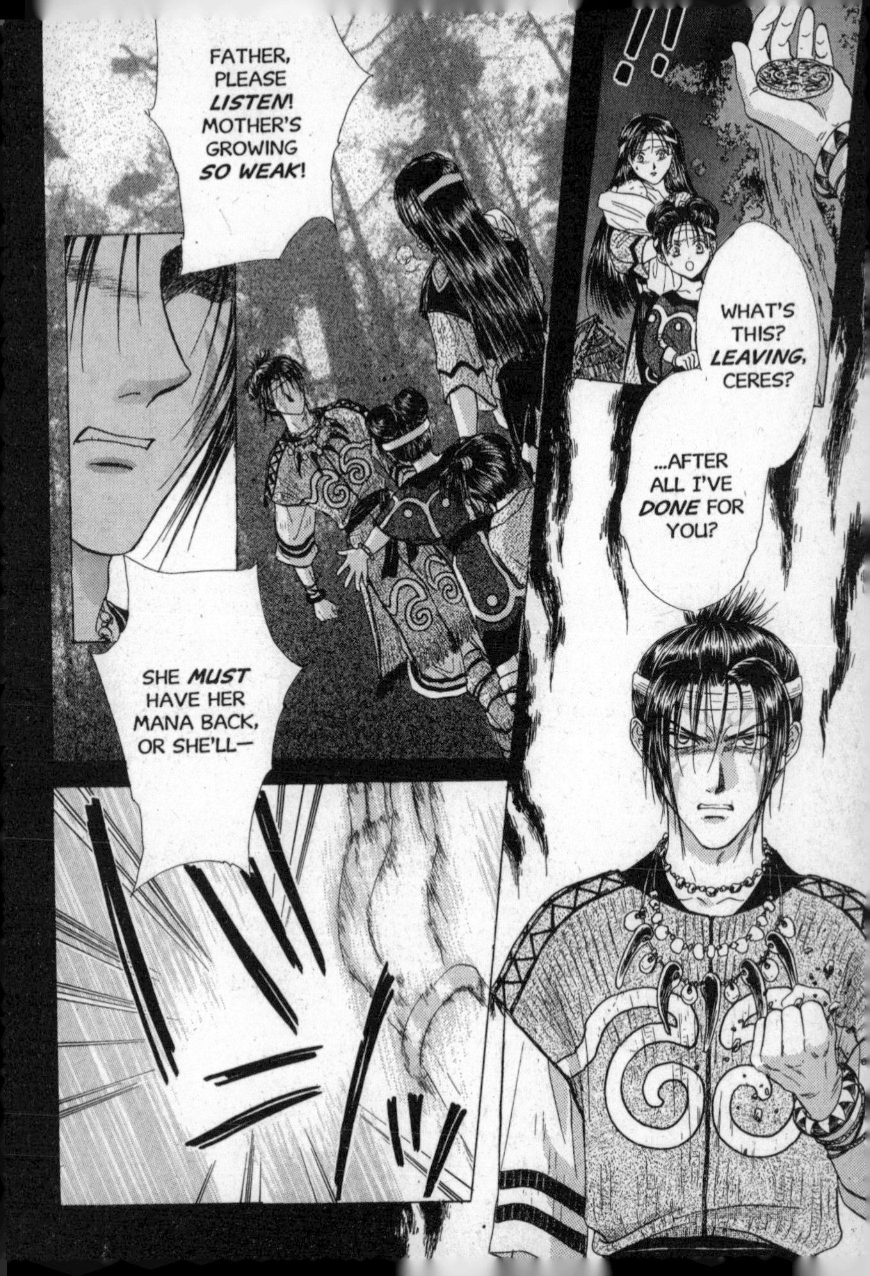
!!
WHAT'S THIS? LEAVING, CERES?
...AFTER ALL I'VE DONE FOR YOU?
FATHER, PLEASE LISTEN! MOTHER'S GROWING SO WEAK!
SHE MUST HAVE HER MANA BACK, OR SHE'LL—

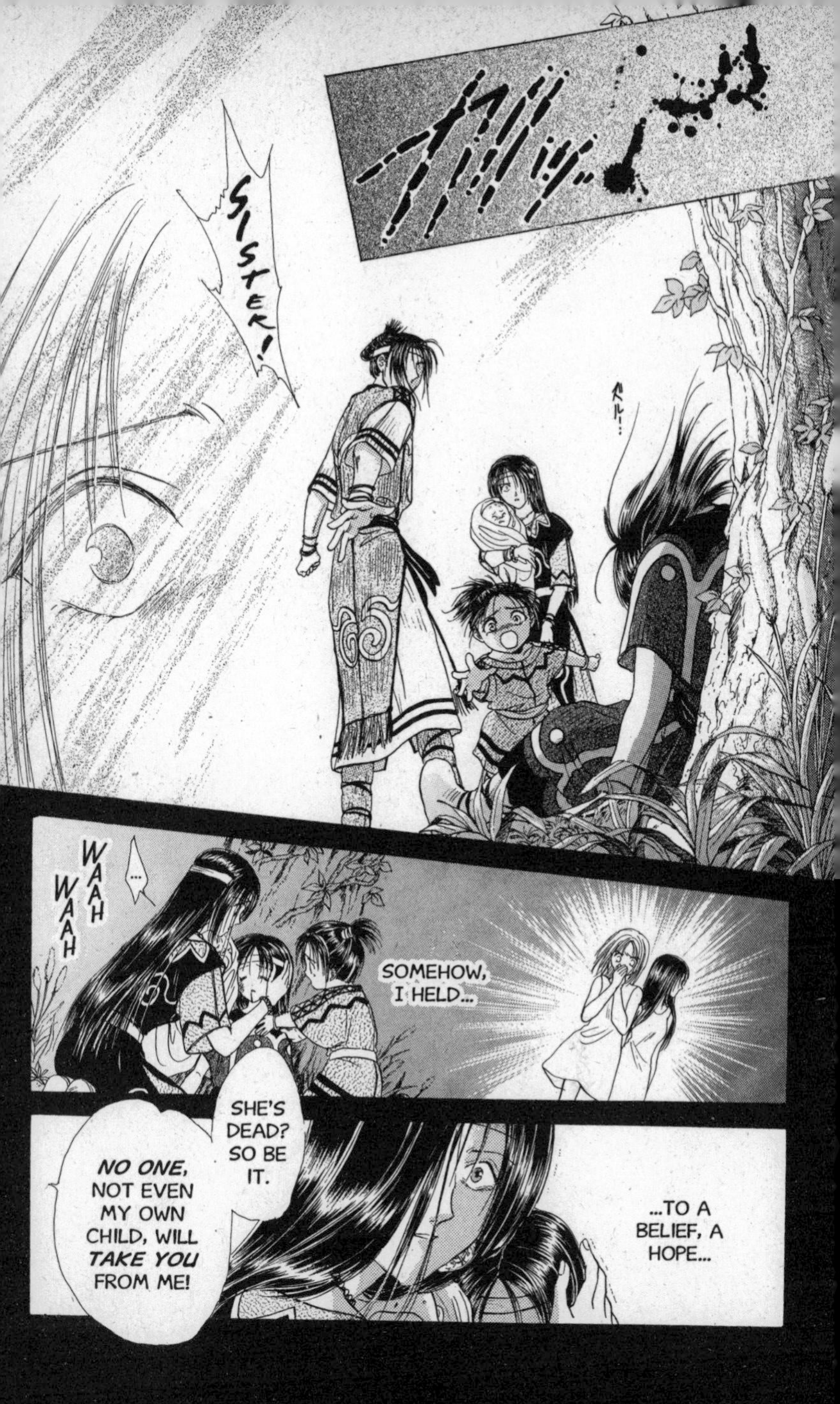
SISTER!
SOMEHOW, I HELD...
...
WAAH WAAH
...TO A BELIEF, A HOPE...
SHE'S DEAD? SO BE IT.
NO ONE, NOT EVEN MY OWN CHILD, WILL TAKE YOU FROM ME!

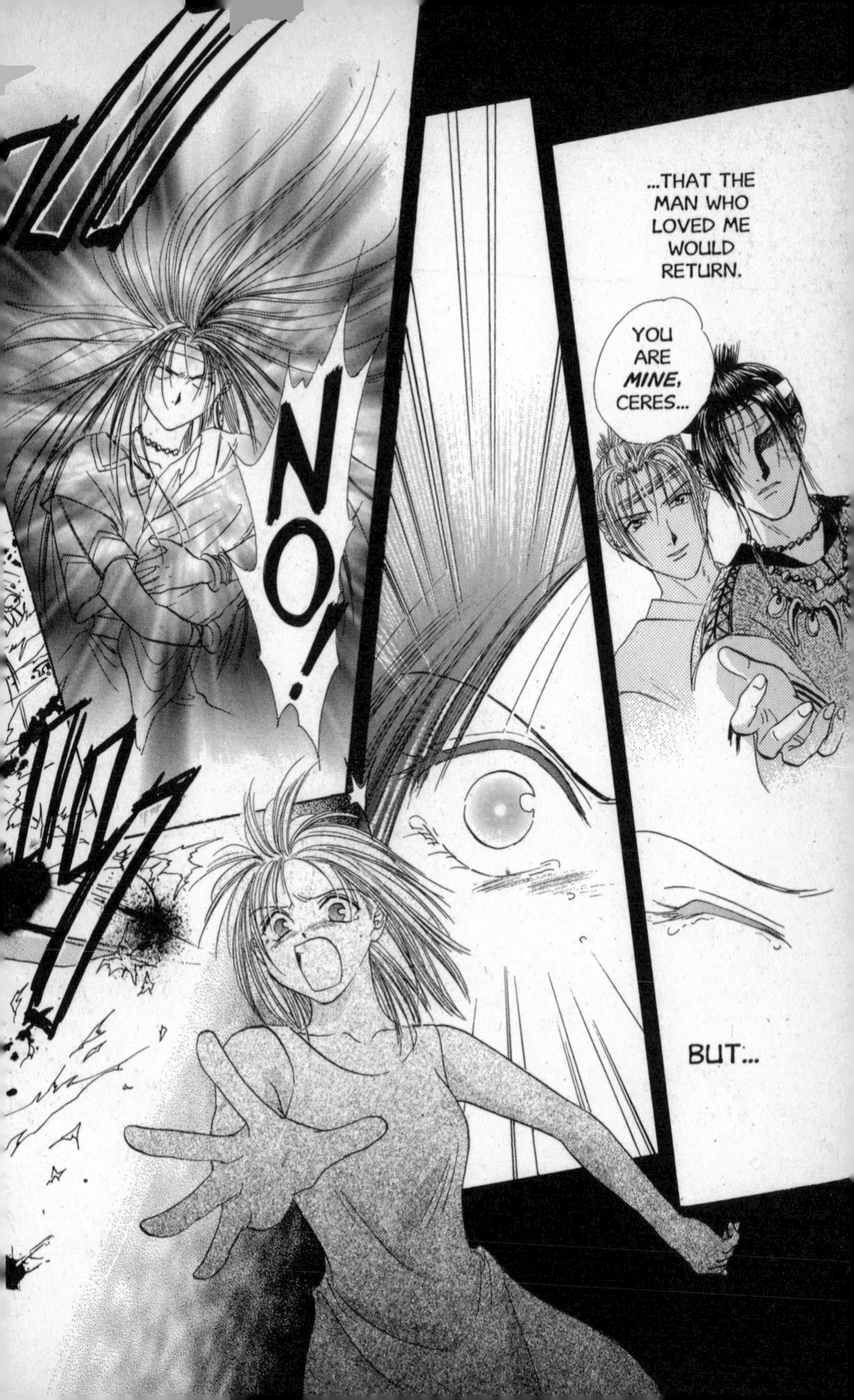
...THAT THE MAN WHO LOVED ME WOULD RETURN.
YOU ARE *MINE*, CERES...
BUT...
NO!

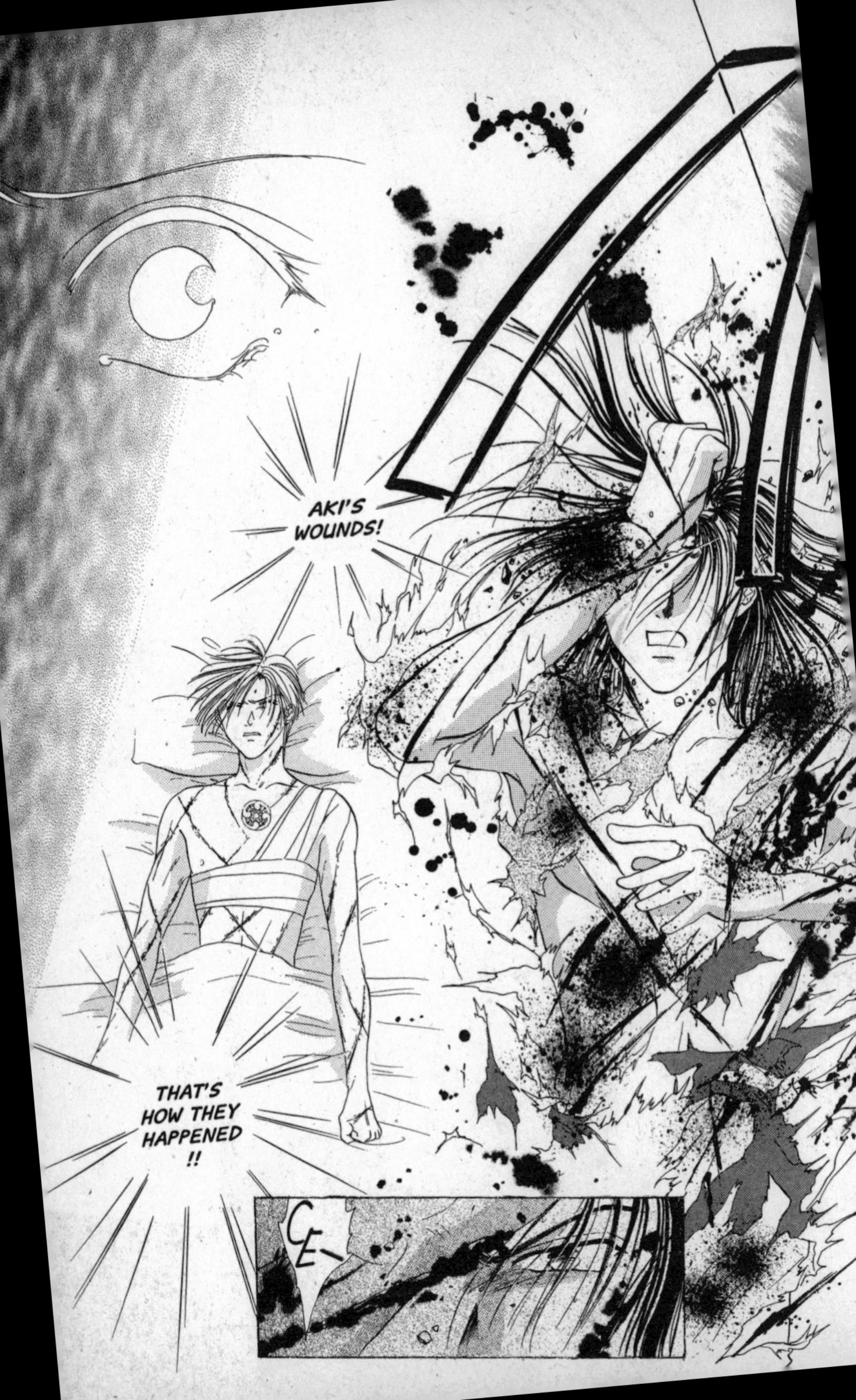
AKI'S WOUNDS!
THAT'S HOW THEY HAPPENED !!
CE-

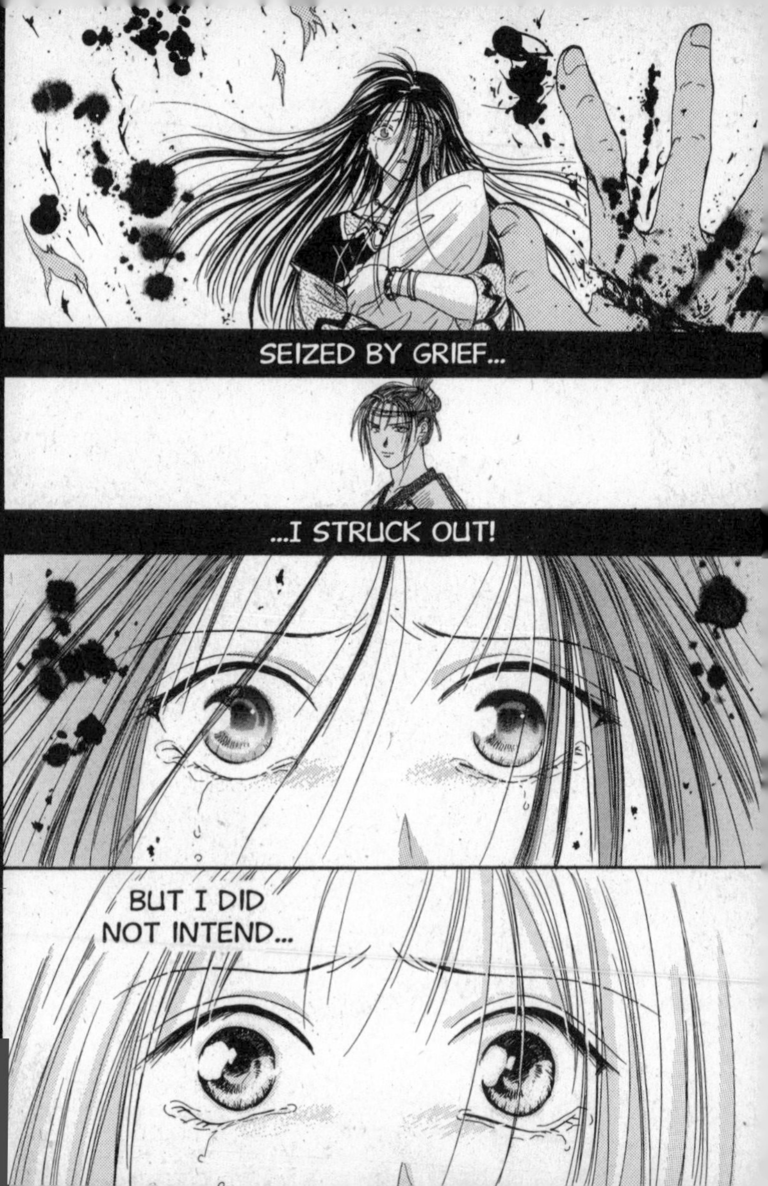
SEIZED BY GRIEF...
...I STRUCK OUT!
BUT I DID NOT INTEND...

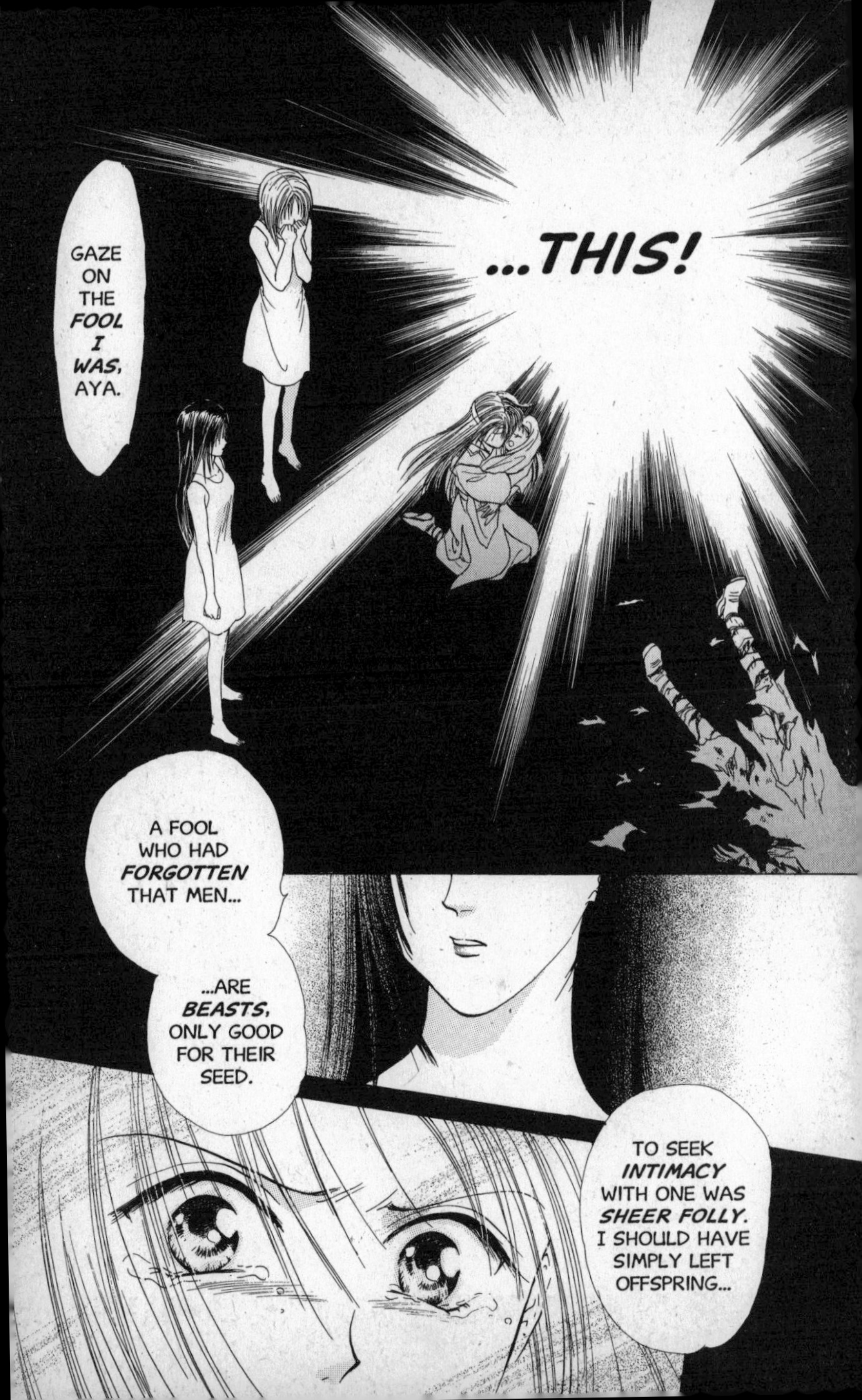
...THIS!
GAZE ON THE FOOL I WAS, AYA.
A FOOL WHO HAD FORGOTTEN THAT MEN...
...ARE BEASTS, ONLY GOOD FOR THEIR SEED.
TO SEEK INTIMACY WITH ONE WAS SHEER FOLLY. I SHOULD HAVE SIMPLY LEFT OFFSPRING...

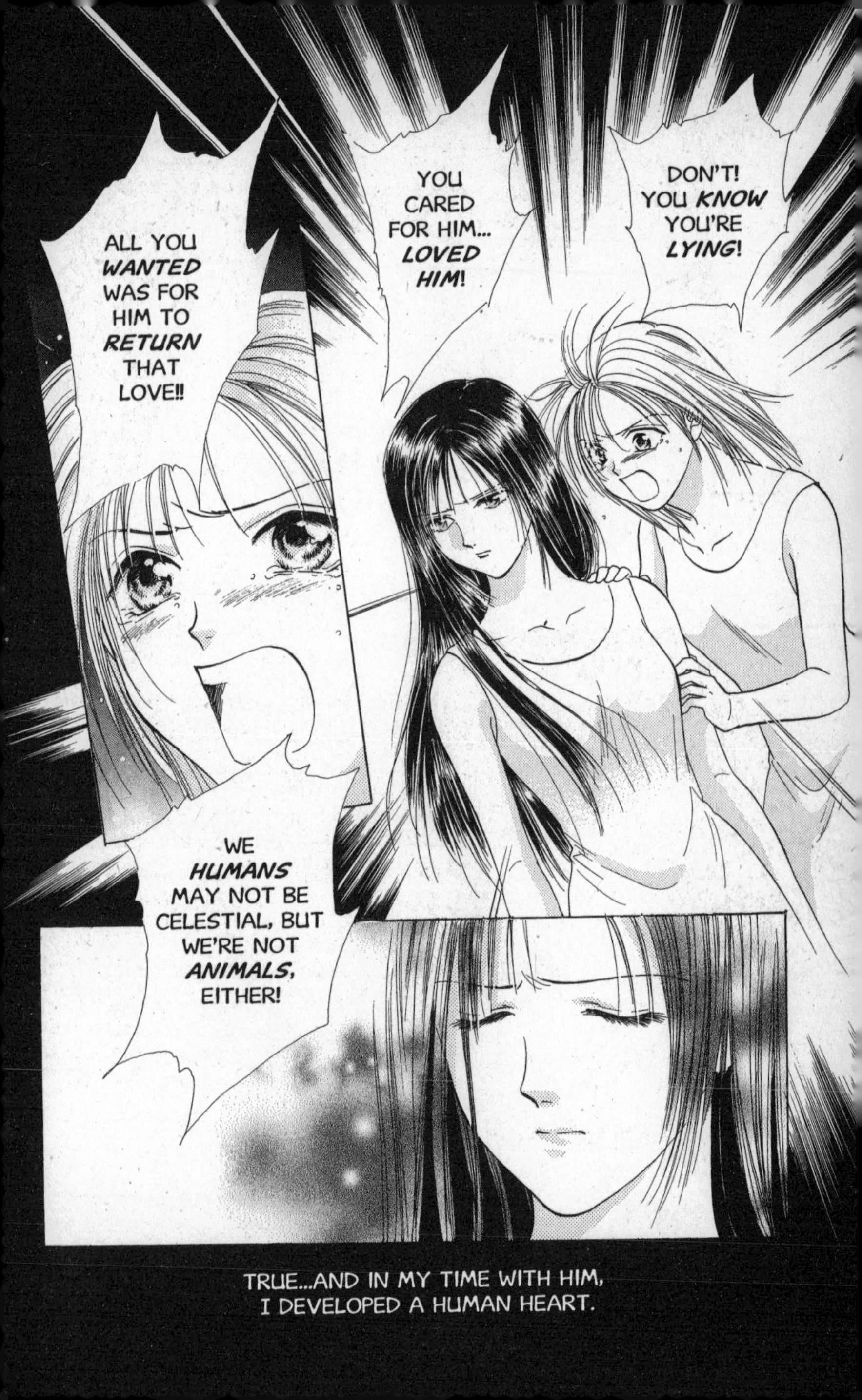
DON'T! YOU *KNOW* YOU'RE *LYING*!
YOU CARED FOR HIM... *LOVED HIM*!
ALL YOU *WANTED* WAS FOR HIM TO *RETURN* THAT LOVE!!
WE *HUMANS* MAY NOT BE CELESTIAL, BUT WE'RE NOT *ANIMALS*, EITHER!
TRUE...AND IN MY TIME WITH HIM, I DEVELOPED A HUMAN HEART.

WITHOUT THAT, I WOULD NEVER HAVE LEARNED OF LOVE, OF HOPE...OF SUFFERING.

AND I...*WANTED* TO LOVE HIM.

"I WANT NOTHING MORE IN LIFE—AND WOULD GIVE MY LIFE—TO BE WITH YOU."

ALL I SOUGHT...

...WAS HIS LOVE IN RETURN.

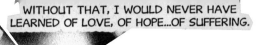

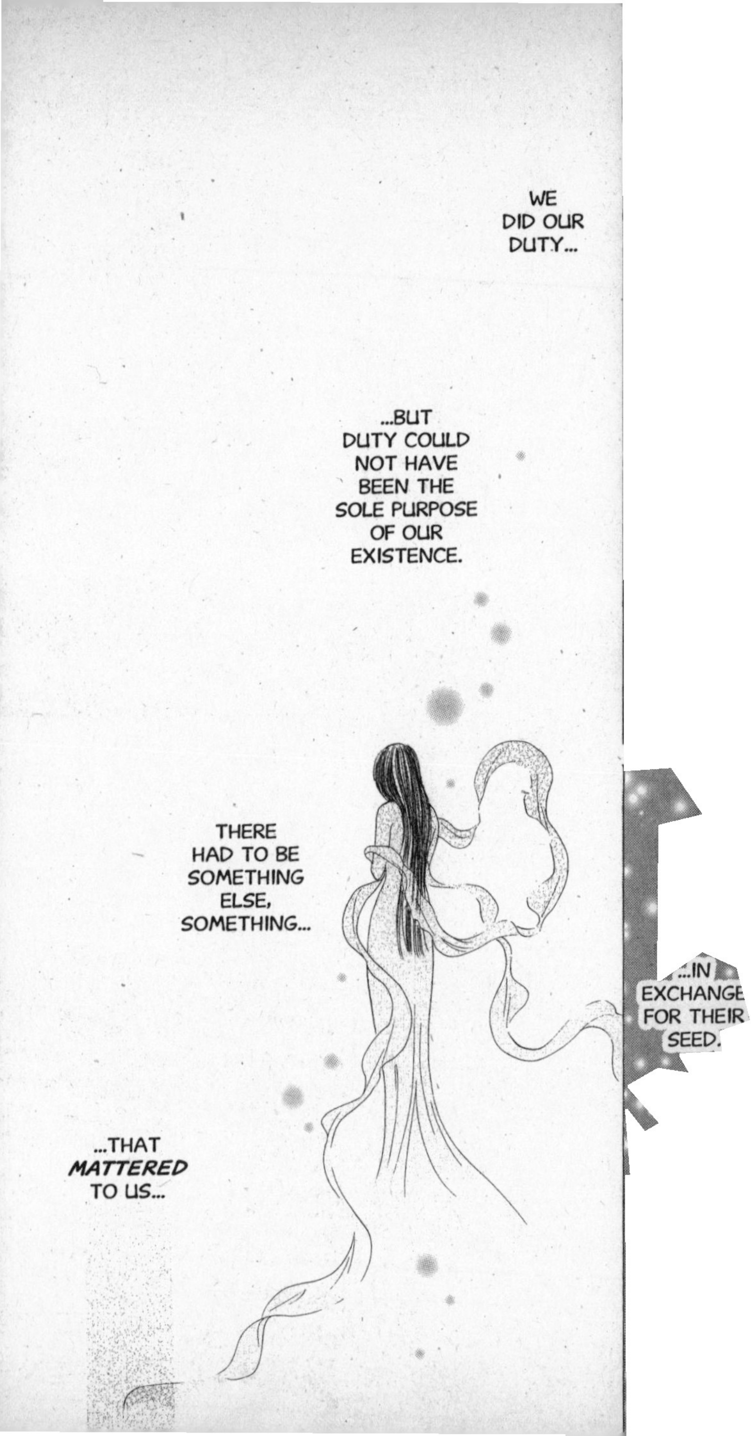
...IN EXCHANGE FOR THEIR SEED.
WE DID OUR DUTY...
...BUT DUTY COULD NOT HAVE BEEN THE SOLE PURPOSE OF OUR EXISTENCE.
THERE HAD TO BE SOMETHING ELSE, SOMETHING...
...THAT *MATTERED* TO US...

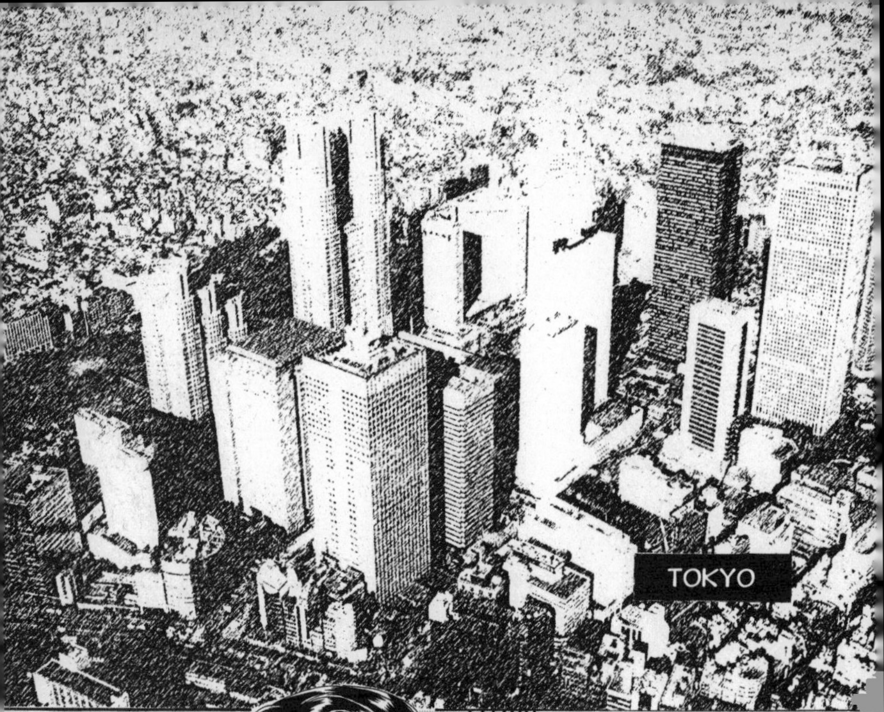
TOKYO

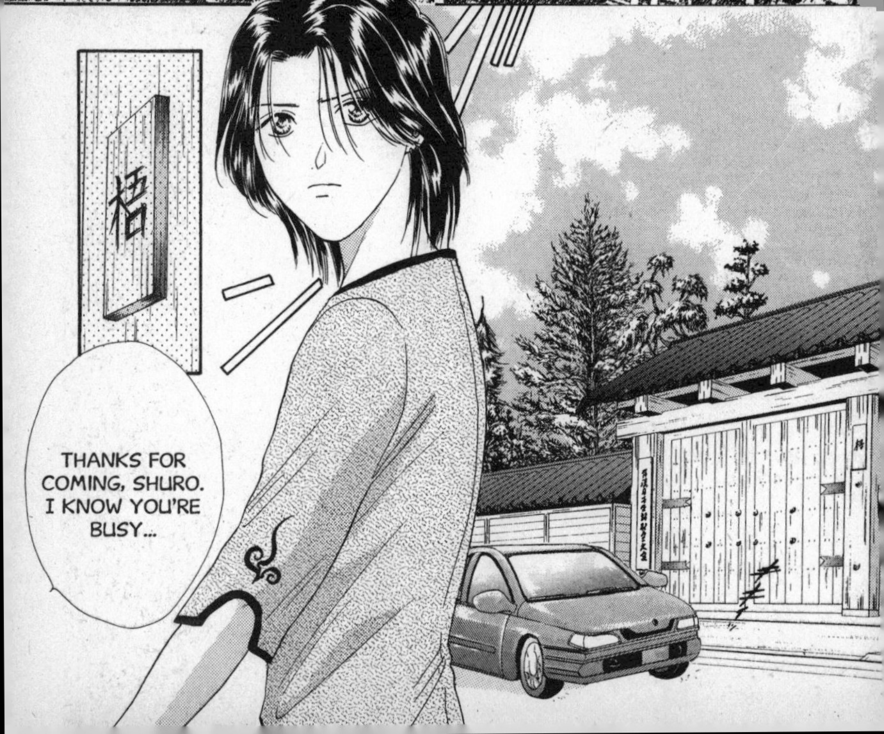
梧
THANKS FOR COMING, SHURO. I KNOW YOU'RE BUSY...

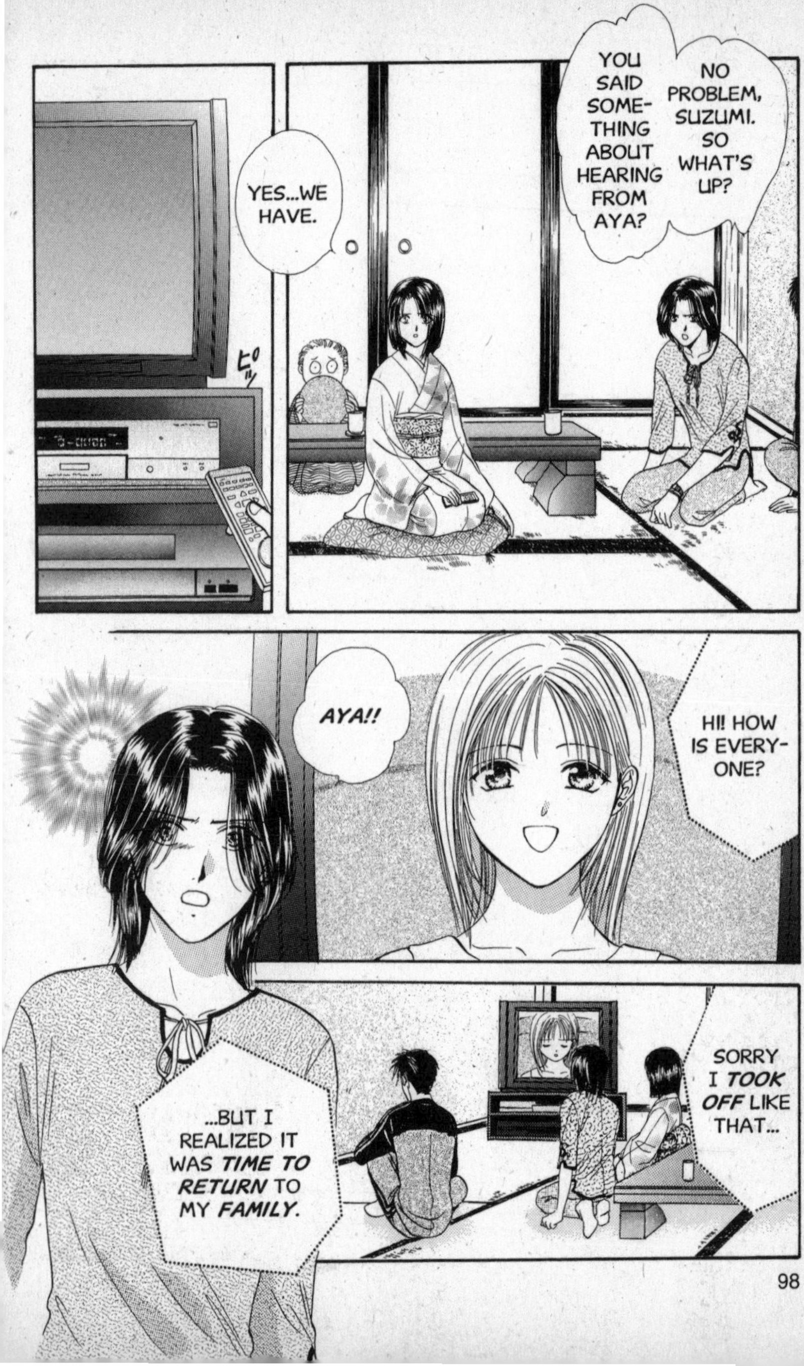
NO PROBLEM, SUZUMI. SO WHAT'S UP?
YOU SAID SOME-THING ABOUT HEARING FROM AYA?
YES...WE HAVE.
ピッ
HI! HOW IS EVERY-ONE?
AYA!!
SORRY I *TOOK OFF* LIKE THAT...
...BUT I REALIZED IT WAS *TIME TO RETURN* TO MY *FAMILY.*

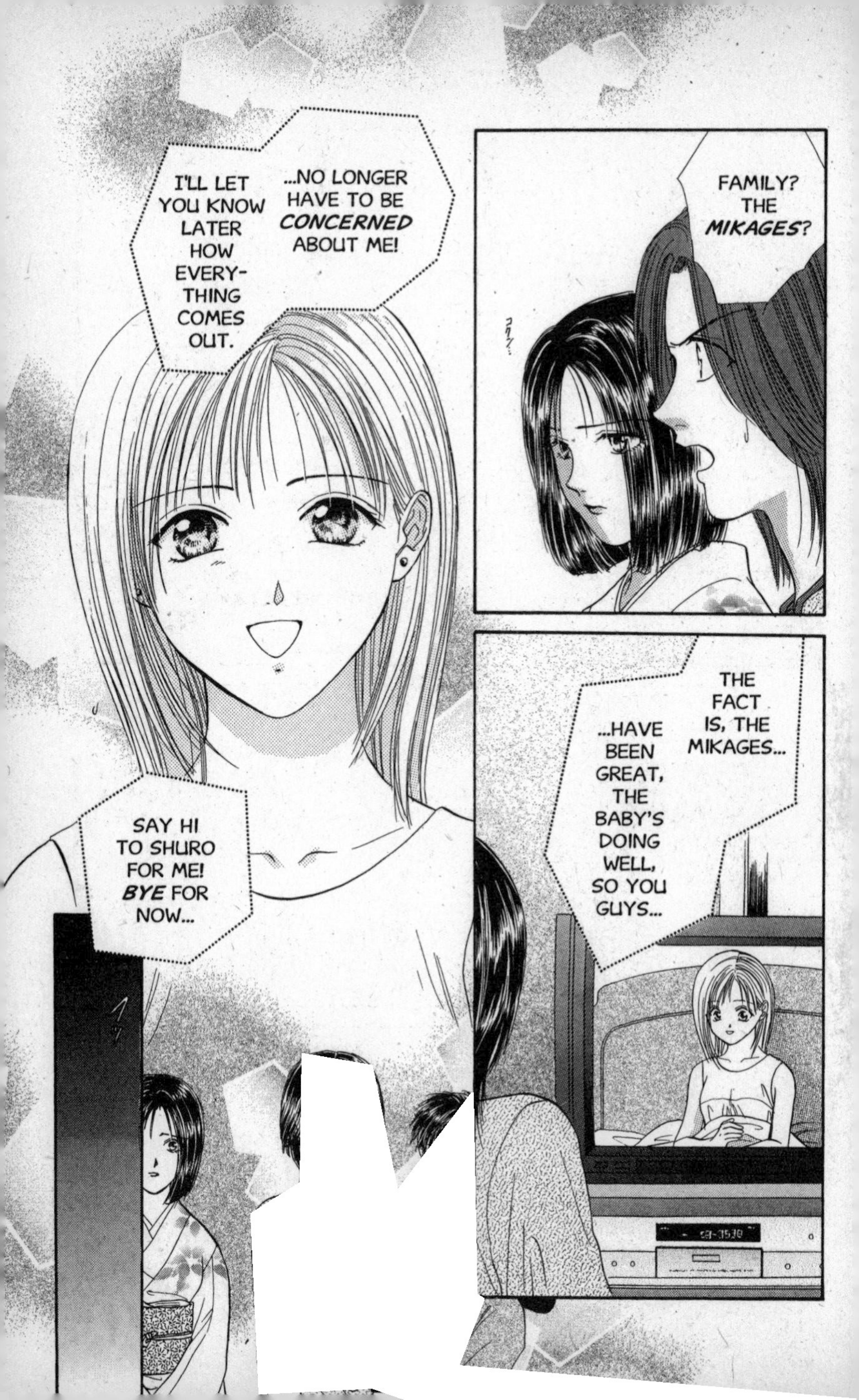
FAMILY? THE MIKAGES?
THE FACT IS, THE MIKAGES...
...HAVE BEEN GREAT, THE BABY'S DOING WELL, SO YOU GUYS...
...NO LONGER HAVE TO BE CONCERNED ABOUT ME!
I'LL LET YOU KNOW LATER HOW EVERY-THING COMES OUT.
SAY HI TO SHURO FOR ME! BYE FOR NOW...

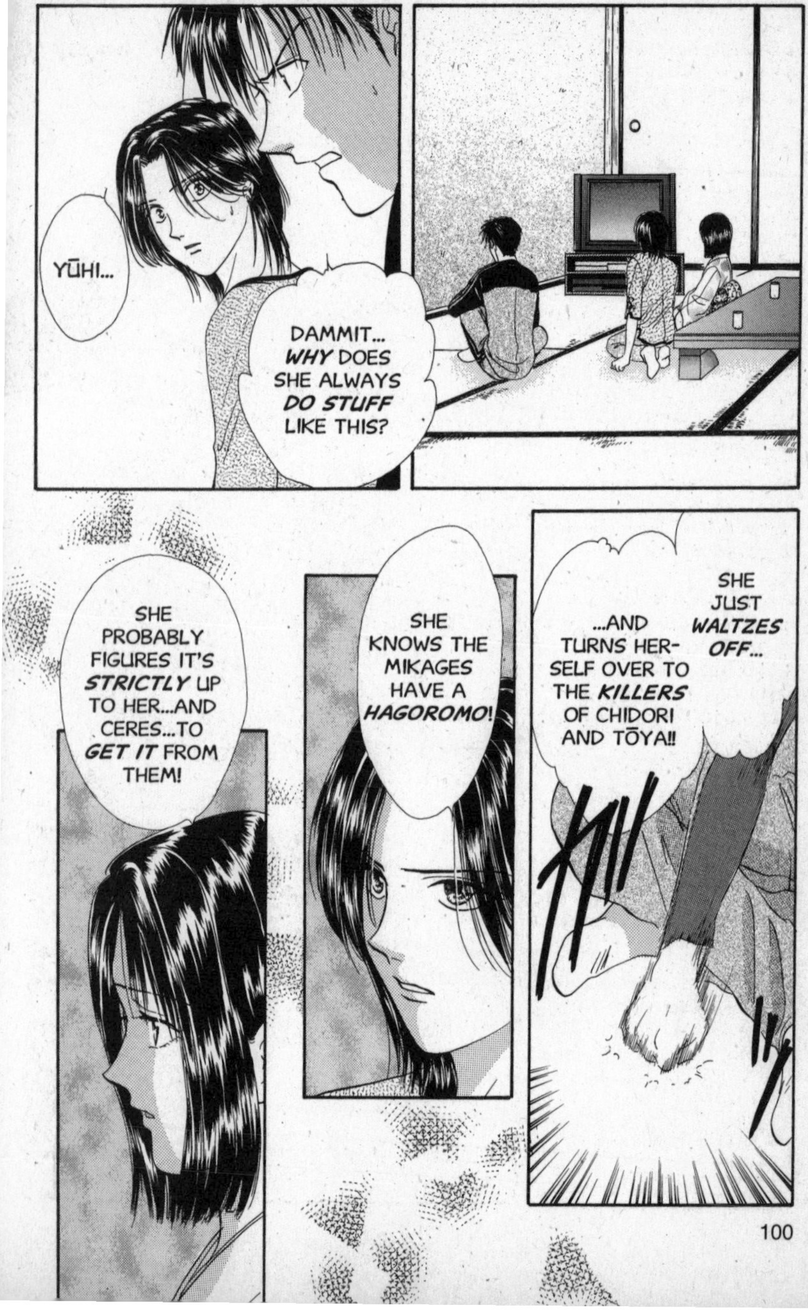
DAMMIT... *WHY* DOES SHE ALWAYS *DO STUFF* LIKE THIS?
YŪHI...
SHE JUST *WALTZES OFF*...
...AND TURNS HER-SELF OVER TO THE *KILLERS* OF CHIDORI AND TŌYA!!
SHE KNOWS THE MIKAGES HAVE A *HAGOROMO*!
SHE PROBABLY FIGURES IT'S *STRICTLY* UP TO HER...AND CERES...TO *GET IT* FROM THEM!

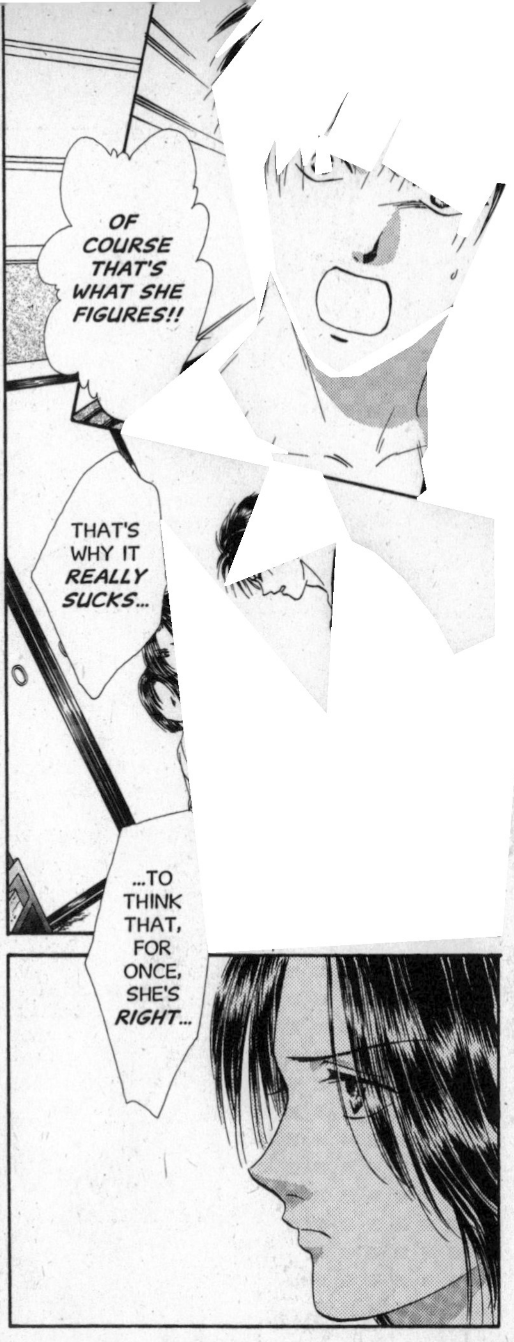
OF COURSE THAT'S WHAT SHE FIGURES!!
THAT'S WHY IT *REALLY SUCKS...*
...TO THINK THAT, FOR ONCE, SHE'S *RIGHT...*

Changing the subject...talking about similarities reminds me that readers constantly say Tōya looks like TERU from the band GLAY! R-really? It's not just the color of his hair? (I didn't suggest it, so don't get mad at me!) There's no particular real-life model for Tōya, by the way. My references for him include every guy I see who I think is beautiful. ☺ I only recently got the hang of drawing him.

And so the Progenitor finally appears for the first time! I'm glad he's been well-received. I added him to the back cover of this volume, too.

They're supposed to be in the late Jomon Period (1500-1000BC). There weren't really any Jomon people like that, though. ☺ It's half fiction...I read that the hagoromo legend spread in Japan around the Yayoi Period (300BC-300AD), so I thought the clothing should be accordingly colorful. They used lots of adornments...so much that it makes me think the modern use of earrings, bracelets, and tattoos are vestiges from the Jomon Period.

A lot of people told me they cried when they read Ceres and Mikagi's story (not to mention the heart-tugging tale of Shuro). I put a lot of effort into the art, I tellya! ☺

Ceres gave Mikagi her powers out of love, but my assistants hypothesized that the gift infused and developed the ugly side of his humanity.

The people in the Jomon period didn't have war, and were actually peaceful and cooperative...

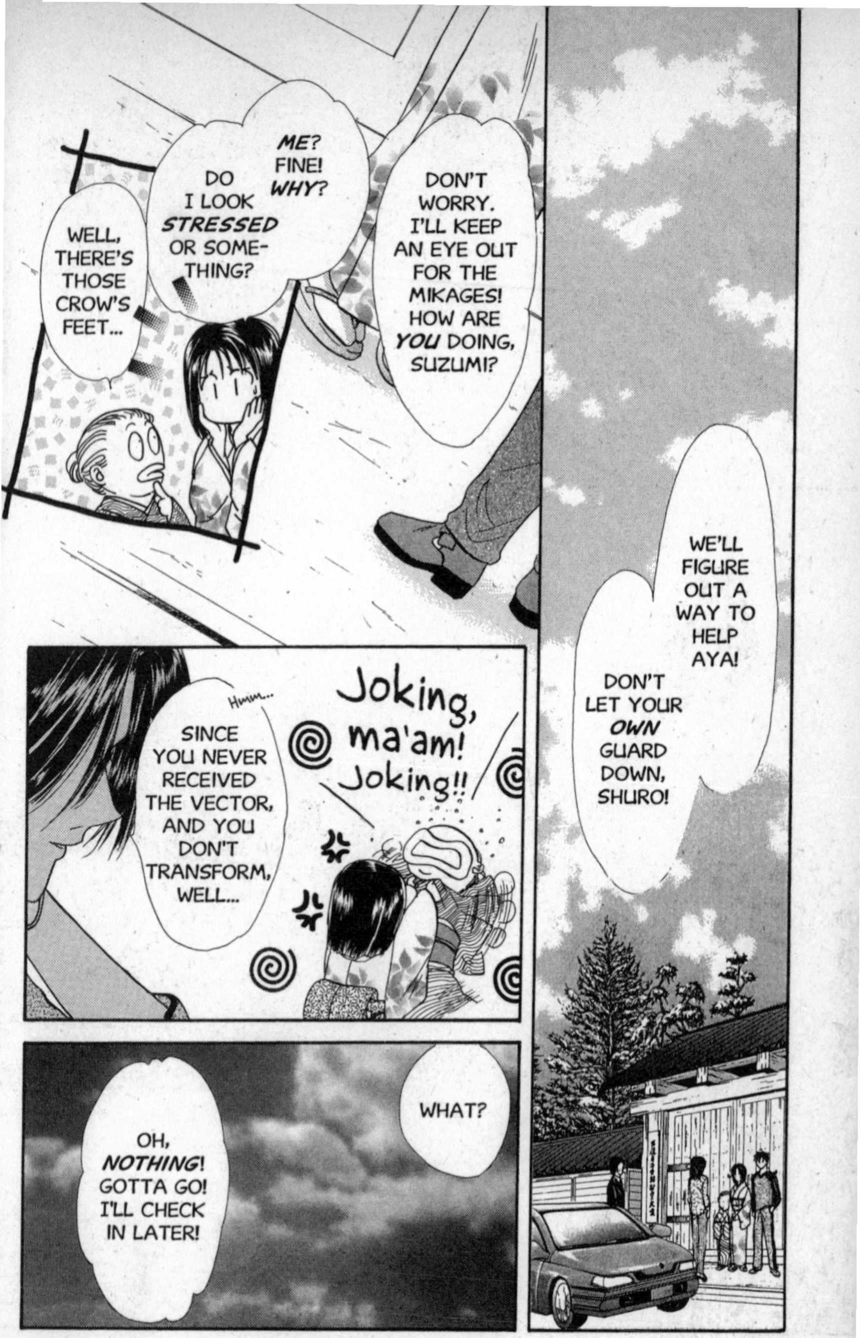

WE'LL FIGURE OUT A WAY TO HELP AYA!
DON'T LET YOUR *OWN* GUARD DOWN, SHURO!
DON'T WORRY. I'LL KEEP AN EYE OUT FOR THE MIKAGES! HOW ARE *YOU* DOING, SUZUMI?
ME? FINE! *WHY*?
DO I LOOK *STRESSED* OR SOME-THING?
WELL, THERE'S THOSE CROW'S FEET...
Joking, ma'am! Joking!!
Hmm...
SINCE YOU NEVER RECEIVED THE VECTOR, AND YOU DON'T TRANSFORM, WELL...
WHAT?
OH, *NOTHING*! GOTTA GO! I'LL CHECK IN LATER!

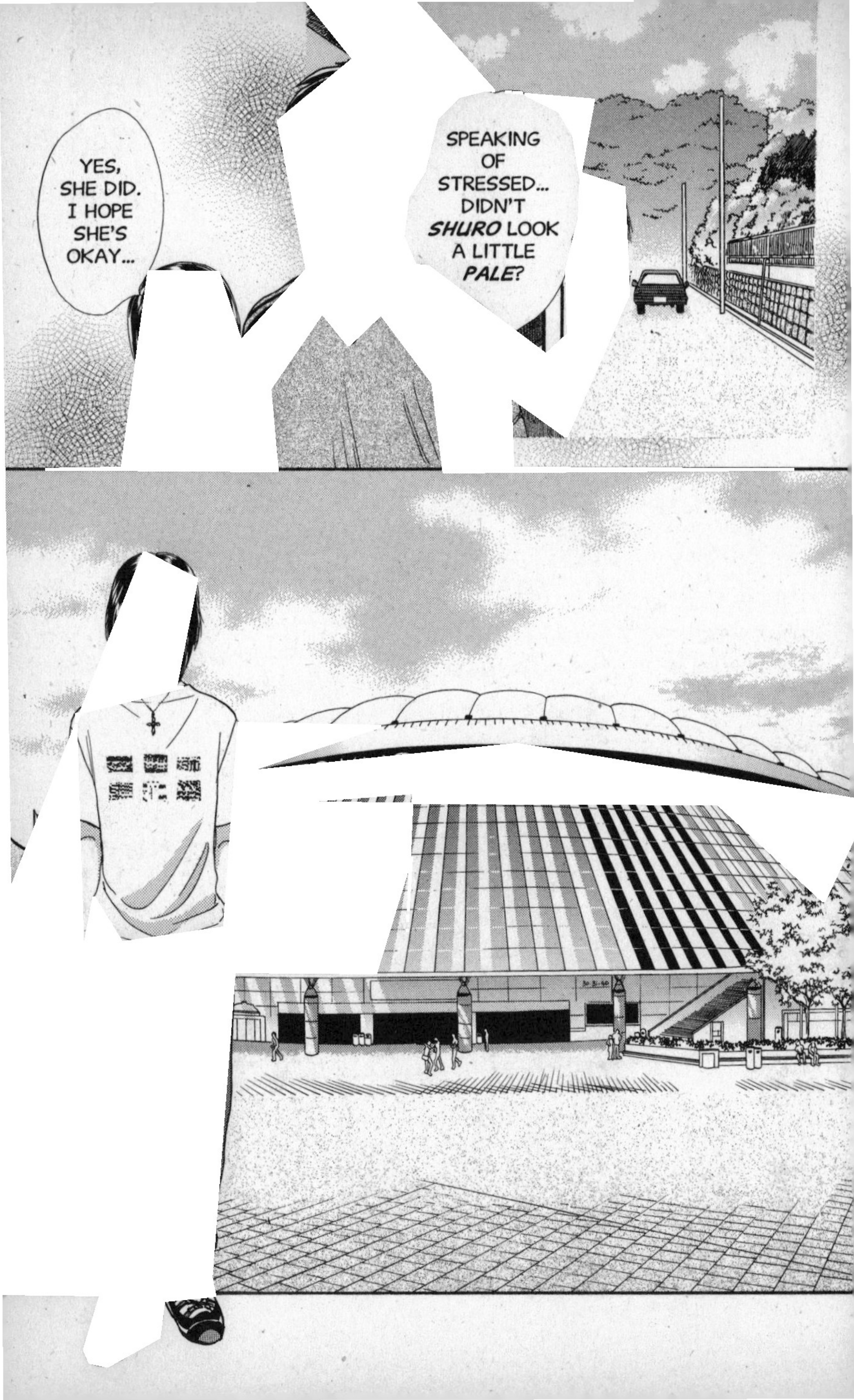
SPEAKING OF STRESSED... DIDN'T *SHURO* LOOK A LITTLE *PALE*?
YES, SHE DID. I HOPE SHE'S OKAY...

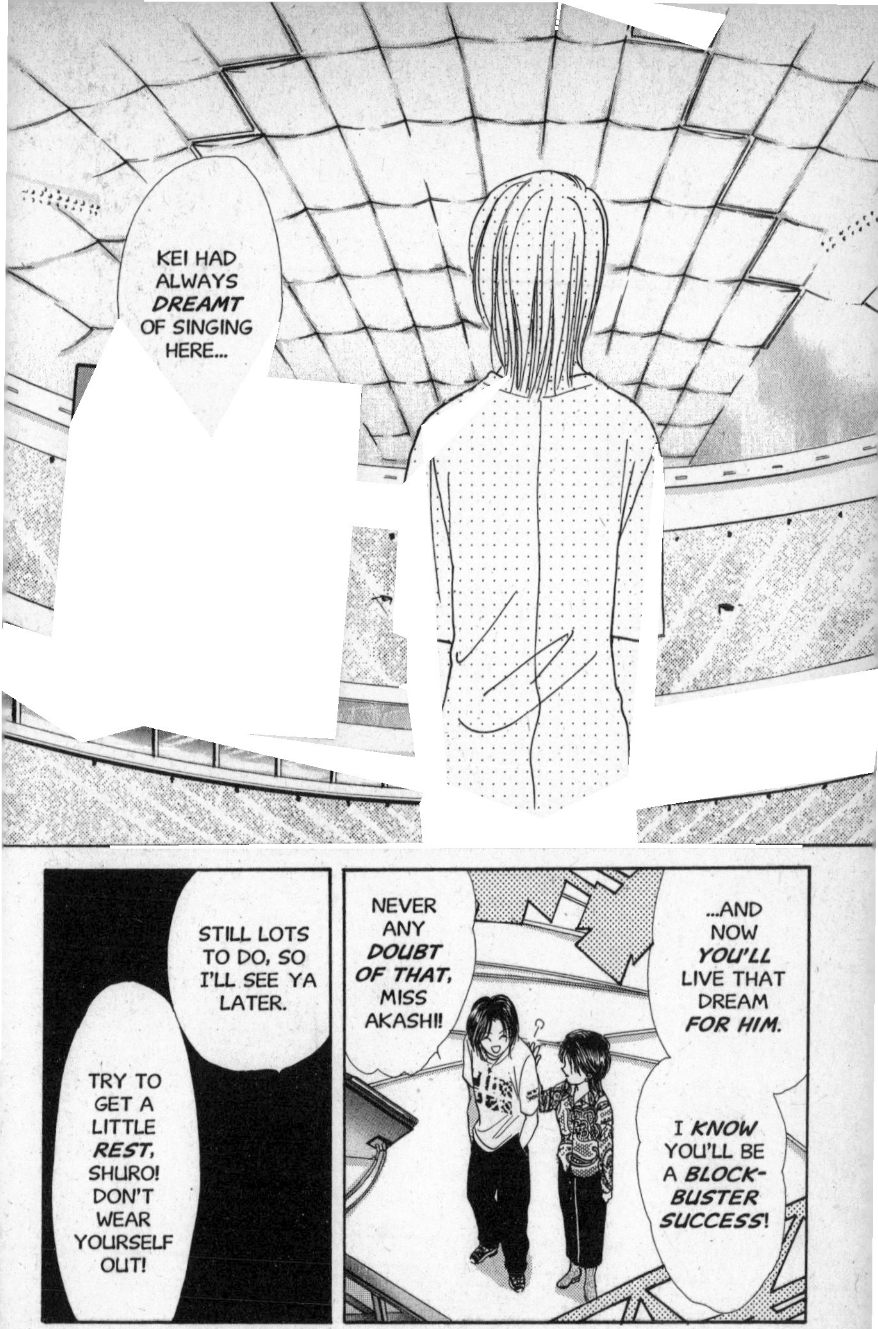
KEI HAD ALWAYS *DREAMT* OF SINGING HERE...
...AND NOW *YOU'LL* LIVE THAT DREAM *FOR HIM.*
I *KNOW* YOU'LL BE A *BLOCK-BUSTER SUCCESS*!
NEVER ANY *DOUBT OF THAT,* MISS AKASHI!
STILL LOTS TO DO, SO I'LL SEE YA LATER.
TRY TO GET A LITTLE *REST,* SHURO! DON'T WEAR YOURSELF OUT!

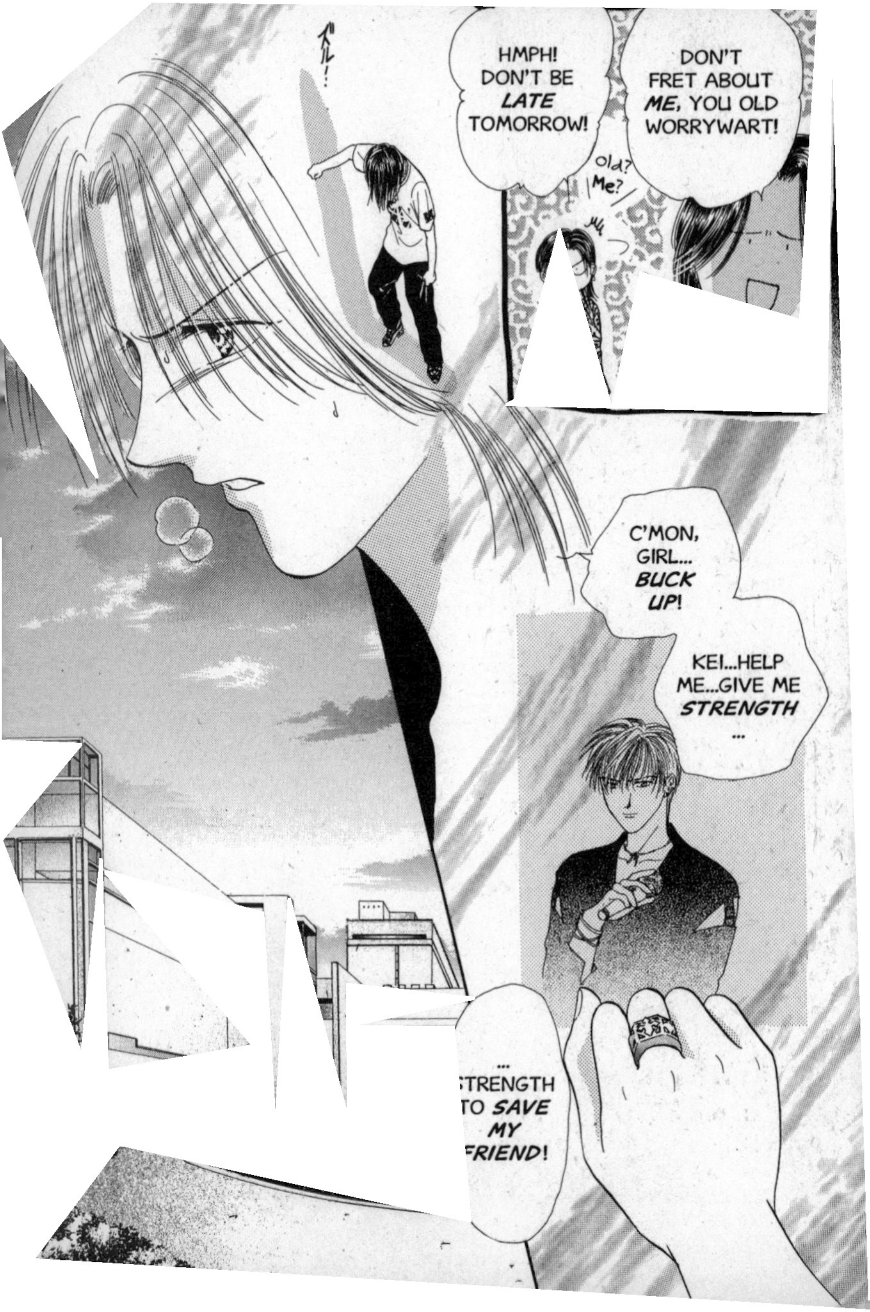
DON'T FRET ABOUT ME, YOU OLD WORRYWART!
HMPH! DON'T BE LATE TOMORROW!
Old? Me?
ズル!
C'MON, GIRL... BUCK UP!
KEI...HELP ME...GIVE ME STRENGTH ...
... STRENGTH TO SAVE MY FRIEND!

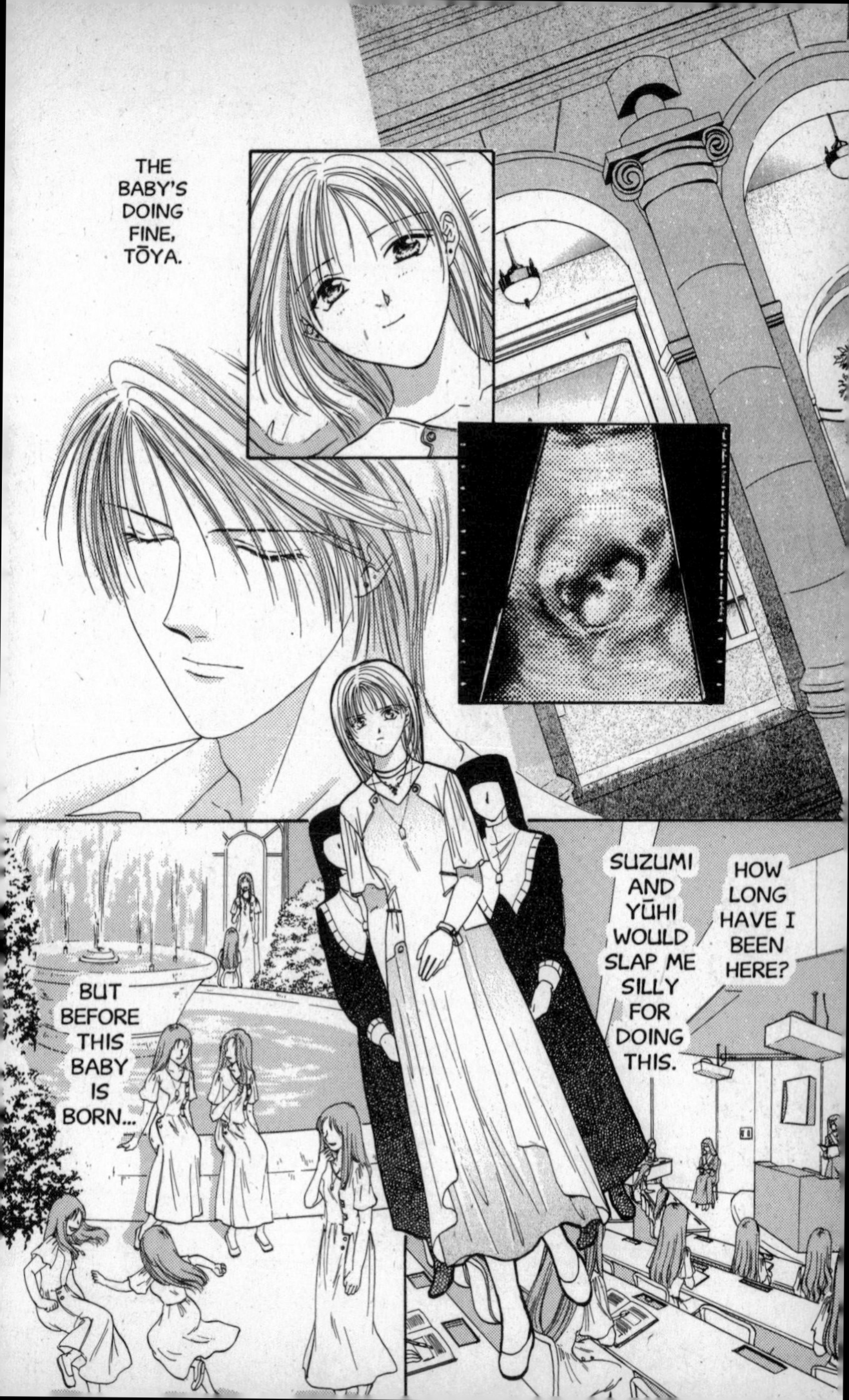
THE BABY'S DOING FINE, TŌYA.
HOW LONG HAVE I BEEN HERE?
SUZUMI AND YŪHI WOULD SLAP ME SILLY FOR DOING THIS.
BUT BEFORE THIS BABY IS BORN...

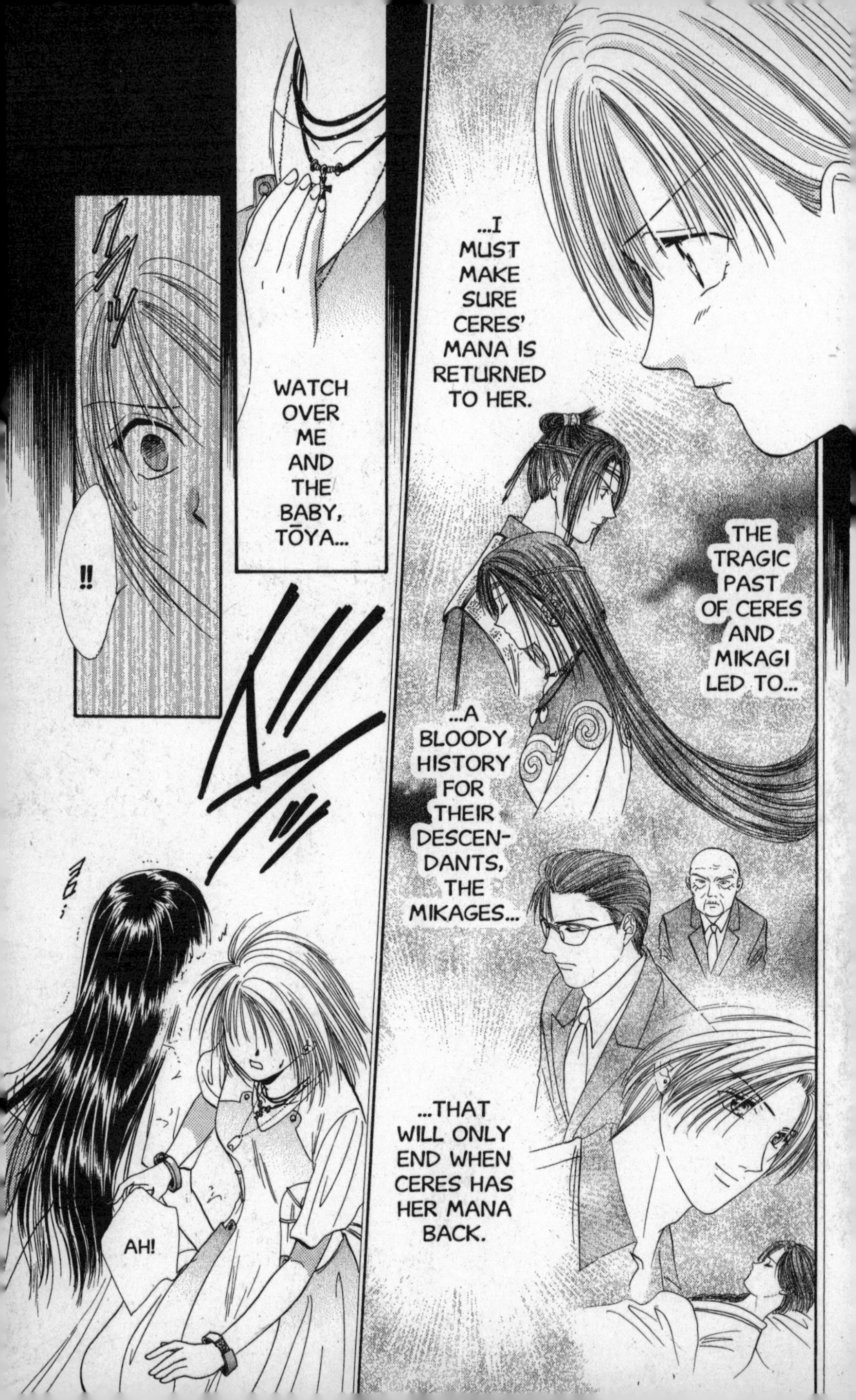

...I MUST MAKE SURE CERES' MANA IS RETURNED TO HER.
THE TRAGIC PAST OF CERES AND MIKAGI LED TO...
...A BLOODY HISTORY FOR THEIR DESCENDANTS, THE MIKAGES...
...THAT WILL ONLY END WHEN CERES HAS HER MANA BACK.
WATCH OVER ME AND THE BABY, TŌYA...
!!
AH!

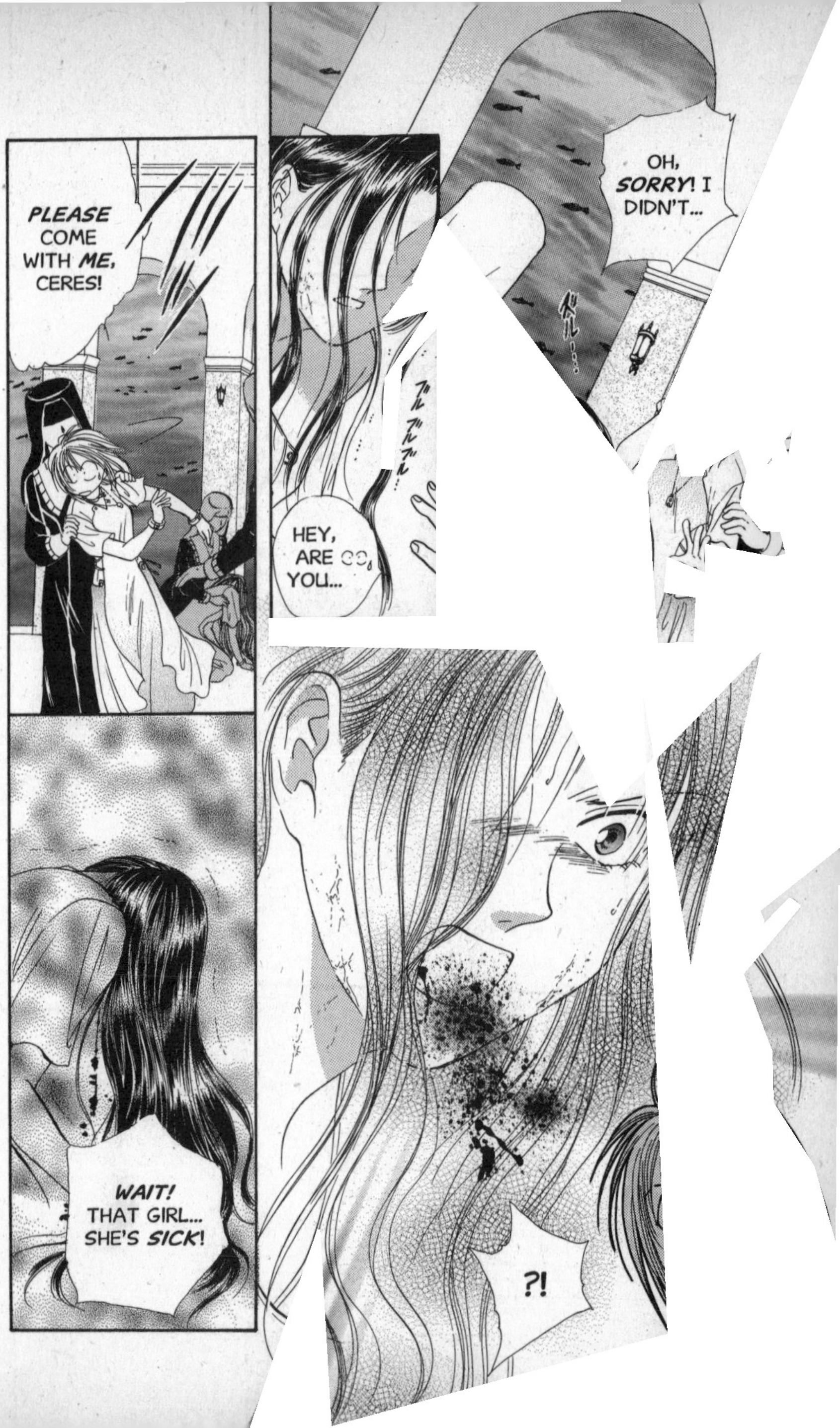
OH, SORRY! I DIDN'T...
ブルブルブル…
HEY, ARE YOU...
PLEASE COME WITH ME, CERES!
?!
WAIT! THAT GIRL... SHE'S SICK!

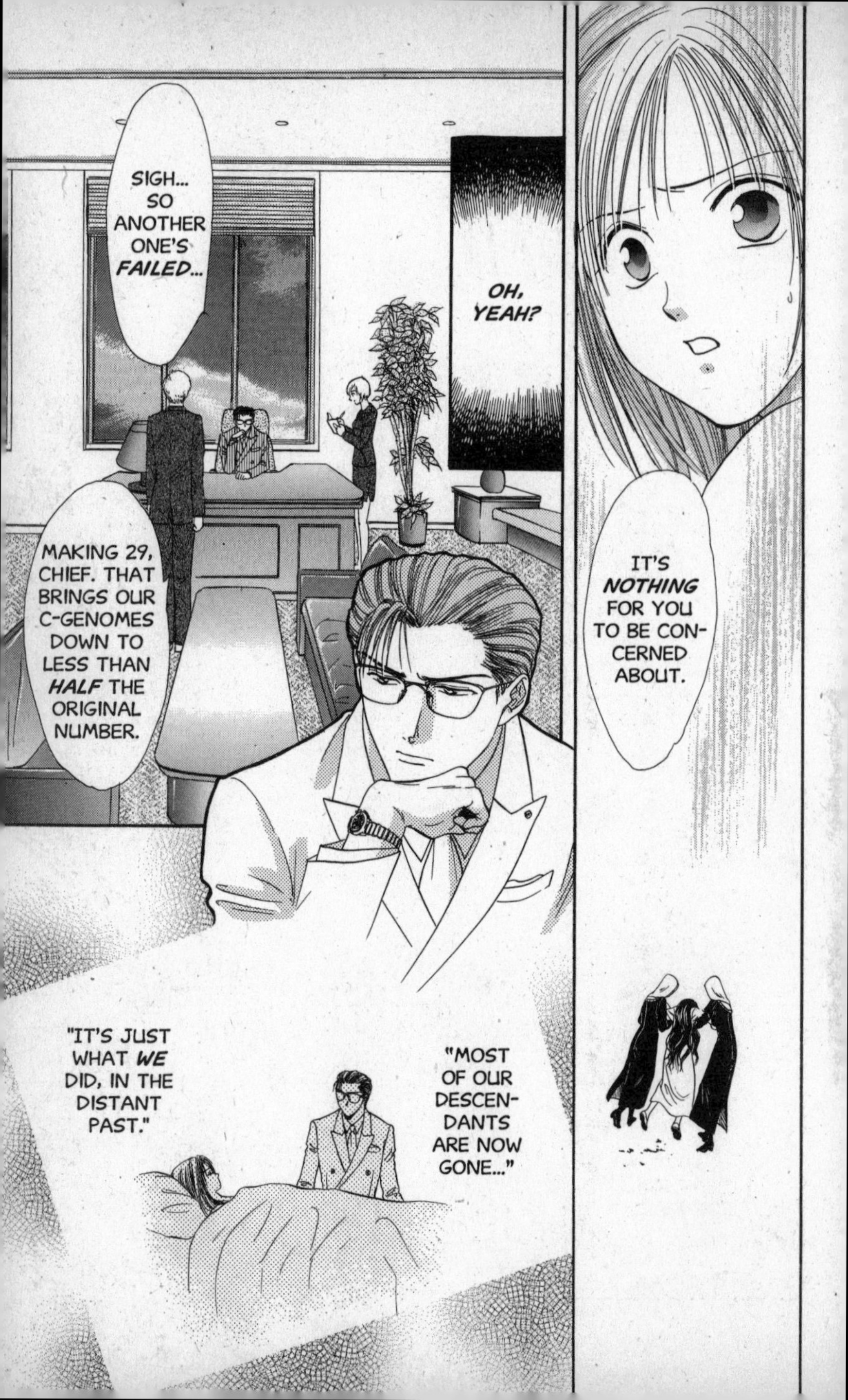
IT'S *NOTHING* FOR YOU TO BE CONCERNED ABOUT.
OH, YEAH?
SIGH... SO ANOTHER ONE'S *FAILED*...
MAKING 29, CHIEF. THAT BRINGS OUR C-GENOMES DOWN TO LESS THAN *HALF* THE ORIGINAL NUMBER.
"MOST OF OUR DESCENDANTS ARE NOW GONE..."
"IT'S JUST WHAT *WE* DID, IN THE DISTANT PAST."

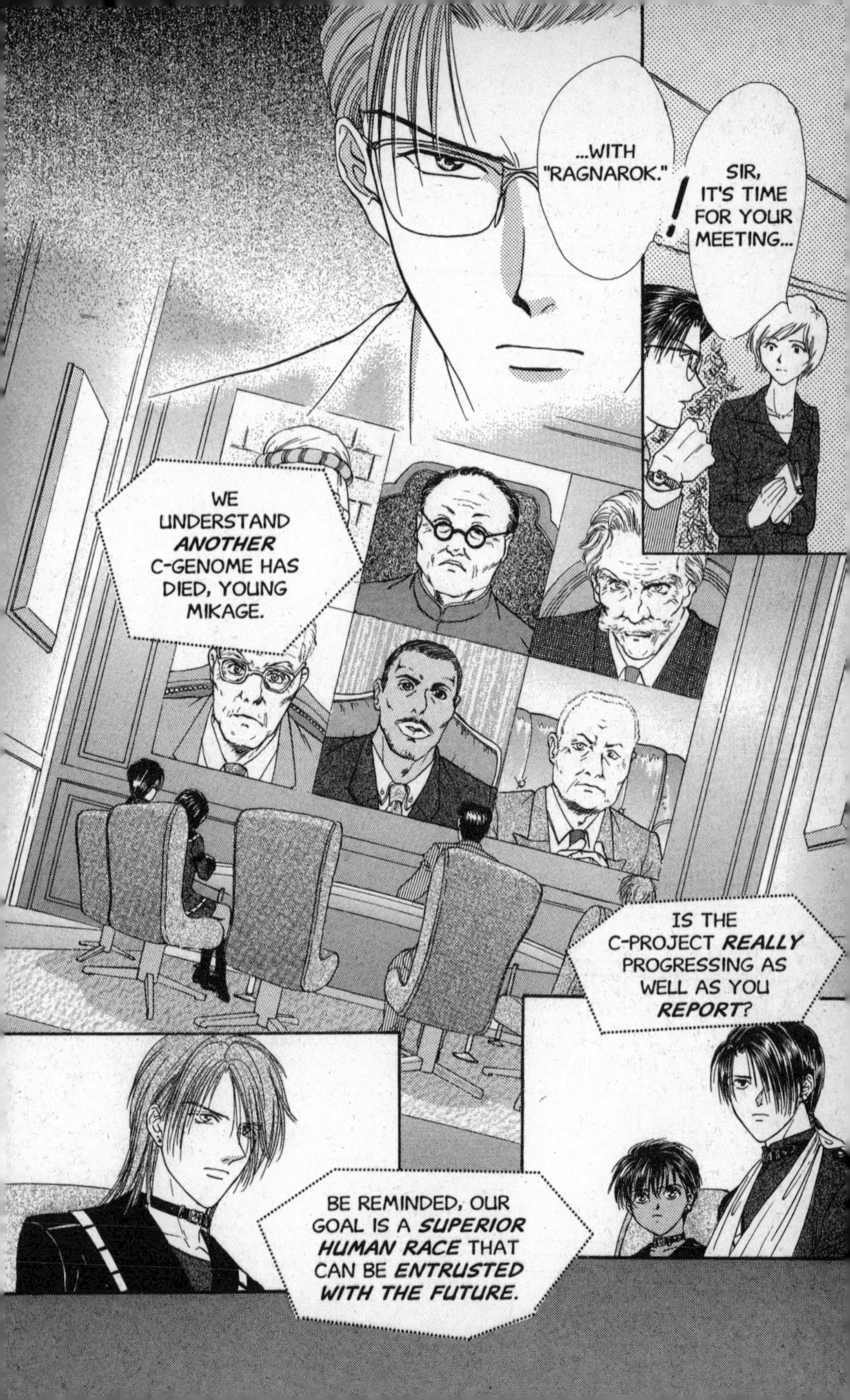
...WITH "RAGNAROK."
!
SIR, IT'S TIME FOR YOUR MEETING...
WE UNDERSTAND ANOTHER C-GENOME HAS DIED, YOUNG MIKAGE.
IS THE C-PROJECT REALLY PROGRESSING AS WELL AS YOU REPORT?
BE REMINDED, OUR GOAL IS A SUPERIOR HUMAN RACE THAT CAN BE ENTRUSTED WITH THE FUTURE.

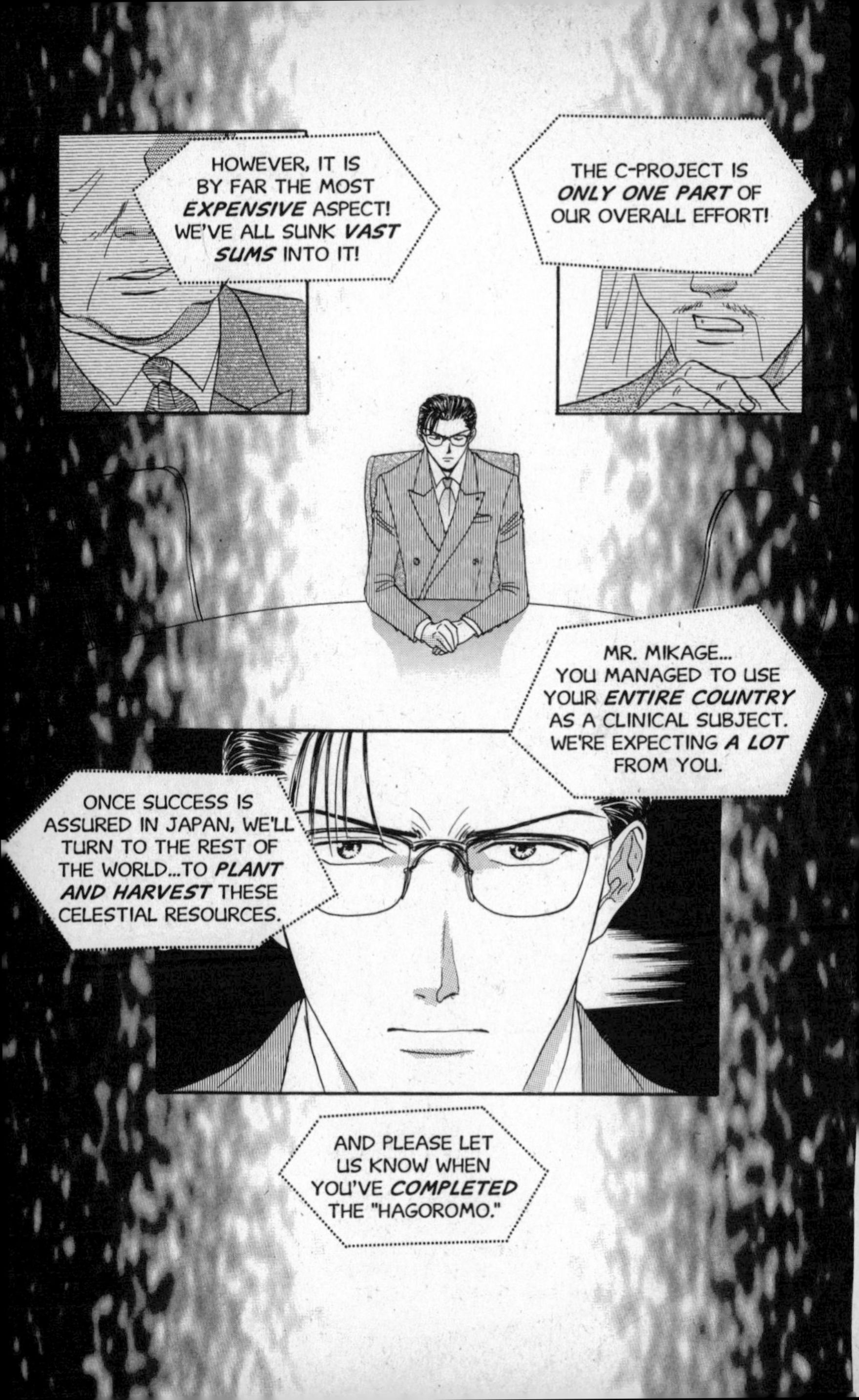
THE C-PROJECT IS ONLY ONE PART OF OUR OVERALL EFFORT!
HOWEVER, IT IS BY FAR THE MOST EXPENSIVE ASPECT! WE'VE ALL SUNK VAST SUMS INTO IT!
MR. MIKAGE... YOU MANAGED TO USE YOUR ENTIRE COUNTRY AS A CLINICAL SUBJECT. WE'RE EXPECTING A LOT FROM YOU.
ONCE SUCCESS IS ASSURED IN JAPAN, WE'LL TURN TO THE REST OF THE WORLD...TO PLANT AND HARVEST THESE CELESTIAL RESOURCES.
AND PLEASE LET US KNOW WHEN YOU'VE COMPLETED THE "HAGOROMO."

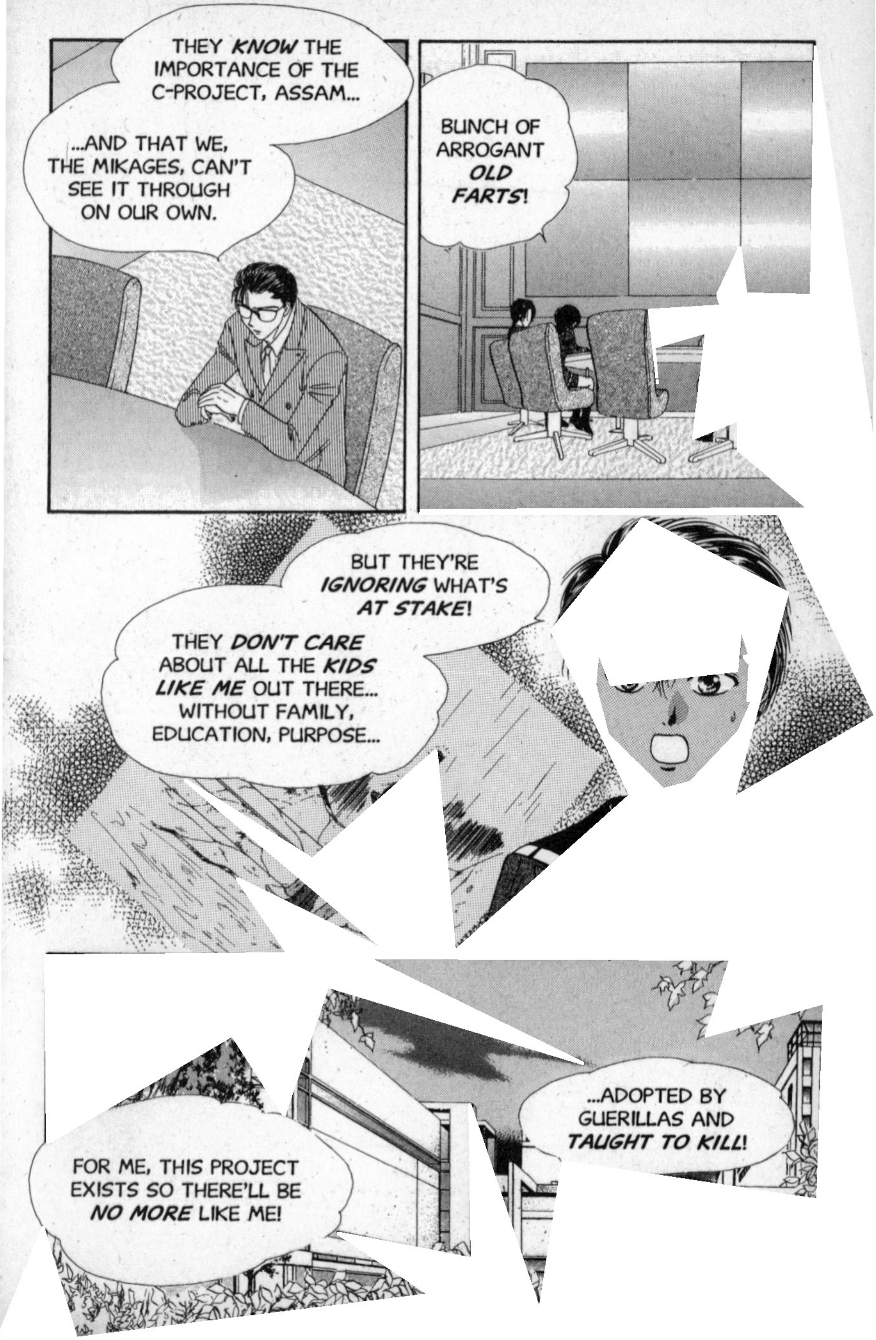
BUNCH OF ARROGANT OLD FARTS!
THEY KNOW THE IMPORTANCE OF THE C-PROJECT, ASSAM...
...AND THAT WE, THE MIKAGES, CAN'T SEE IT THROUGH ON OUR OWN.
BUT THEY'RE IGNORING WHAT'S AT STAKE!
THEY DON'T CARE ABOUT ALL THE KIDS LIKE ME OUT THERE... WITHOUT FAMILY, EDUCATION, PURPOSE...
...ADOPTED BY GUERILLAS AND TAUGHT TO KILL!
FOR ME, THIS PROJECT EXISTS SO THERE'LL BE NO MORE LIKE ME!

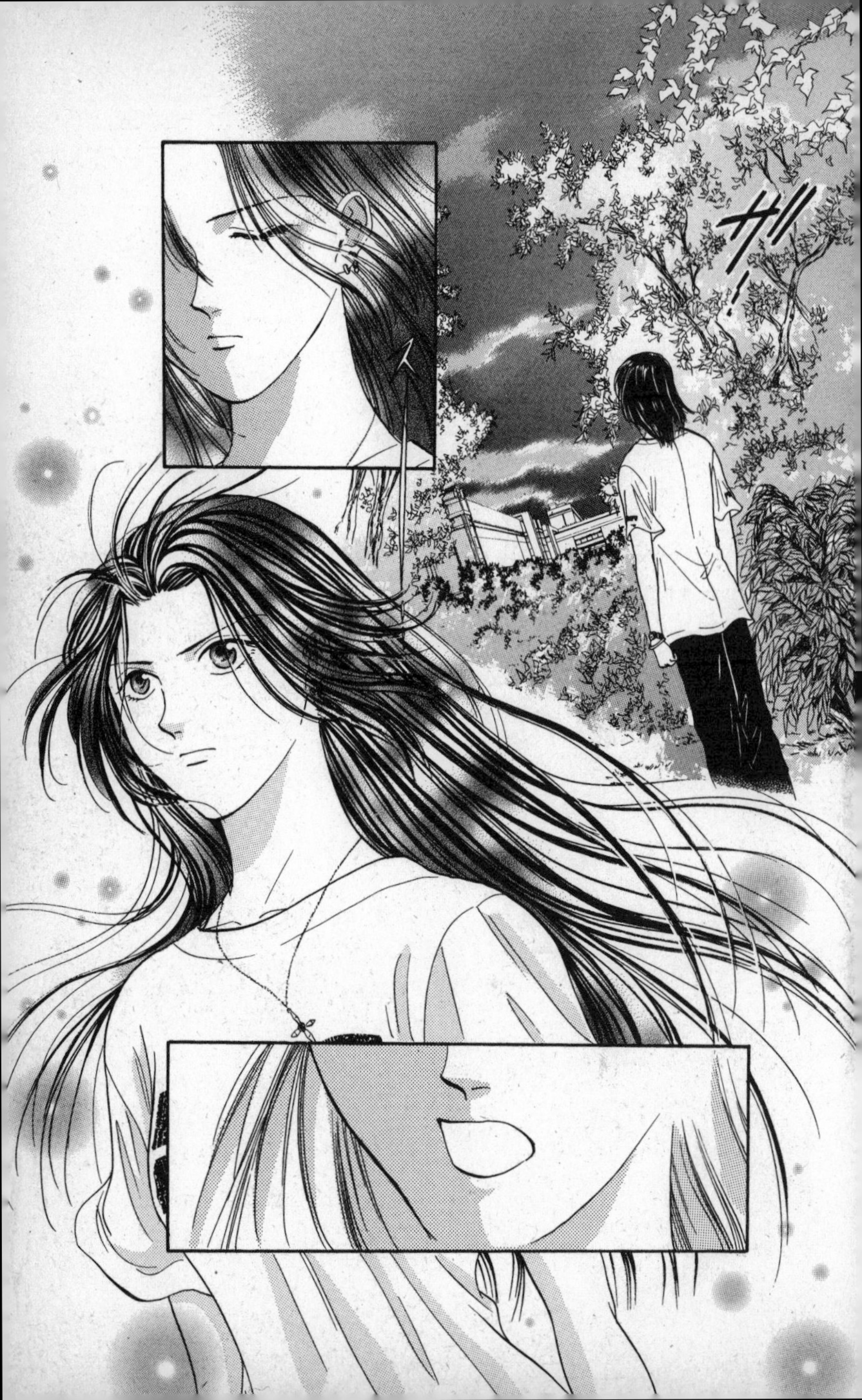
ザ!

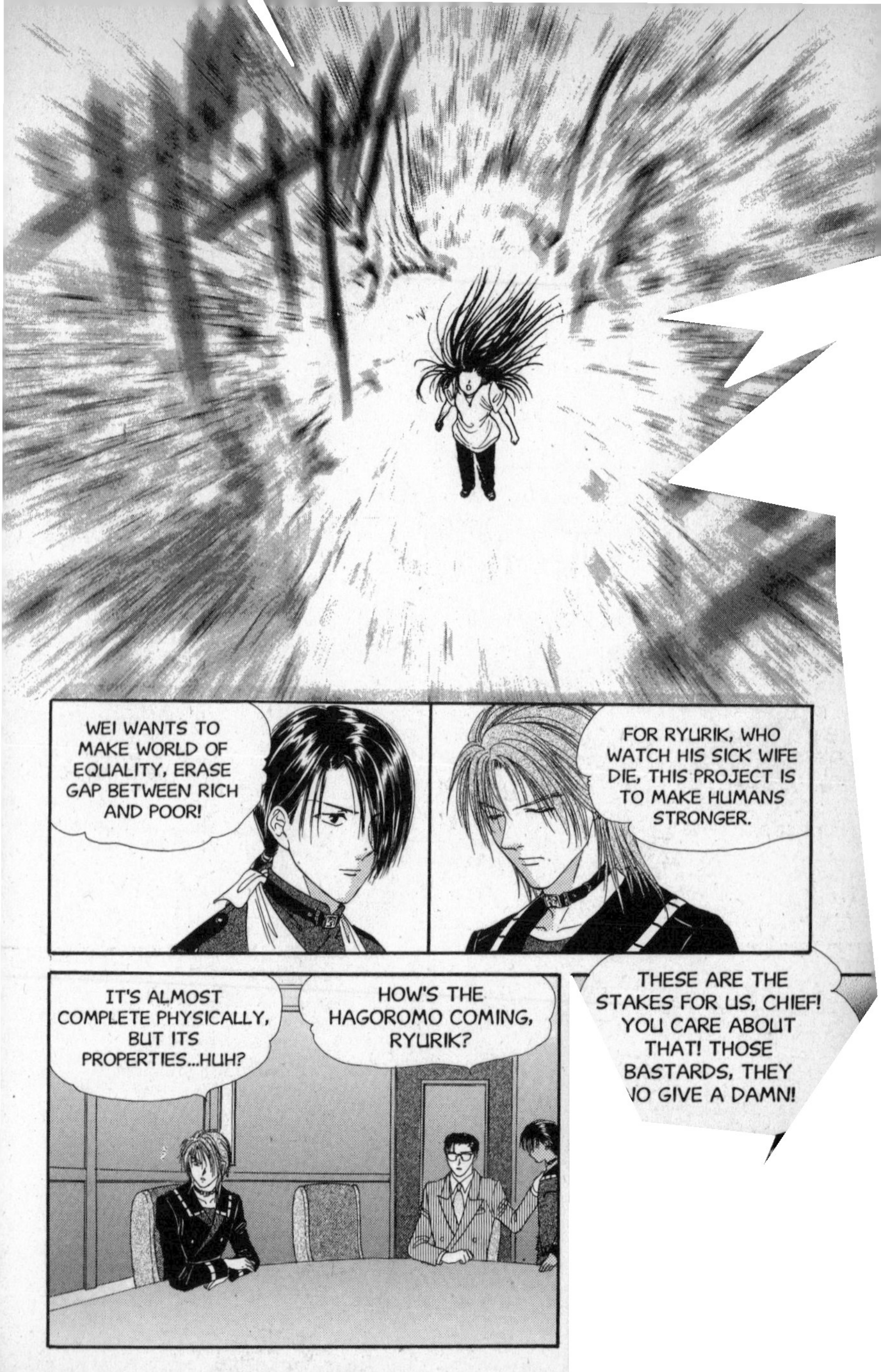
FOR RYURIK, WHO WATCH HIS SICK WIFE DIE, THIS PROJECT IS TO MAKE HUMANS STRONGER.
WEI WANTS TO MAKE WORLD OF EQUALITY, ERASE GAP BETWEEN RICH AND POOR!
THESE ARE THE STAKES FOR US, CHIEF! YOU CARE ABOUT THAT! THOSE BASTARDS, THEY NO GIVE A DAMN!
HOW'S THE HAGOROMO COMING, RYURIK?
IT'S ALMOST COMPLETE PHYSICALLY, BUT ITS PROPERTIES...HUH?

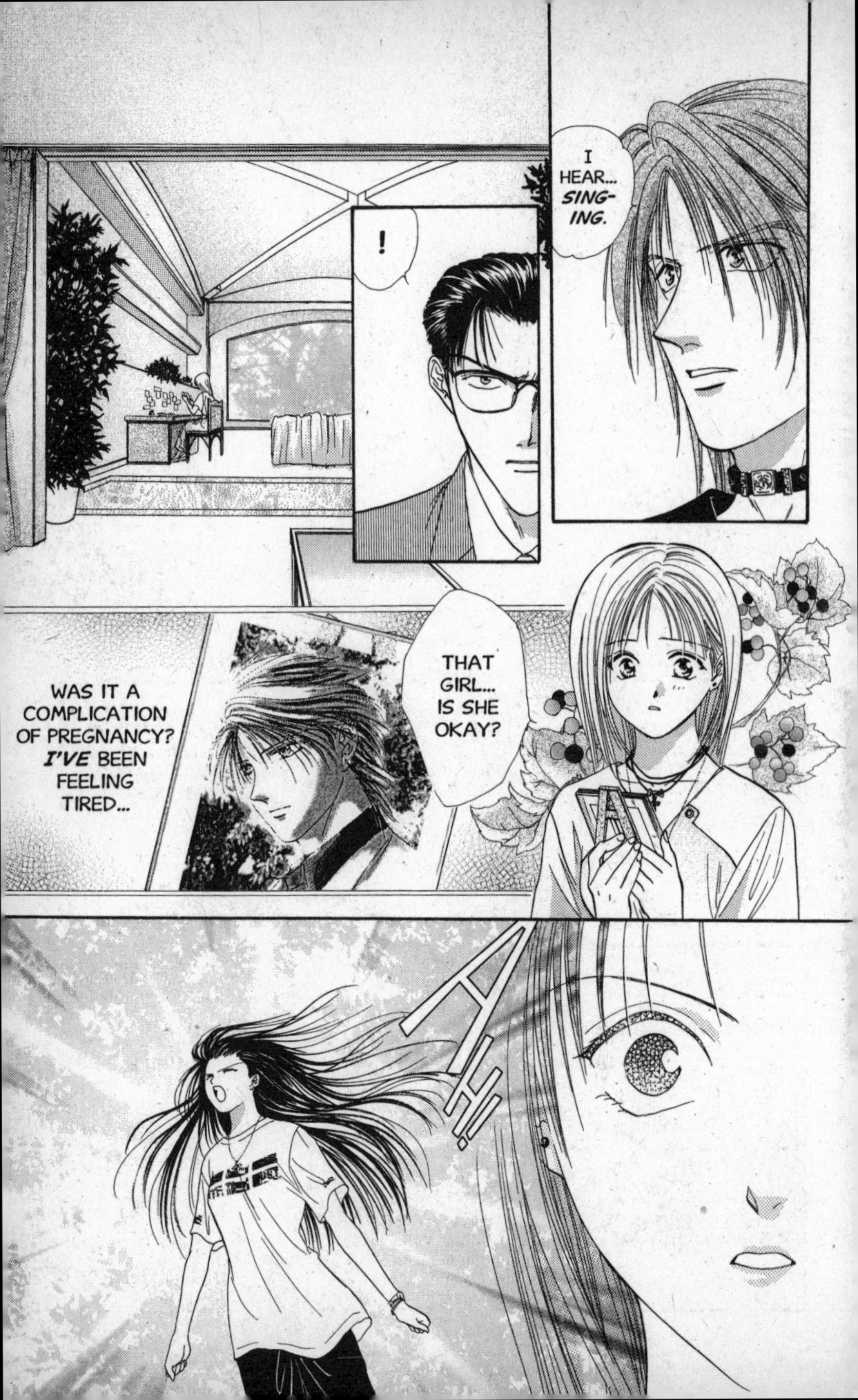
I HEAR... SING-ING.
!
THAT GIRL... IS SHE OKAY?
WAS IT A COMPLICATION OF PREGNANCY? I'VE BEEN FEELING TIRED...
AH!

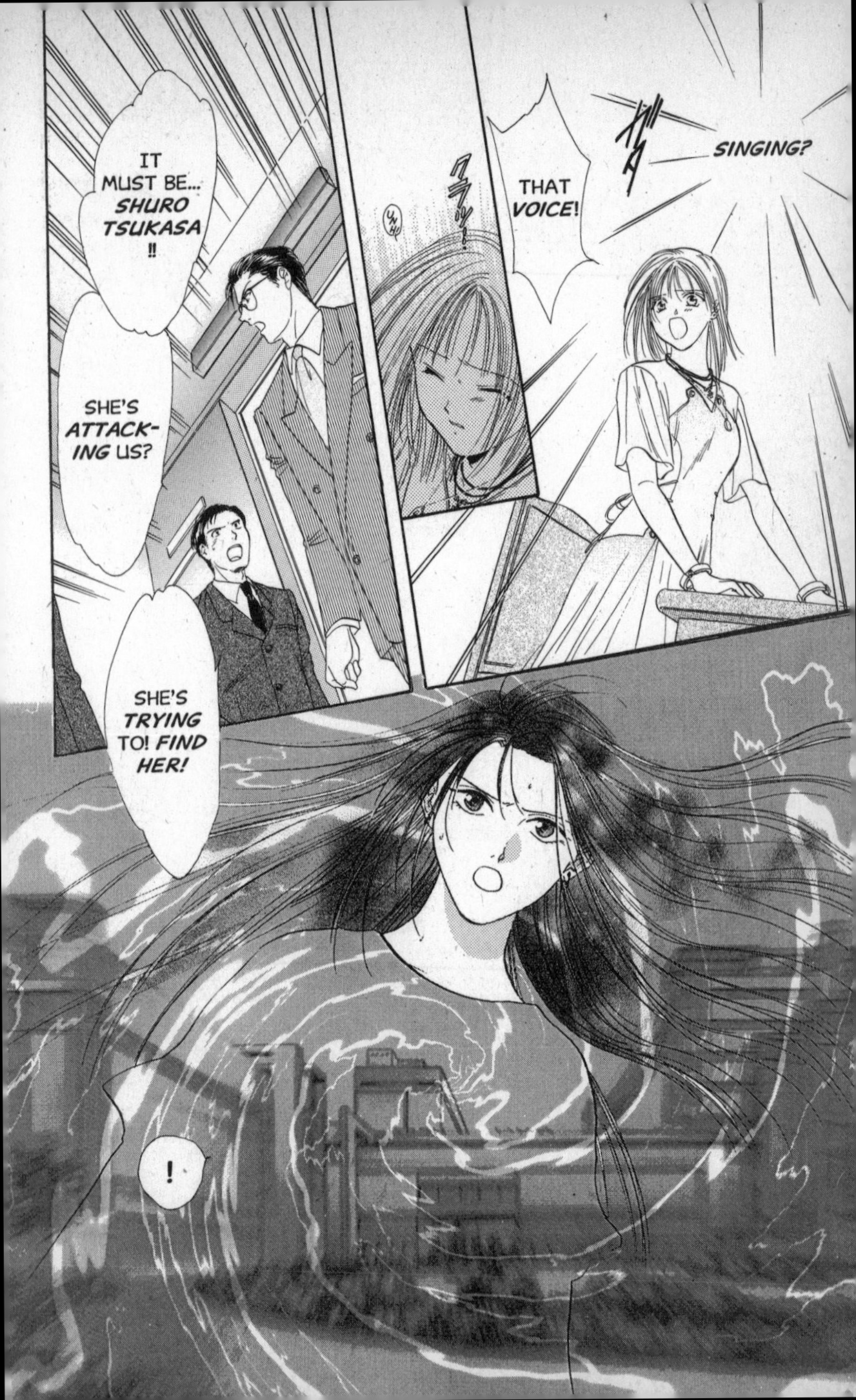
SINGING?
THAT VOICE!
UNH!
IT MUST BE... SHURO TSUKASA!!
SHE'S ATTACKING US?
SHE'S TRYING TO! FIND HER!
!

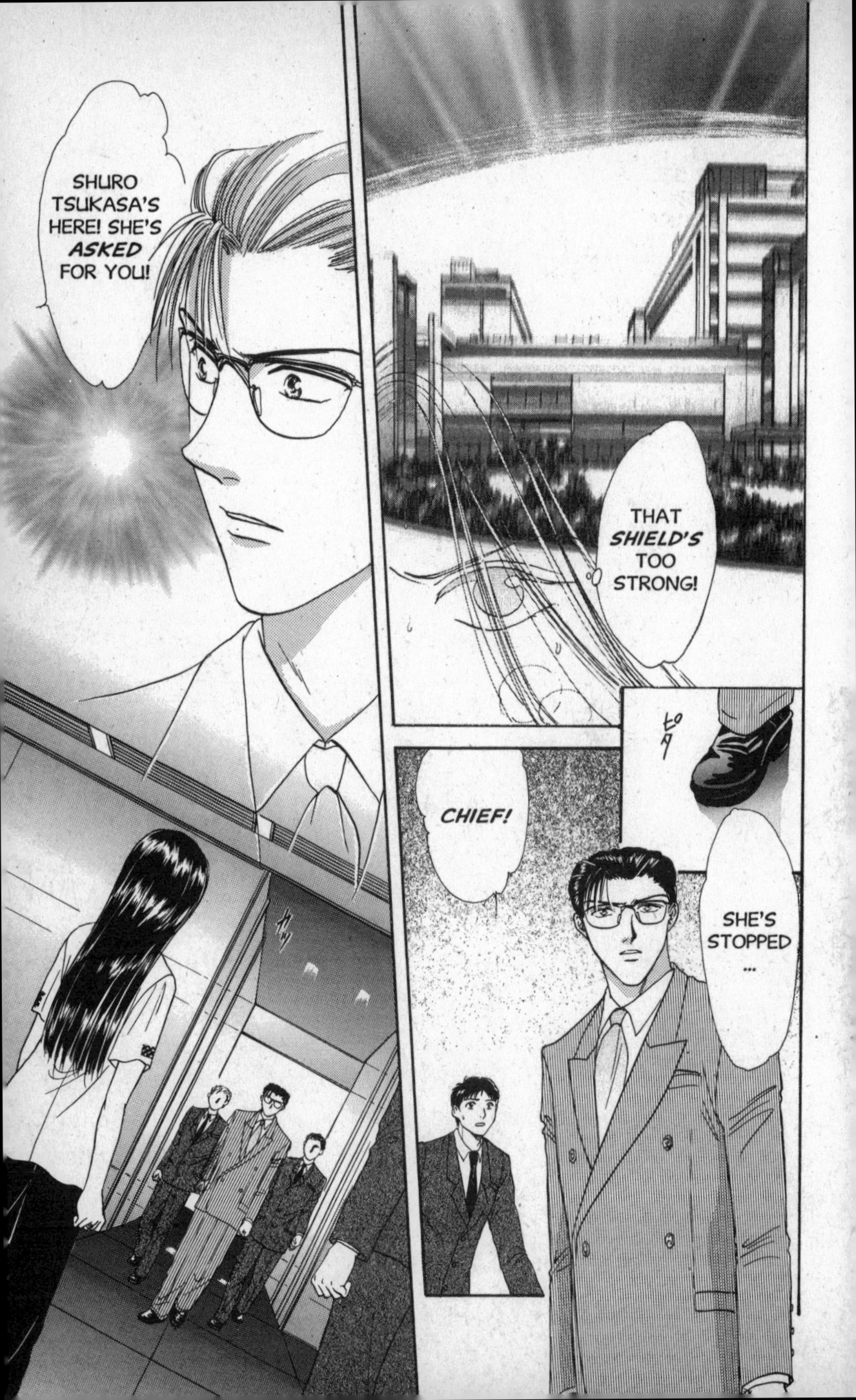
THAT *SHIELD'S* TOO STRONG!
ピタ
CHIEF!
SHE'S STOPPED ...
SHURO TSUKASA'S HERE! SHE'S *ASKED* FOR YOU!

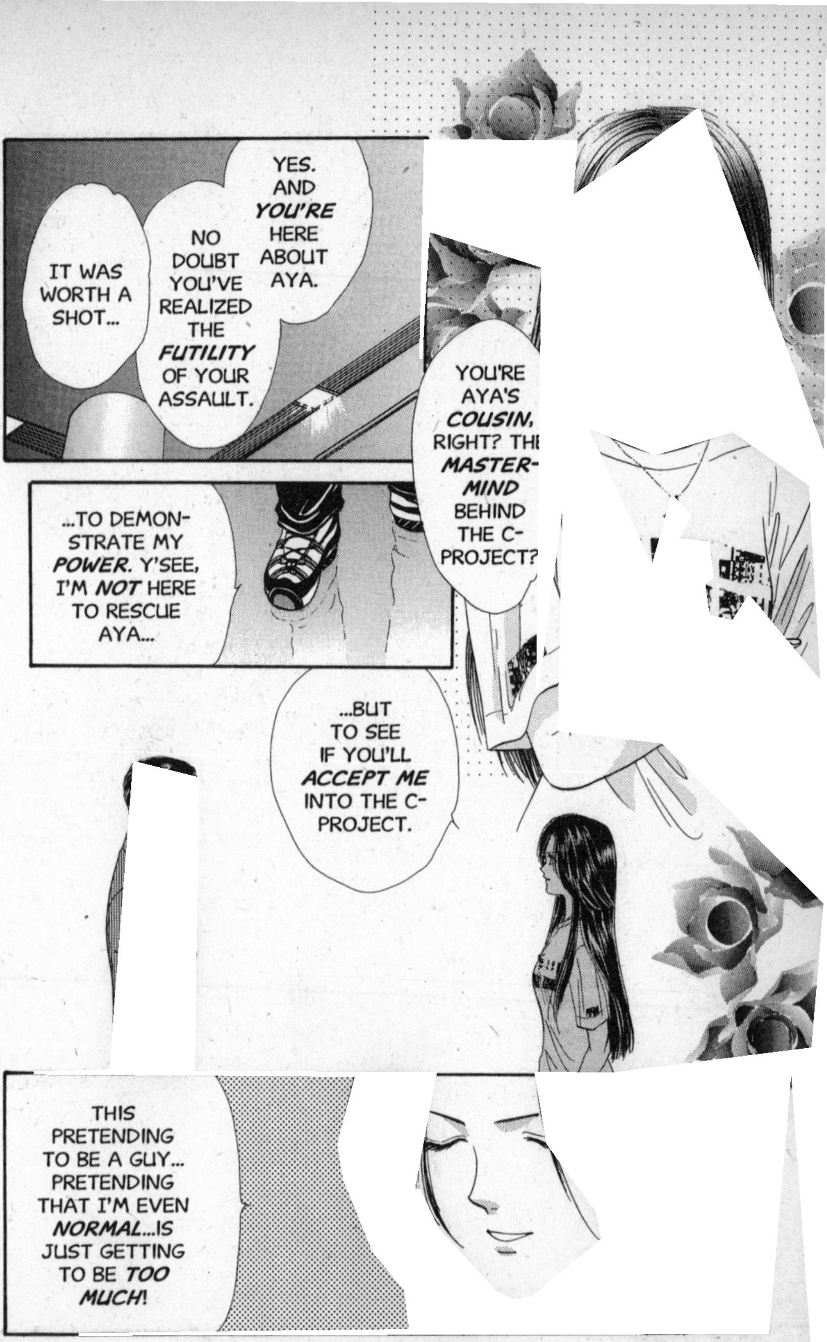
YOU'RE AYA'S COUSIN, RIGHT? THE MASTER-MIND BEHIND THE C-PROJECT?
YES. AND YOU'RE HERE ABOUT AYA.
NO DOUBT YOU'VE REALIZED THE FUTILITY OF YOUR ASSAULT.
IT WAS WORTH A SHOT...
...TO DEMON-STRATE MY POWER. Y'SEE, I'M NOT HERE TO RESCUE AYA...
...BUT TO SEE IF YOU'LL ACCEPT ME INTO THE C-PROJECT.
THIS PRETENDING TO BE A GUY... PRETENDING THAT I'M EVEN NORMAL...IS JUST GETTING TO BE TOO MUCH!

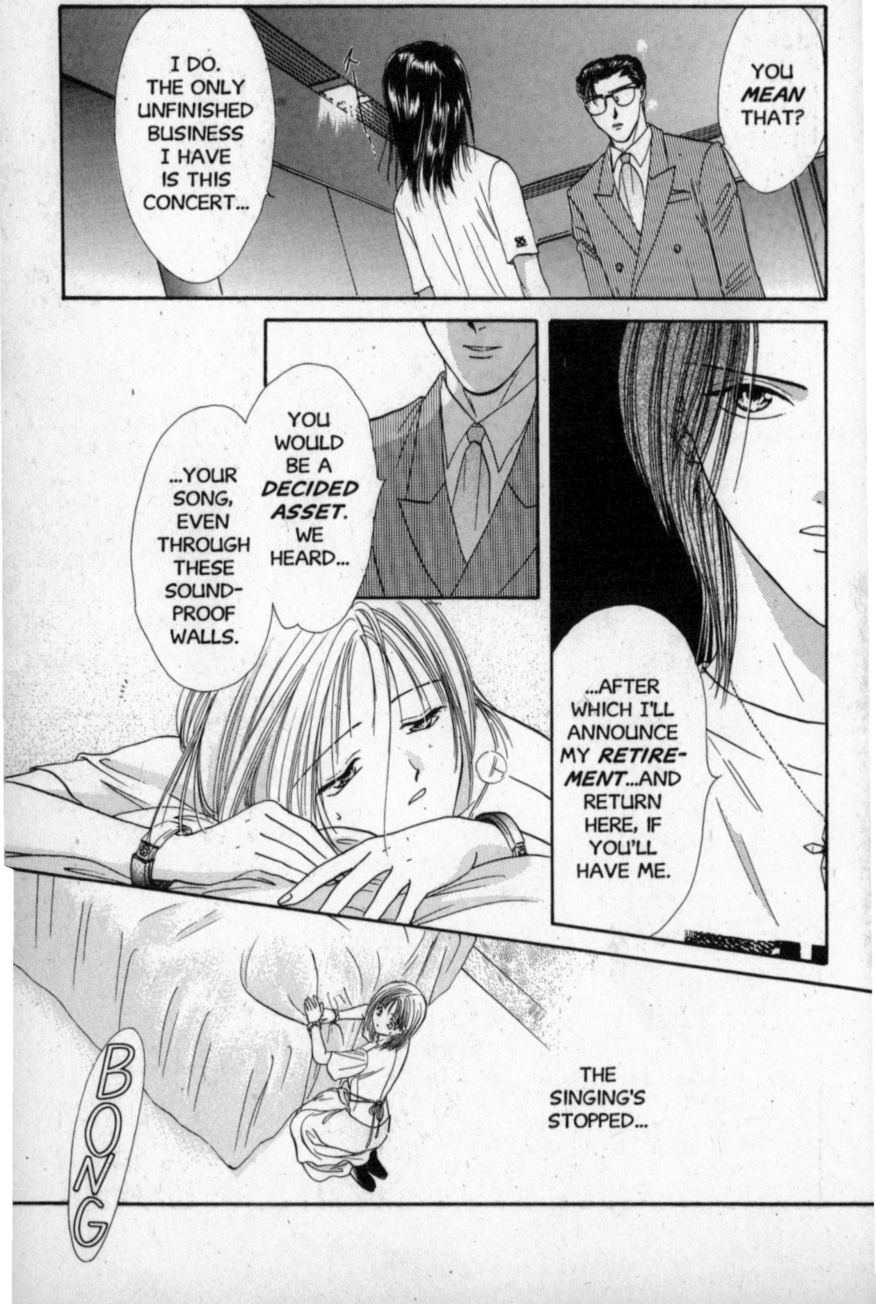
YOU MEAN THAT?
I DO. THE ONLY UNFINISHED BUSINESS I HAVE IS THIS CONCERT...
...AFTER WHICH I'LL ANNOUNCE MY RETIREMENT...AND RETURN HERE, IF YOU'LL HAVE ME.
YOU WOULD BE A DECIDED ASSET. WE HEARD...
...YOUR SONG, EVEN THROUGH THESE SOUNDPROOF WALLS.
THE SINGING'S STOPPED...
BONG

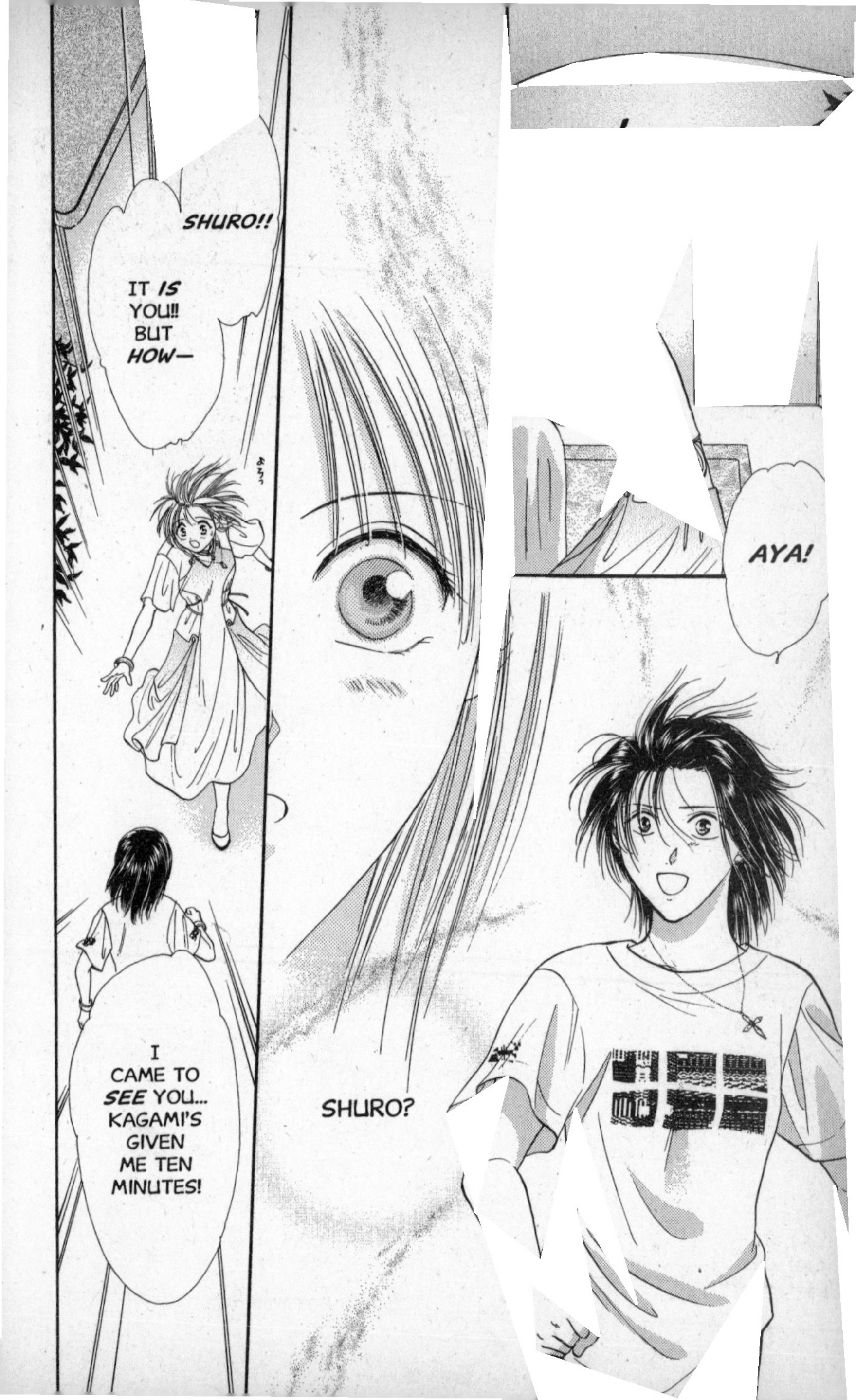
AYA!
SHURO?
SHURO!!
IT IS YOU!! BUT HOW—
I CAME TO SEE YOU... KAGAMI'S GIVEN ME TEN MINUTES!

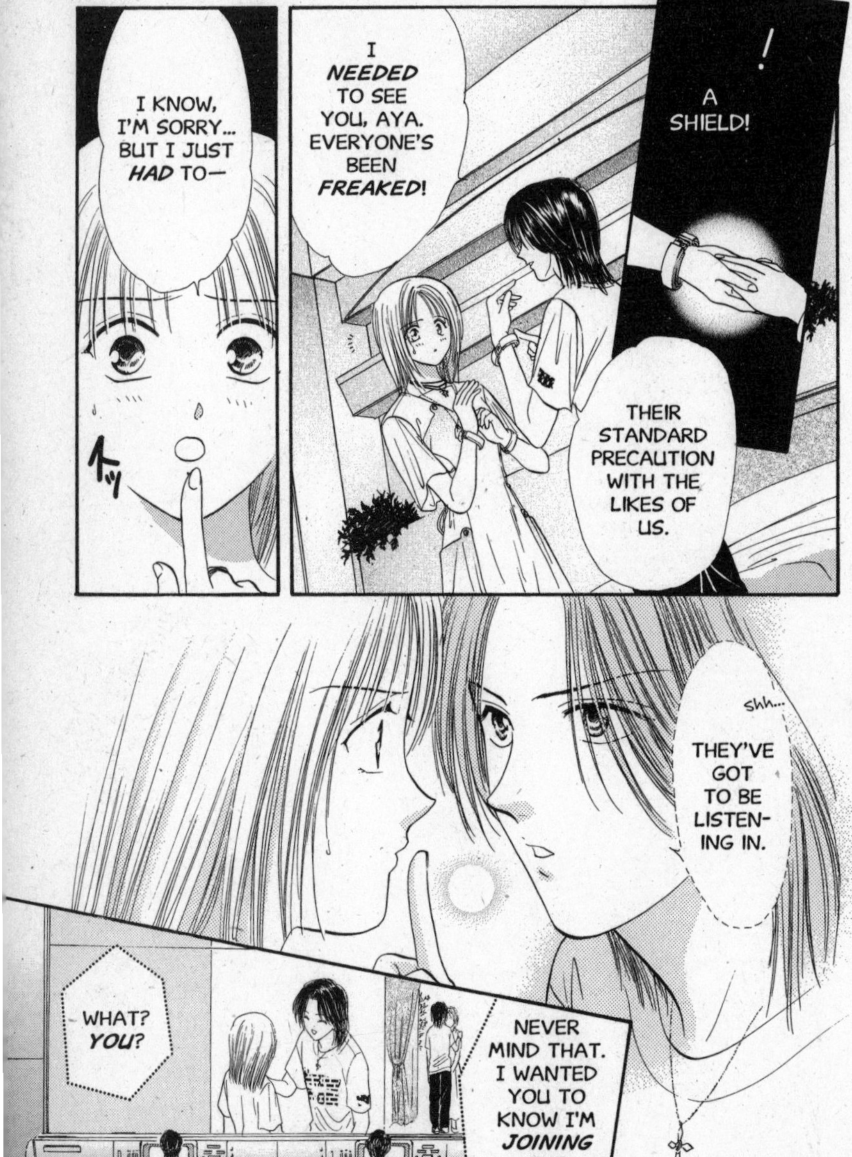
!
A SHIELD!
THEIR STANDARD PRECAUTION WITH THE LIKES OF US.
I *NEEDED* TO SEE YOU, AYA. EVERYONE'S BEEN *FREAKED*!
I KNOW, I'M SORRY... BUT I JUST *HAD* TO—
イッ
shh...
THEY'VE GOT TO BE LISTENING IN.
NEVER MIND THAT. I WANTED YOU TO KNOW I'M *JOINING* THE PROJECT.
WHAT? *YOU*?

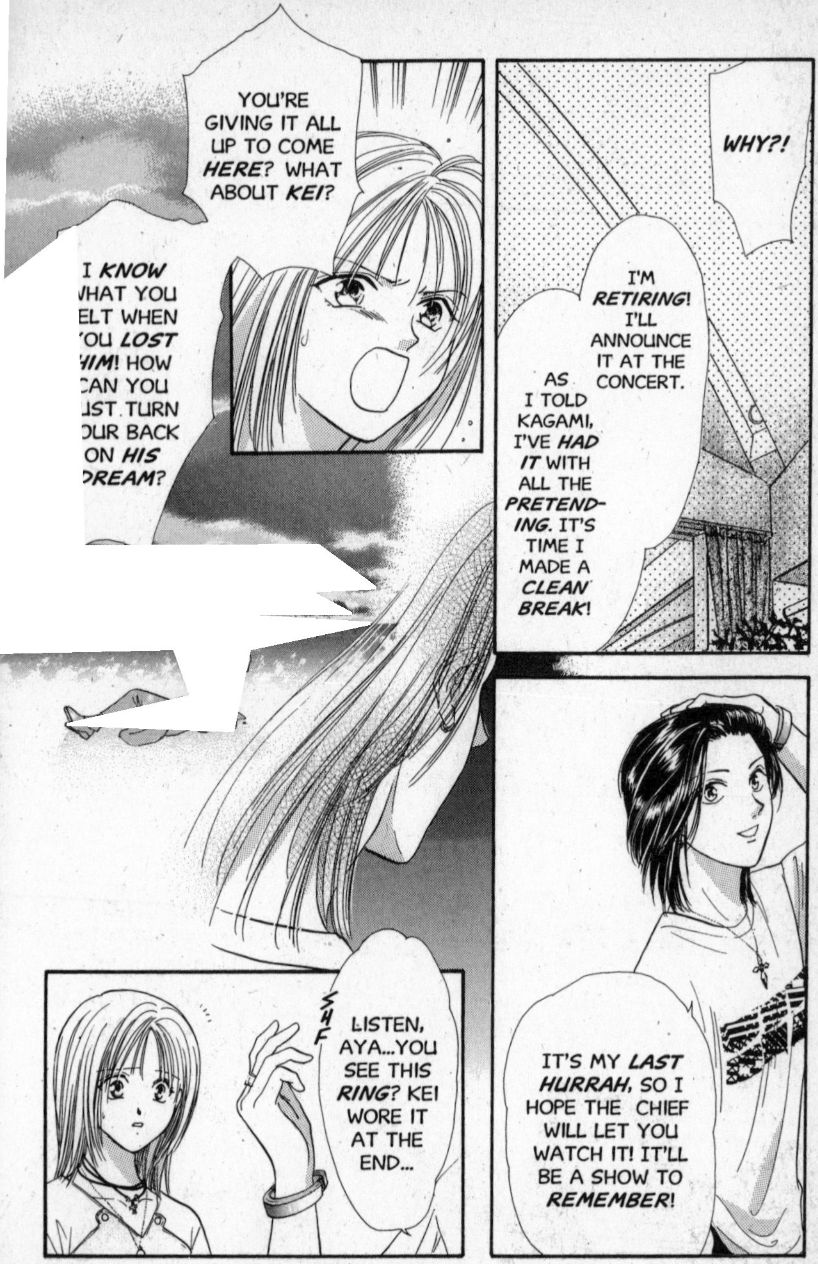
WHY?!
I'M RETIRING! I'LL ANNOUNCE IT AT THE CONCERT.
AS I TOLD KAGAMI, I'VE HAD IT WITH ALL THE PRETEND-ING. IT'S TIME I MADE A CLEAN BREAK!
YOU'RE GIVING IT ALL UP TO COME HERE? WHAT ABOUT KEI?
I KNOW WHAT YOU ELT WHEN OU LOST HIM! HOW CAN YOU UST TURN OUR BACK ON HIS DREAM?
IT'S MY LAST HURRAH, SO I HOPE THE CHIEF WILL LET YOU WATCH IT! IT'LL BE A SHOW TO REMEMBER!
SHF
LISTEN, AYA...YOU SEE THIS RING? KEI WORE IT AT THE END...

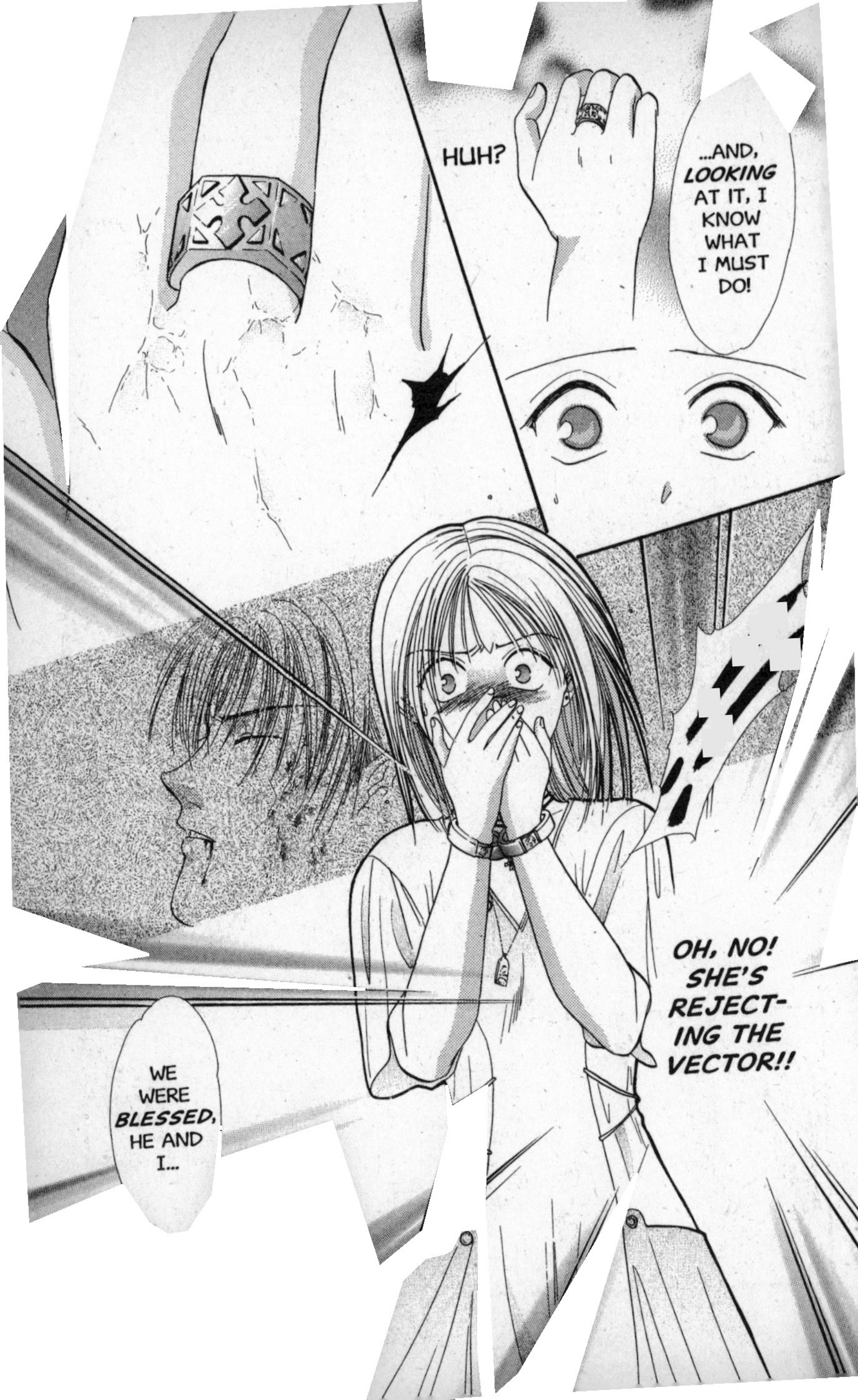
...AND, *LOOKING* AT IT, I KNOW WHAT I MUST DO!
HUH?
OH, NO! SHE'S REJECT-ING THE VECTOR!!
WE WERE *BLESSED*, HE AND I...

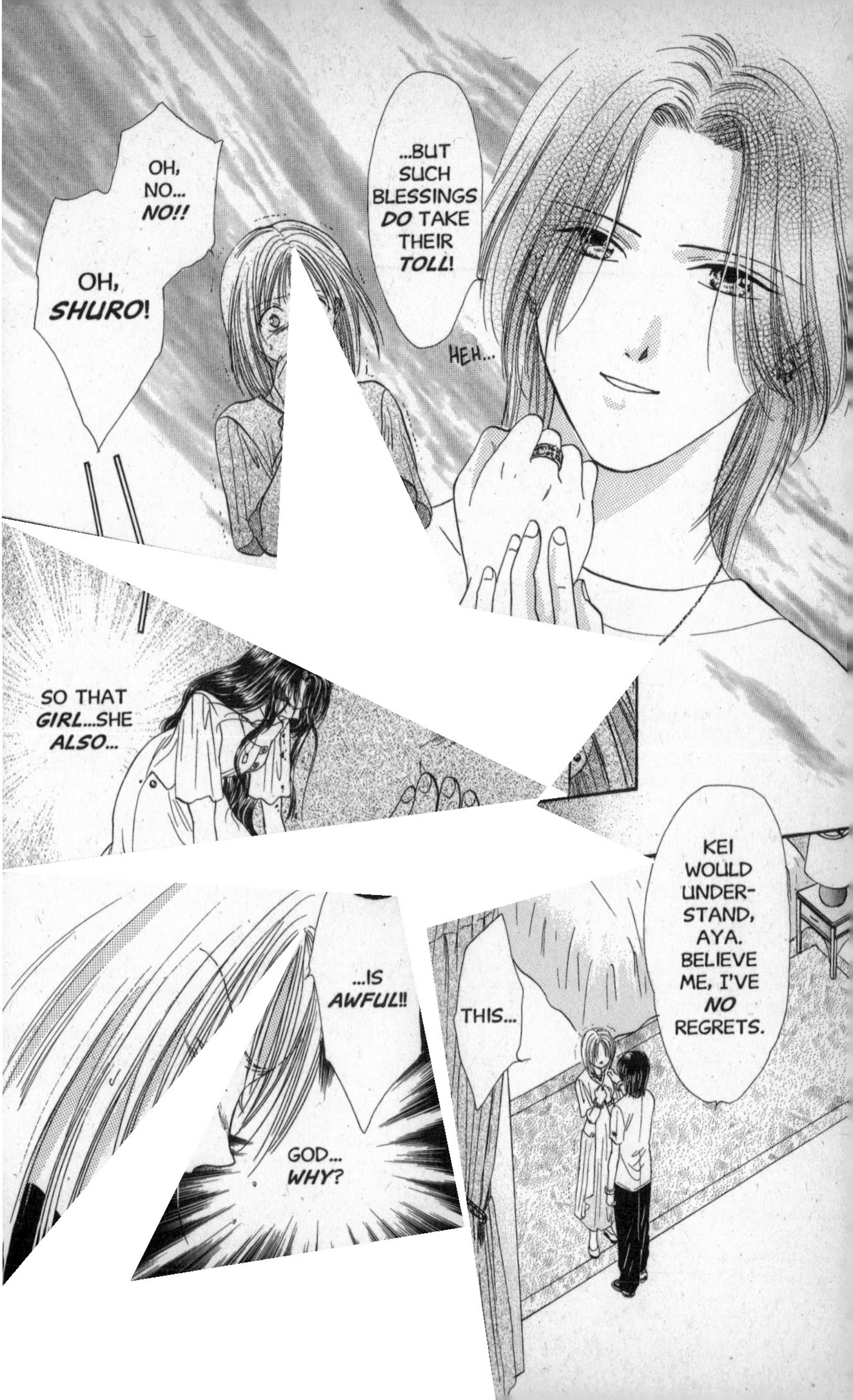

...BUT SUCH BLESSINGS DO TAKE THEIR TOLL!
HEH...
OH, NO... NO!!
OH, SHURO!
SO THAT GIRL...SHE ALSO...
KEI WOULD UNDERSTAND, AYA. BELIEVE ME, I'VE NO REGRETS.
THIS...
...IS AWFUL!!
GOD... WHY?

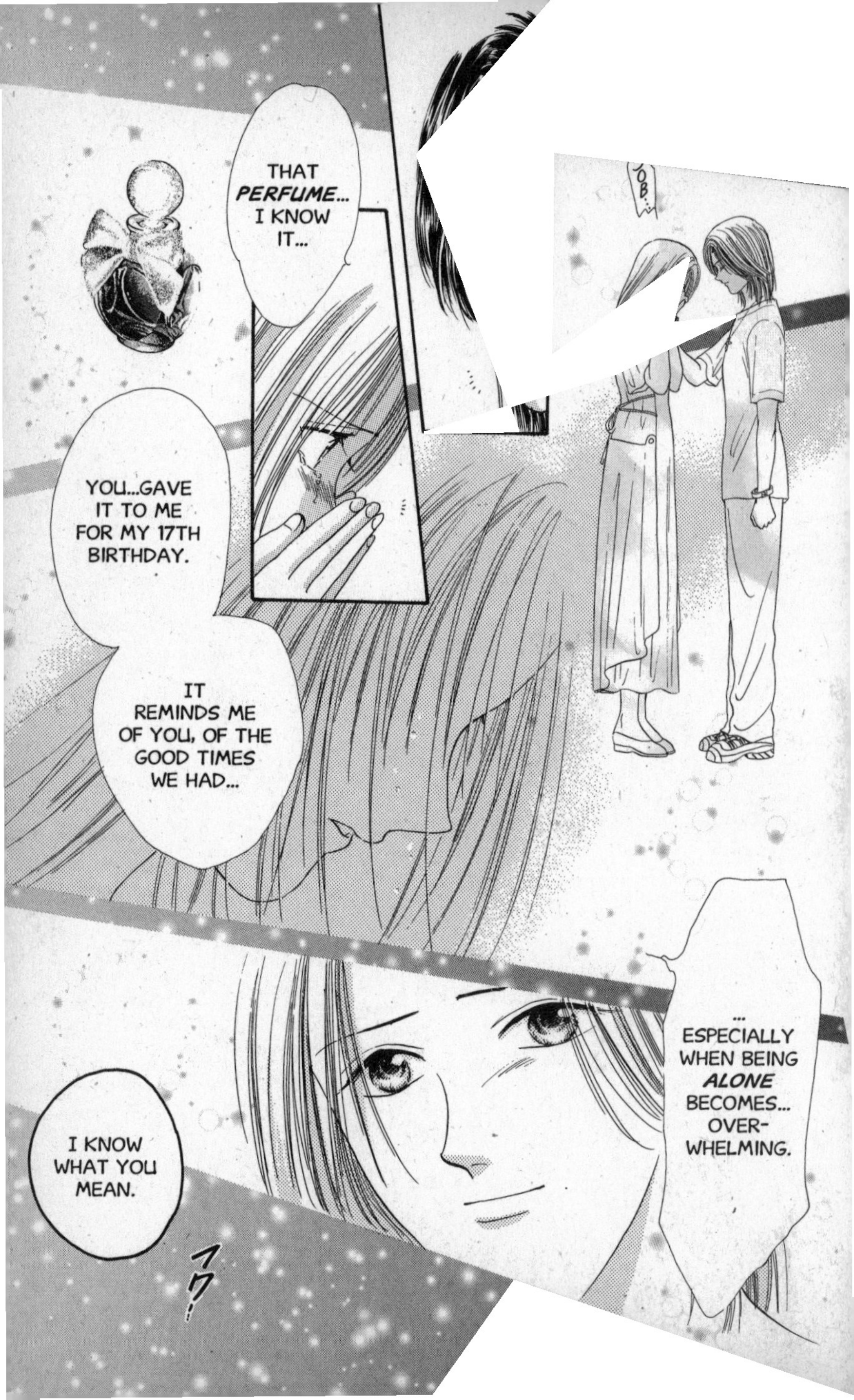
THAT *PERFUME*... I KNOW IT...
YOU...GAVE IT TO ME FOR MY 17TH BIRTHDAY.
IT REMINDS ME OF YOU, OF THE GOOD TIMES WE HAD...
...ESPECIALLY WHEN BEING *ALONE* BECOMES... OVER-WHELMING.
I KNOW WHAT YOU MEAN.
フワ

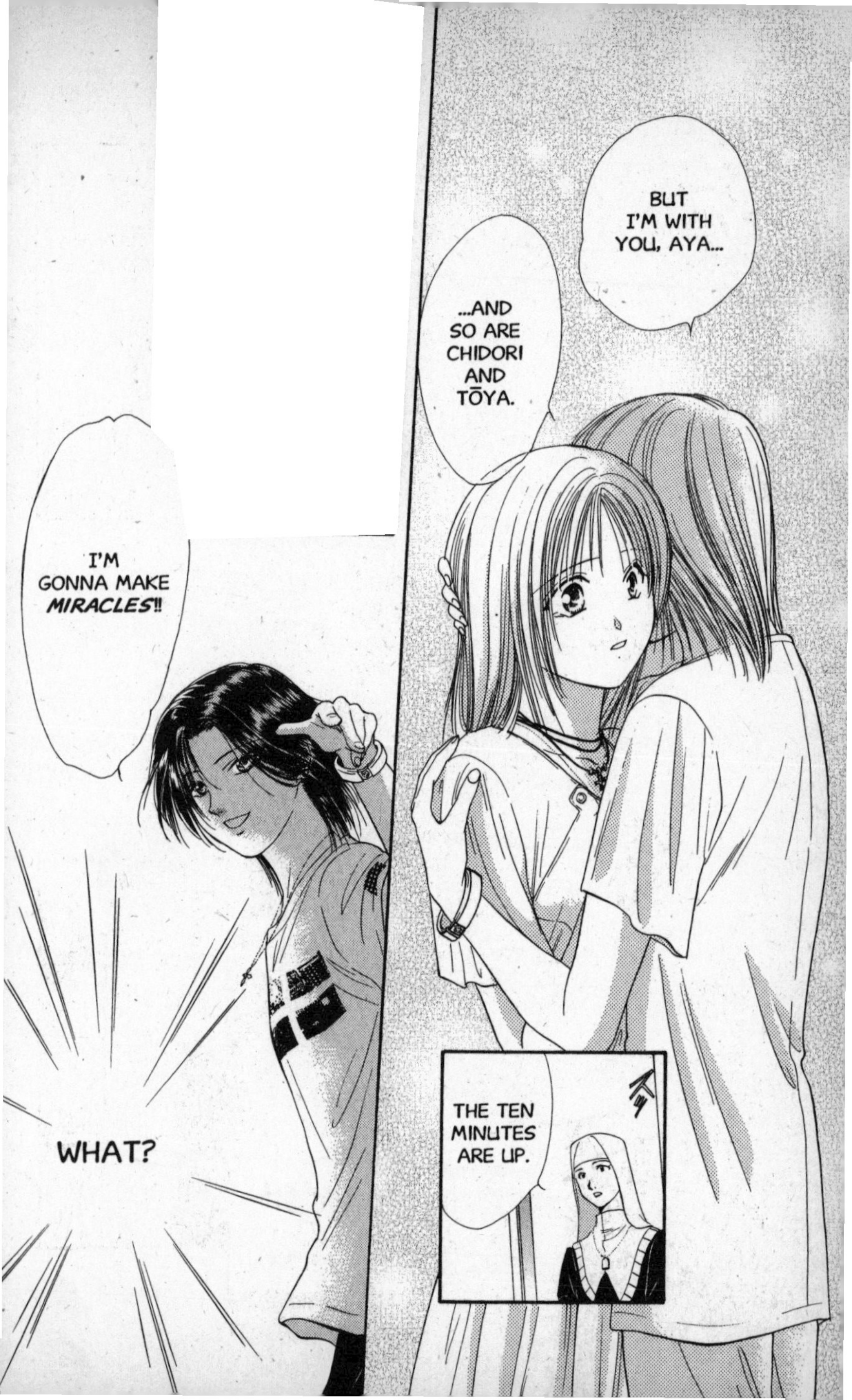
BUT I'M WITH YOU, AYA...
...AND SO ARE CHIDORI AND TŌYA.
THE TEN MINUTES ARE UP.
I'M GONNA MAKE *MIRACLES*!!
WHAT?

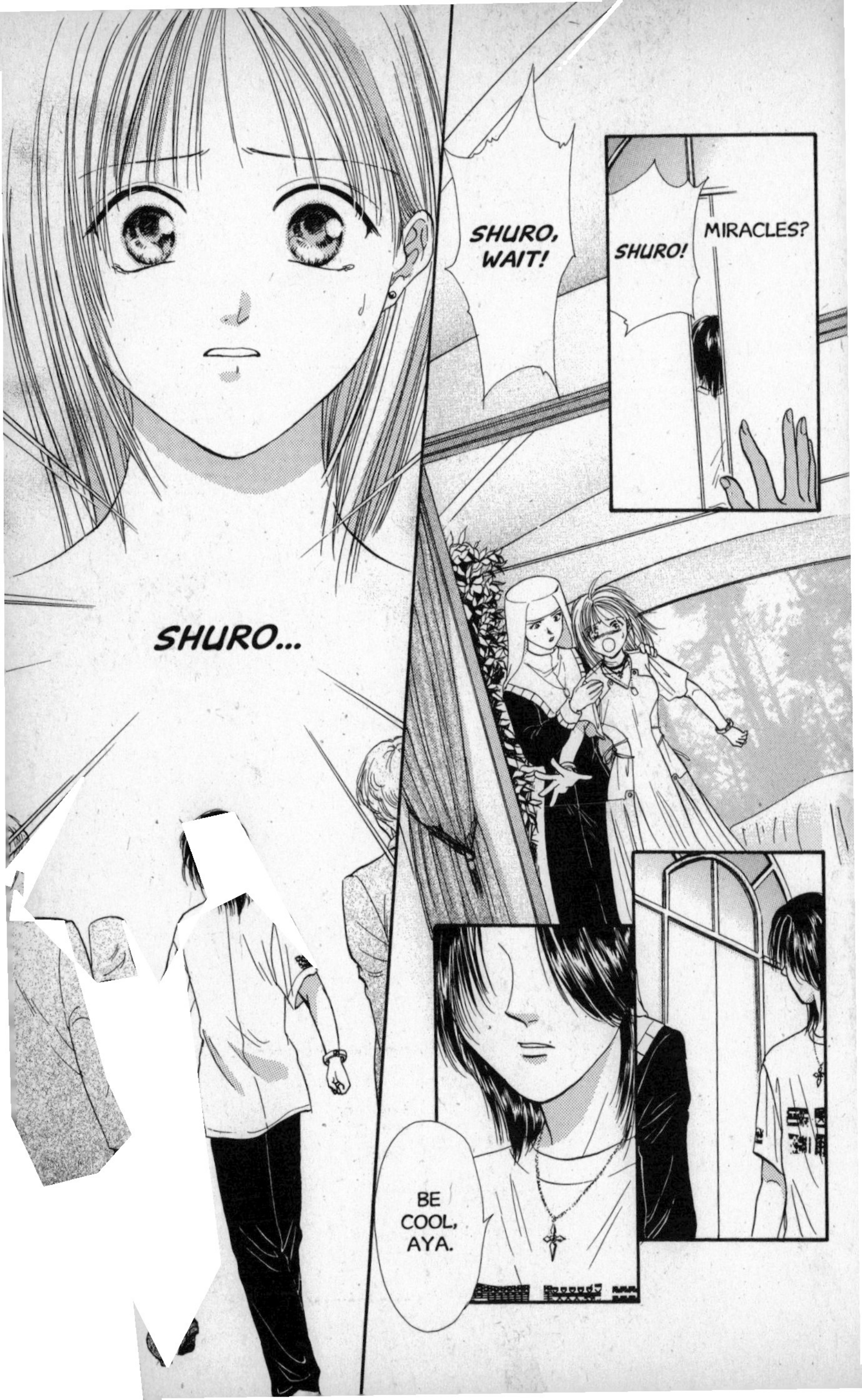
MIRACLES?
SHURO!
SHURO, WAIT!
BE COOL, AYA.
SHURO...

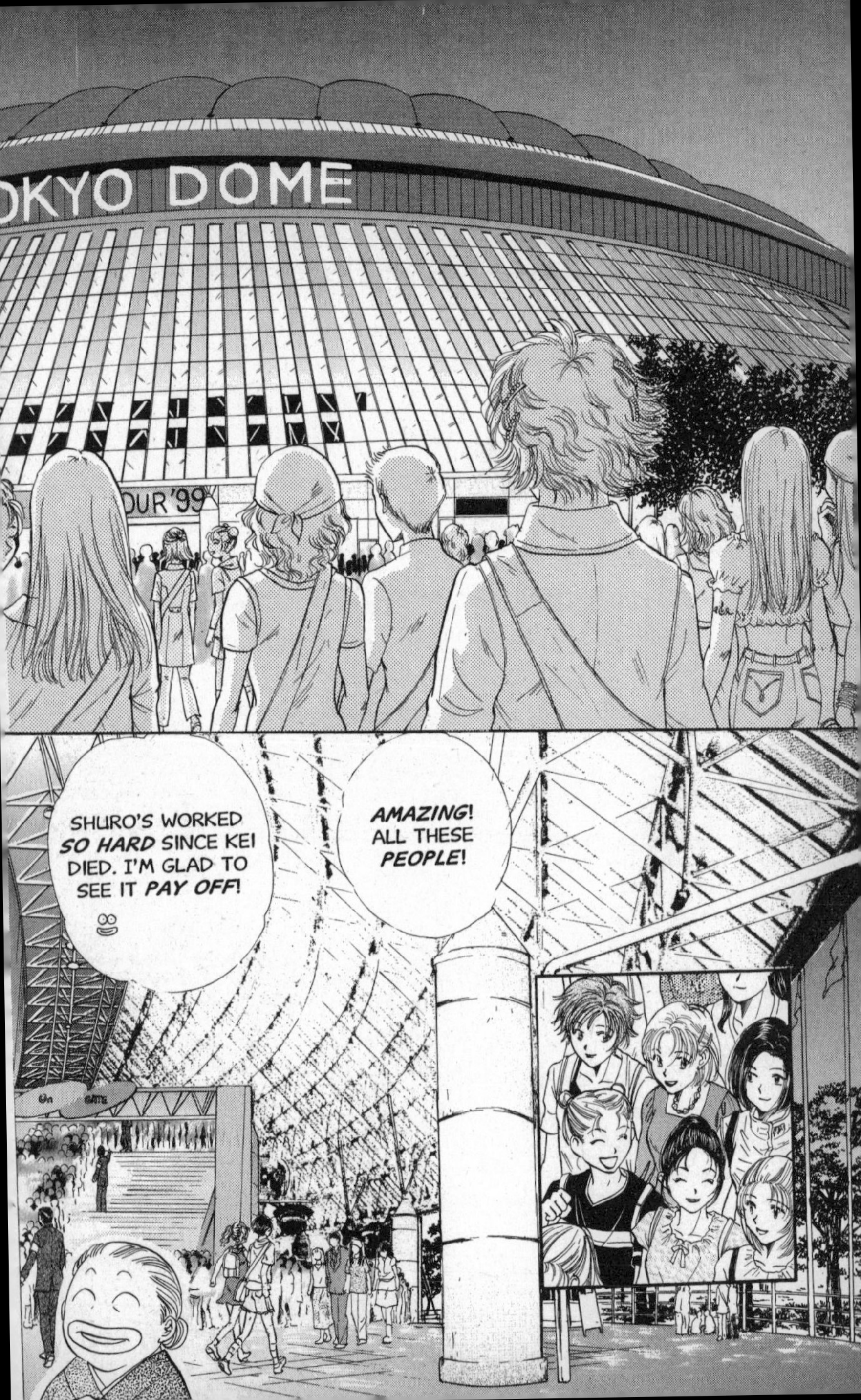
OKYO DOME
OUR'99
AMAZING! ALL THESE *PEOPLE!*
SHURO'S WORKED *SO HARD* SINCE KEI DIED. I'M GLAD TO SEE IT *PAY OFF!*

I'll explain the deeper elements of **Ceres** in the next, final volume. I got a letter the other day that said, "I like how you depict both the good and the ugly sides of humanity." She liked the realism of the bad guys not being purely evil...ooh, good insight there! ◡̈ Yes, that's right. I don't have any "bad guys" in this story. You might, of course, think the Progenitor and Kagami are evil, but they're only exhibiting human foolishness and frailty.

It's easy to understand "good vs. evil" in a piece of entertainment. People like that kind of story, and it's a nice feeling when the good guys win...I **know** that, but...I couldn't bring myself to do that this time. Aya and Kagami aren't "enemies." They simply have different objectives, and the story is meant to compare two people heading in completely opposite directions. They both want the hagoromo for different reasons, and, as for the breeding project...well, I can't go into more detail now, but I hope you can catch on to the deeper meanings...though I realize that's not always easy. ◡̈

Right in the middle of it all is Tōya and Aya's baby...and the meaning of his existence. ◡̈ Hmm, I don't think you could guess at any of these intentions by reading the beginning of **Ceres**...unfortunately, that just shows my inexperience. ◊ Sigh... I don't know what I'm saying. Well, I'll do my best until the end. Will I be able to convey my message, and will people be able to interpret it? Bear with me for one more volume!

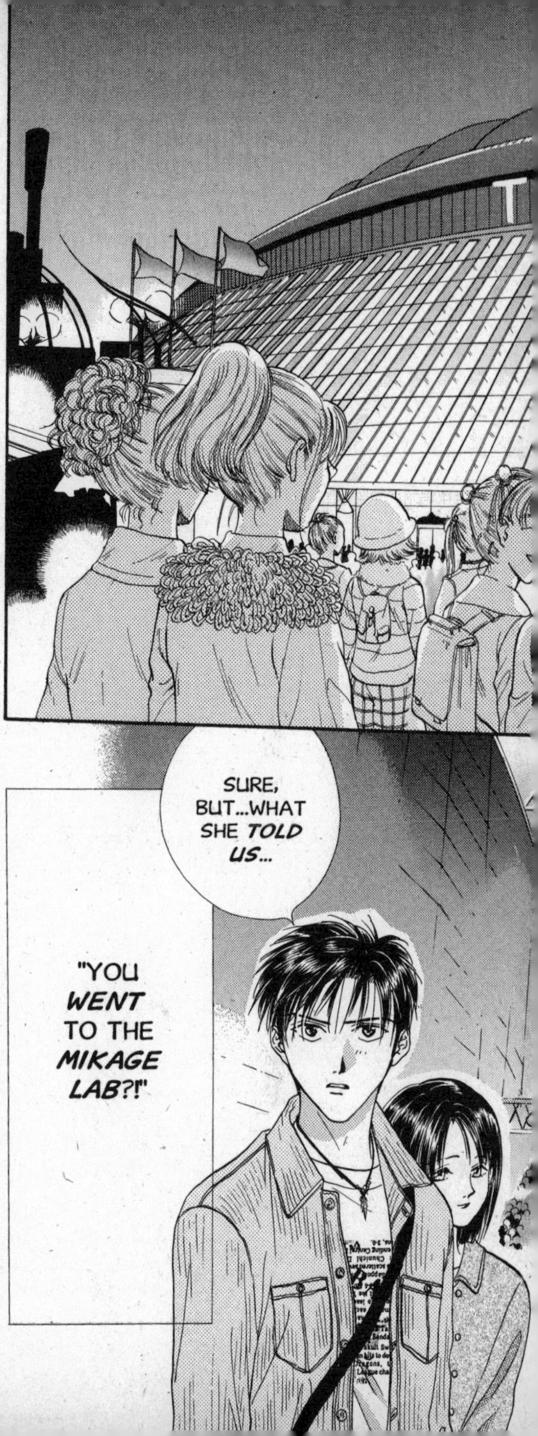
SURE, BUT...WHAT SHE *TOLD* US...
"YOU *WENT* TO THE *MIKAGE* *LAB*?!"

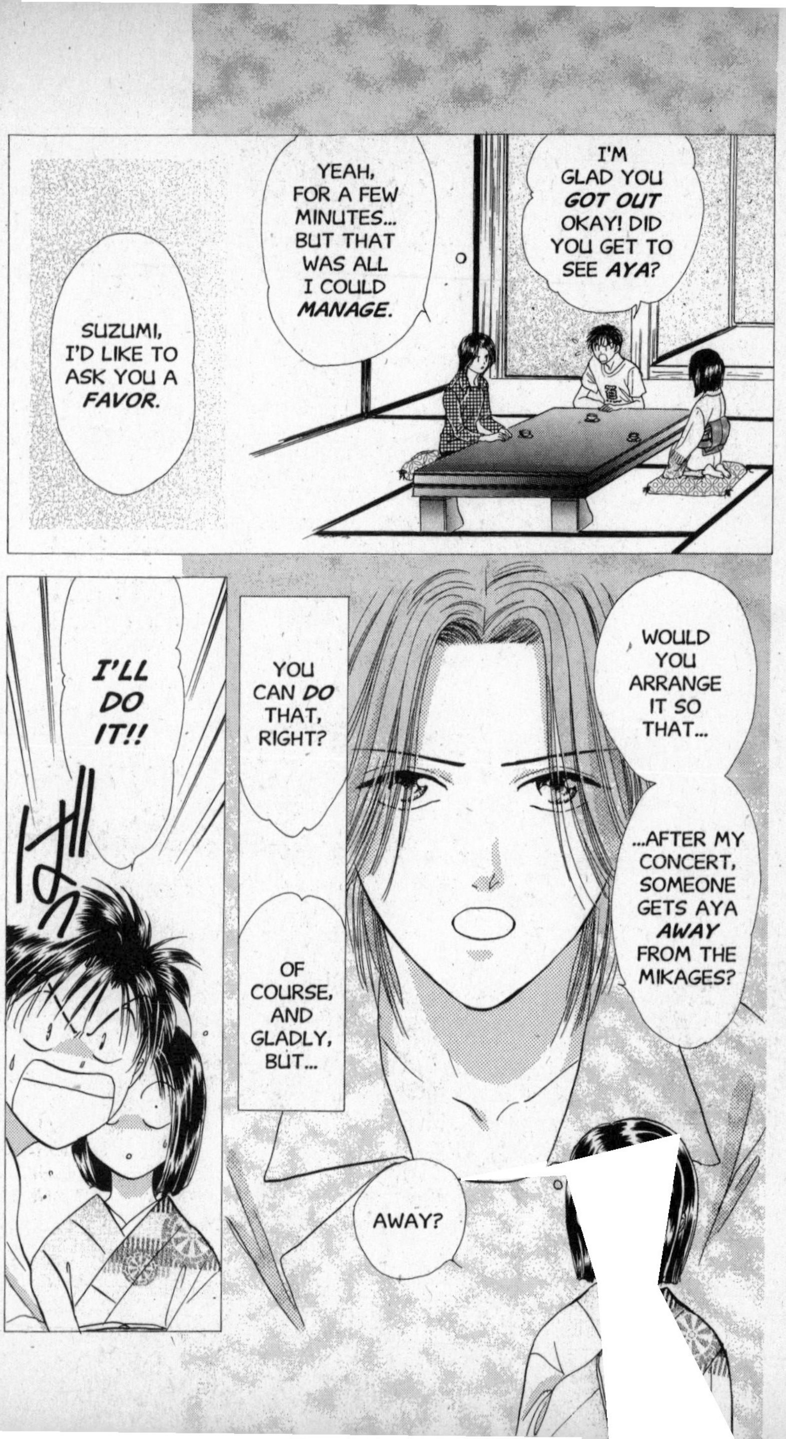
I'M GLAD YOU *GOT OUT* OKAY! DID YOU GET TO SEE *AYA*?
YEAH, FOR A FEW MINUTES... BUT THAT WAS ALL I COULD *MANAGE*.
SUZUMI, I'D LIKE TO ASK YOU A *FAVOR*.
WOULD YOU ARRANGE IT SO THAT...
...AFTER MY CONCERT, SOMEONE GETS AYA *AWAY* FROM THE MIKAGES?
YOU CAN *DO* THAT, RIGHT?
OF COURSE, AND GLADLY, BUT...
AWAY?
はっ
I'LL DO IT!!

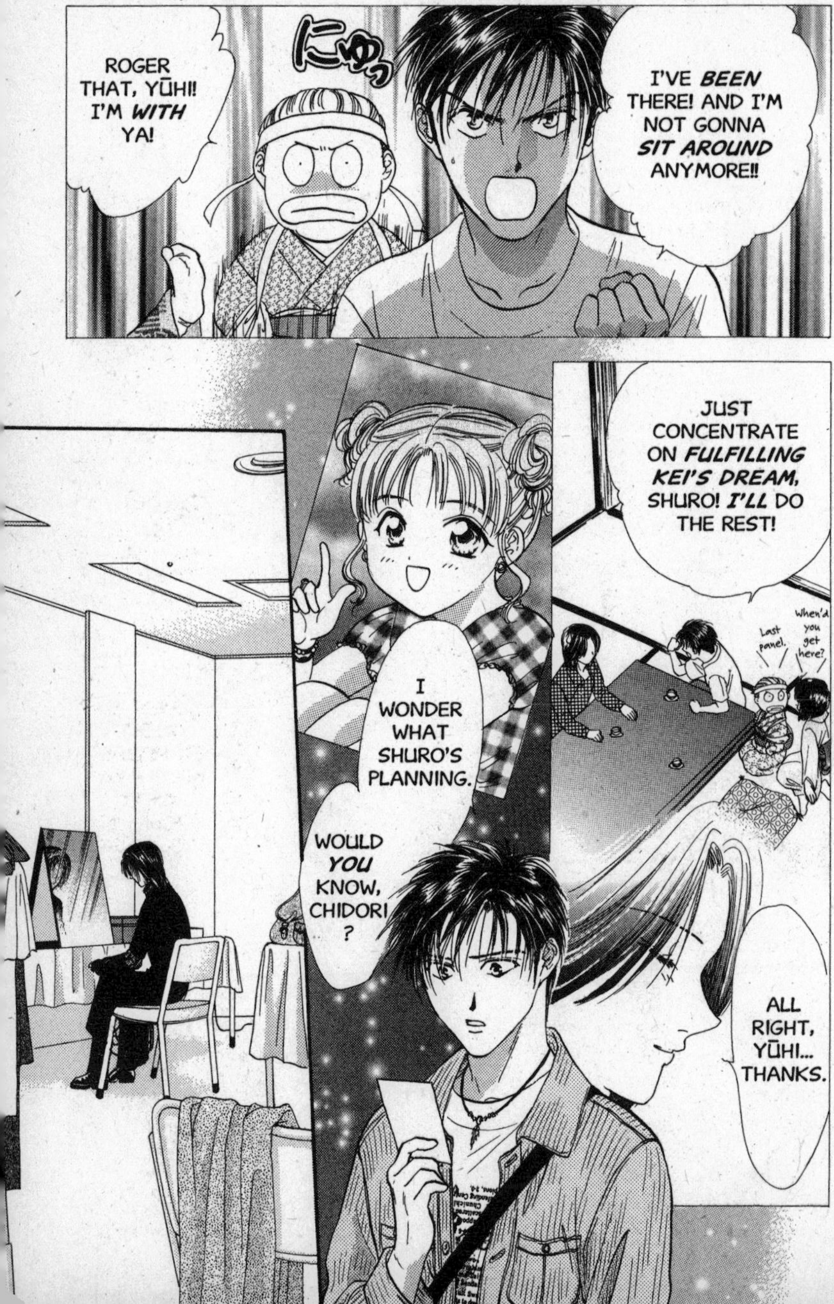
I'VE BEEN THERE! AND I'M NOT GONNA SIT AROUND ANYMORE!!
にゅっ
ROGER THAT, YŪHI! I'M WITH YA!
JUST CONCENTRATE ON FULFILLING KEI'S DREAM, SHURO! I'LL DO THE REST!
When'd you get here?
Last panel.
ALL RIGHT, YŪHI... THANKS.
I WONDER WHAT SHURO'S PLANNING.
WOULD YOU KNOW, CHIDORI?

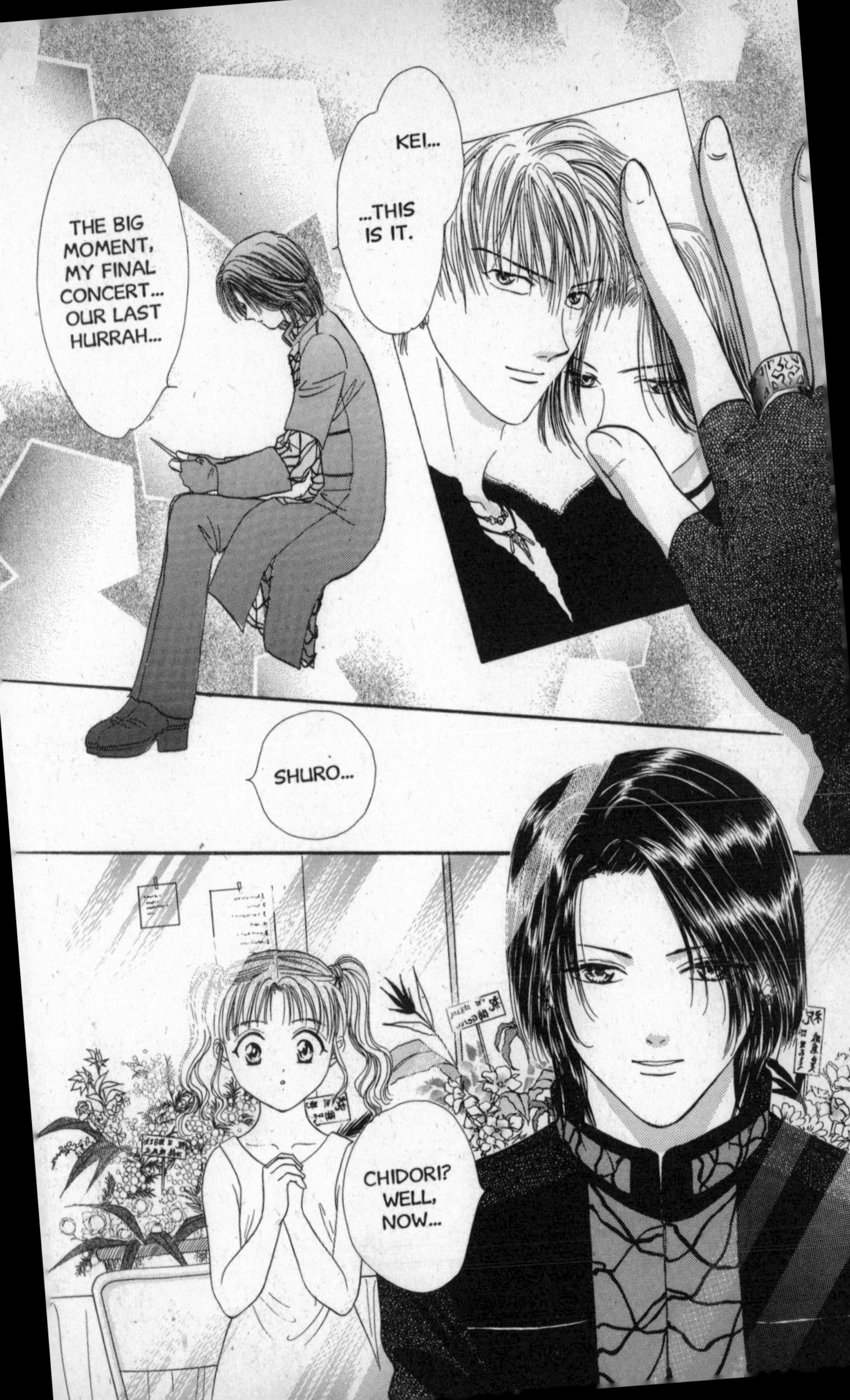
KEI...
...THIS IS IT.
THE BIG MOMENT, MY FINAL CONCERT... OUR LAST HURRAH...
SHURO...
CHIDORI? WELL, NOW...

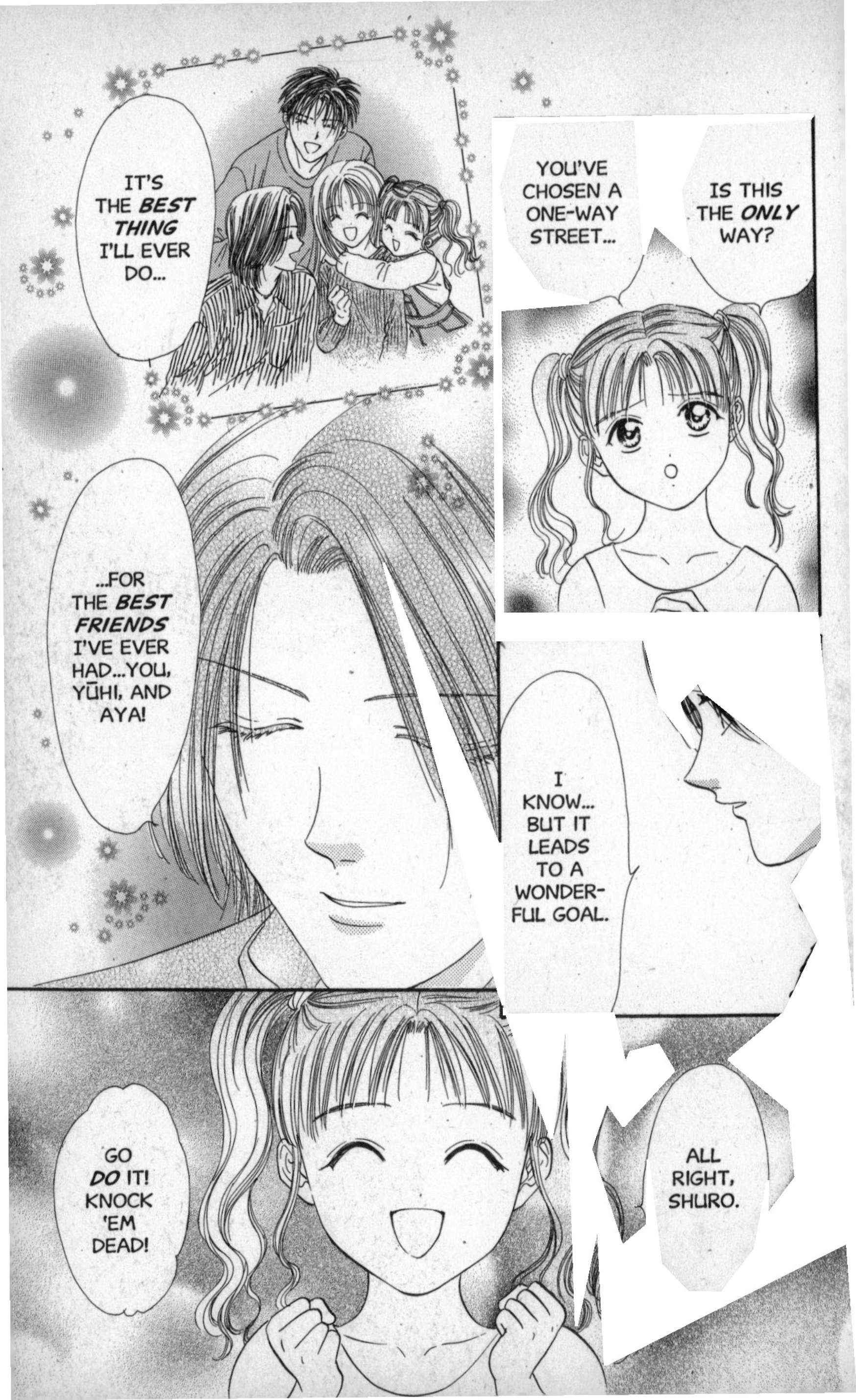
IS THIS THE *ONLY* WAY?
YOU'VE CHOSEN A ONE-WAY STREET...
I KNOW... BUT IT LEADS TO A WONDER-FUL GOAL.
IT'S THE *BEST THING* I'LL EVER DO...
...FOR THE *BEST FRIENDS* I'VE EVER HAD...YOU, YŪHI, AND AYA!
ALL RIGHT, SHURO.
GO *DO* IT! KNOCK 'EM DEAD!

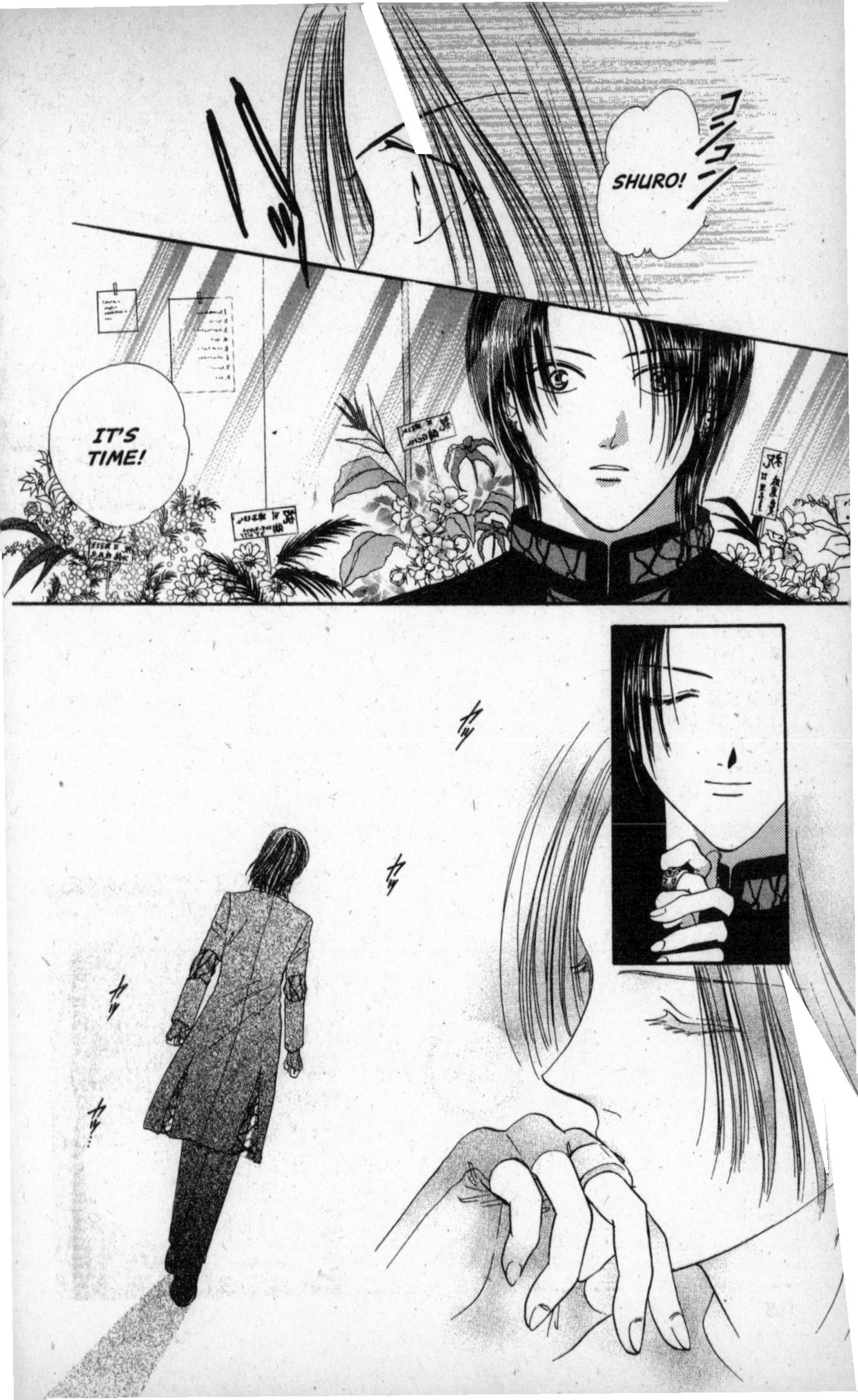
SHURO!
IT'S TIME!

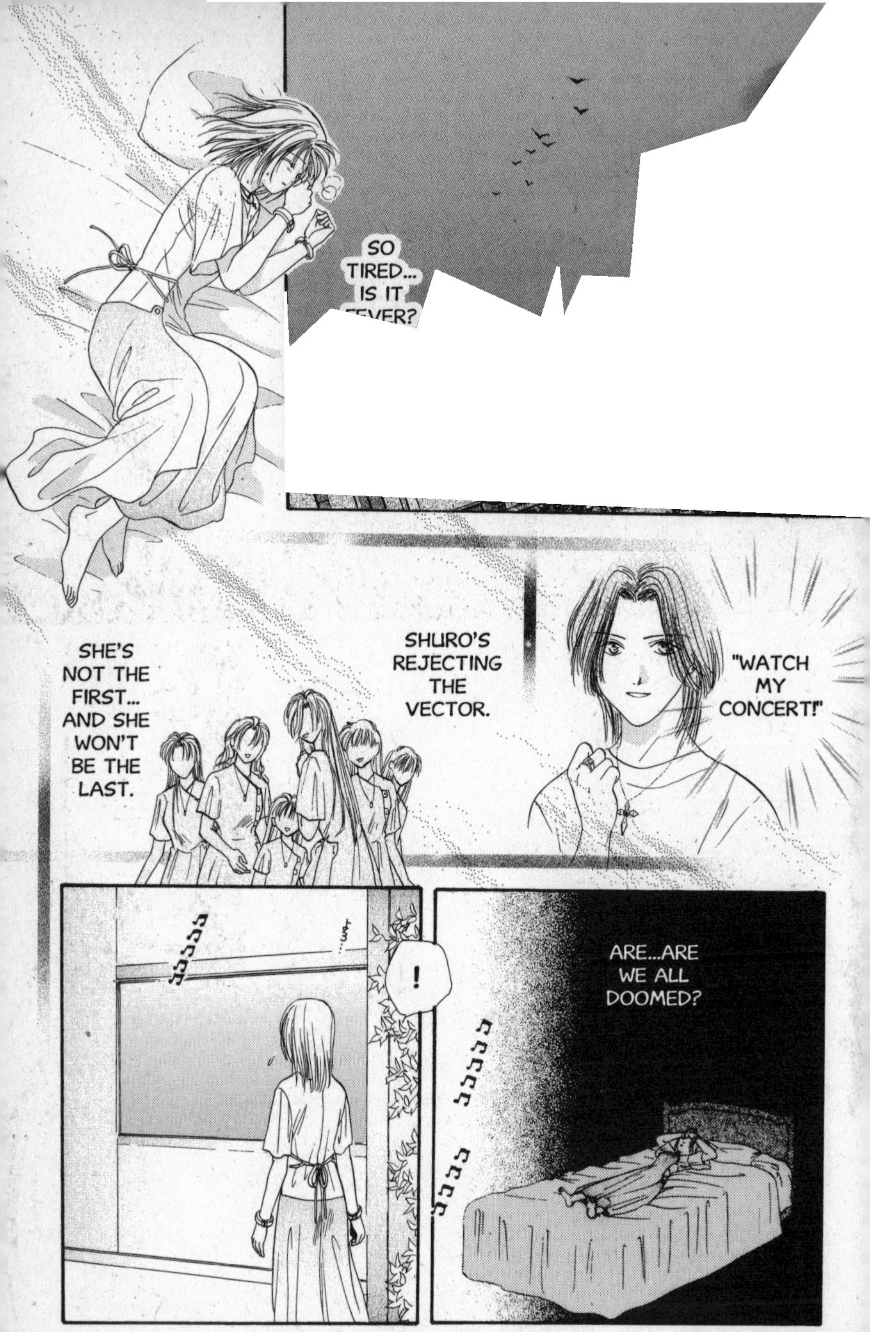
SO TIRED... IS IT
"WATCH MY CONCERT!"
SHURO'S REJECTING THE VECTOR.
SHE'S NOT THE FIRST... AND SHE WON'T BE THE LAST.
ARE...ARE WE ALL DOOMED?
!

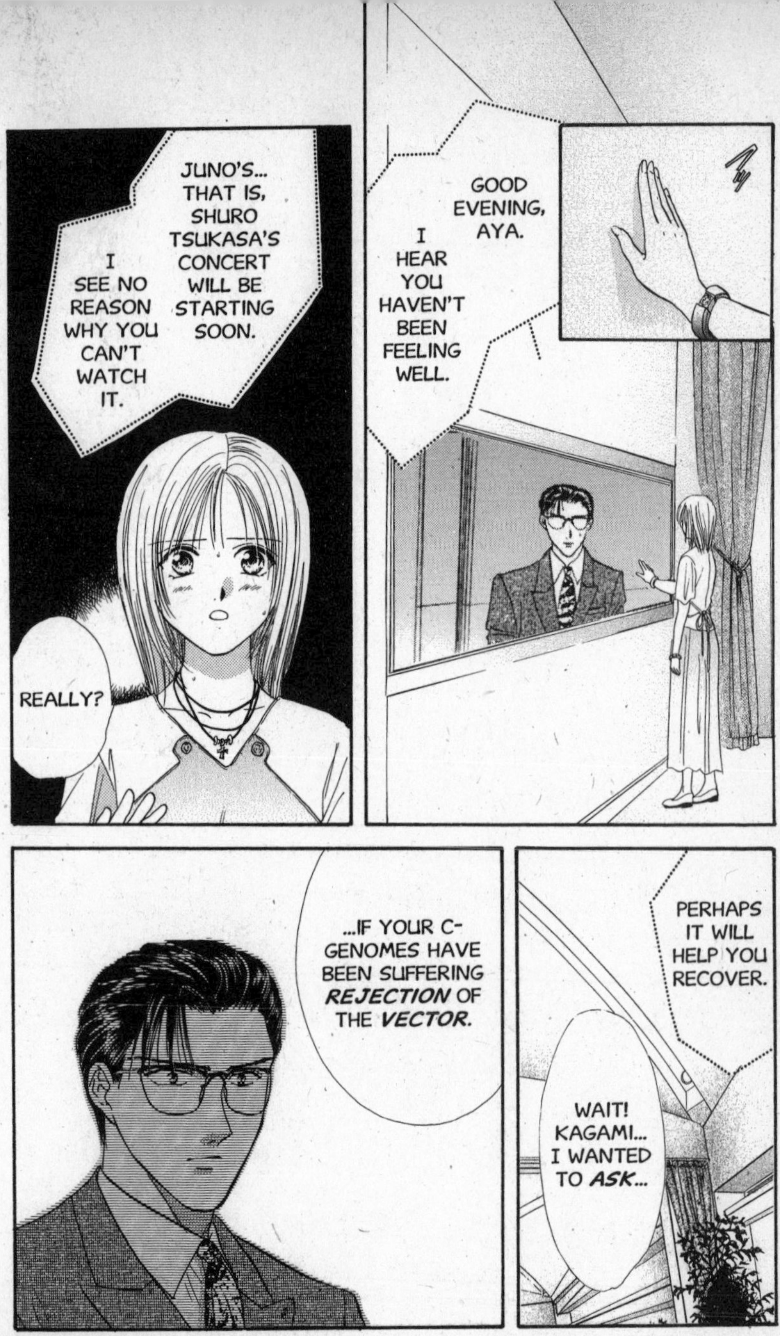
GOOD EVENING, AYA.
I HEAR YOU HAVEN'T BEEN FEELING WELL.
JUNO'S... THAT IS, SHURO TSUKASA'S CONCERT WILL BE STARTING SOON.
I SEE NO REASON WHY YOU CAN'T WATCH IT.
REALLY?
PERHAPS IT WILL HELP YOU RECOVER.
WAIT! KAGAMI... I WANTED TO *ASK*...
...IF YOUR C-GENOMES HAVE BEEN SUFFERING *REJECTION* OF THE *VECTOR*.

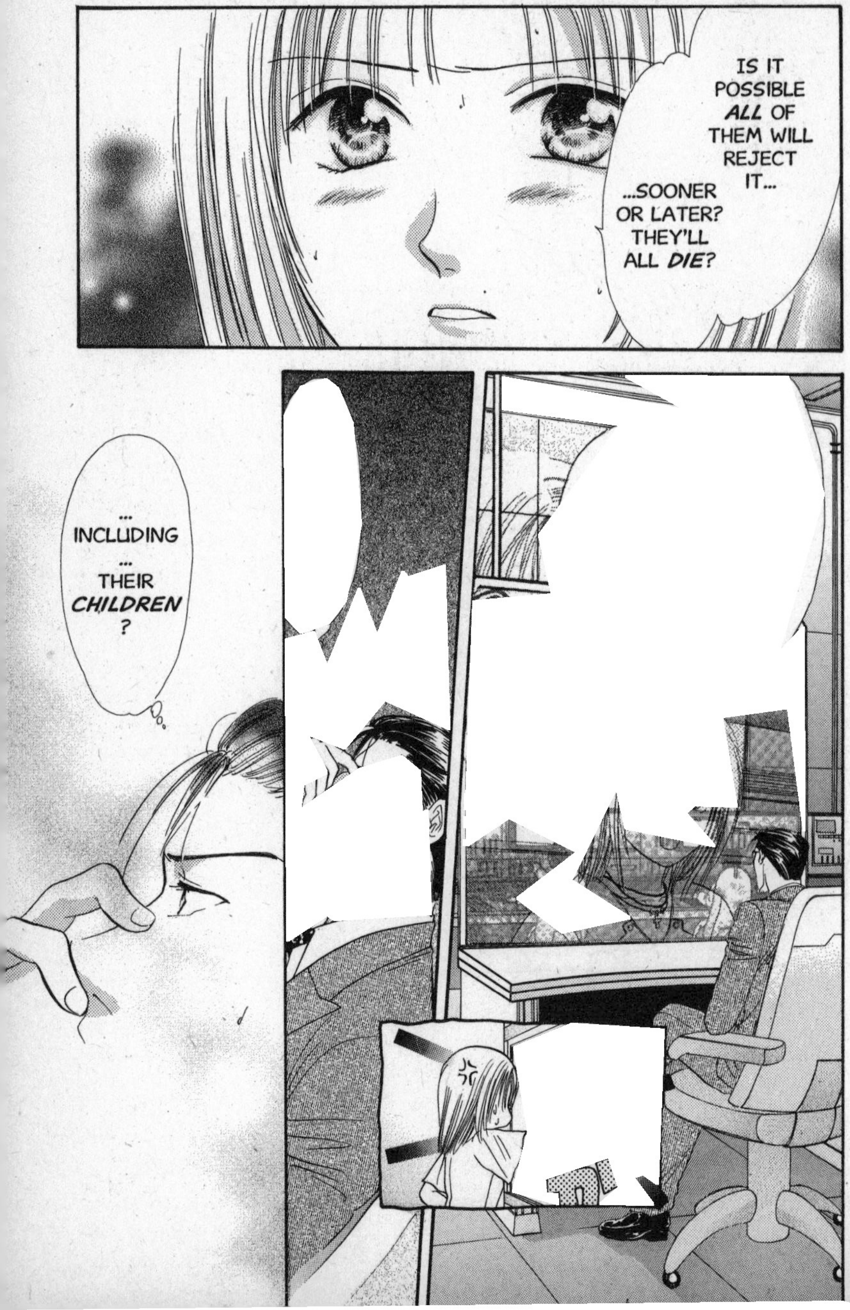
IS IT POSSIBLE ALL OF THEM WILL REJECT IT...
...SOONER OR LATER? THEY'LL ALL DIE?
... INCLUDING ... THEIR CHILDREN ?

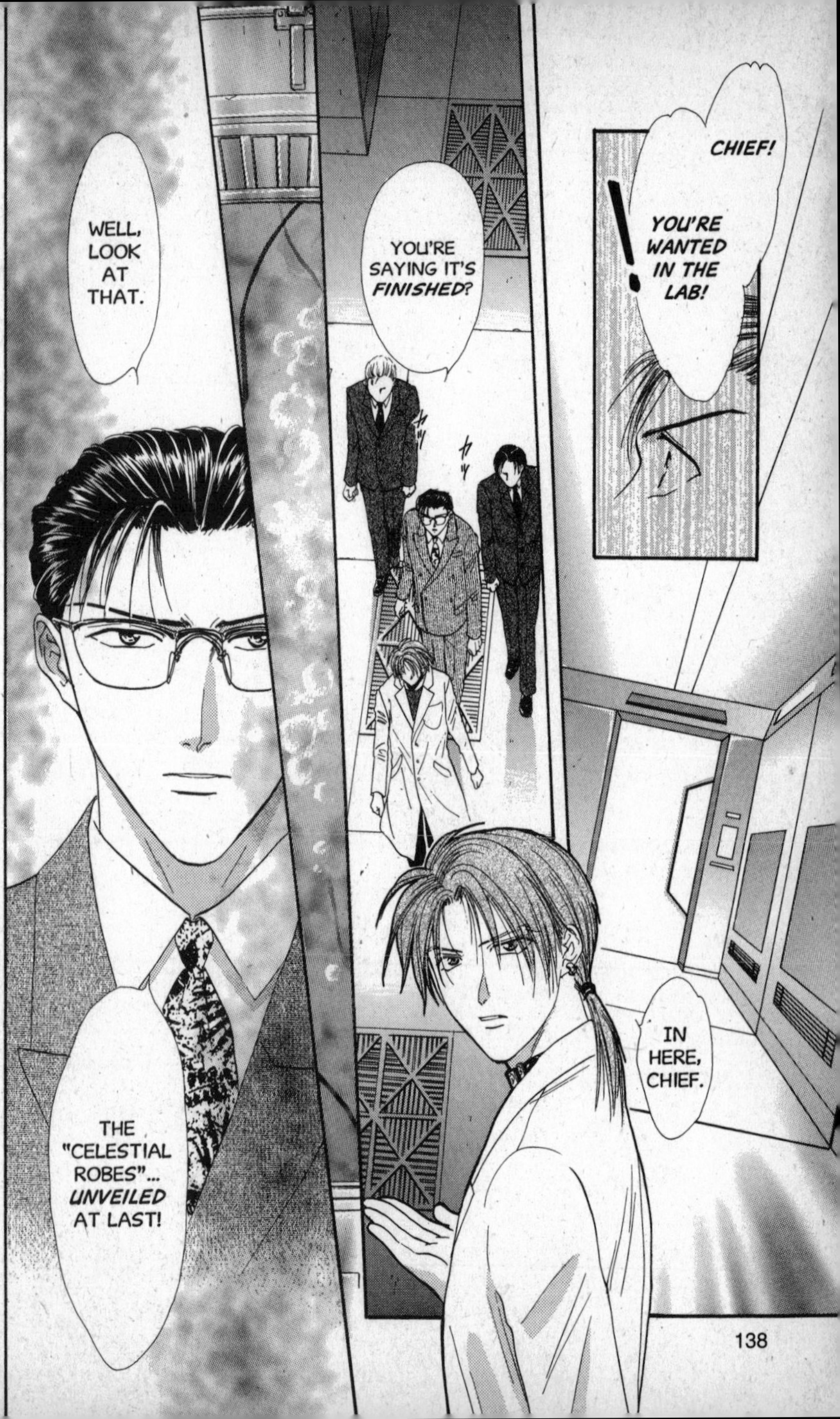
CHIEF!
YOU'RE WANTED IN THE LAB!
YOU'RE SAYING IT'S *FINISHED*?
IN HERE, CHIEF.
WELL, LOOK AT THAT.
THE "CELESTIAL ROBES"... *UNVEILED* AT LAST!

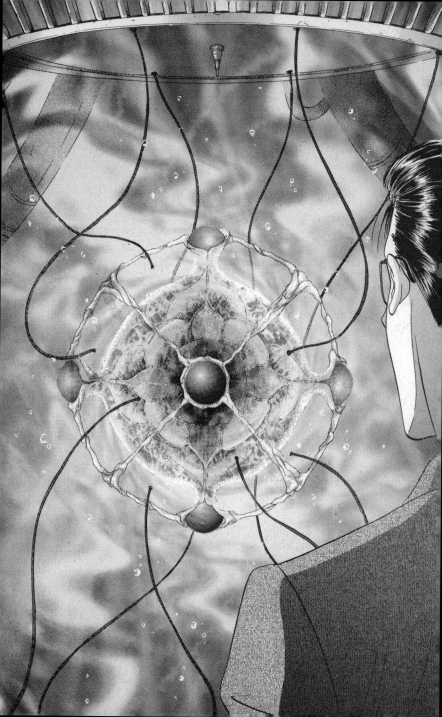

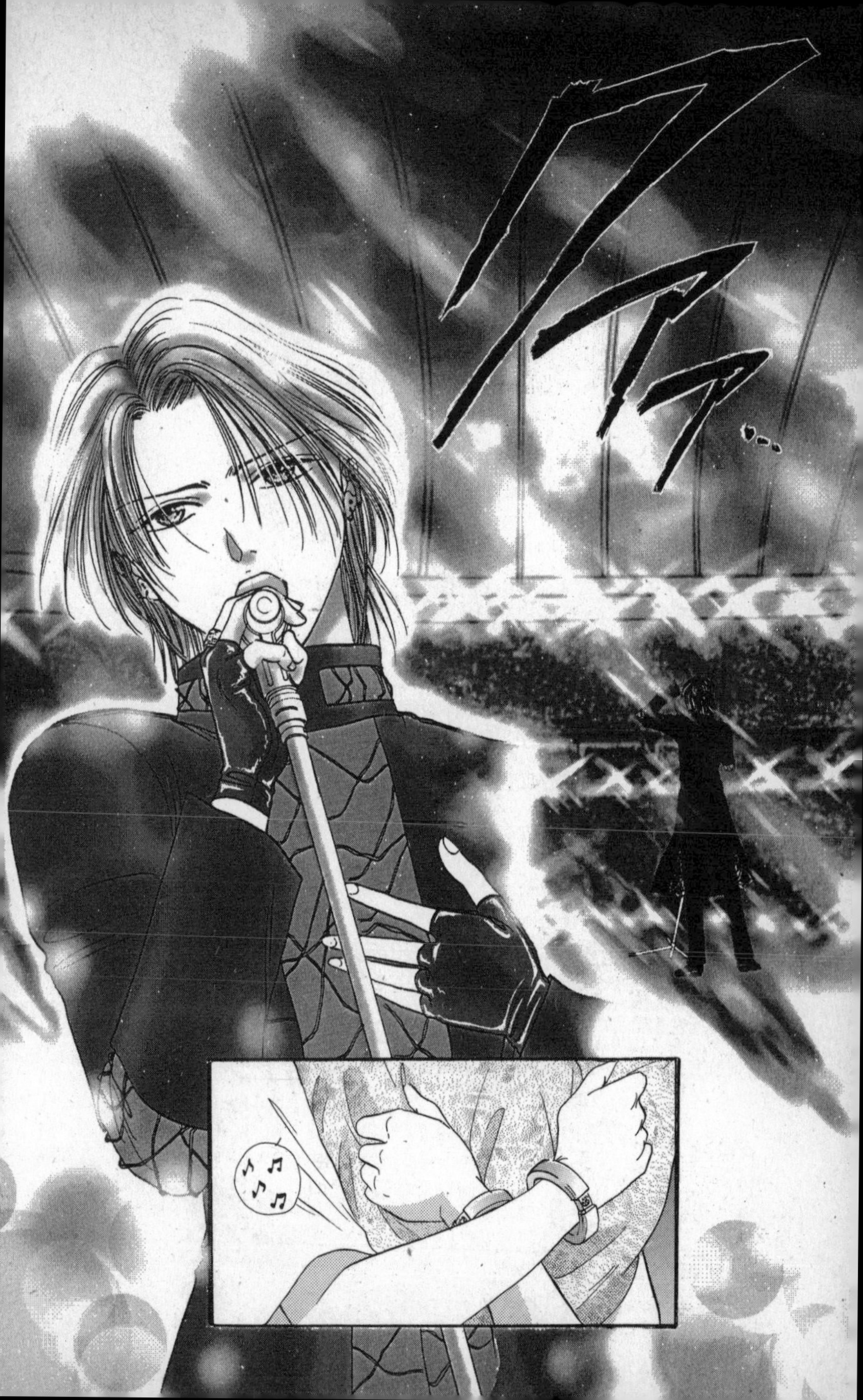
ワアア…

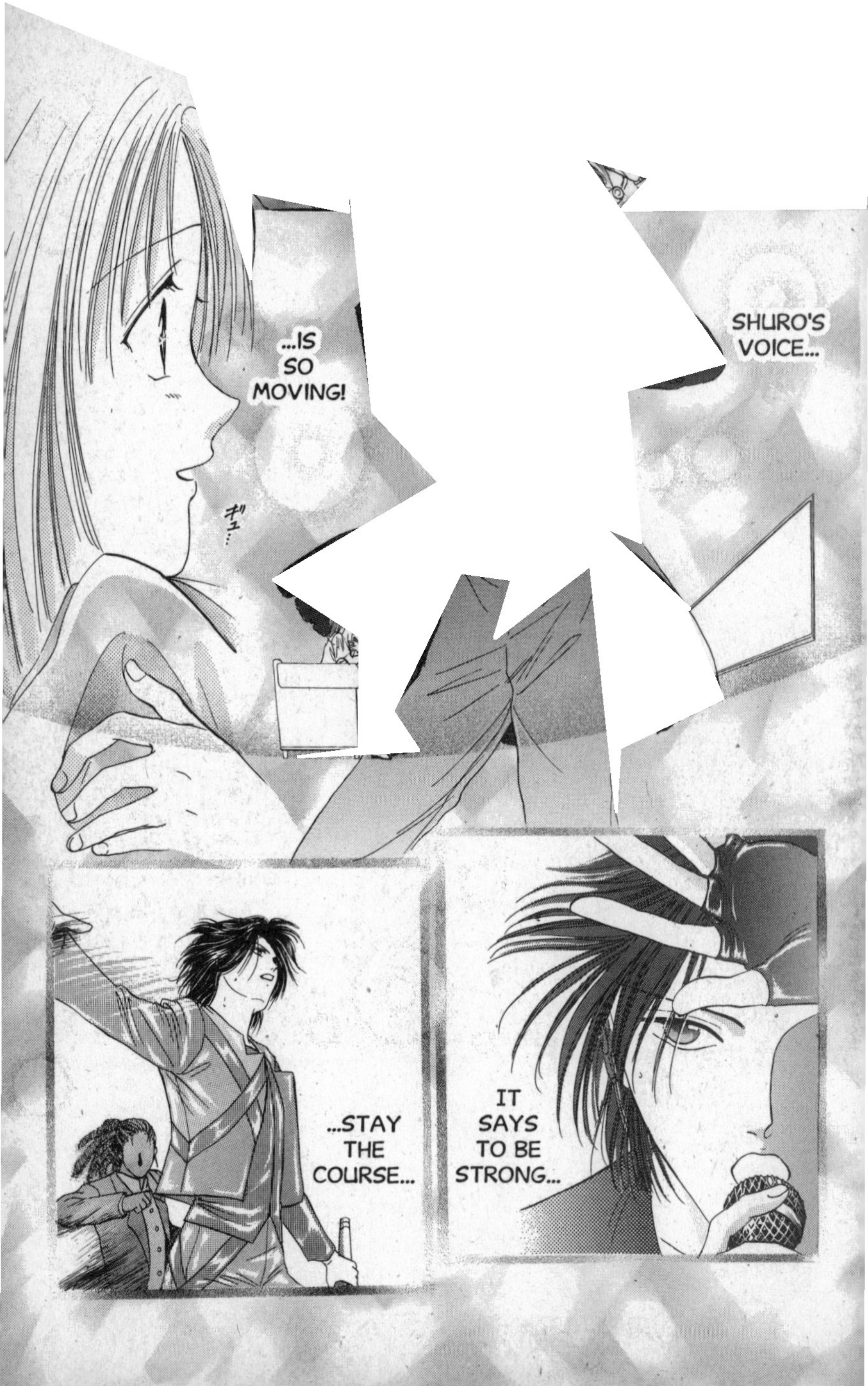
SHURO'S VOICE...
...IS SO MOVING!
ギュ...
IT SAYS TO BE STRONG...
...STAY THE COURSE...

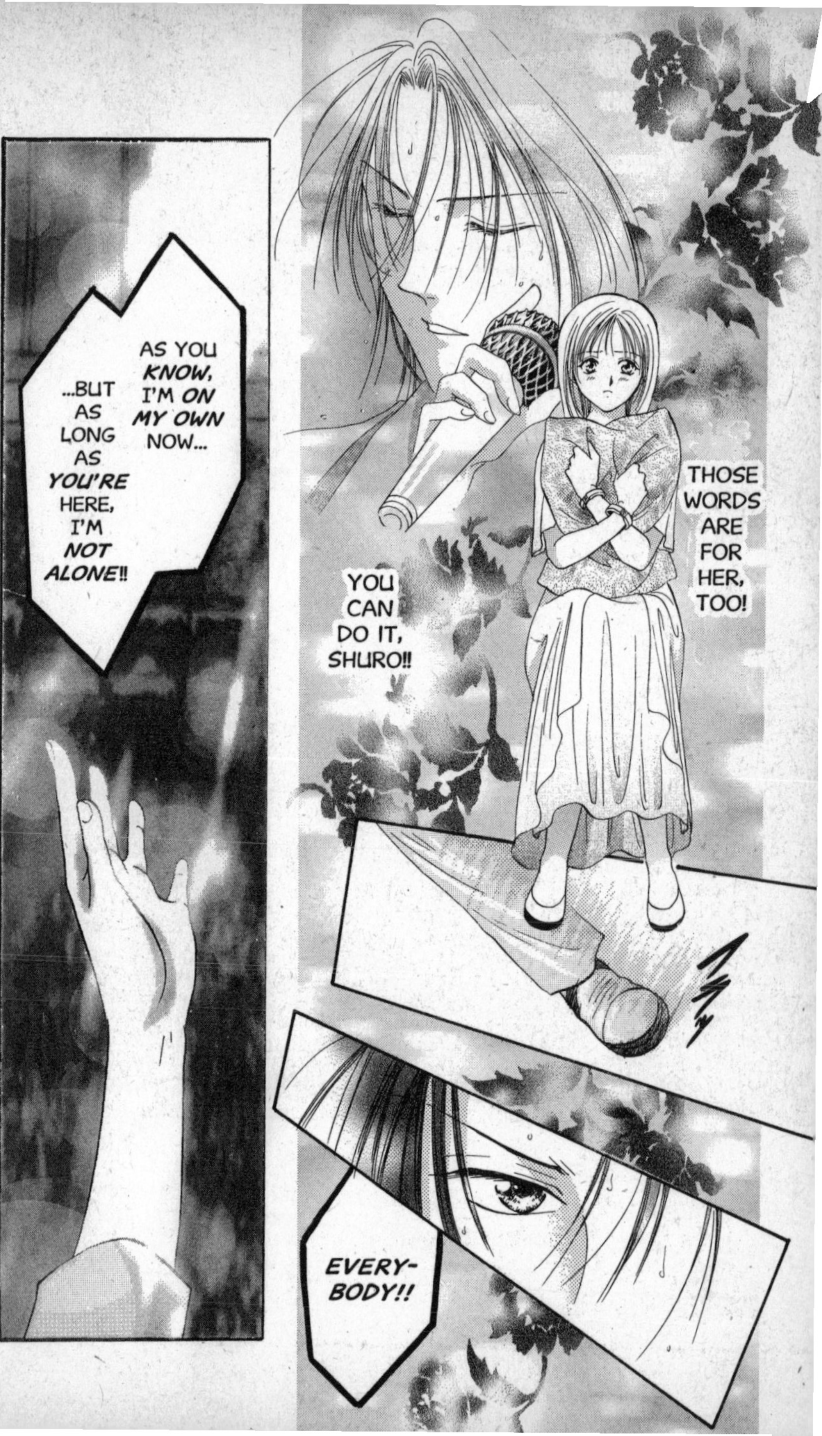
THOSE WORDS ARE FOR HER, TOO!
YOU CAN DO IT, SHURO!!
EVERY-BODY!!
AS YOU KNOW, I'M ON MY OWN NOW...
...BUT AS LONG AS YOU'RE HERE, I'M NOT ALONE!!

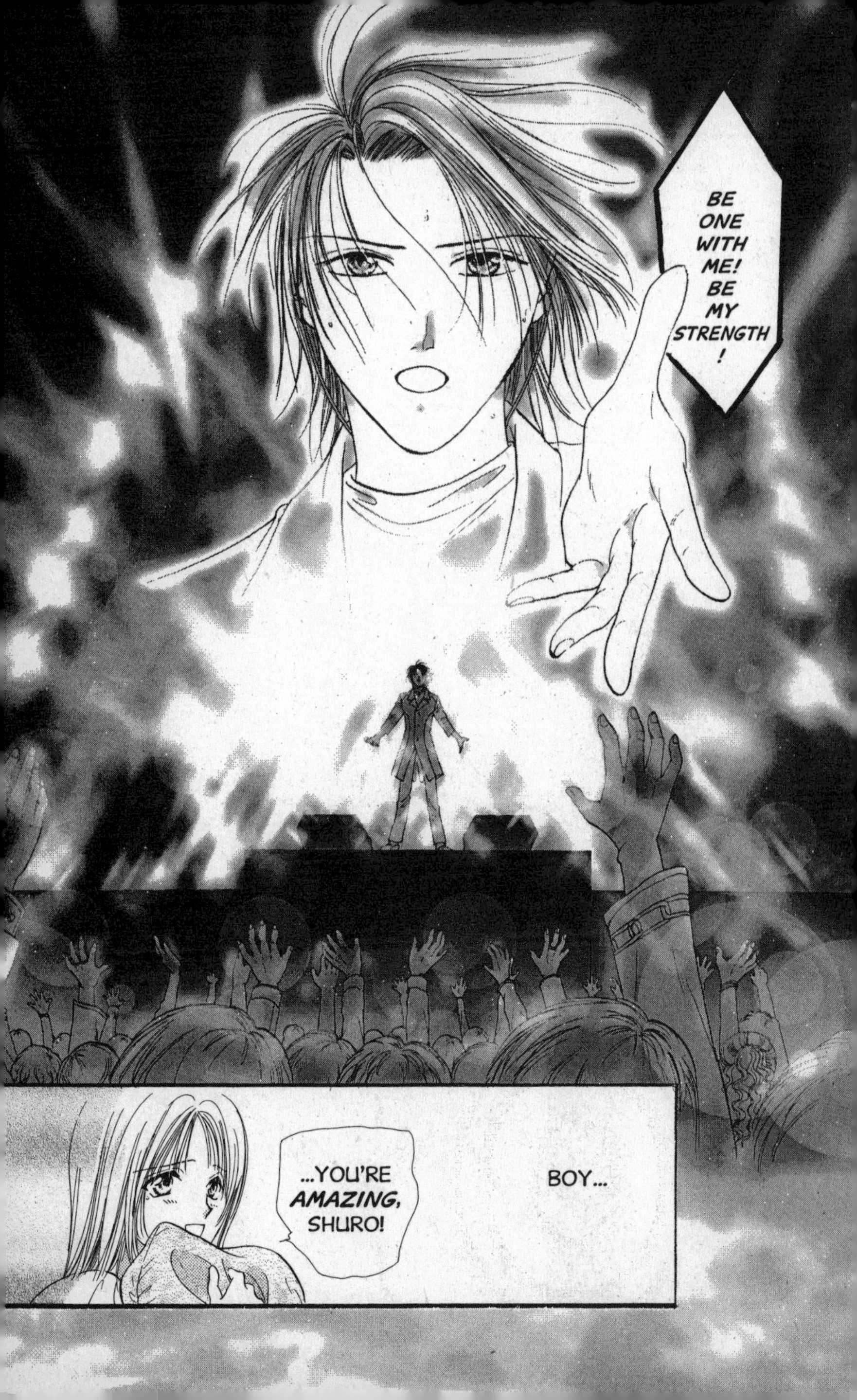
BE ONE WITH ME! BE MY STRENGTH!
BOY...
...YOU'RE AMAZING, SHURO!

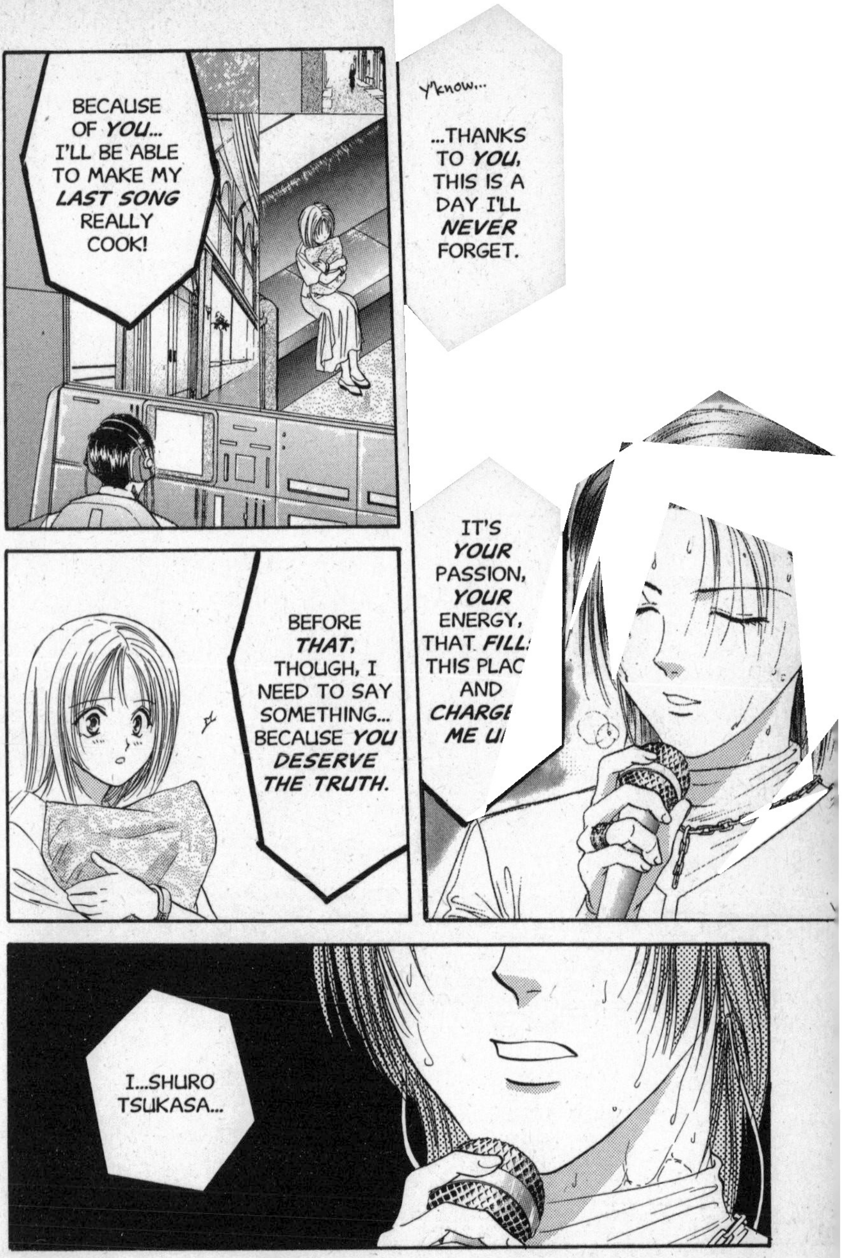
Y'know...
...THANKS TO *YOU*, THIS IS A DAY I'LL *NEVER* FORGET.
BECAUSE OF *YOU*... I'LL BE ABLE TO MAKE MY *LAST SONG* REALLY COOK!
IT'S *YOUR* PASSION, *YOUR* ENERGY, THAT *FILL* THIS PLAC AND *CHARGE ME U*
BEFORE *THAT*, THOUGH, I NEED TO SAY SOMETHING... BECAUSE *YOU DESERVE THE TRUTH*.
I...SHURO TSUKASA...

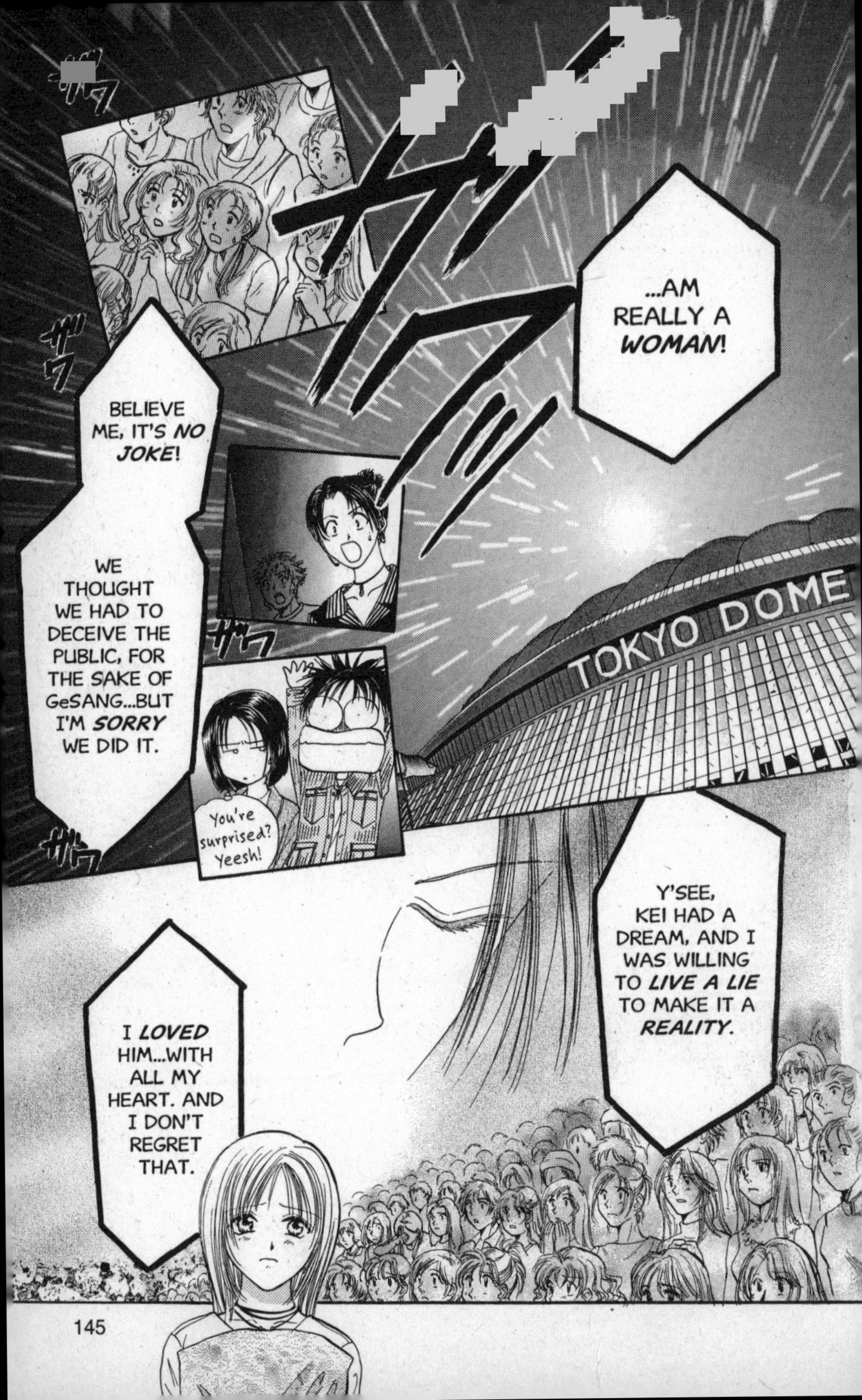
...AM REALLY A *WOMAN*!
BELIEVE ME, IT'S *NO JOKE*!
WE THOUGHT WE HAD TO DECEIVE THE PUBLIC, FOR THE SAKE OF GeSANG...BUT I'M *SORRY* WE DID IT.
You're surprised? Yeesh!
TOKYO DOME
Y'SEE, KEI HAD A DREAM, AND I WAS WILLING TO *LIVE A LIE* TO MAKE IT A *REALITY*.
I *LOVED* HIM...WITH ALL MY HEART. AND I DON'T REGRET THAT.

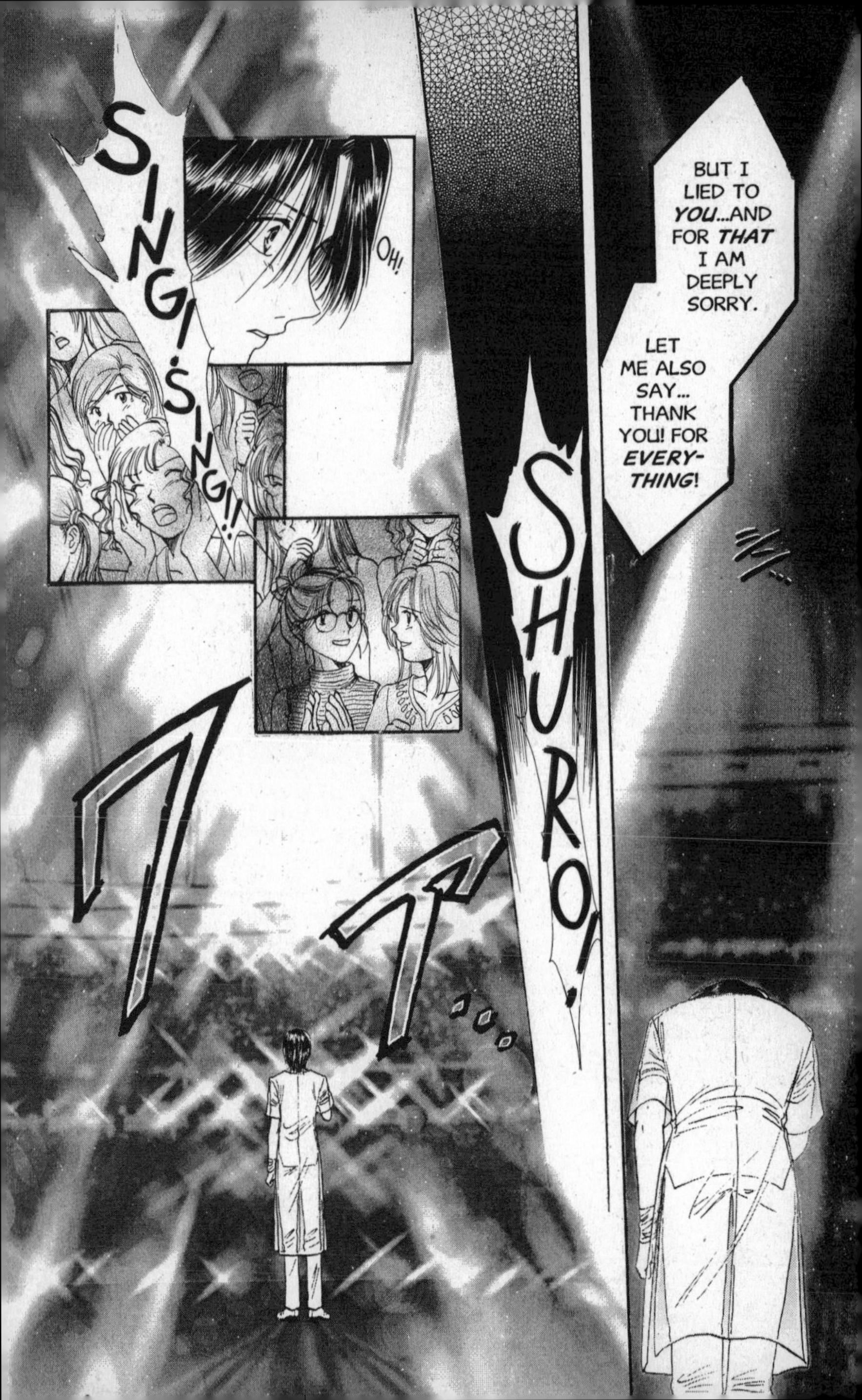
BUT I LIED TO *YOU*...AND FOR *THAT* I AM DEEPLY SORRY.
LET ME ALSO SAY... THANK YOU! FOR *EVERY-THING*!
SHURO!
OH!
SING! SING! SING!!!

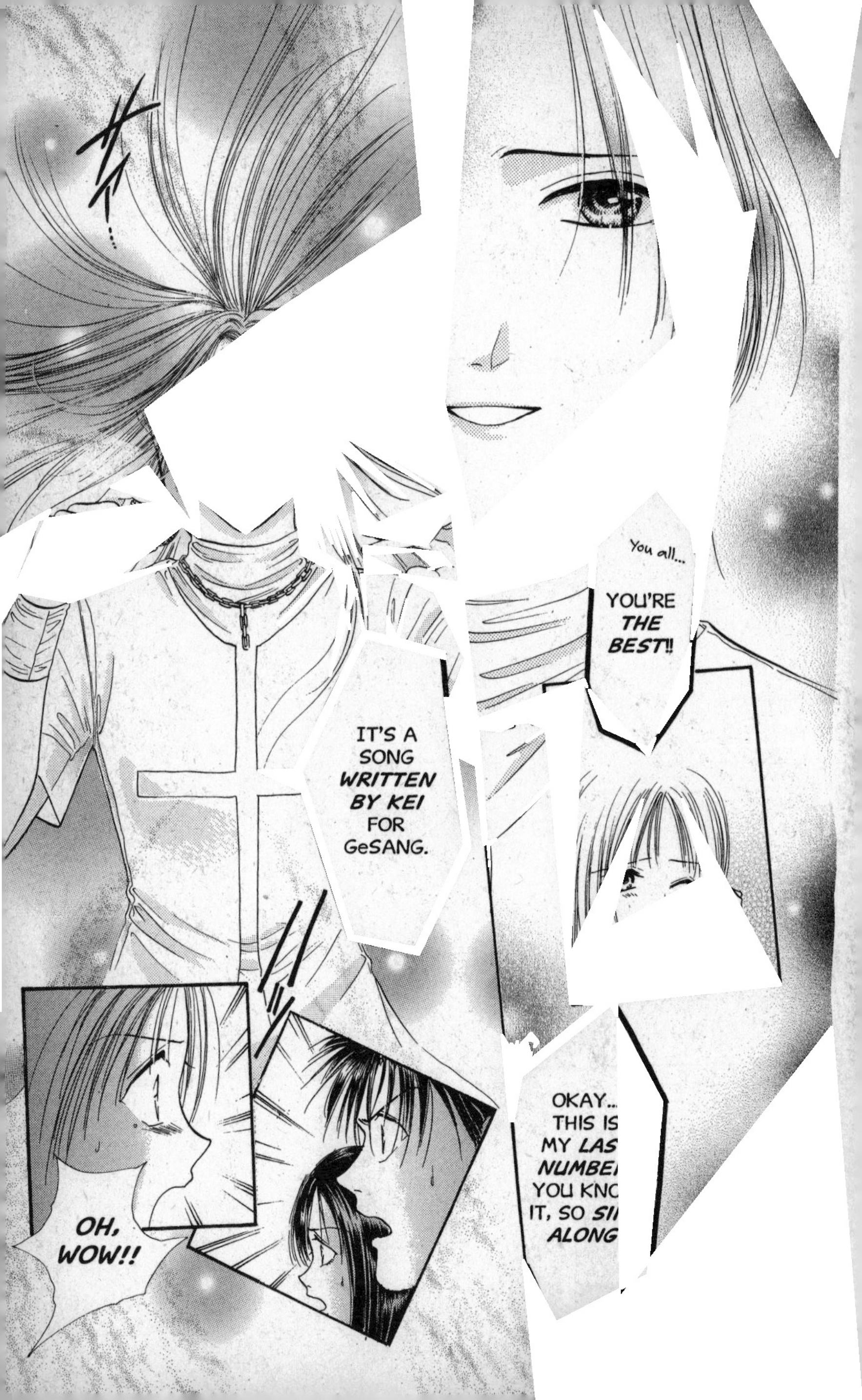
You all...
YOU'RE THE BEST!!
IT'S A SONG WRITTEN BY KEI FOR GeSANG.
OKAY... THIS IS MY LAS NUMBE YOU KNO IT, SO SI ALONG
OH, WOW!!

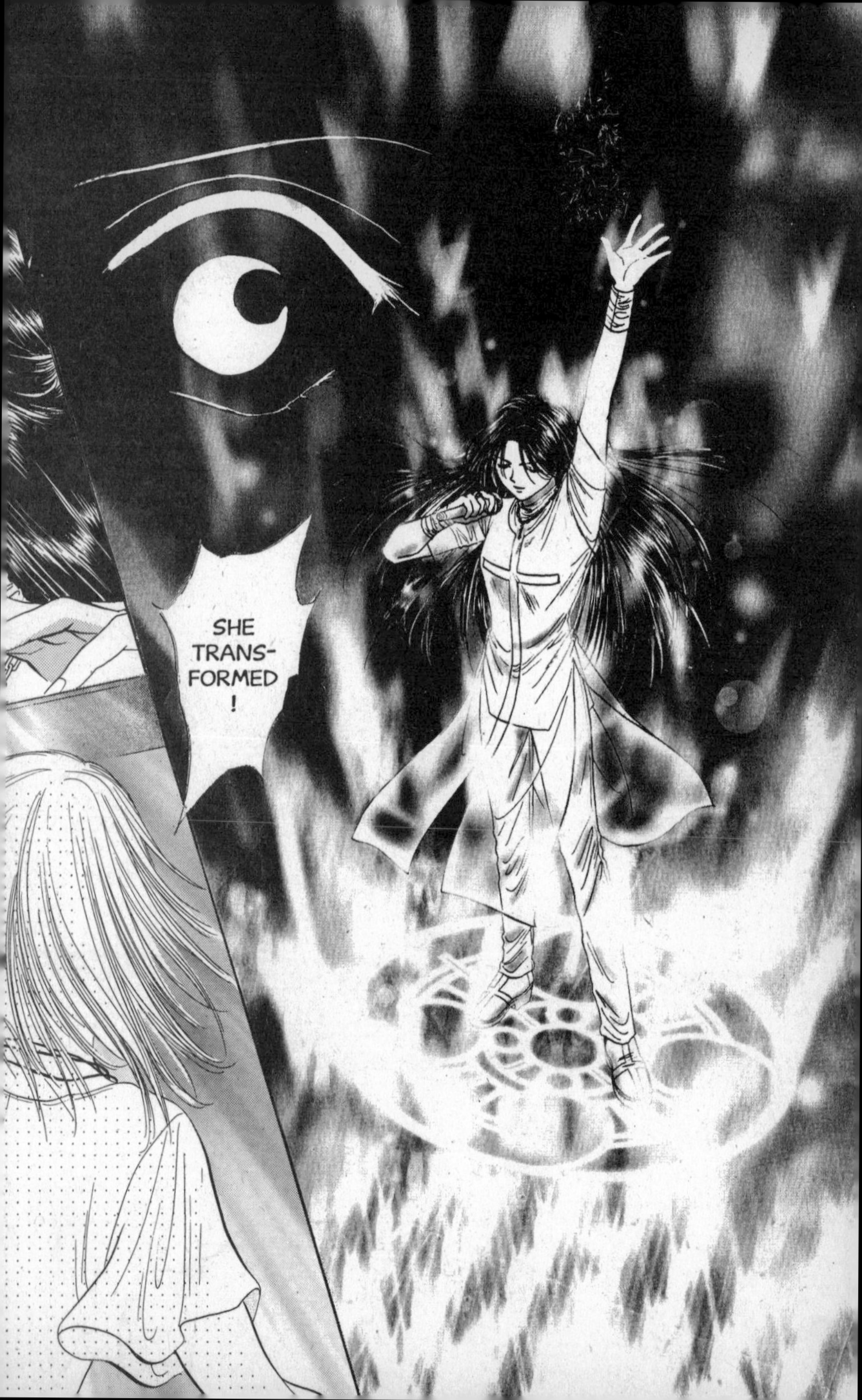
SHE TRANSFORMED!

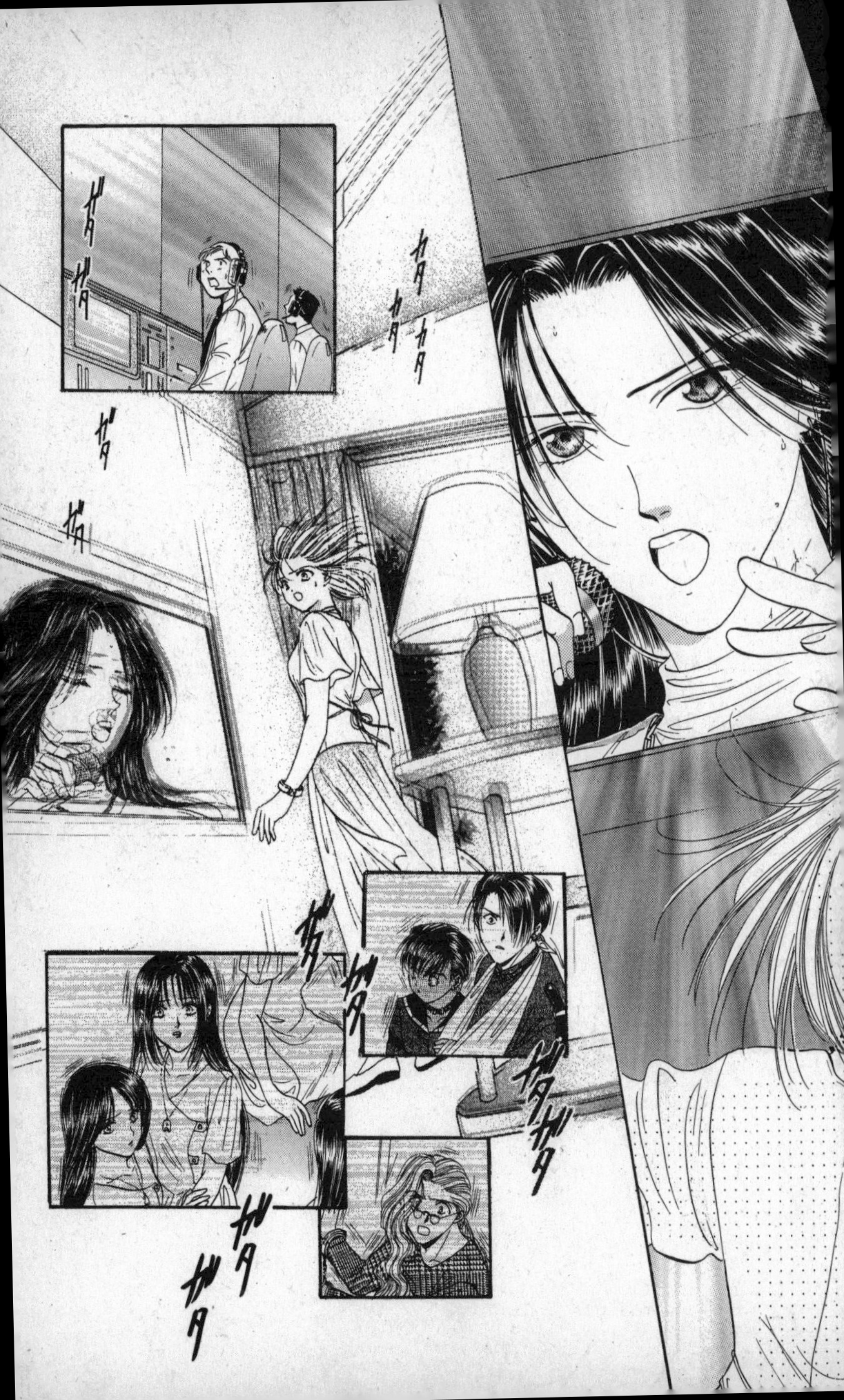
カタ カタ
ガタ ガタ
ガタ ガタ
ガタ ガタ
ガタ ガタ
ガタ ガタ

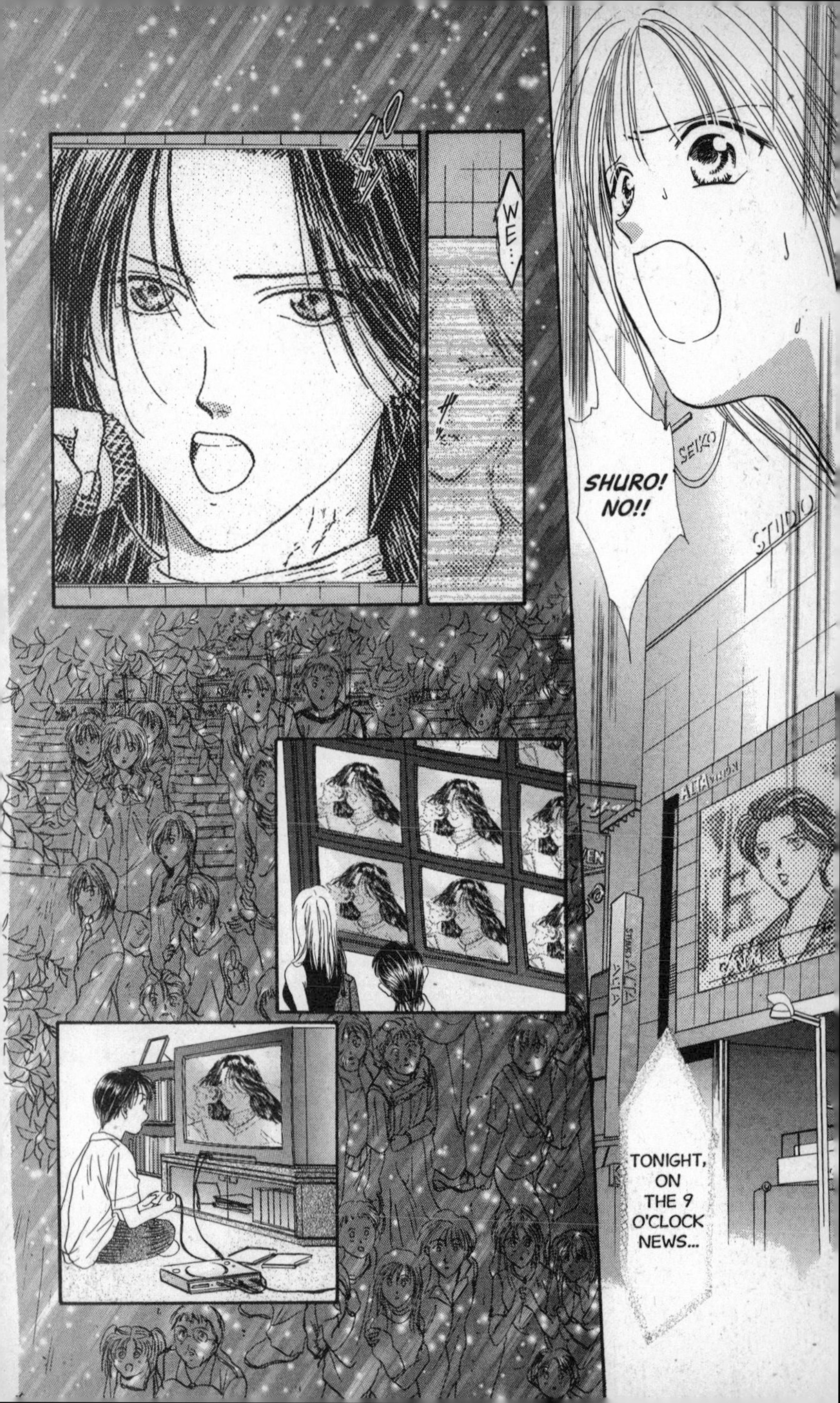
SHURO! NO!!
SEIKO
STUDIO
TONIGHT, ON THE 9 O'CLOCK NEWS...
WE...

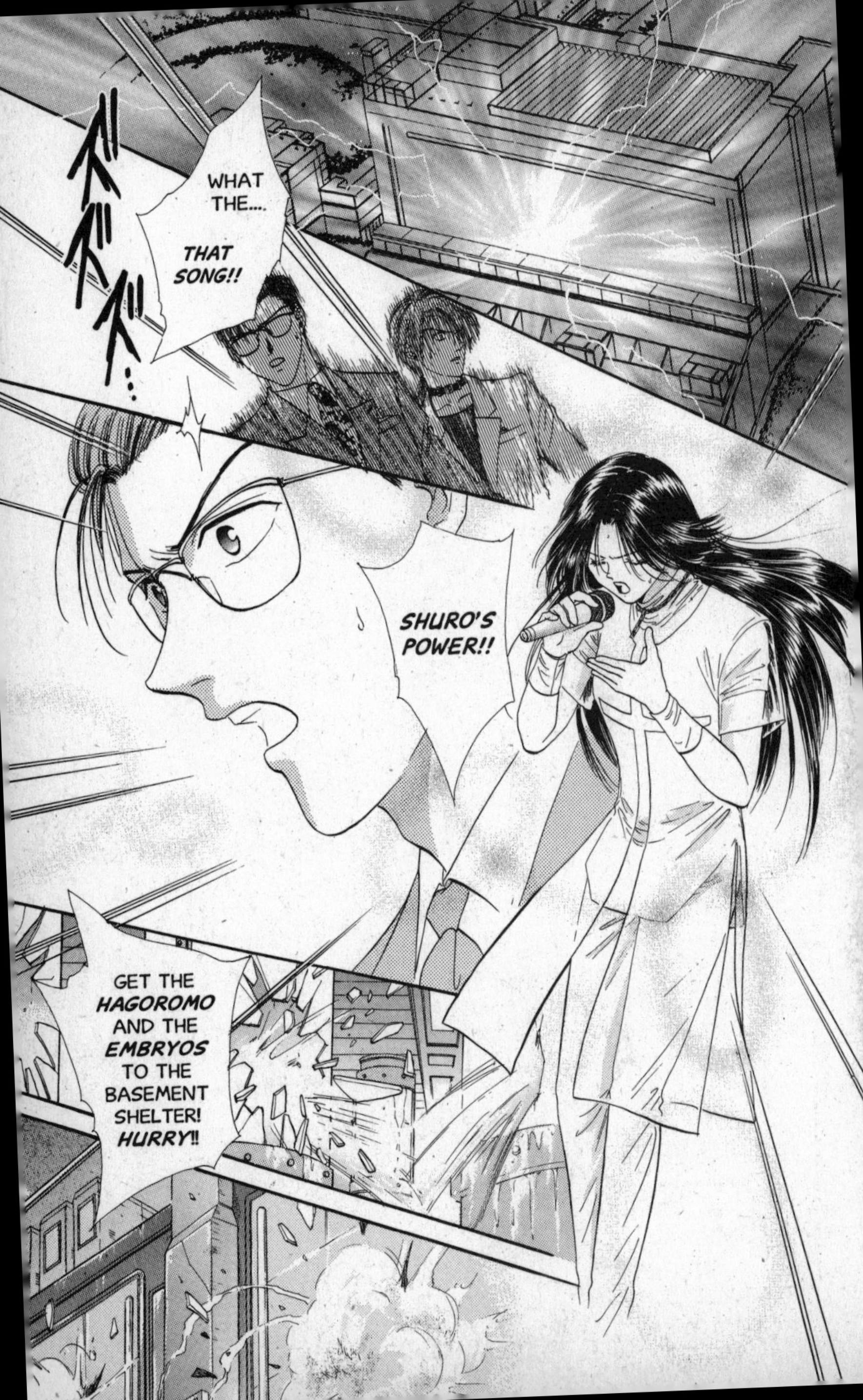
WHAT THE....
THAT SONG!!
ズズズ…
SHURO'S POWER!!
GET THE HAGOROMO AND THE EMBRYOS TO THE BASEMENT SHELTER! HURRY!!

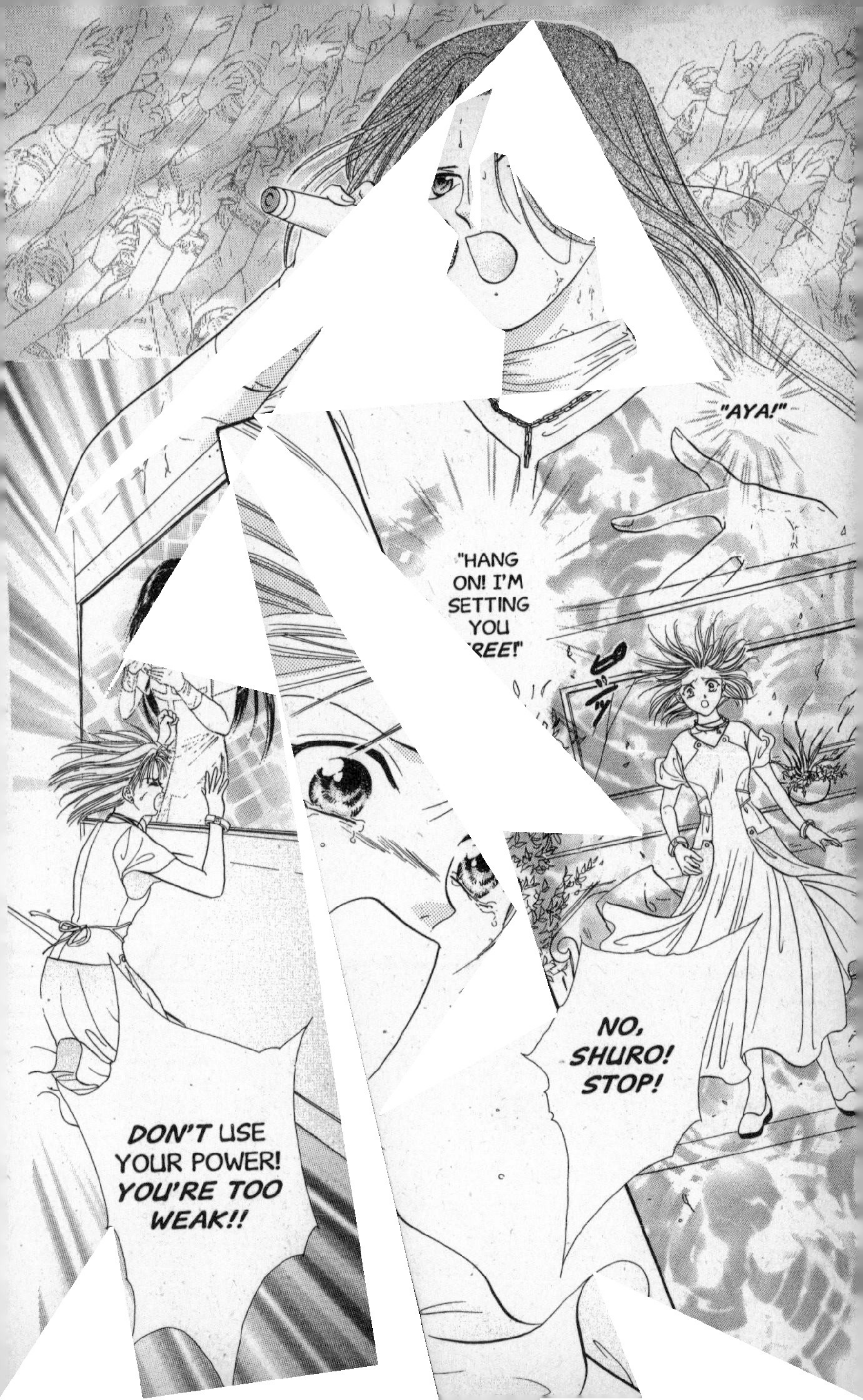
"AYA!"
"HANG ON! I'M SETTING YOU FREE!"
NO, SHURO! STOP!
DON'T USE YOUR POWER! YOU'RE TOO WEAK!!

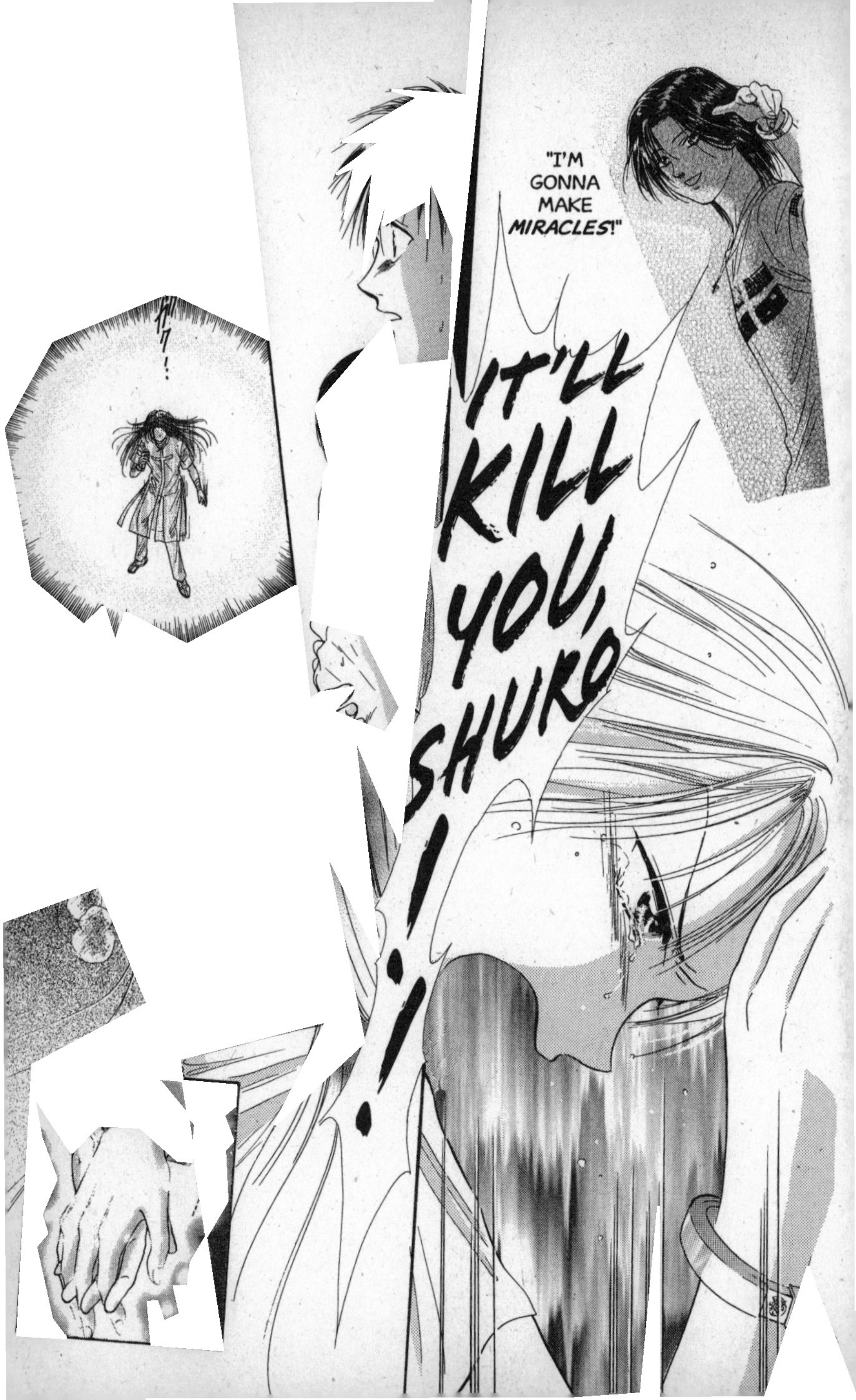
"I'M GONNA MAKE *MIRACLES!*"
IT'LL KILL YOU, SHURO!!

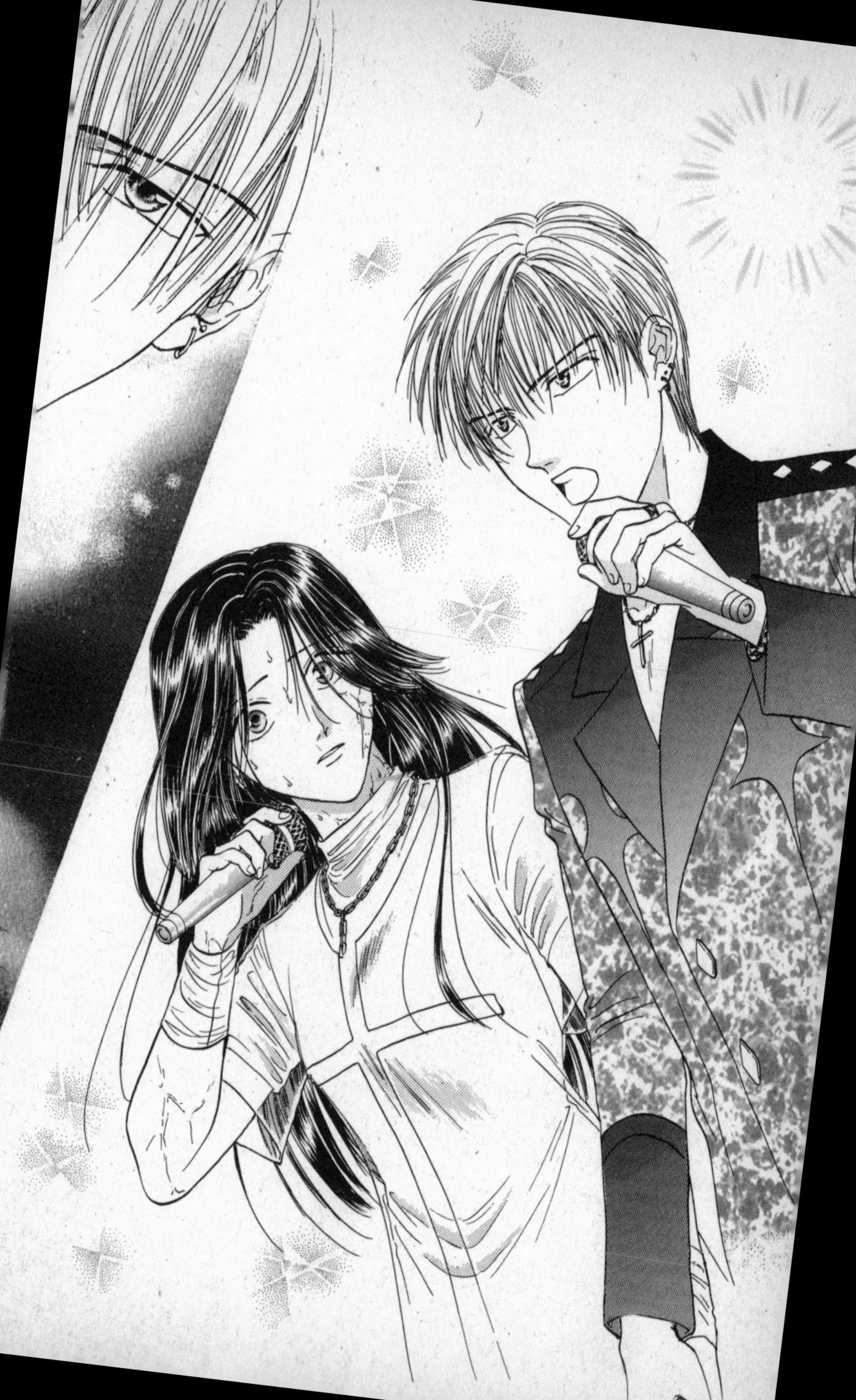

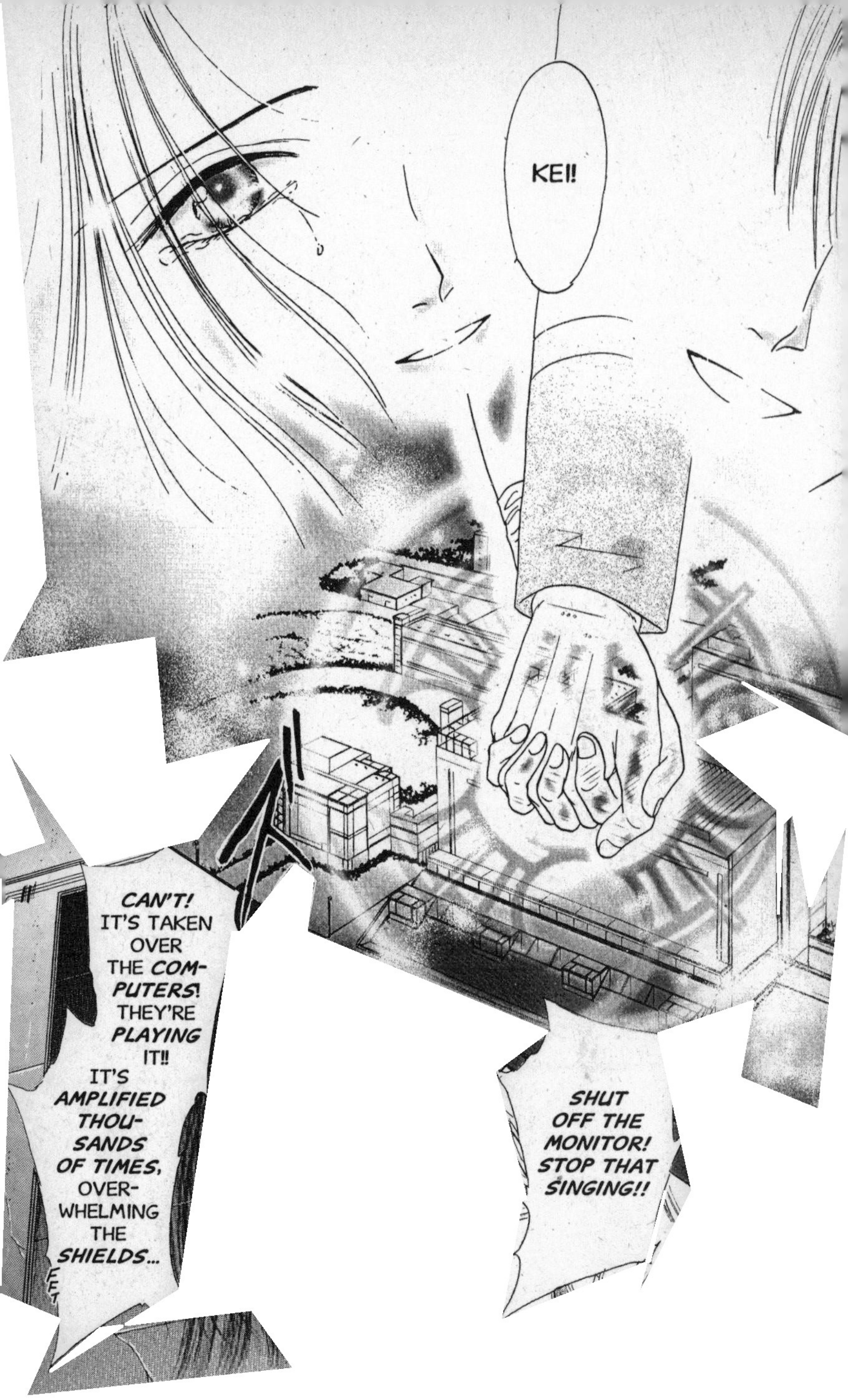
KEI!
SHUT OFF THE MONITOR! STOP THAT SINGING!!
CAN'T! IT'S TAKEN OVER THE COMPUTERS! THEY'RE PLAYING IT!! IT'S AMPLIFIED THOUSANDS OF TIMES, OVERWHELMING THE SHIELDS...

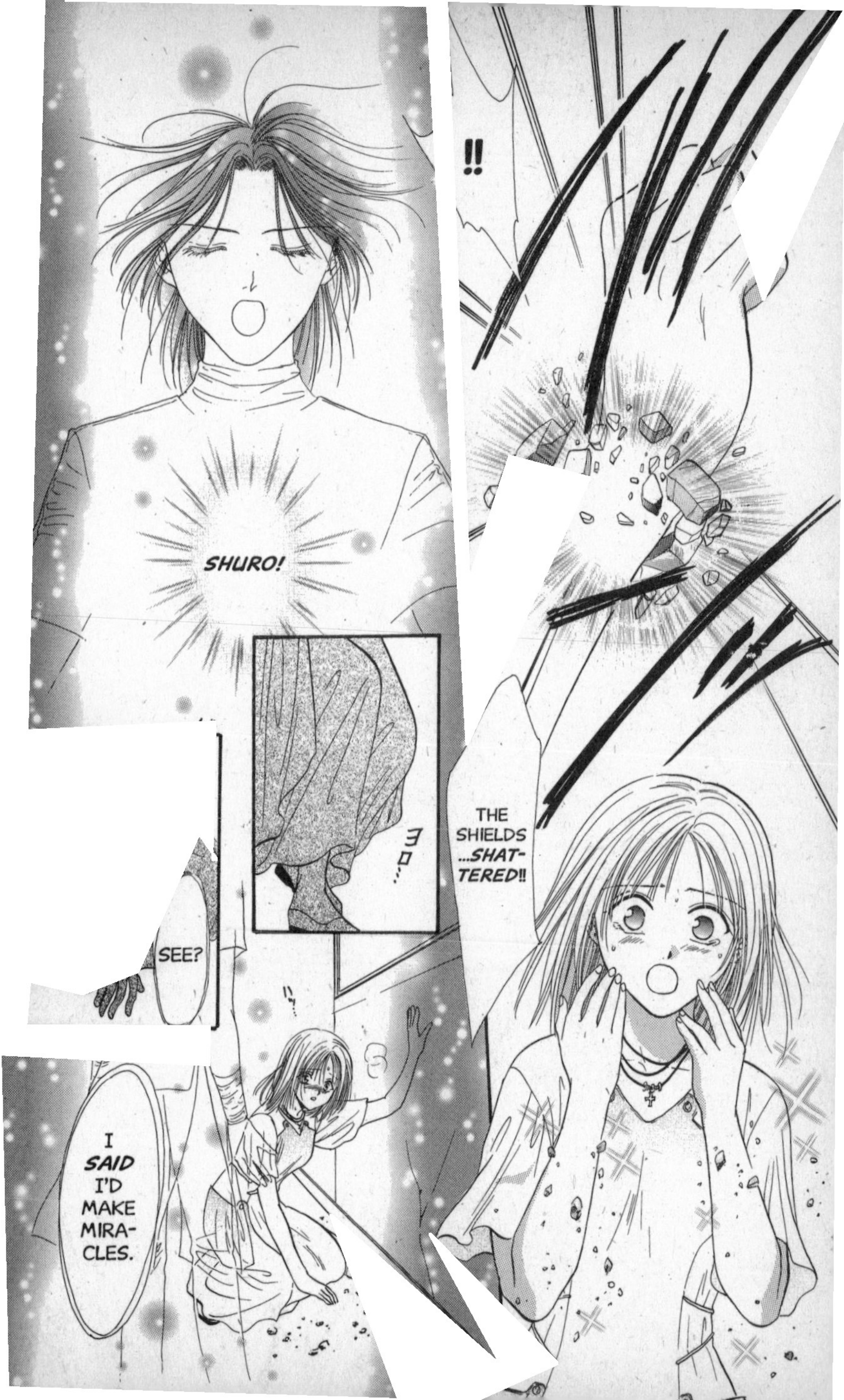
!!
THE SHIELDS ...SHATTERED!!
SHURO!
ヨロ…
SEE?
ハッ…
I SAID I'D MAKE MIRACLES.

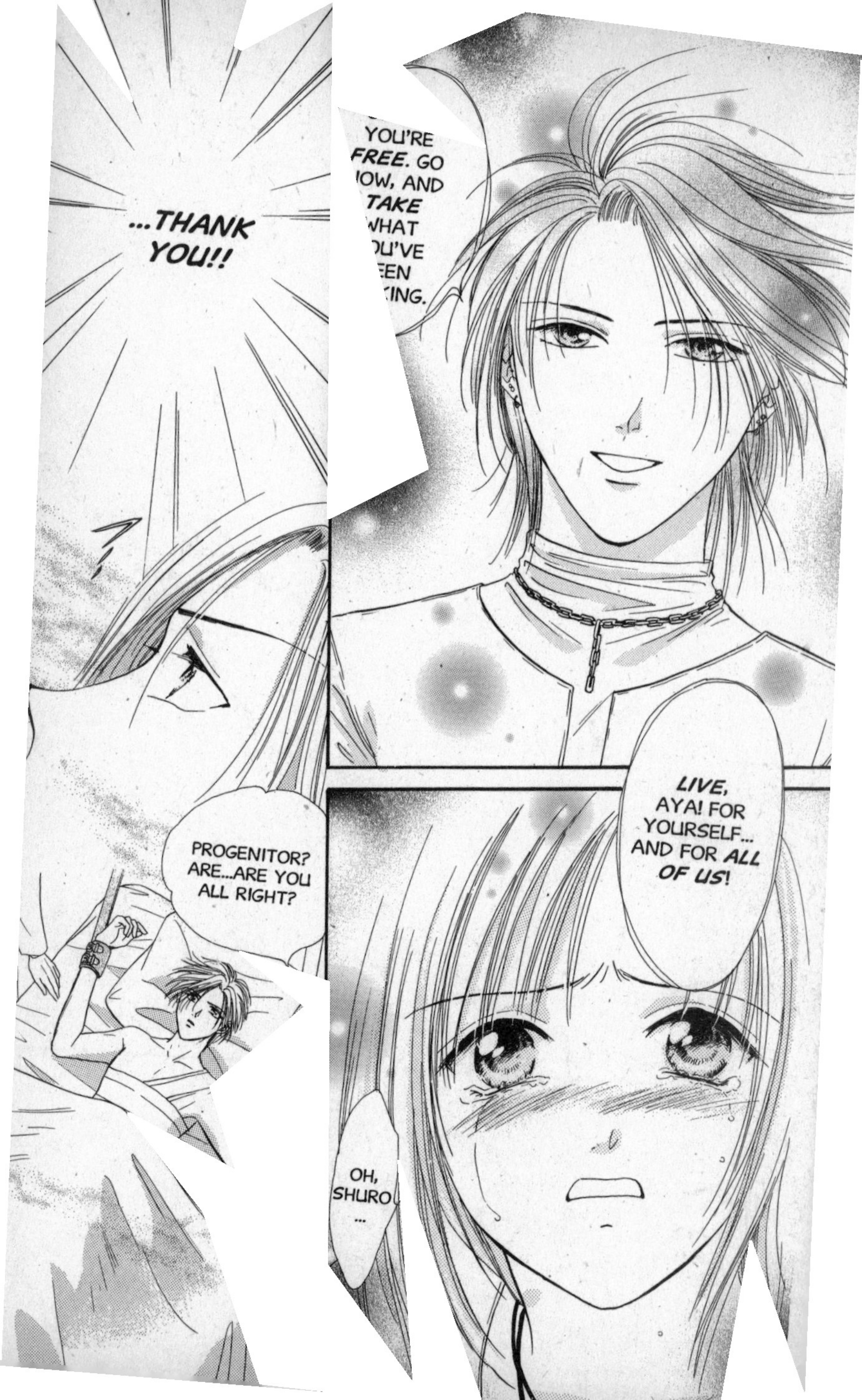
YOU'RE FREE. GO OW, AND TAKE WHAT OU'VE EEN KING.
LIVE, AYA! FOR YOURSELF... AND FOR ALL OF US!
OH, SHURO ...
...THANK YOU!!
PROGENITOR? ARE...ARE YOU ALL RIGHT?

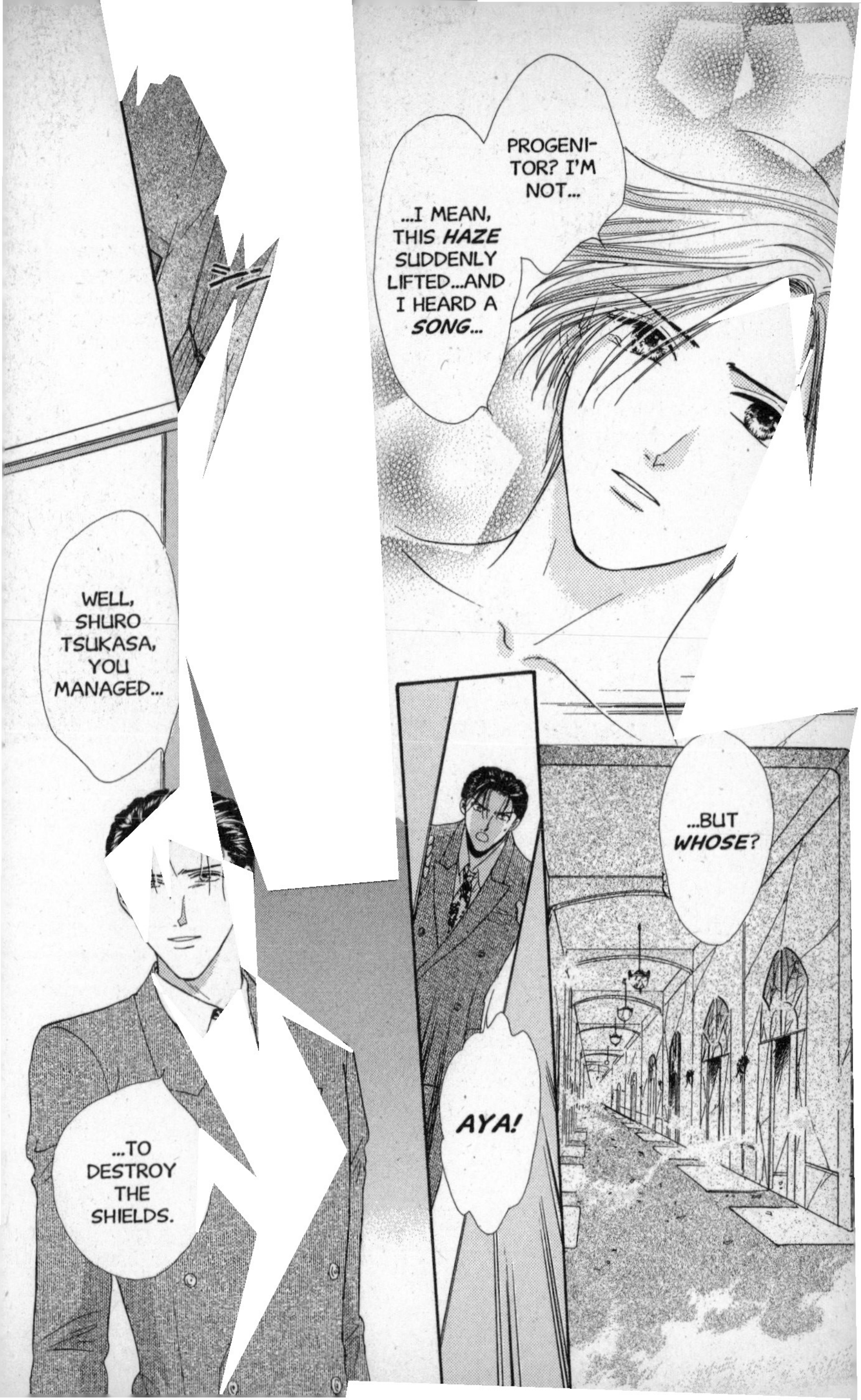
PROGENI-TOR? I'M NOT...
...I MEAN, THIS HAZE SUDDENLY LIFTED...AND I HEARD A SONG...
...BUT WHOSE?
AYA!
WELL, SHURO TSUKASA, YOU MANAGED...
...TO DESTROY THE SHIELDS.

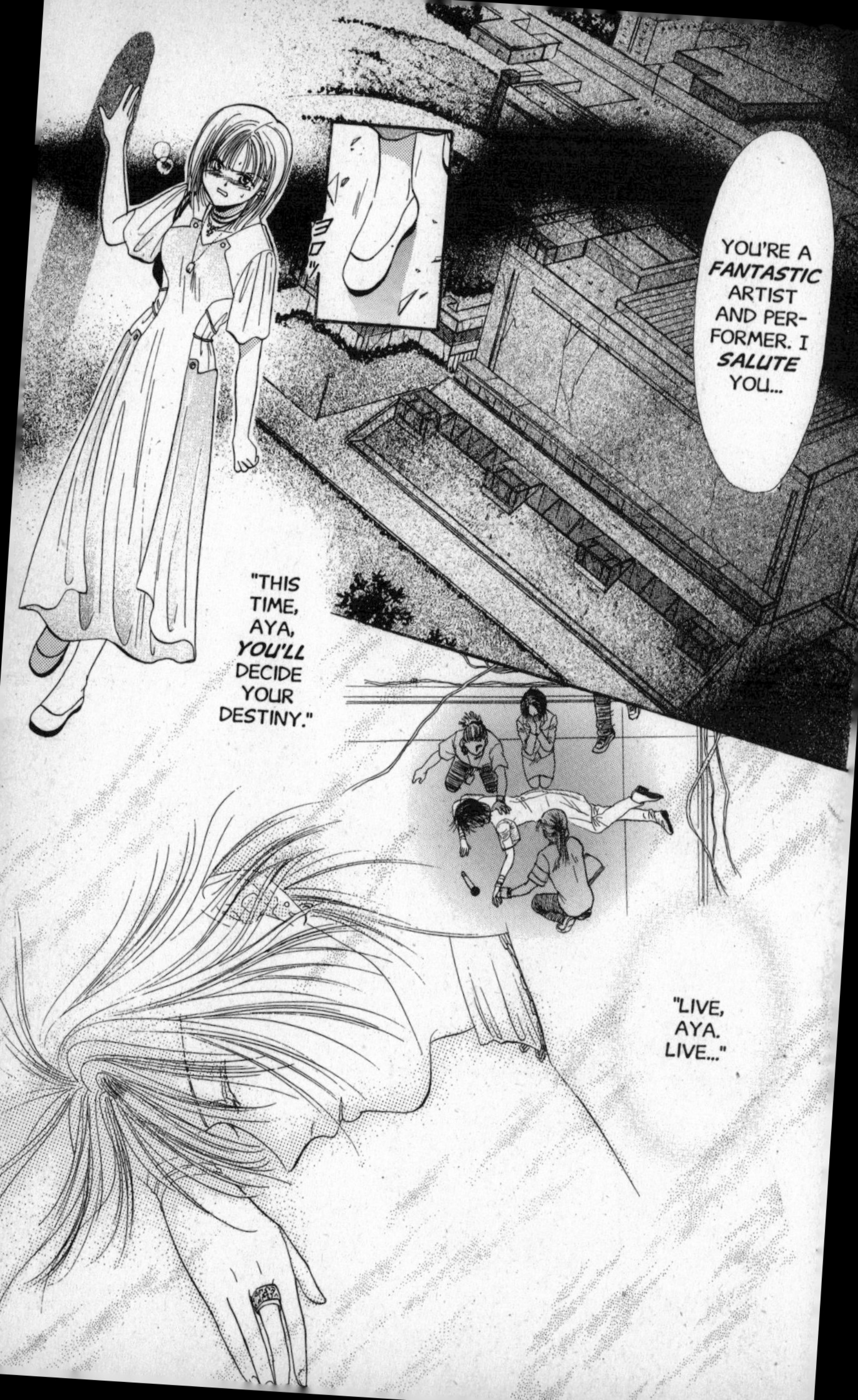
YOU'RE A *FANTASTIC* ARTIST AND PER-FORMER. I *SALUTE* YOU...
"THIS TIME, AYA, *YOU'LL* DECIDE YOUR DESTINY."
"LIVE, AYA. LIVE..."

I never learn...
The Maniac's Guide to "Ceres" ③!!

Probably the last one!!

GUARDINALS → The term for those assembled to carry out the C-Project. It's a made-up word (I think), using "guard" and "national" as roots. These are the five superior (physically, mentally, and in skill) men and women chosen to manage the Project. They saw to it that sperm donors for the C-genomes were gathered from all over the world.

THE MIKAGES' UNIFORMS → A distinct design worn by Wei, Assam, and Tôya (in the beginning). Rumor has it that they were designed by Alec. They're made of special fabrics that are very durable and can withstand plenty of abuse.

PALLAS → Chidori's celestial name. The first asteroid ever discovered was named "Ceres," and Chidori was named after the second. Shuro was the third, then Juno, and the series continues with Vesta, Astraea, Hebe, Iris, etc... so there must've been C-genomes with those names, too (named either in the order they transformed, or in order of the magnitude of their powers). If they are descended from the same celestial maiden, or if they have equivalent powers, they are categorized under one name and ranked as Type A, B, C, etc.

RAGNAROK (THE TWILIGHT OF THE GODS) → A nongovernmental organization with which the Mikages are affiliated. It is composed of gray eminences from various countries...a rich men's club, so to speak. They invest in various research projects, and sponsor the C-Project. My editor came up with their name, equivalent to the Biblical Armageddon, but they're really just rich guys with too much time and money on their hands, not plotting anything nefarious so much as trying to stay occupied.

MANA → An indispensable item for celestial maidens (or goddesses), likened in legends to feathered cloaks ("hagoromo"), white robes, furs, sashes, hair ornaments, etc. However, some legends exist of celestial maidens coming down from (or going back to) heaven without one. In the Christian Bible, "manna" is a Greek word for a miraculous food that seems to descend from Heaven, although there is no known relation between this and "mana."

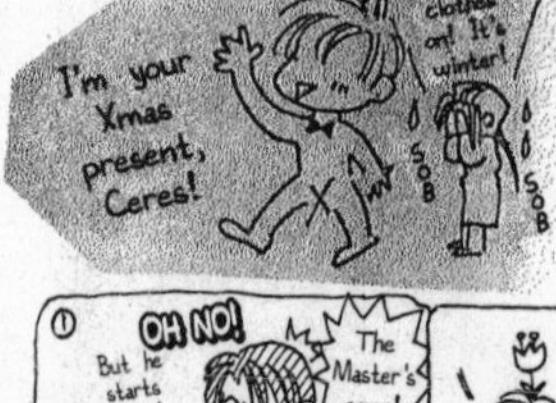

I'm your Xmas present, Ceres!
Get some clothes on! It's winter!
SOB
SOB

← Bonus
My Aki-loving assistant J's original comics featuring the Progenitor and Wei. She started drawing these when he got naked in Volume 5. She always draws them on her fax cover sheets...

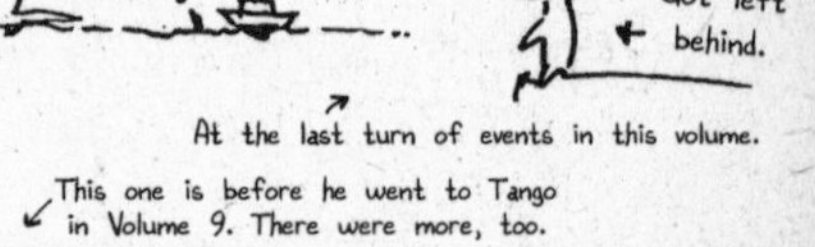

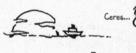

Ceres...
Got left behind.

At the last turn of events in this volume.

This one is before he went to Tango in Volume 9. There were more, too.

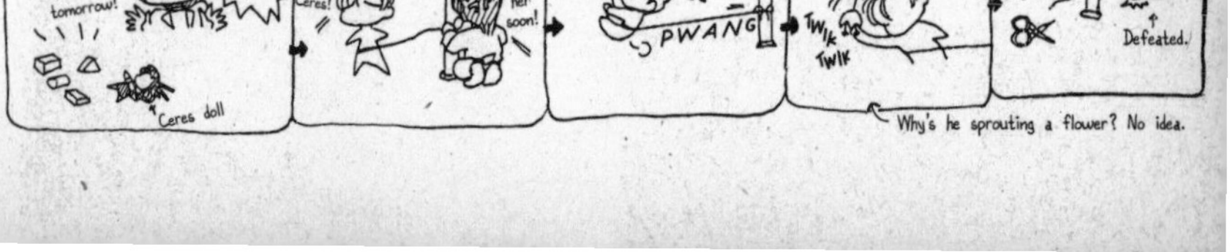

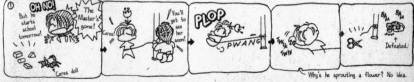

①
OH NO!
But he starts school tomorrow!
The Master's gone!
Ceres doll
Ceres!
You'll get to see her soon!
PLOP
PWANG
TWIK TWIK
BA BA
Defeated.

Why's he sprouting a flower? No idea.

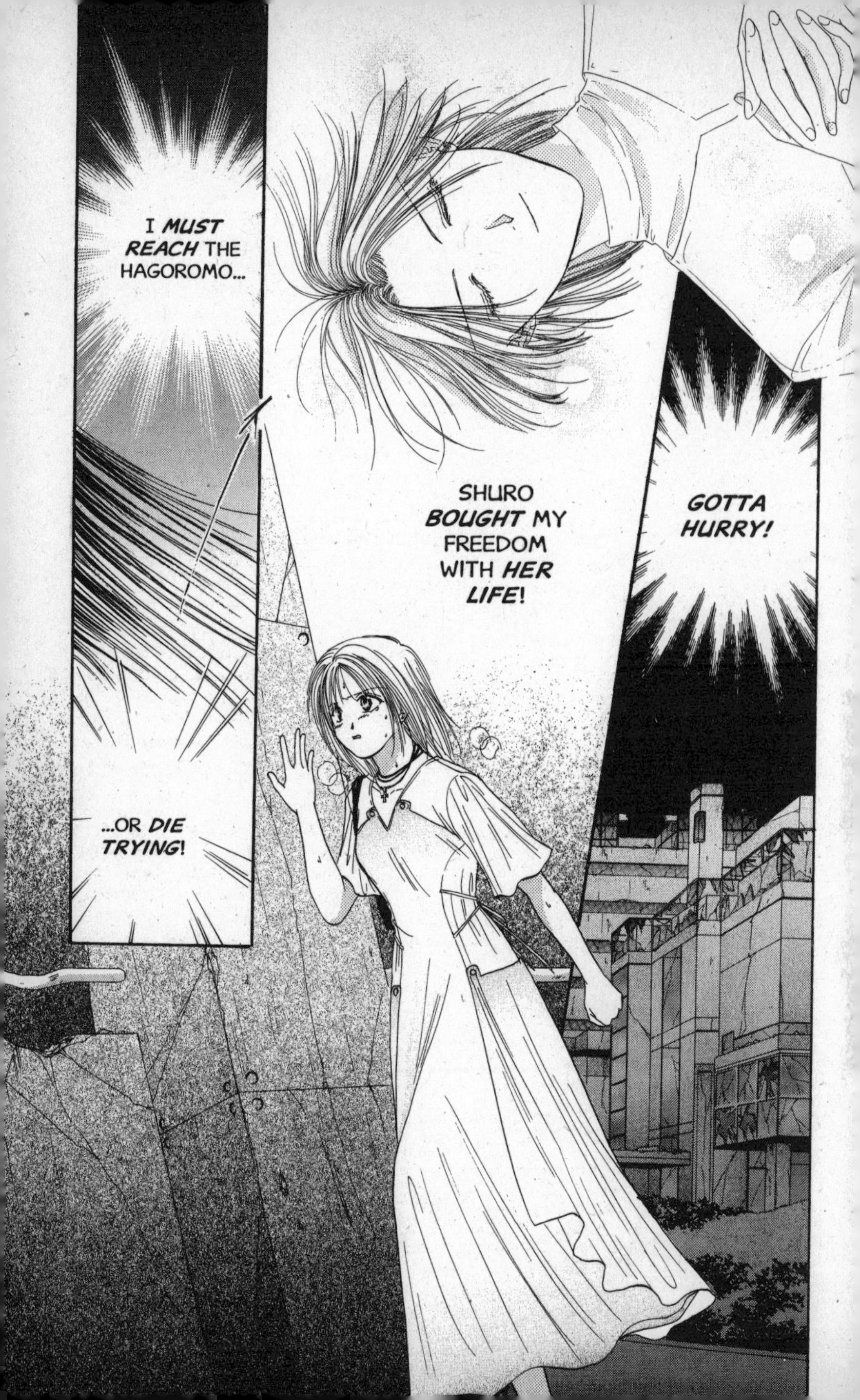
GOTTA HURRY!
SHURO BOUGHT MY FREEDOM WITH HER LIFE!
I MUST REACH THE HAGOROMO...
...OR DIE TRYING!

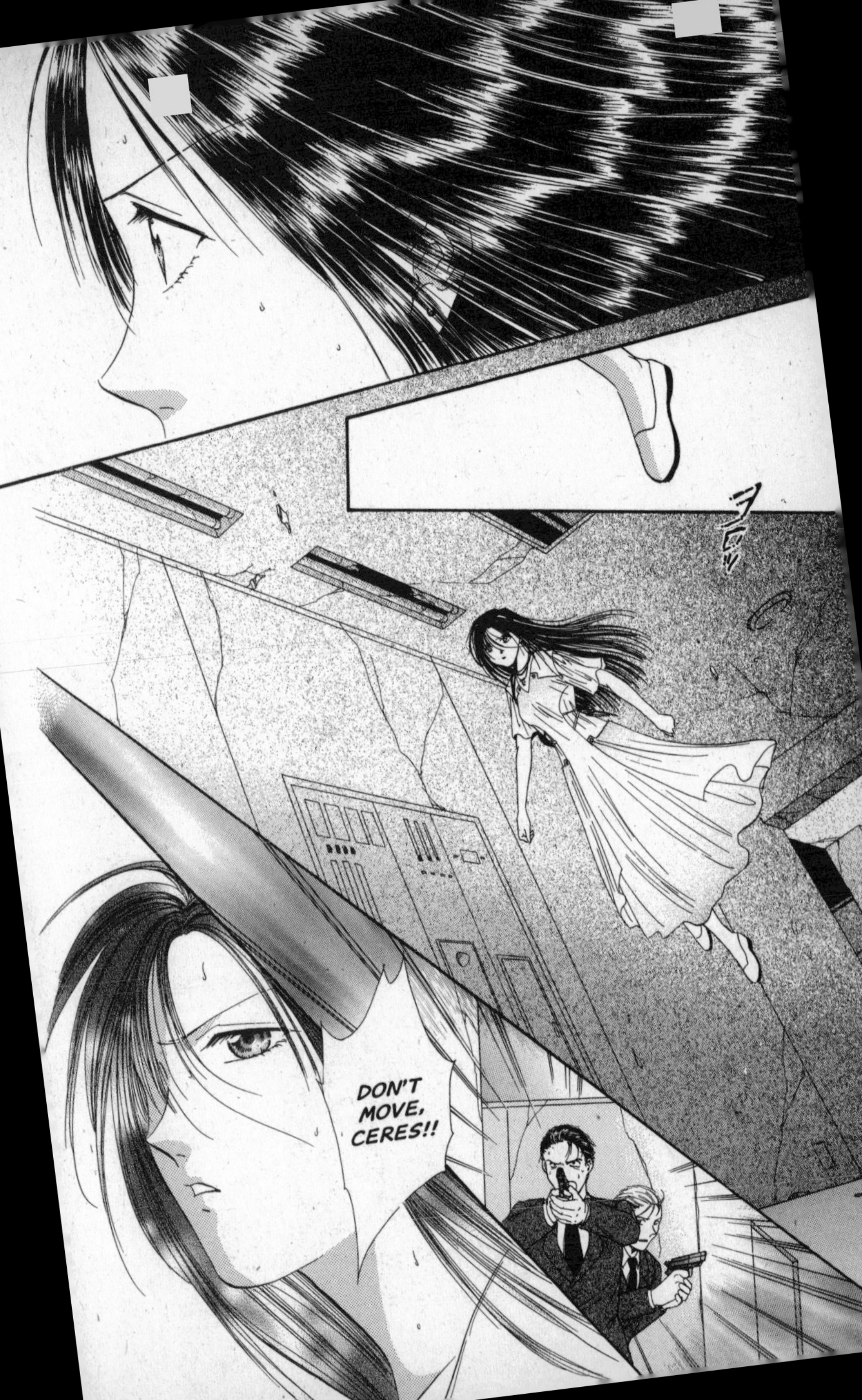
DON'T MOVE, CERES!!

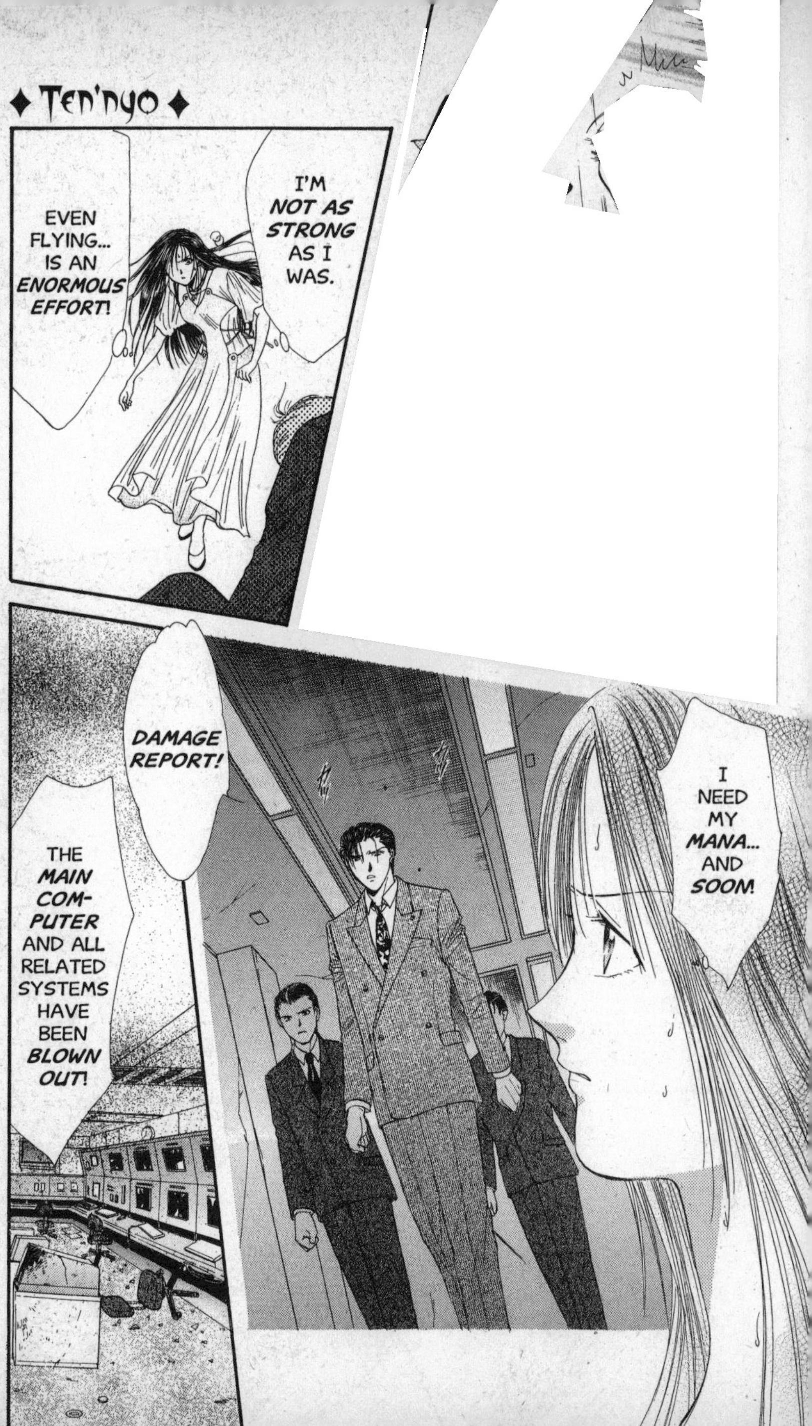
I'M NOT AS STRONG AS I WAS.
EVEN FLYING... IS AN ENORMOUS EFFORT!
I NEED MY MANA... AND SOON!
DAMAGE REPORT!
THE MAIN COMPUTER AND ALL RELATED SYSTEMS HAVE BEEN BLOWN OUT!

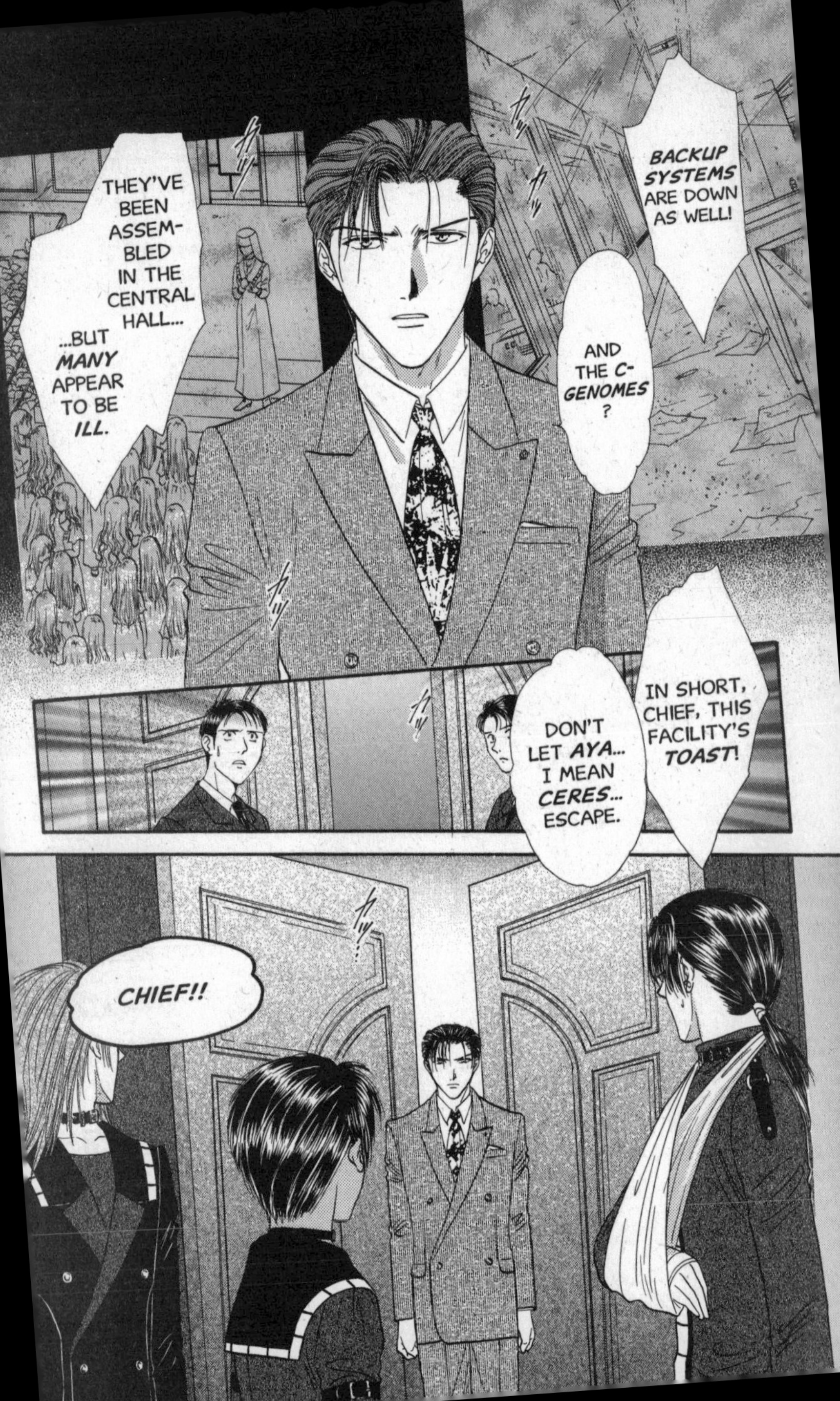
BACKUP SYSTEMS ARE DOWN AS WELL!
AND THE C-GENOMES?
THEY'VE BEEN ASSEMBLED IN THE CENTRAL HALL...
...BUT MANY APPEAR TO BE ILL.
IN SHORT, CHIEF, THIS FACILITY'S TOAST!
DON'T LET AYA... I MEAN CERES... ESCAPE.
CHIEF!!

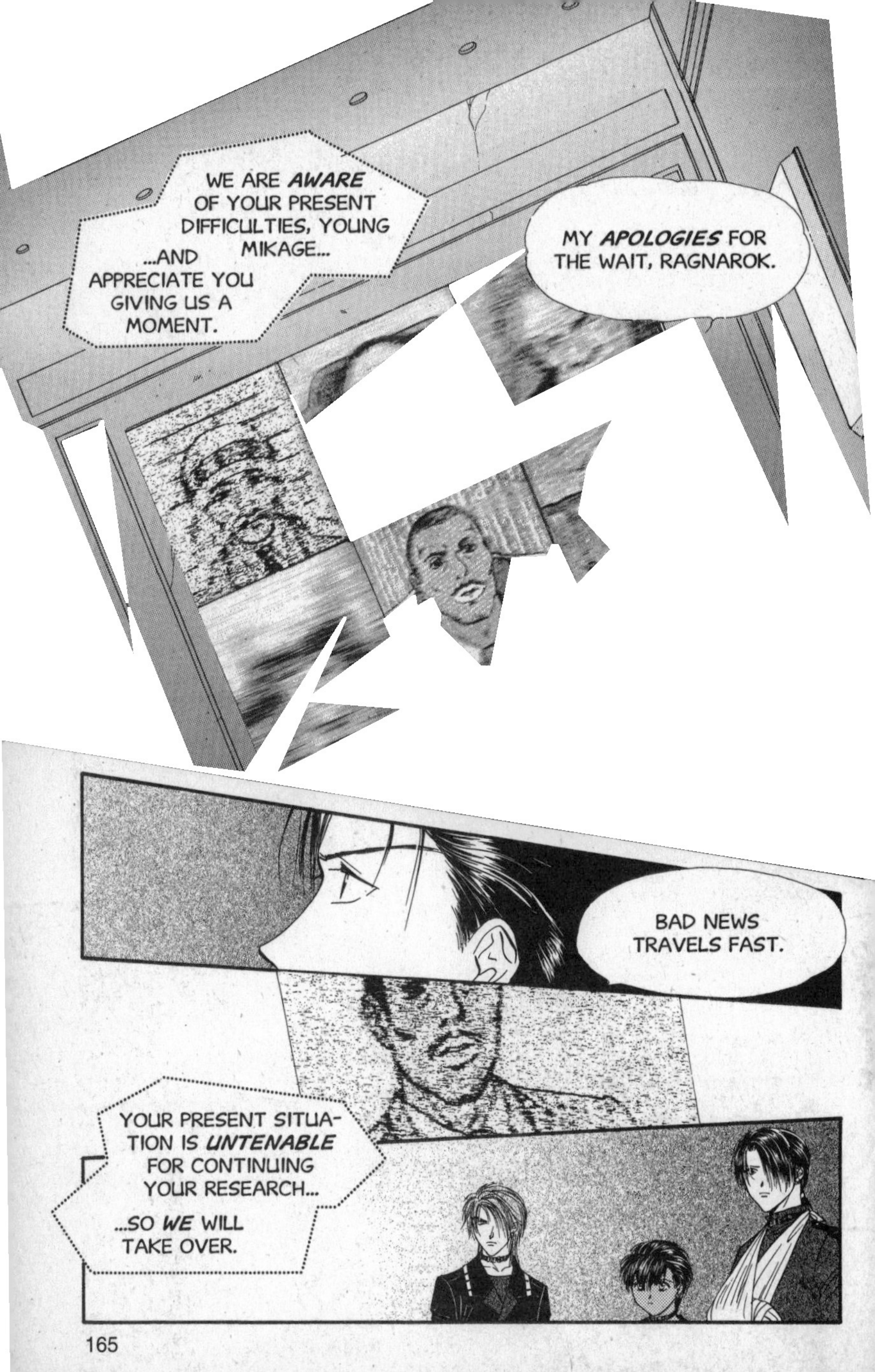
MY *APOLOGIES* FOR THE WAIT, RAGNAROK.
WE ARE *AWARE* OF YOUR PRESENT DIFFICULTIES, YOUNG MIKAGE...
...AND APPRECIATE YOU GIVING US A MOMENT.
BAD NEWS TRAVELS FAST.
YOUR PRESENT SITUATION IS *UNTENABLE* FOR CONTINUING YOUR RESEARCH...
...SO *WE* WILL TAKE OVER.

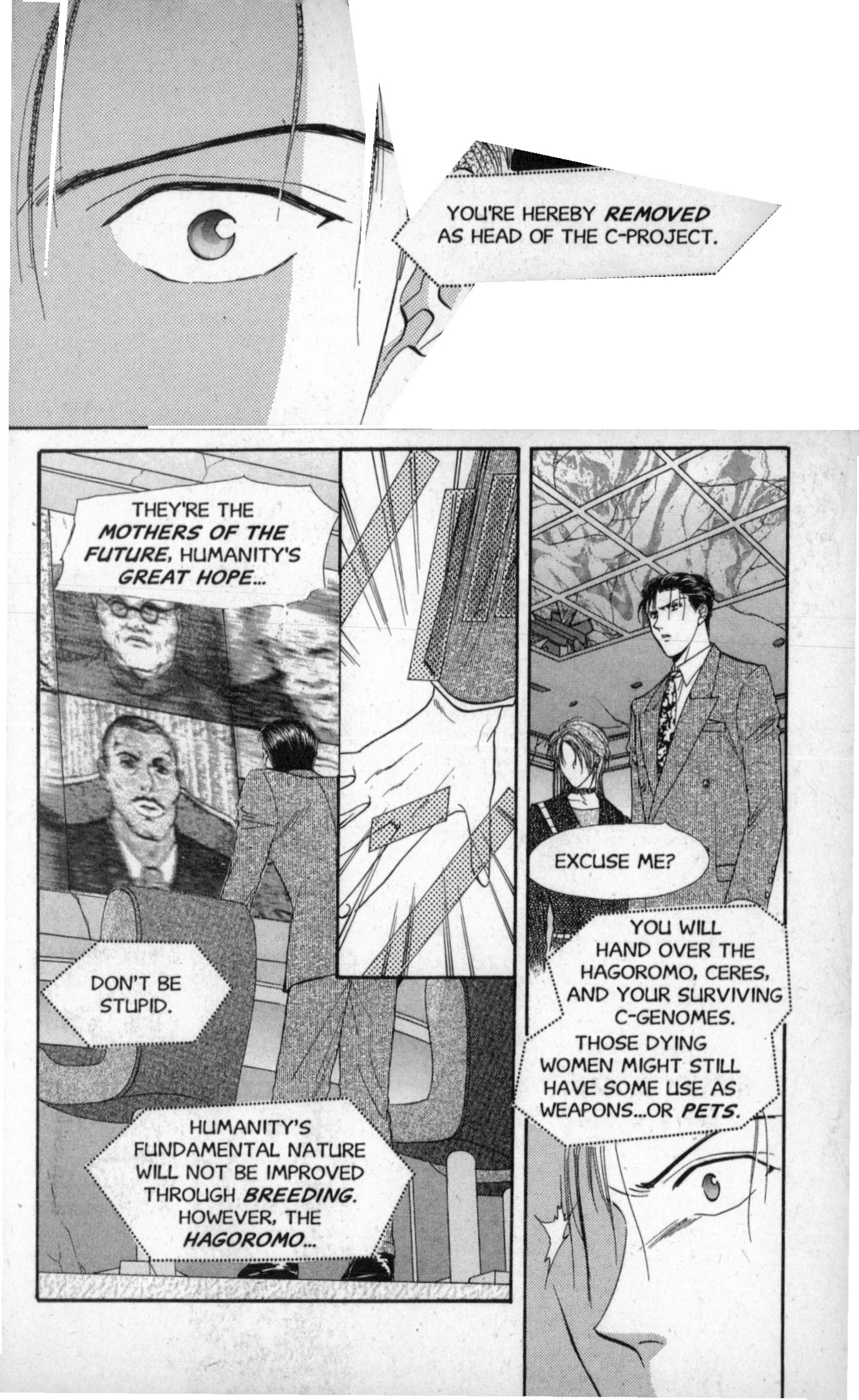

YOU'RE HEREBY *REMOVED* AS HEAD OF THE C-PROJECT.
EXCUSE ME?
YOU WILL HAND OVER THE HAGOROMO, CERES, AND YOUR SURVIVING C-GENOMES.
THOSE DYING WOMEN MIGHT STILL HAVE SOME USE AS WEAPONS...OR *PETS*.
THEY'RE THE *MOTHERS OF THE FUTURE*, HUMANITY'S *GREAT HOPE*...
DON'T BE STUPID.
HUMANITY'S FUNDAMENTAL NATURE WILL NOT BE IMPROVED THROUGH *BREEDING*. HOWEVER, THE *HAGOROMO*...

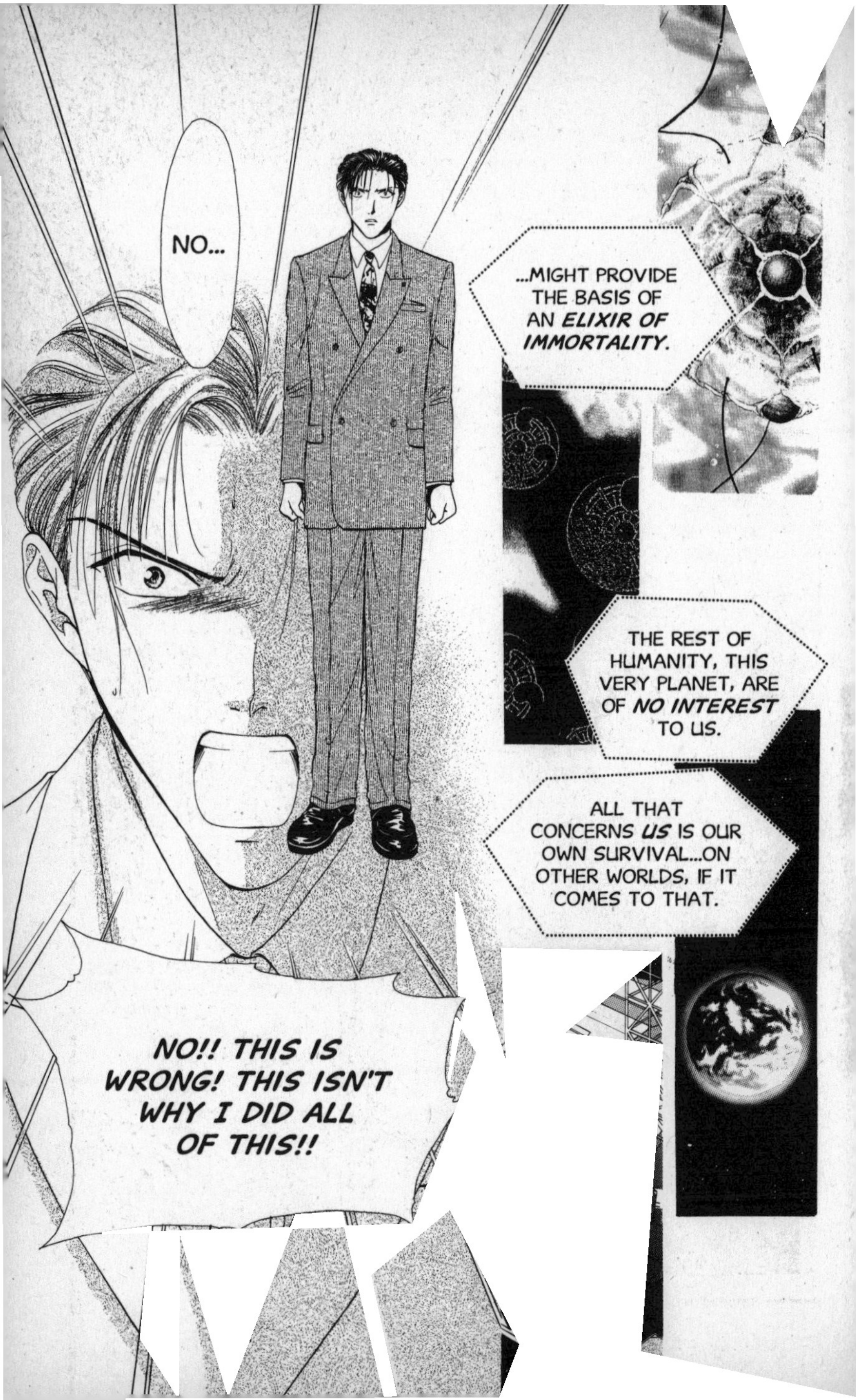
...MIGHT PROVIDE THE BASIS OF AN ELIXIR OF IMMORTALITY.
THE REST OF HUMANITY, THIS VERY PLANET, ARE OF NO INTEREST TO US.
ALL THAT CONCERNS US IS OUR OWN SURVIVAL...ON OTHER WORLDS, IF IT COMES TO THAT.
NO...
NO!! THIS IS WRONG! THIS ISN'T WHY I DID ALL OF THIS!!

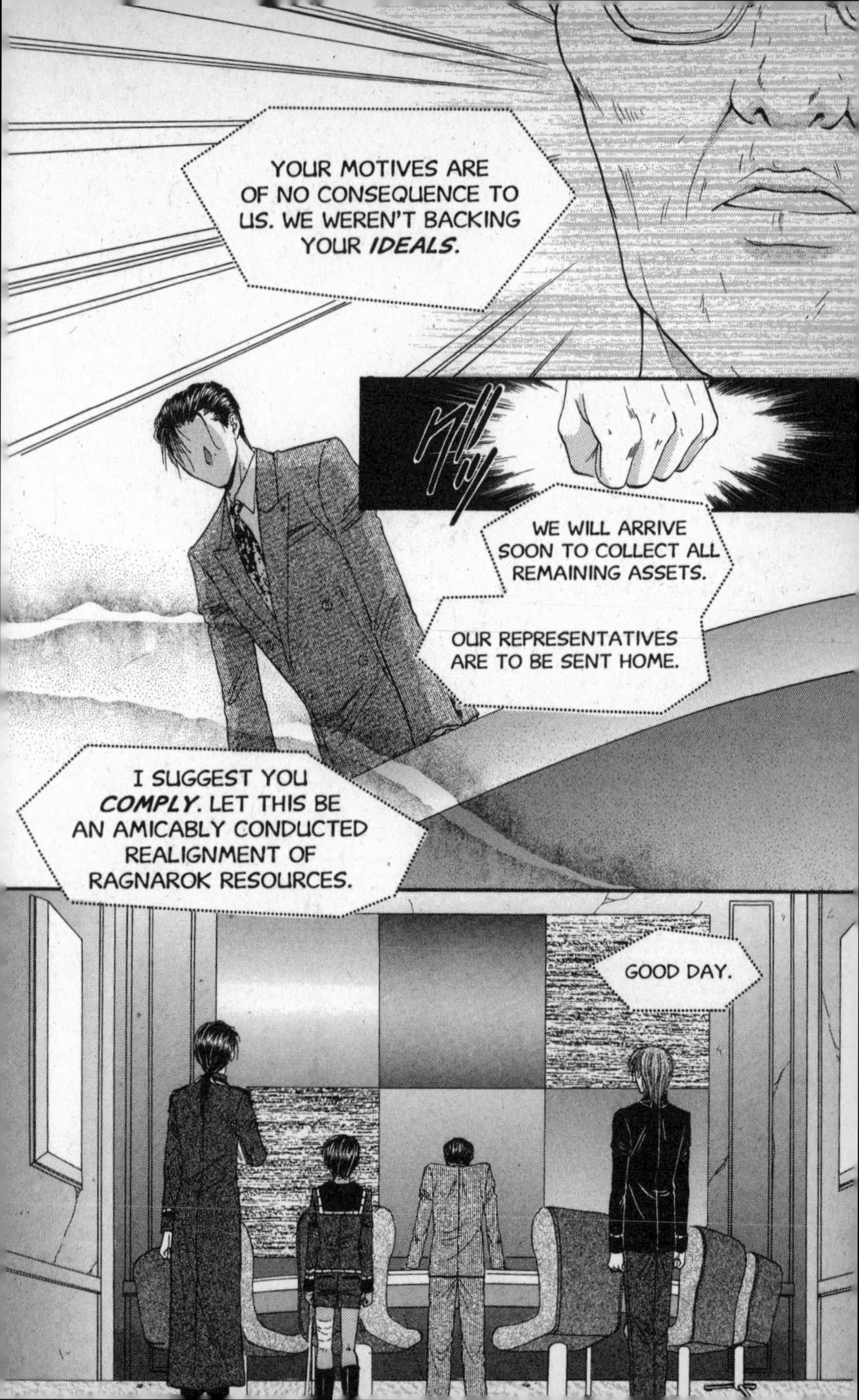
YOUR MOTIVES ARE OF NO CONSEQUENCE TO US. WE WEREN'T BACKING YOUR *IDEALS*.
WE WILL ARRIVE SOON TO COLLECT ALL REMAINING ASSETS.
OUR REPRESENTATIVES ARE TO BE SENT HOME.
I SUGGEST YOU *COMPLY*. LET THIS BE AN AMICABLY CONDUCTED REALIGNMENT OF RAGNAROK RESOURCES.
GOOD DAY.

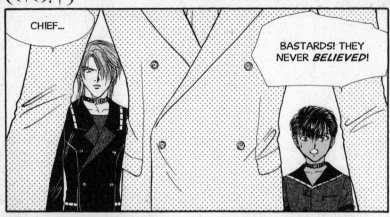

BASTARDS! THEY NEVER BELIEVED!
CHIEF...
I WAS ALWAYS AWARE...
...OF THEIR VIEWS, BUT I NEEDED THEIR MONEY AND INFLUENCE TO MAKE THINGS HAPPEN.
WITH ENOUGH WORK, ENOUGH SACRIFICE...
...I THOUGHT I COULD SECURE OUR POSITION. WISHFUL THINKING, I SUPPOSE...
CHIEF, YOU...
YOU CAN'T GIVE UP!!

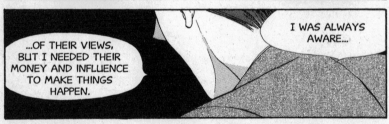

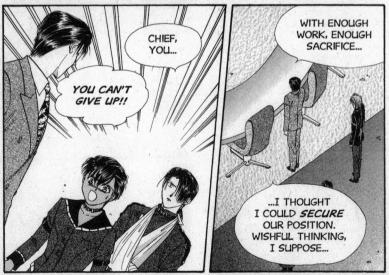

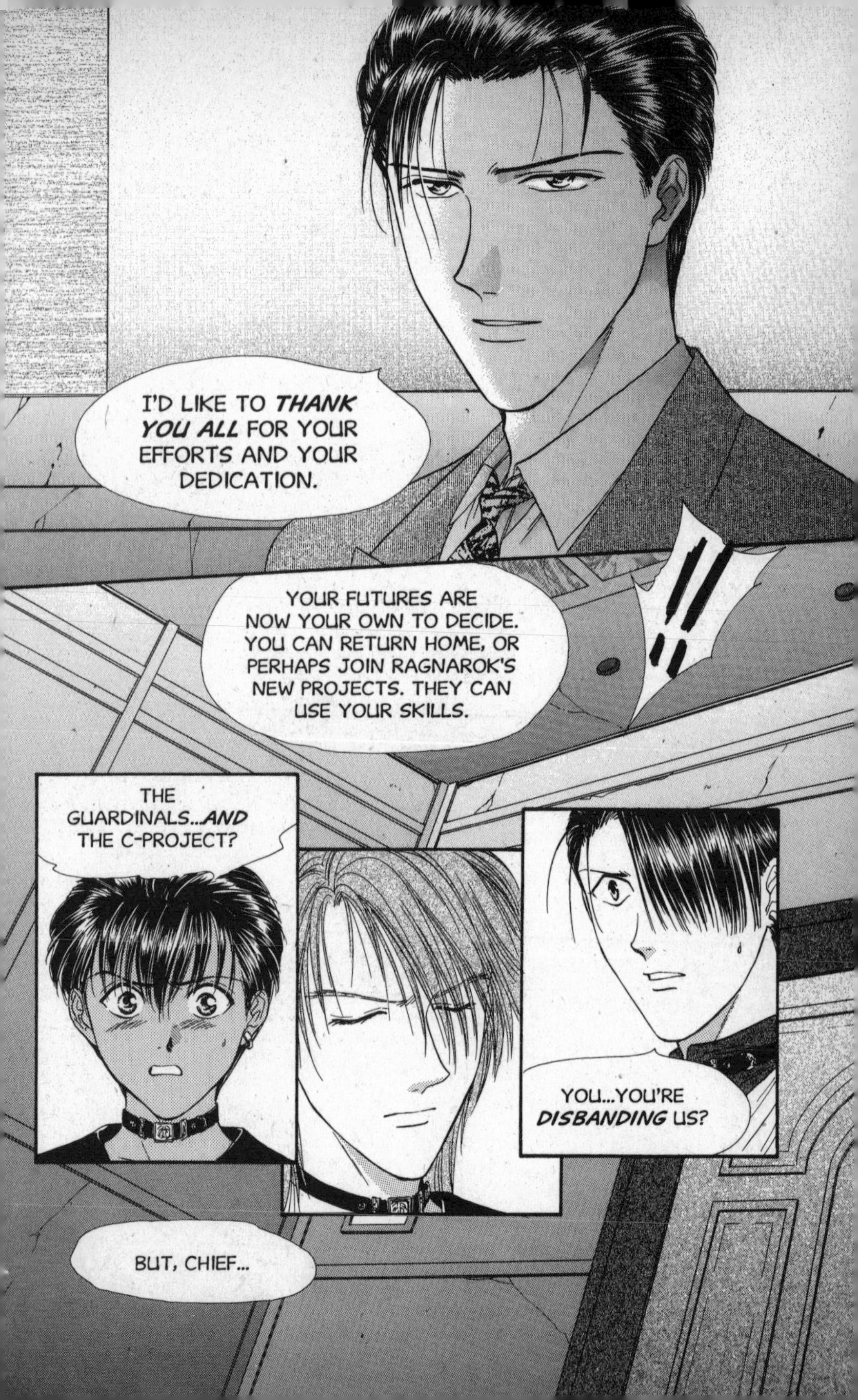
I'D LIKE TO THANK YOU ALL FOR YOUR EFFORTS AND YOUR DEDICATION.
YOUR FUTURES ARE NOW YOUR OWN TO DECIDE. YOU CAN RETURN HOME, OR PERHAPS JOIN RAGNAROK'S NEW PROJECTS. THEY CAN USE YOUR SKILLS.
YOU...YOU'RE DISBANDING US?
THE GUARDINALS...AND THE C-PROJECT?
BUT, CHIEF...

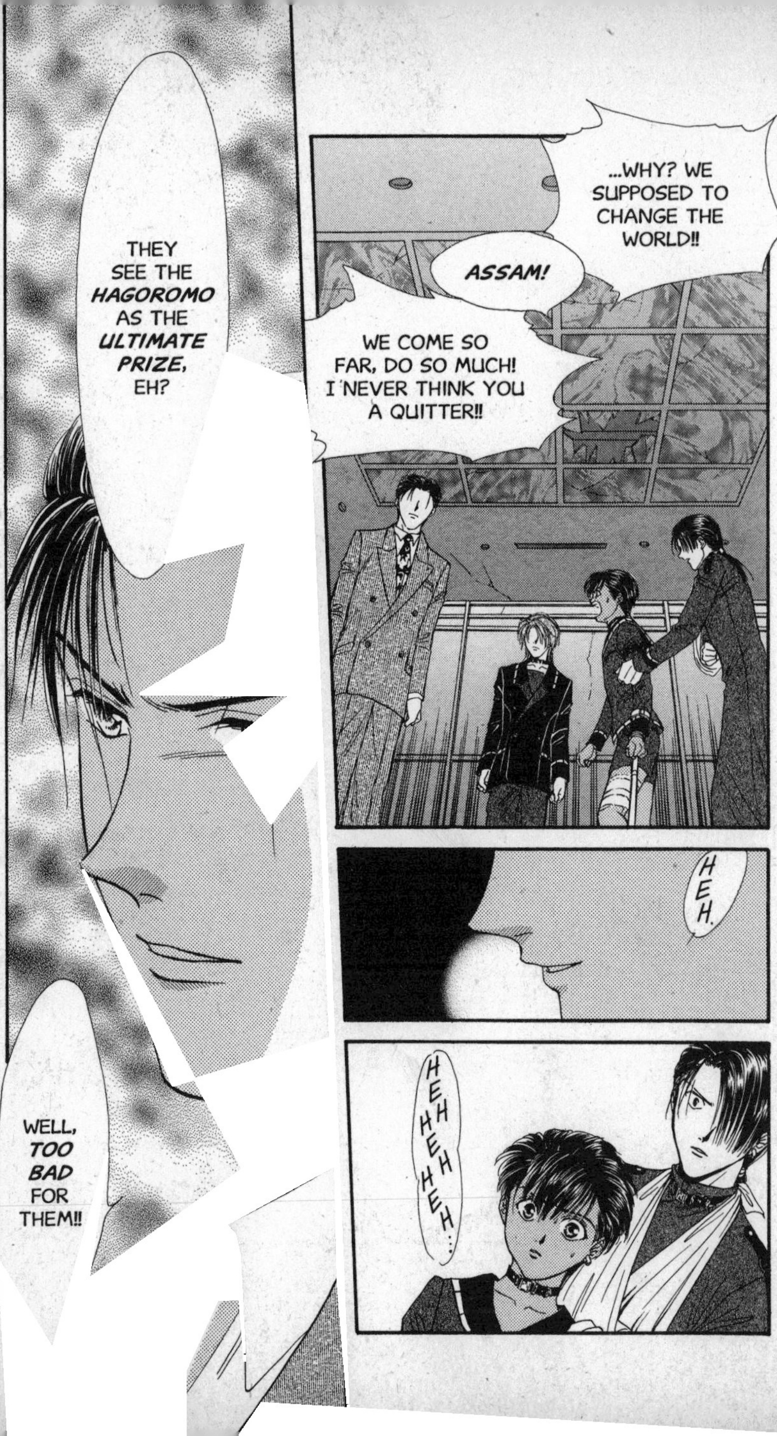
...WHY? WE SUPPOSED TO CHANGE THE WORLD!!
ASSAM!
WE COME SO FAR, DO SO MUCH! I NEVER THINK YOU A QUITTER!!
HEH HEH.
HEH HEH HEH HEH...
THEY SEE THE HAGOROMO AS THE ULTIMATE PRIZE, EH?
WELL, TOO BAD FOR THEM!!

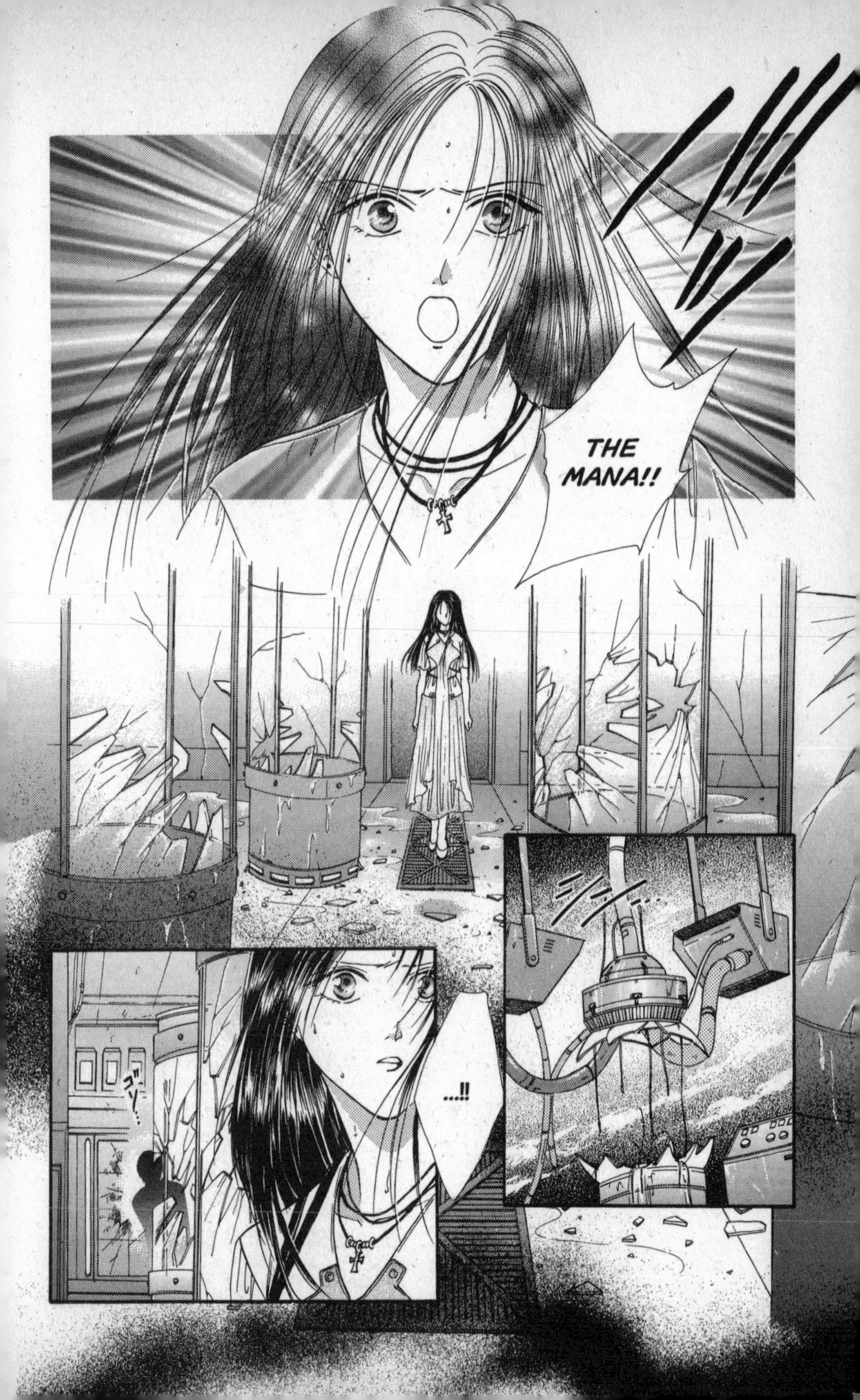
THE MANA!!
...!!

Now, then...lately, the graphic novels have been filled up by the main story, with no room left for bonus material. I know, people have missed the art pages a lot. I don't know the details yet, but...**there's going to be an artbook**. Of **Ceres**, of course. It'll go on sale next March...I think. I'll have more details in the next volume. Knowing me, I'll probably draw new art just for it. Also, the fifth **Fushigi Yugi** novel, "Seiran Legend," came out on December 1. It's Nakago's story, which is my favorite.♡ Tragedies are so dramatic. The next one will come out around next February...and then the series will finally end. **Ceres** will probably be novelized, too.

Also, the Flower Comics deluxe editions of **Prepubescent** will be coming out next spring (2000... wow!). The content is the same as the regular six-volume graphic novel edition, but it'll be packaged into three volumes...and the covers will no doubt feature new art by me. And the "Final Arc" will probably follow. That's a lot of titles coming up... But they're all only "tentative," so plans might change. Keep checking, and please buy them!

I guess that's enough to report right now. (What am I saying?) Ha ha ha... Sigh...we're running out of space...

See you in the next volume, everyone. Will it be a happy ending or not? Stay tuned!

Oh, and what kind of story would you like to see me draw next? Why do I even ask? Don't forget to check Shojo Comics for additional news on **Ceres**.

See you in March!!

Oct./'99

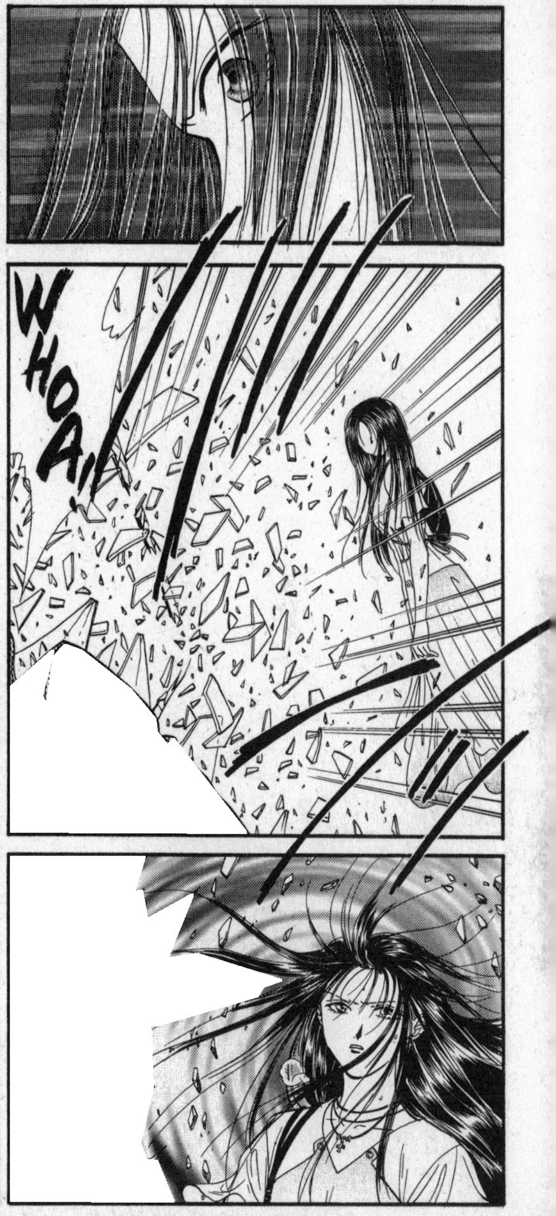
WHOA!!

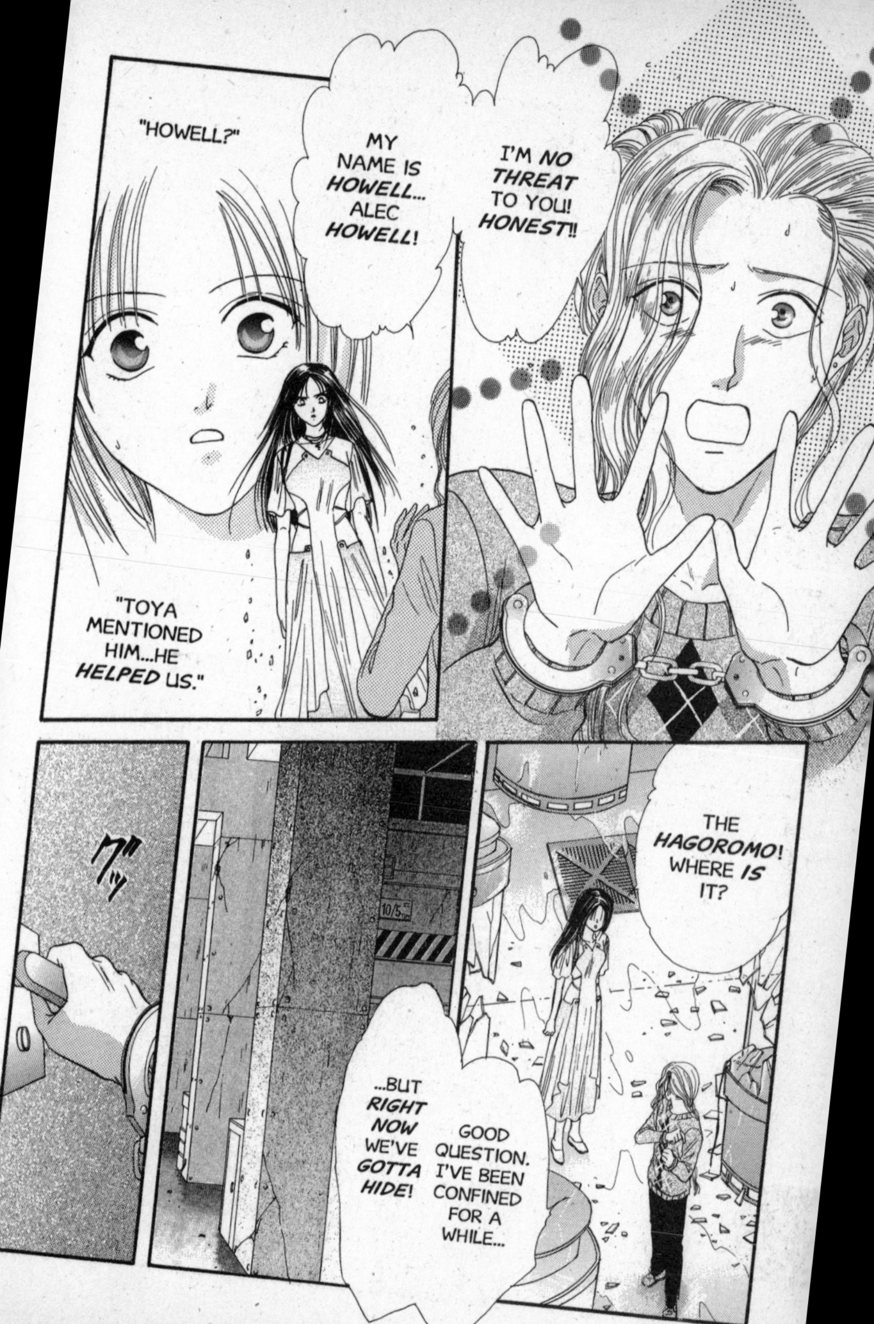
I'M NO THREAT TO YOU! HONEST!!
MY NAME IS HOWELL... ALEC HOWELL!
"HOWELL?"
"TOYA MENTIONED HIM...HE HELPED US."
THE HAGOROMO! WHERE IS IT?
GOOD QUESTION. I'VE BEEN CONFINED FOR A WHILE...
...BUT RIGHT NOW WE'VE GOTTA HIDE!
グッ

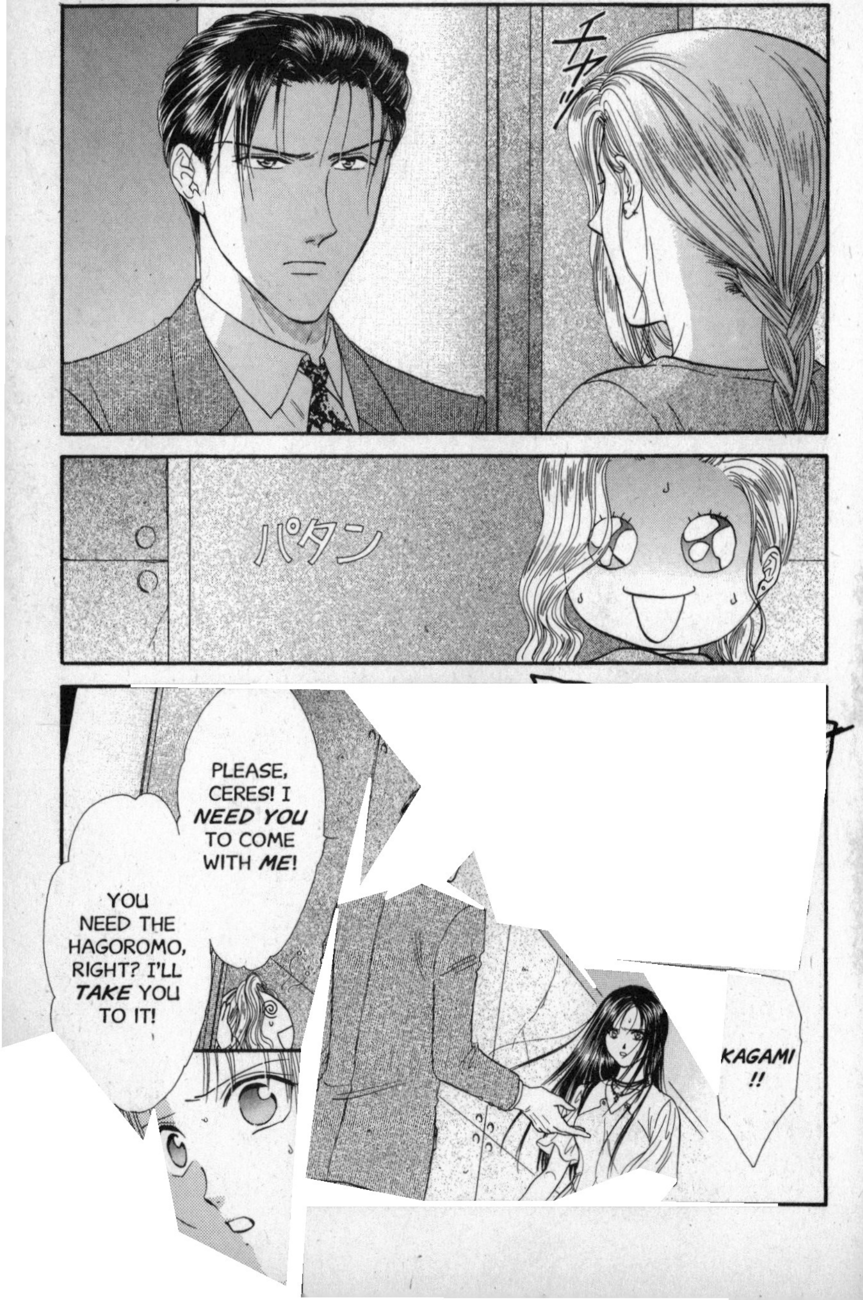
チラッ
パタン
KAGAMI !!
PLEASE, CERES! I *NEED YOU* TO COME WITH *ME*!
YOU NEED THE HAGOROMO, RIGHT? I'LL *TAKE* YOU TO IT!

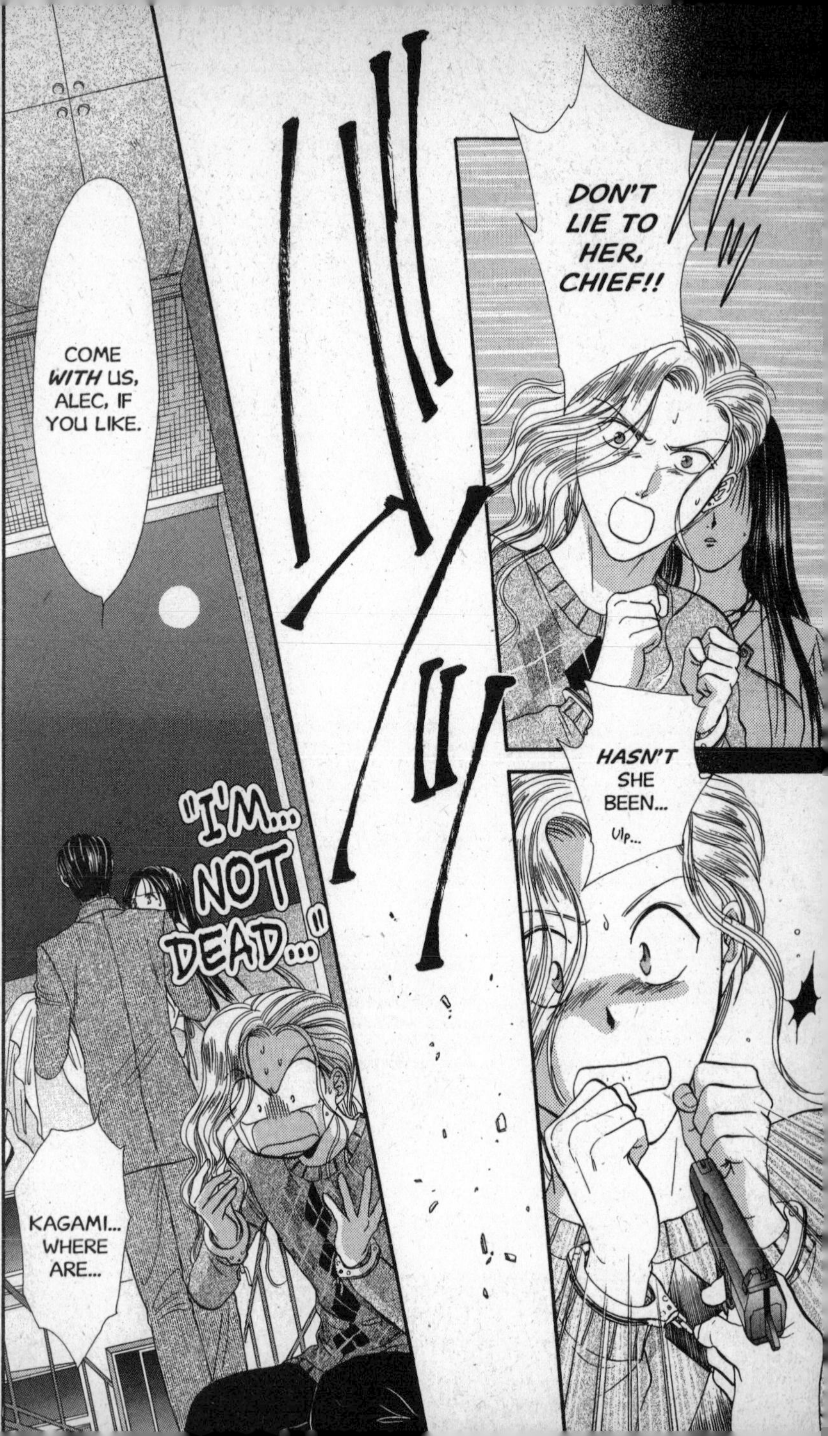
DON'T LIE TO HER, CHIEF!!
HASN'T SHE BEEN...
Ulp...
COME WITH US, ALEC, IF YOU LIKE.
"I'M... NOT DEAD..."
KAGAMI... WHERE ARE...

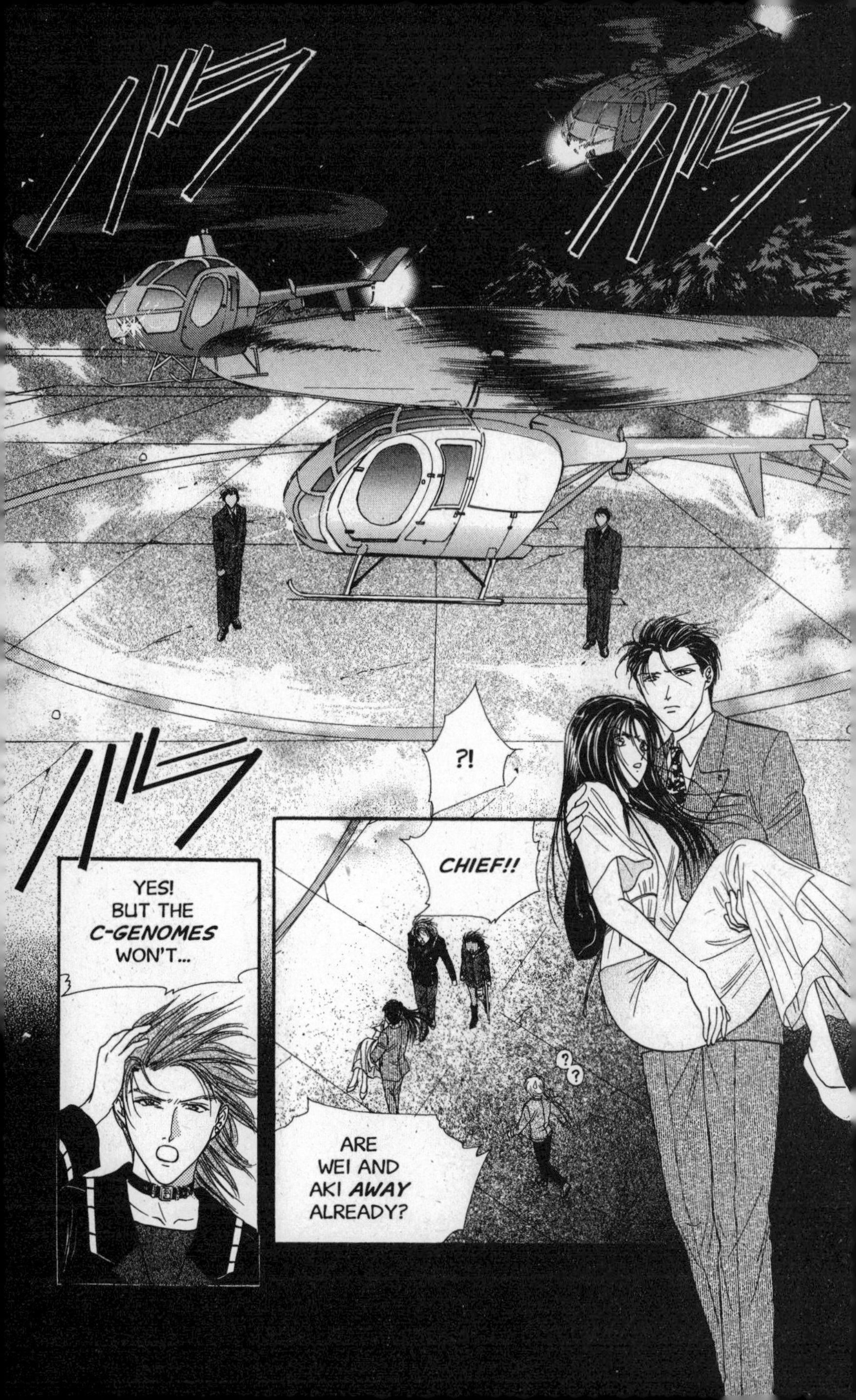
?!
CHIEF!!
ARE WEI AND AKI *AWAY* ALREADY?
??
YES! BUT THE *C-GENOMES* WON'T...

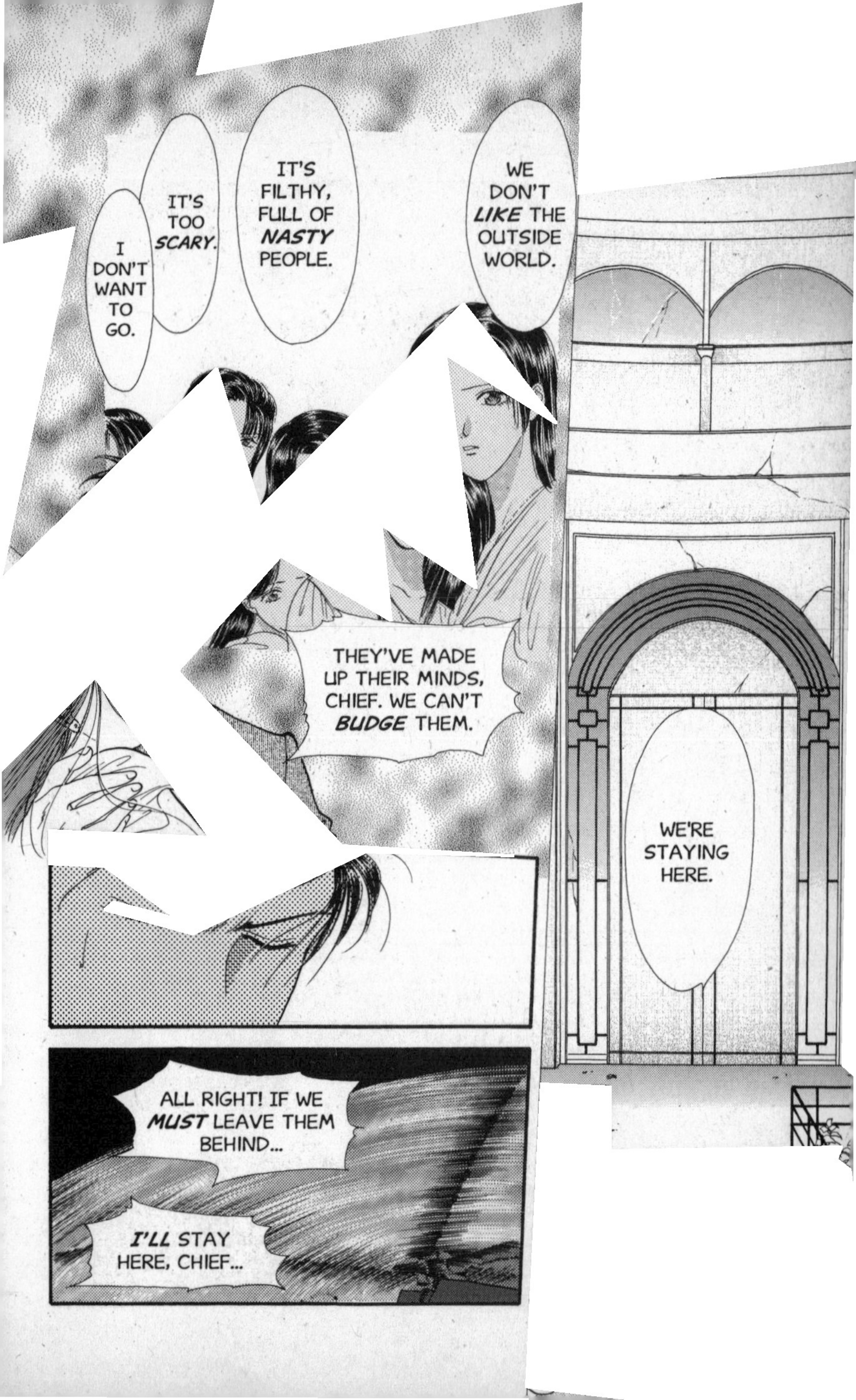
WE DON'T *LIKE* THE OUTSIDE WORLD.
IT'S FILTHY, FULL OF *NASTY* PEOPLE.
IT'S TOO *SCARY*.
I DON'T WANT TO GO.
WE'RE STAYING HERE.
THEY'VE MADE UP THEIR MINDS, CHIEF. WE CAN'T *BUDGE* THEM.
ALL RIGHT! IF WE *MUST* LEAVE THEM BEHIND...
I'LL STAY HERE, CHIEF...

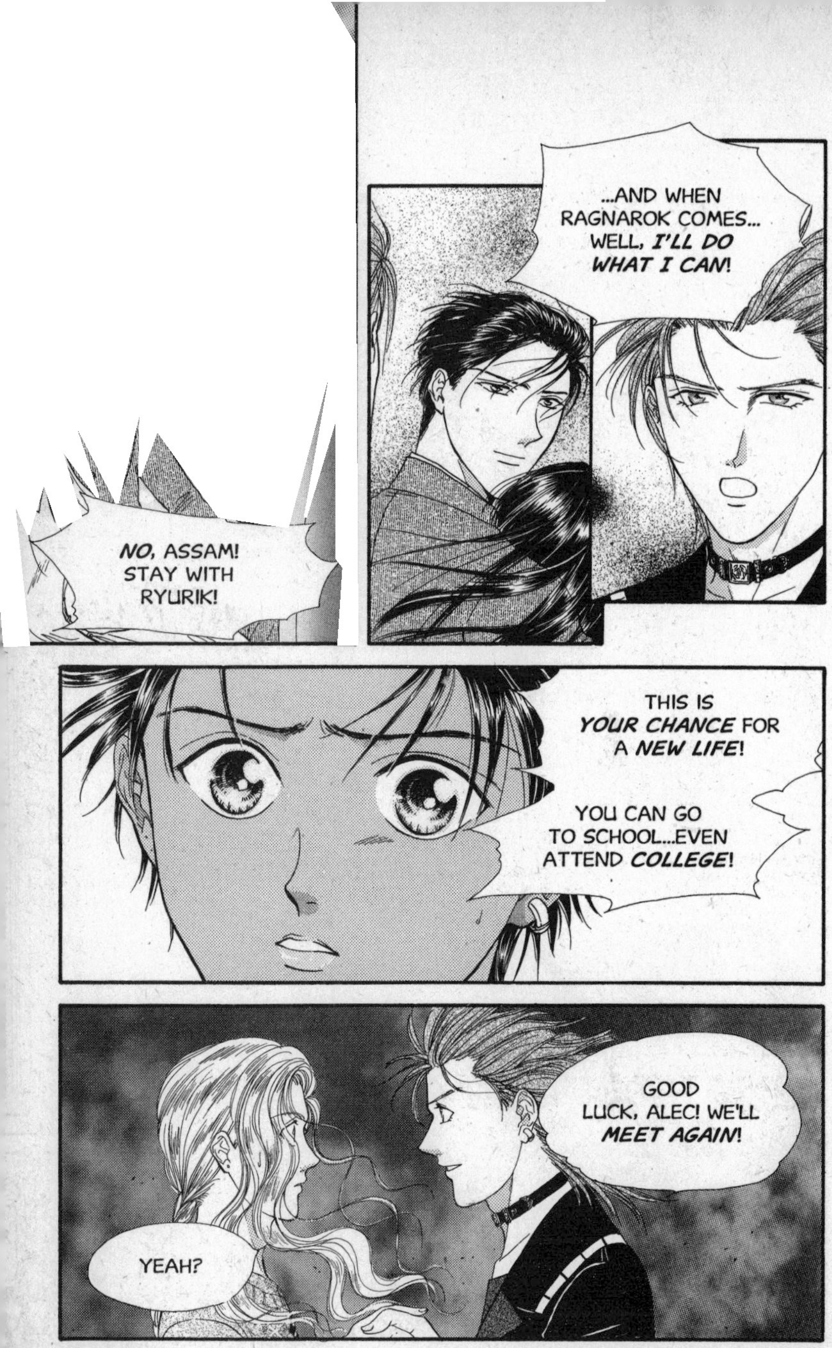
...AND WHEN RAGNAROK COMES... WELL, I'LL DO WHAT I CAN!
NO, ASSAM! STAY WITH RYURIK!
THIS IS YOUR CHANCE FOR A NEW LIFE!
YOU CAN GO TO SCHOOL...EVEN ATTEND COLLEGE!
GOOD LUCK, ALEC! WE'LL MEET AGAIN!
YEAH?

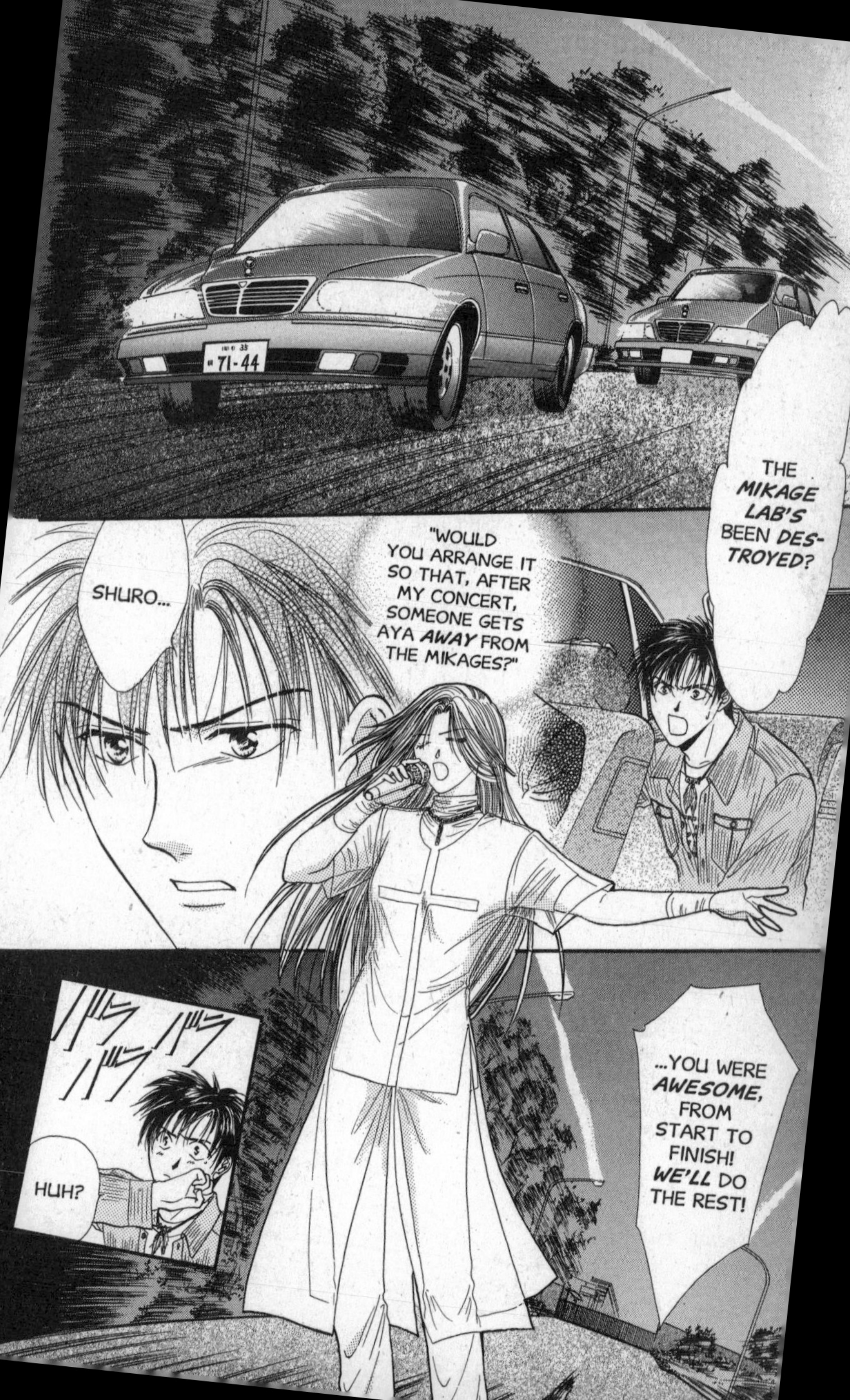
THE MIKAGE LAB'S BEEN DES-TROYED?
"WOULD YOU ARRANGE IT SO THAT, AFTER MY CONCERT, SOMEONE GETS AYA AWAY FROM THE MIKAGES?"
SHURO...
...YOU WERE AWESOME, FROM START TO FINISH! WE'LL DO THE REST!
HUH?

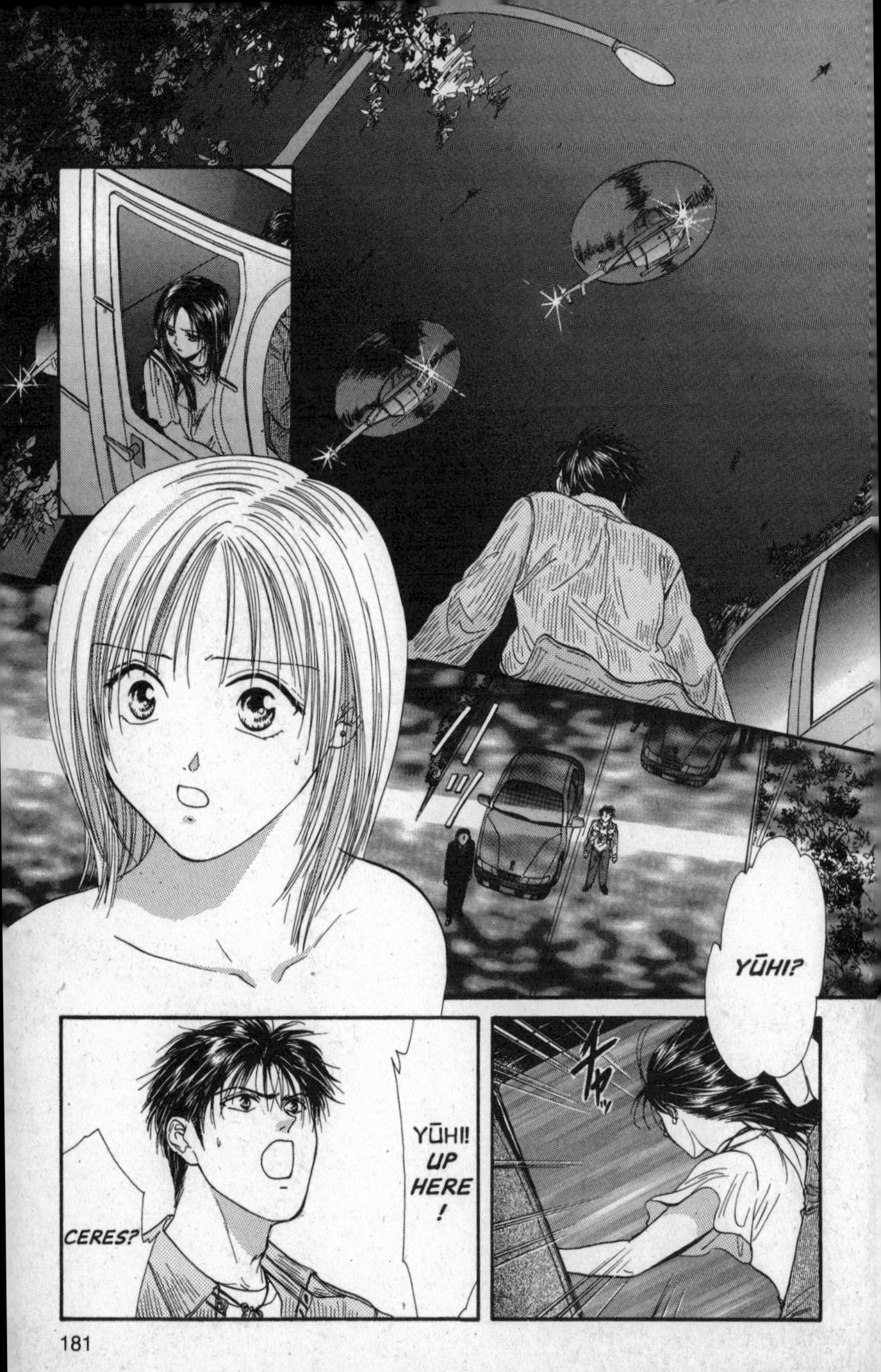
YŪHI?
YŪHI! UP HERE!
CERES?

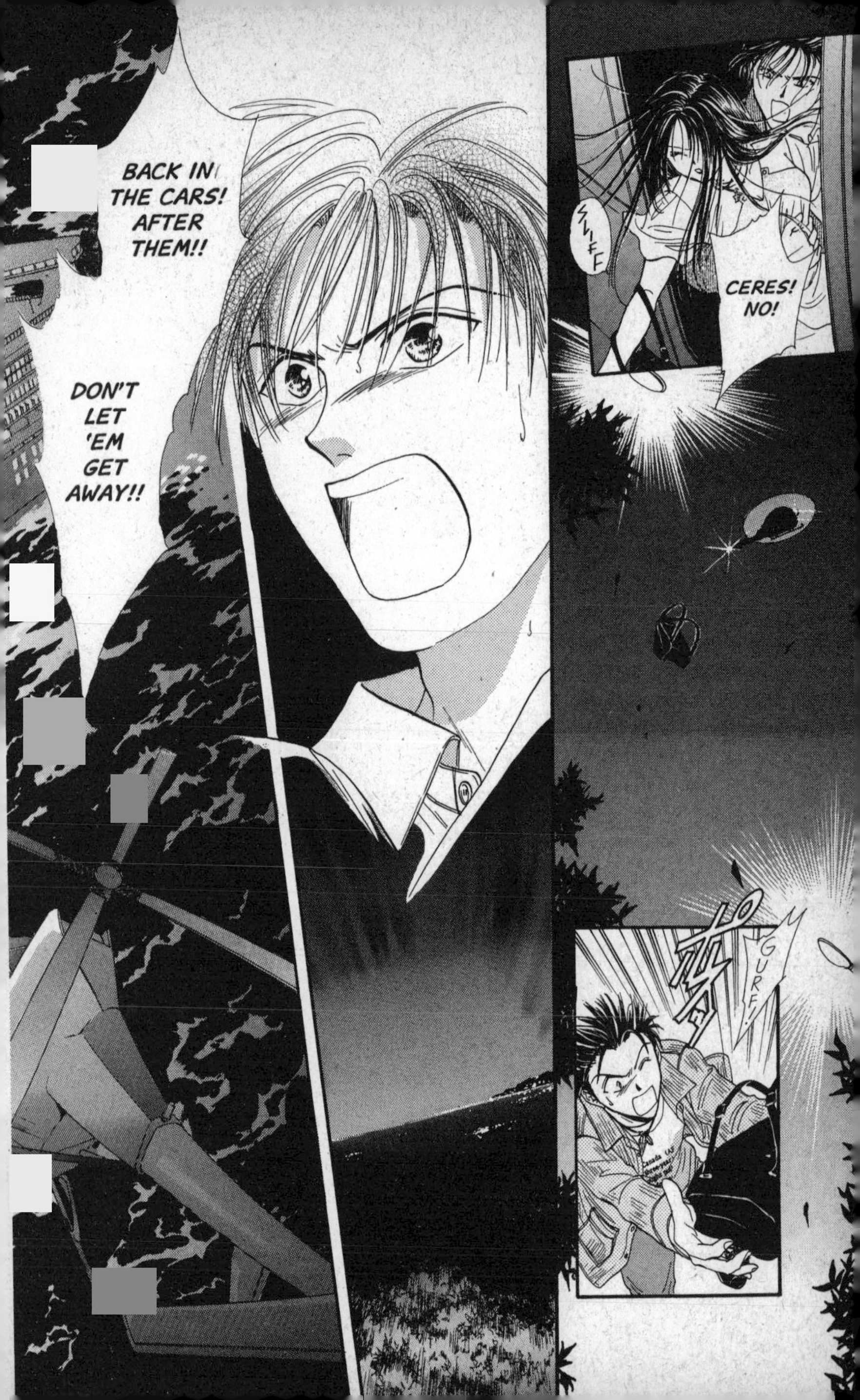
SHIFF
CERES! NO!
GURF!
BACK IN THE CARS! AFTER THEM!!
DON'T LET 'EM GET AWAY!!

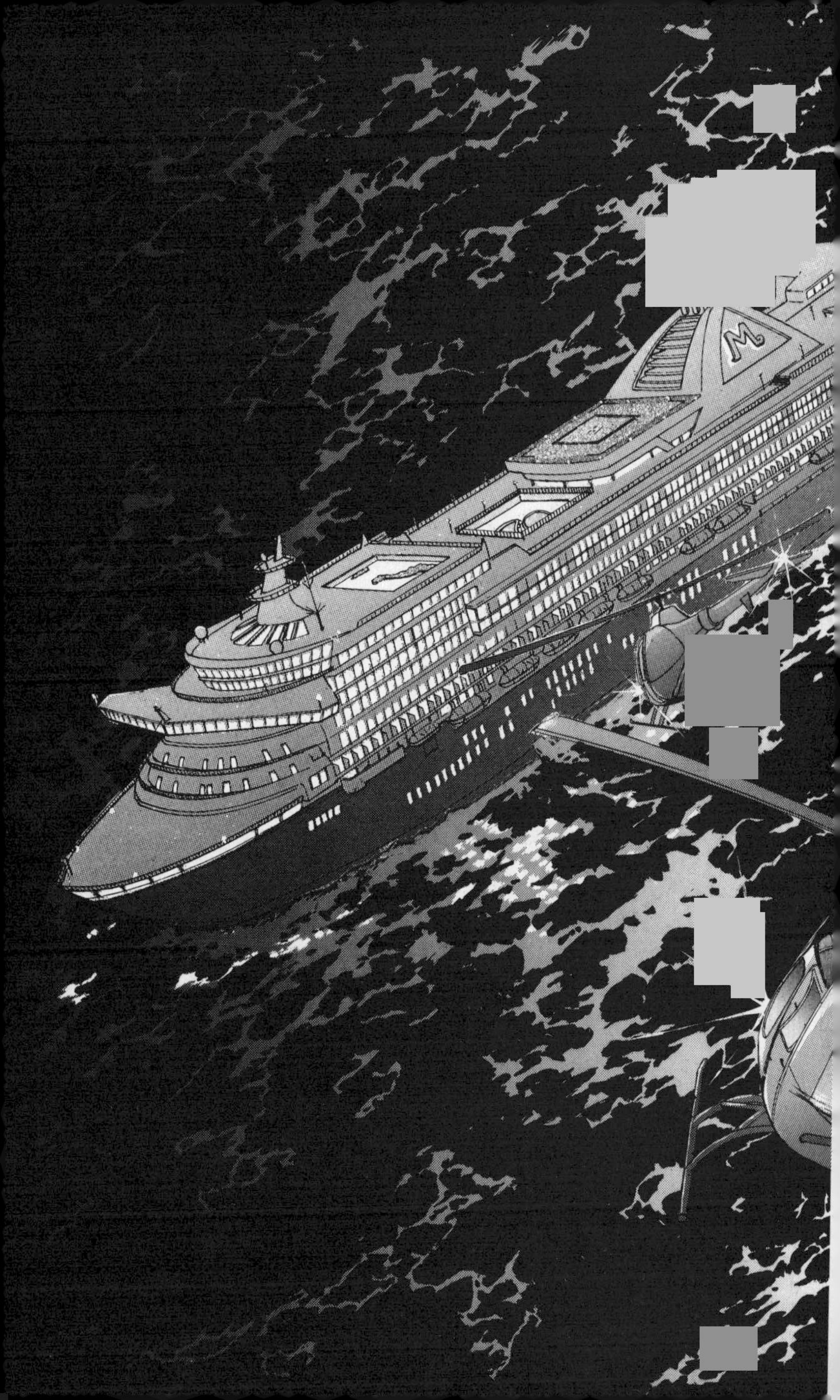

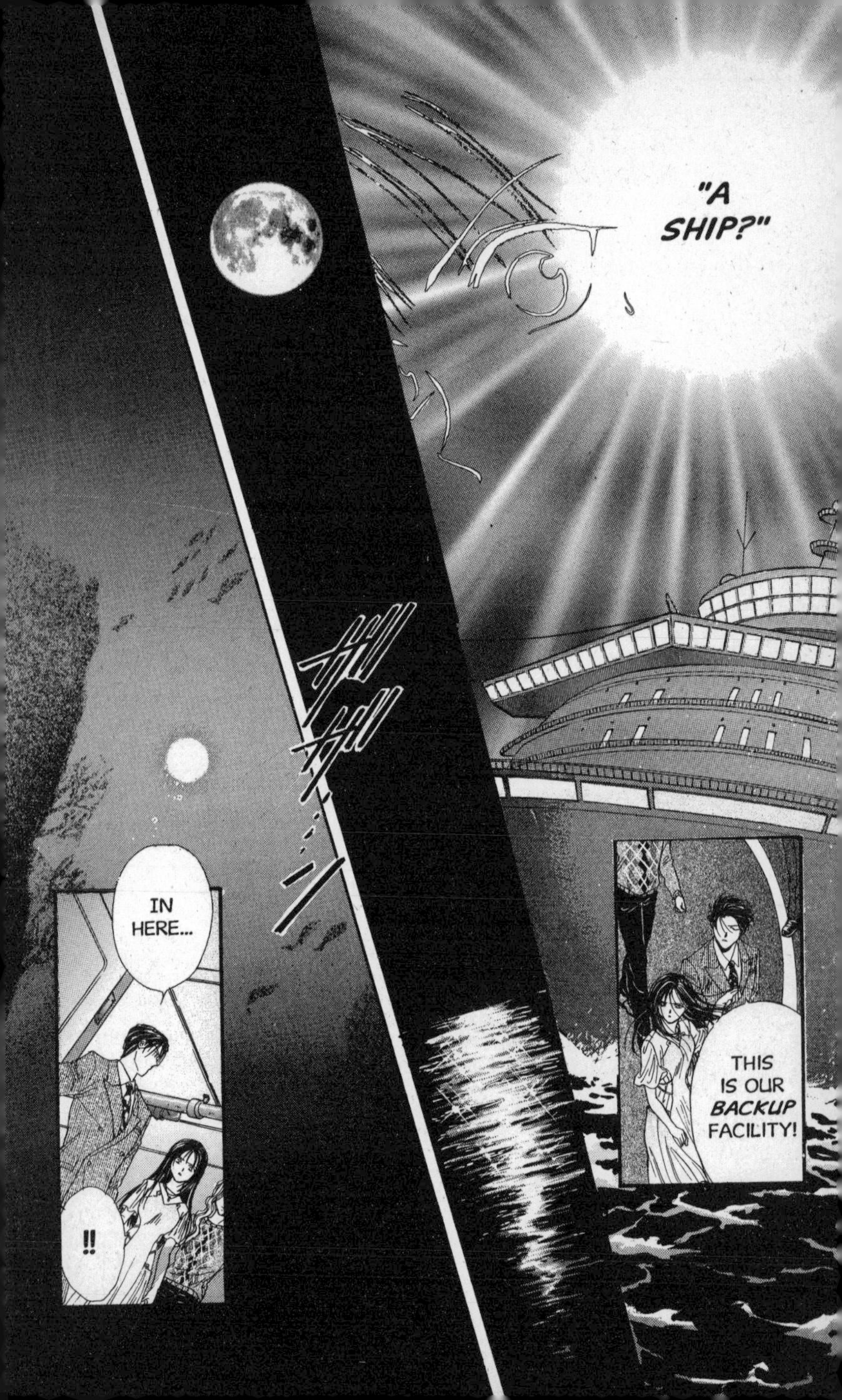
"A SHIP?"
THIS IS OUR *BACKUP* FACILITY!
IN HERE...
!!

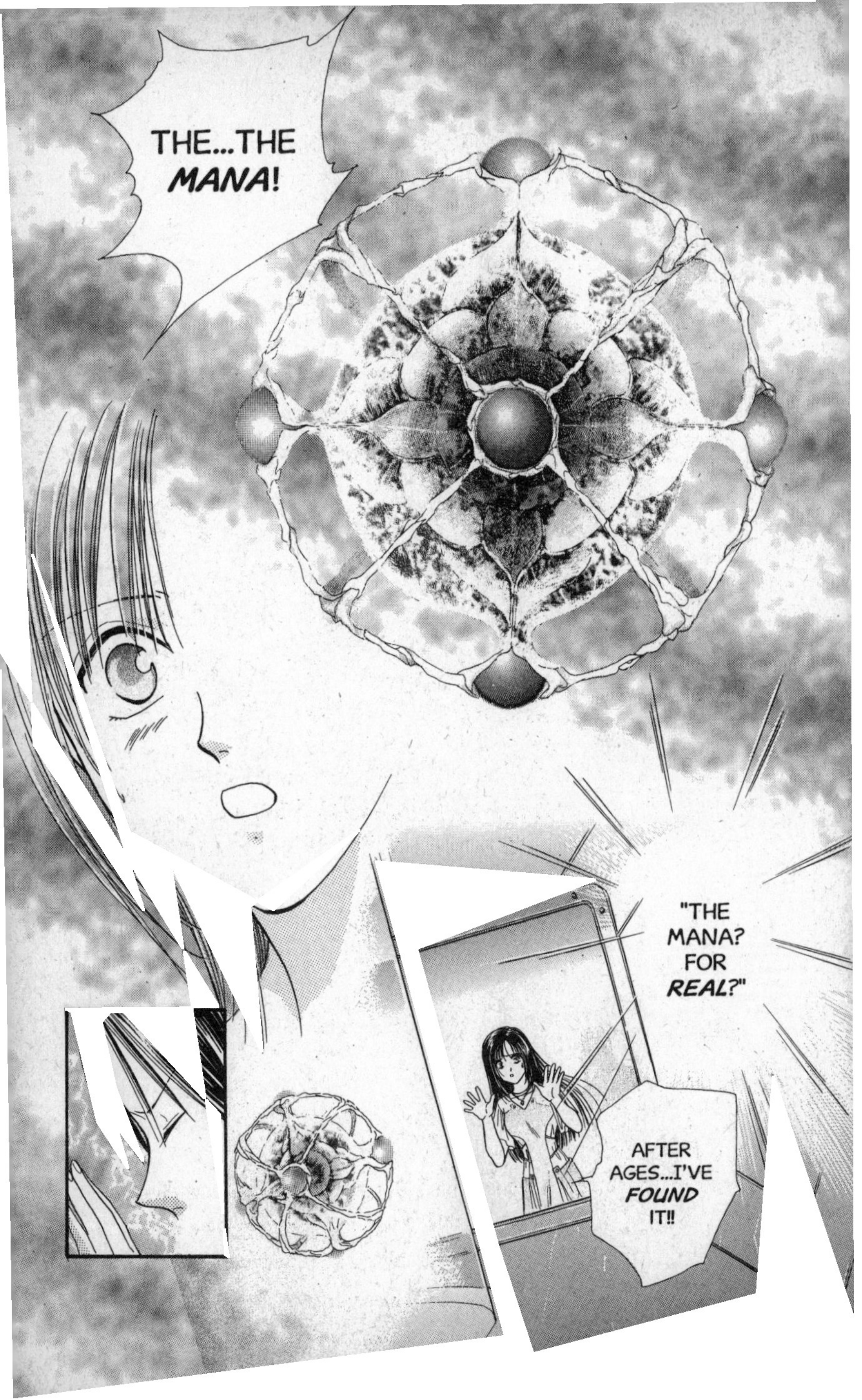
THE...THE *MANA*!
"THE MANA? FOR *REAL*?"
AFTER AGES...I'VE *FOUND* IT!!

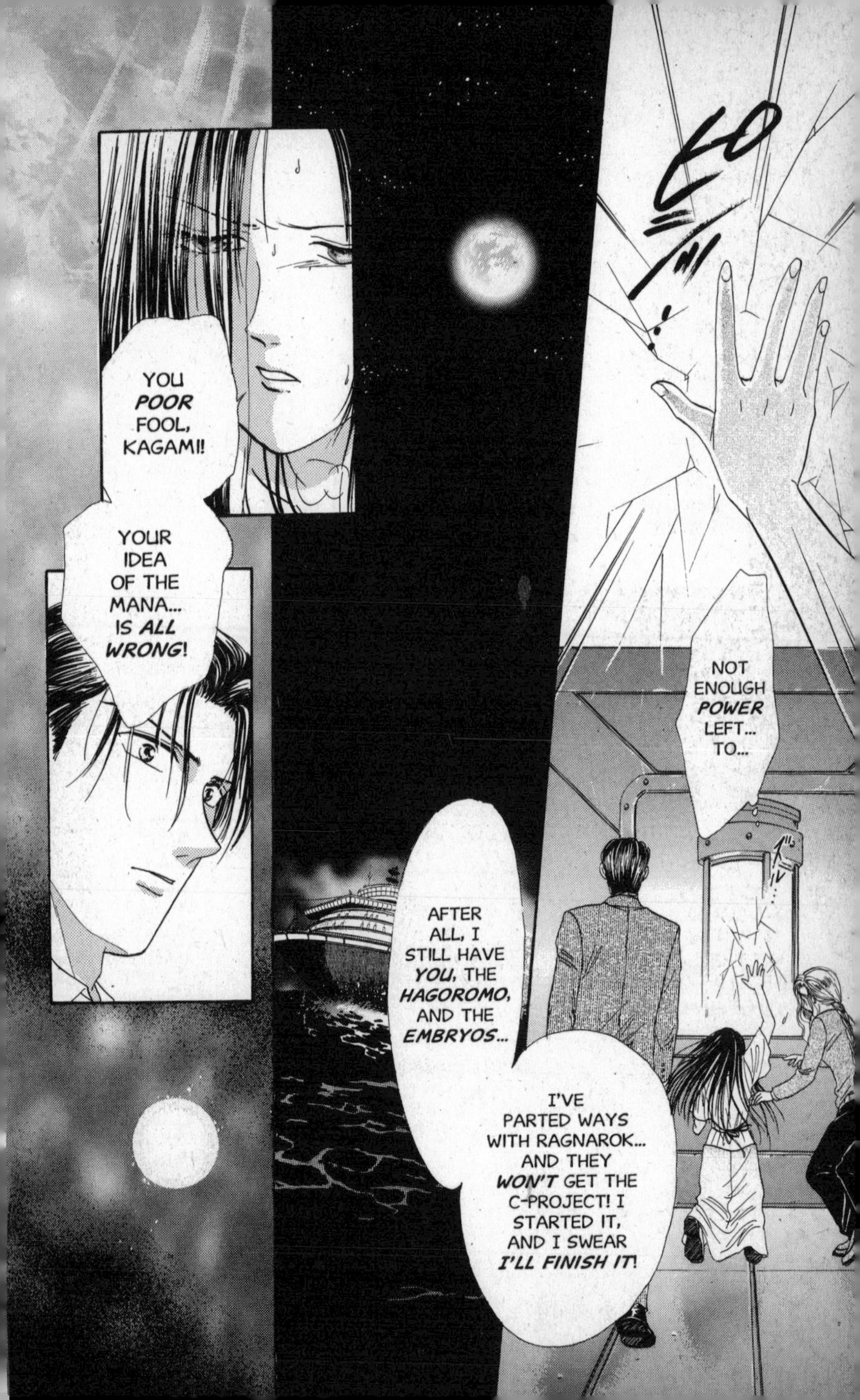
NOT ENOUGH POWER LEFT... TO...
YOU POOR FOOL, KAGAMI!
YOUR IDEA OF THE MANA... IS ALL WRONG!
AFTER ALL, I STILL HAVE YOU, THE HAGOROMO, AND THE EMBRYOS...
I'VE PARTED WAYS WITH RAGNAROK... AND THEY WON'T GET THE C-PROJECT! I STARTED IT, AND I SWEAR I'LL FINISH IT!

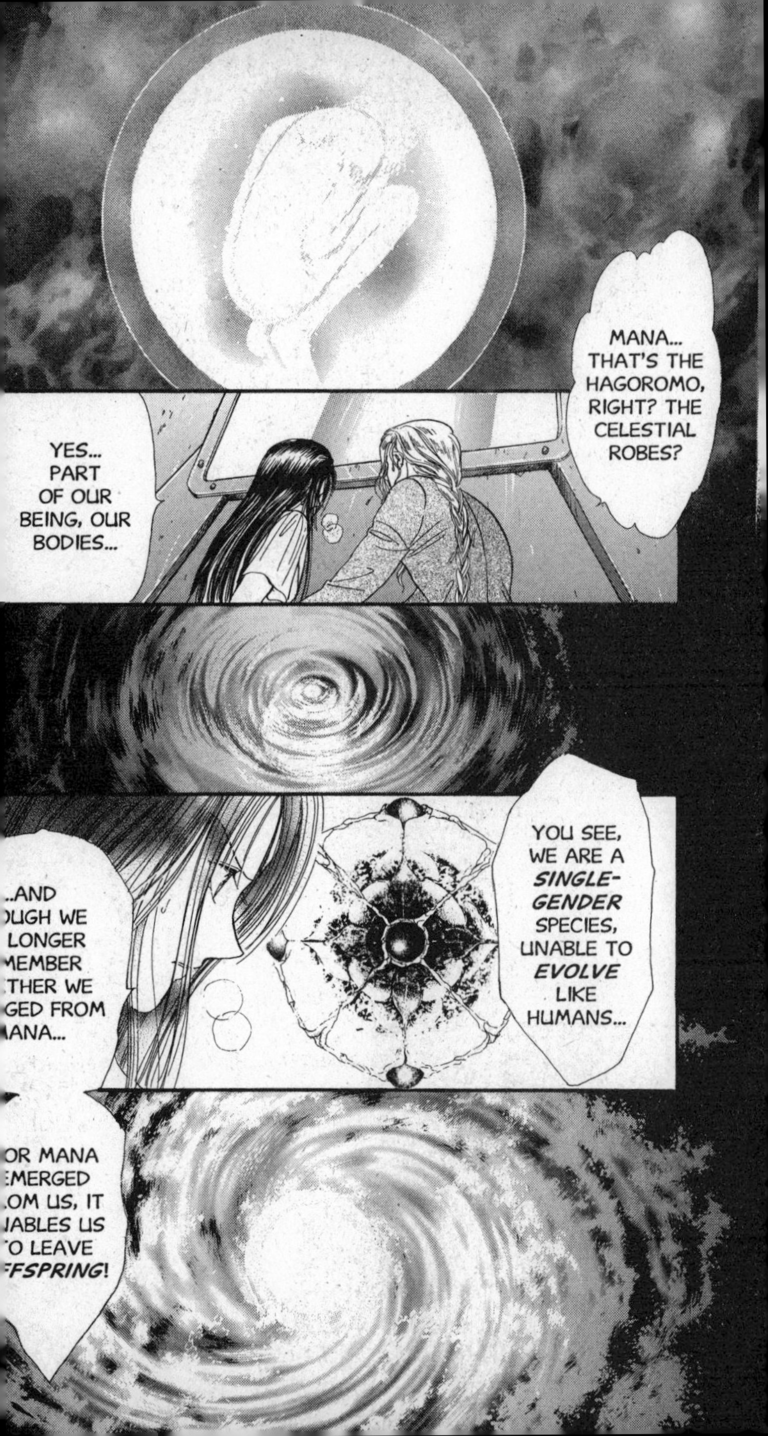
MANA... THAT'S THE HAGOROMO, RIGHT? THE CELESTIAL ROBES?
YES... PART OF OUR BEING, OUR BODIES...
YOU SEE, WE ARE A SINGLE-GENDER SPECIES, UNABLE TO EVOLVE LIKE HUMANS...
...AND OUGH WE LONGER MEMBER THER WE GED FROM ANA...
OR MANA EMERGED OM US, IT NABLES US TO LEAVE FFSPRING!

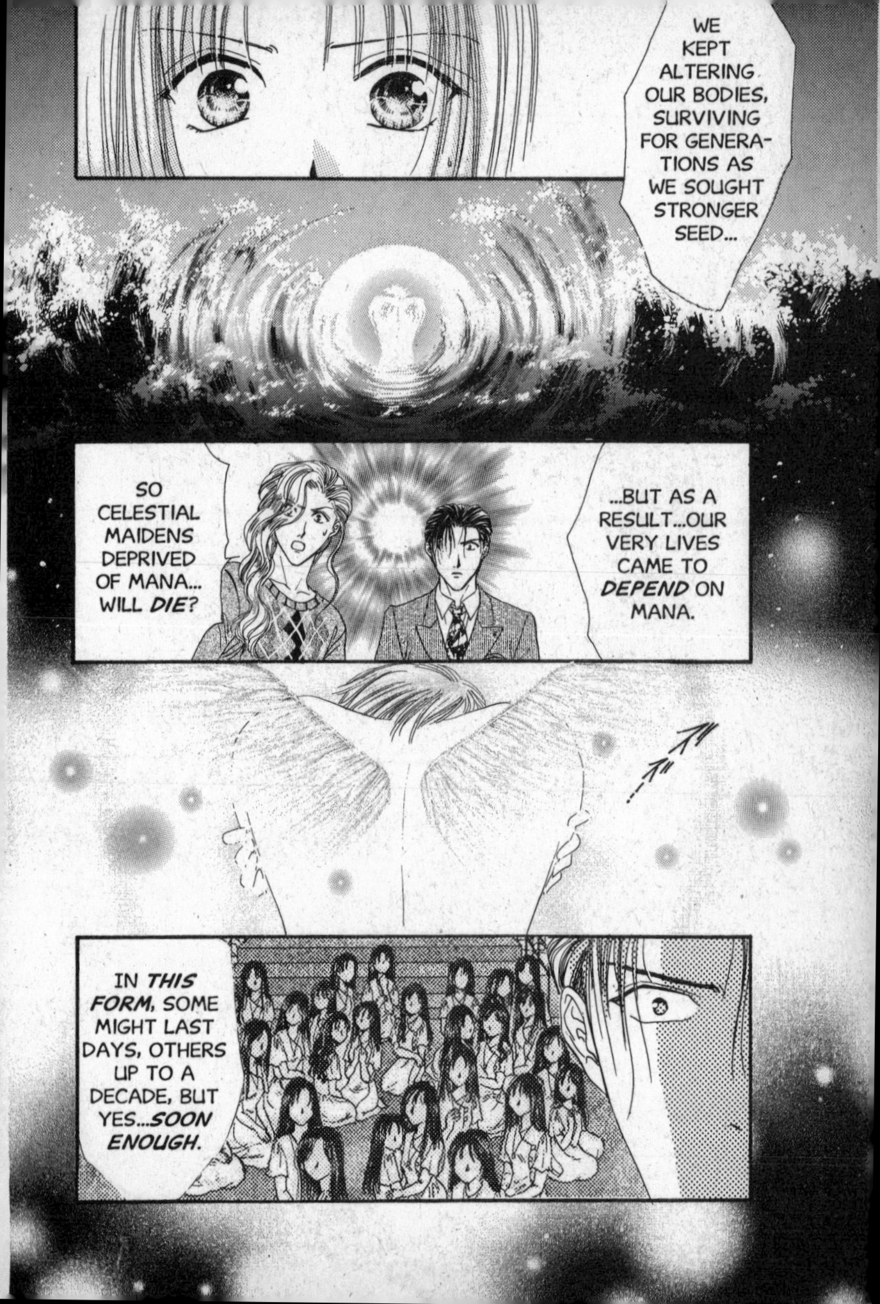
WE KEPT ALTERING OUR BODIES, SURVIVING FOR GENERATIONS AS WE SOUGHT STRONGER SEED...
...BUT AS A RESULT...OUR VERY LIVES CAME TO *DEPEND* ON MANA.
SO CELESTIAL MAIDENS DEPRIVED OF MANA... WILL *DIE*?
IN *THIS FORM*, SOME MIGHT LAST DAYS, OTHERS UP TO A DECADE, BUT YES...*SOON ENOUGH*.

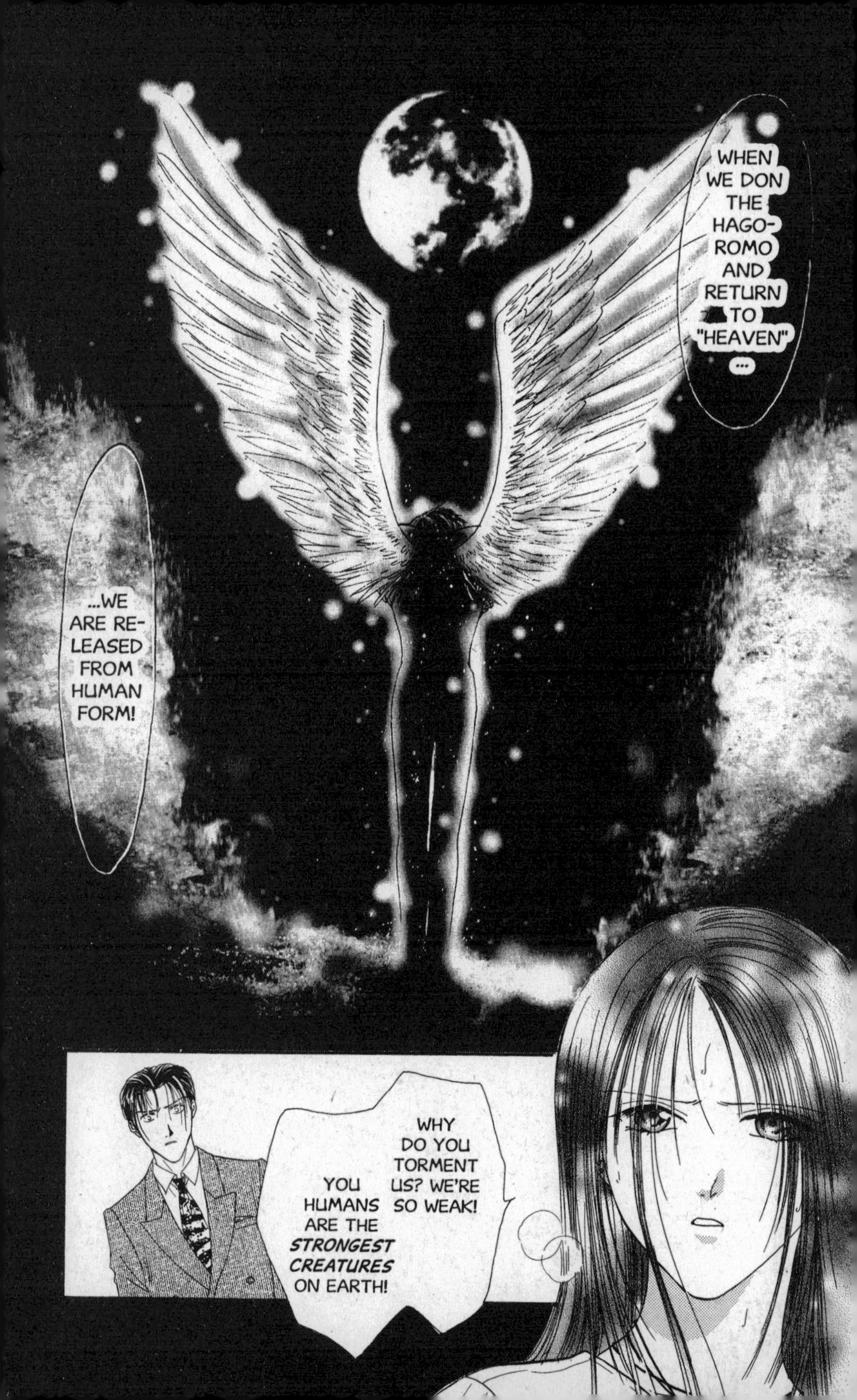
WHEN WE DON THE HAGO-ROMO AND RETURN TO "HEAVEN"...
...WE ARE RE-LEASED FROM HUMAN FORM!
WHY DO YOU TORMENT US? WE'RE SO WEAK!
YOU HUMANS ARE THE *STRONGEST CREATURES* ON EARTH!

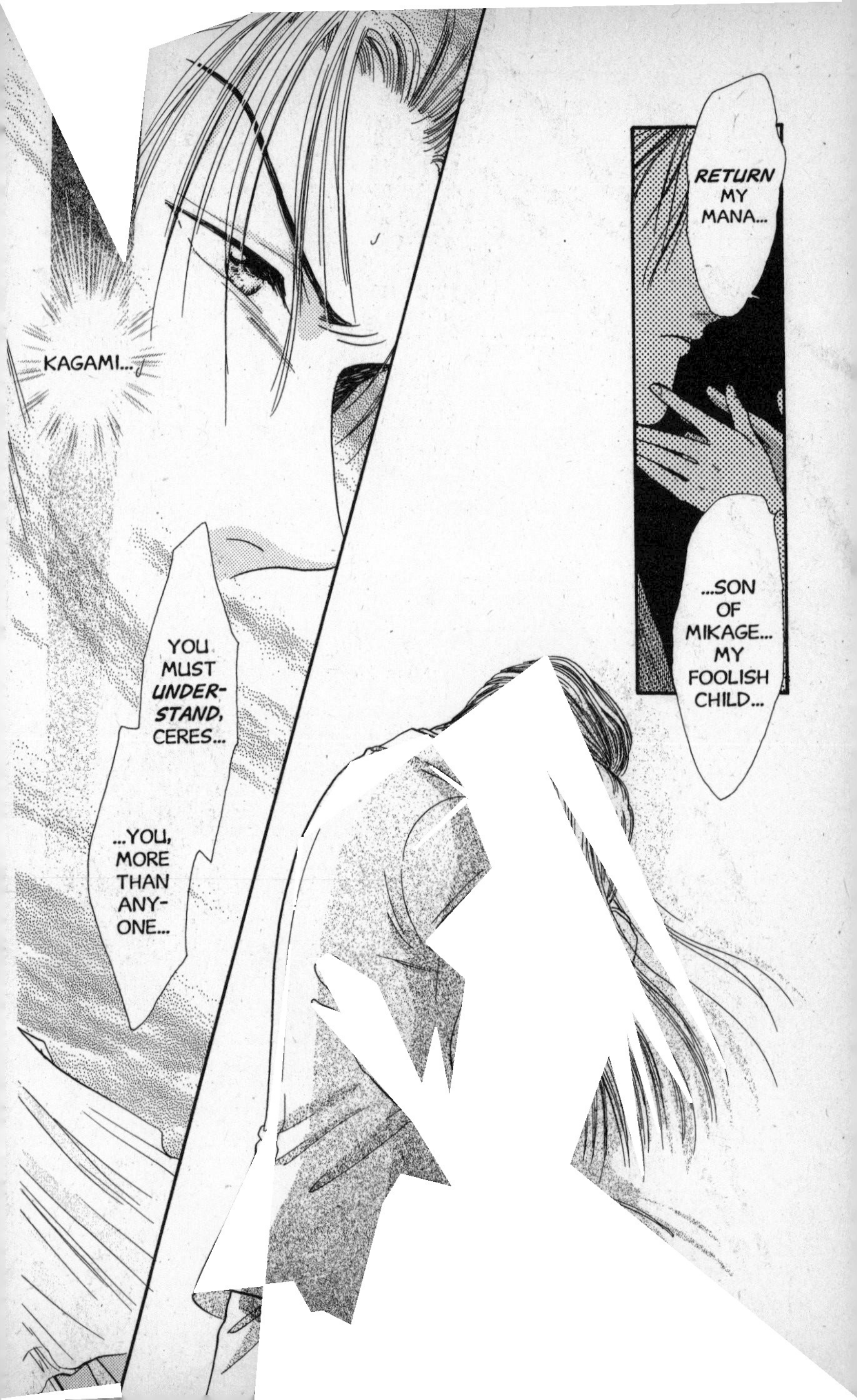
RETURN MY MANA...
...SON OF MIKAGE... MY FOOLISH CHILD...
KAGAMI...
YOU MUST UNDERSTAND, CERES...
...YOU, MORE THAN ANYONE...

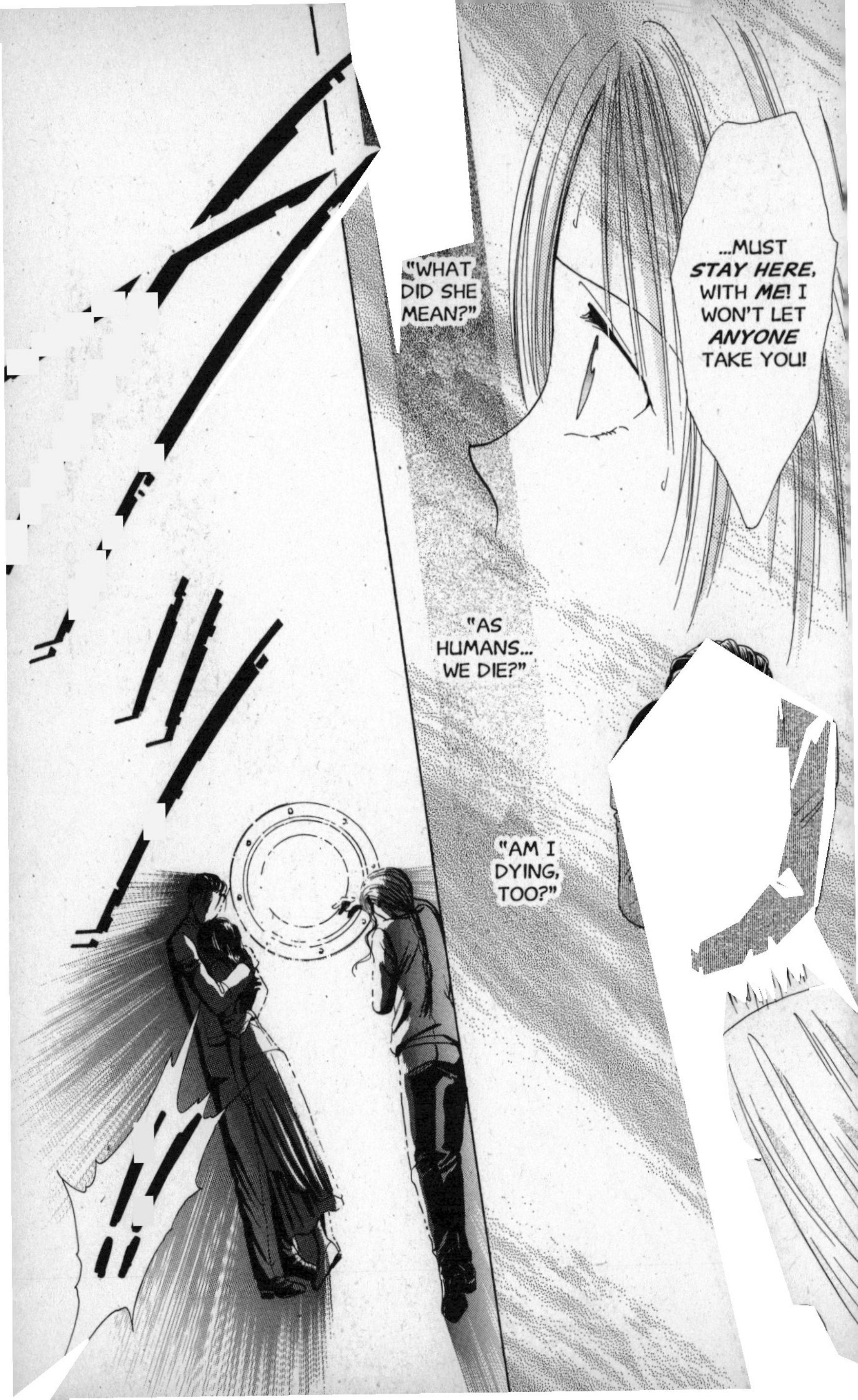
...MUST STAY HERE, WITH ME! I WON'T LET ANYONE TAKE YOU!
"WHAT DID SHE MEAN?"
"AS HUMANS... WE DIE?"
"AM I DYING, TOO?"

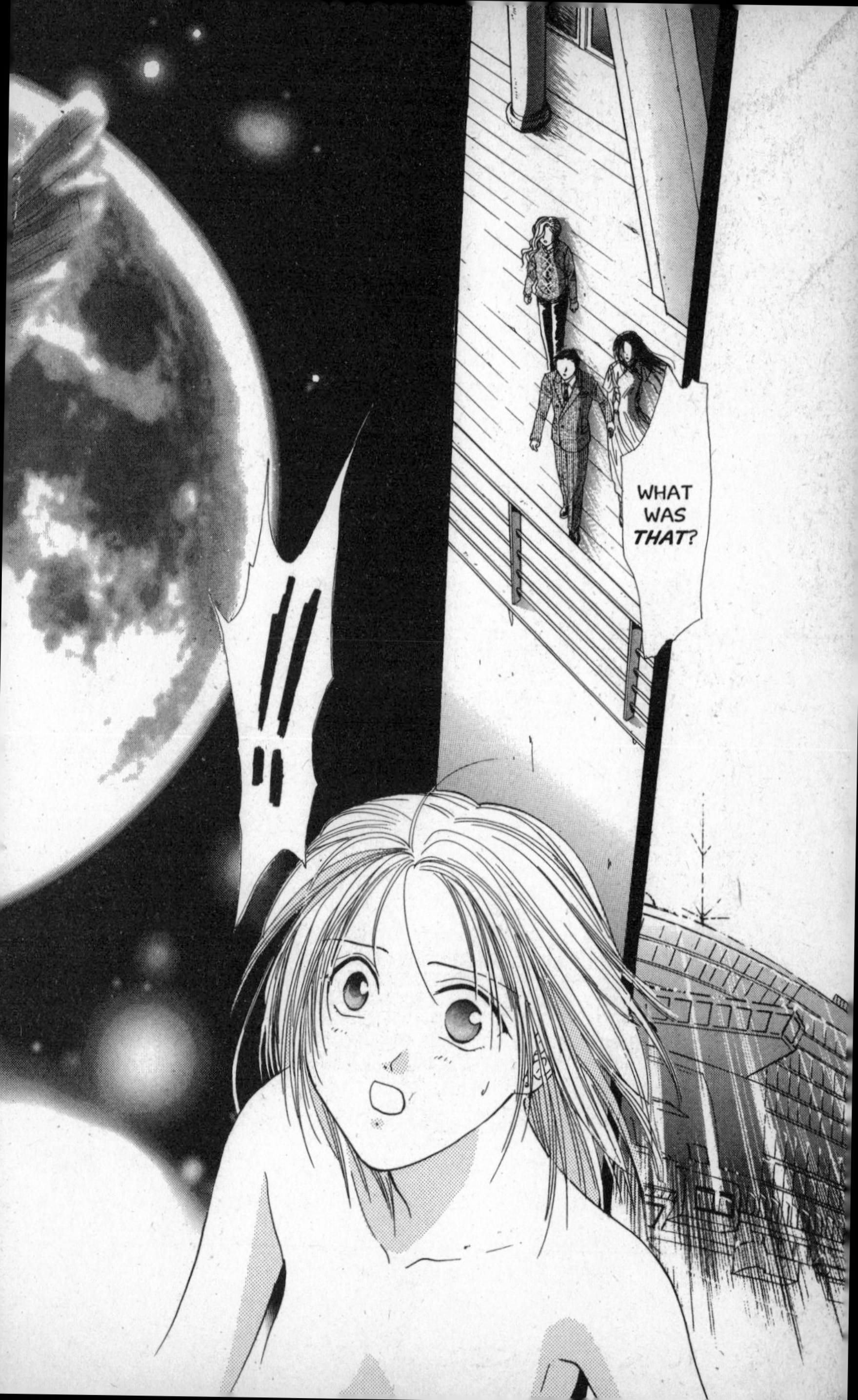
WHAT WAS THAT?
!!

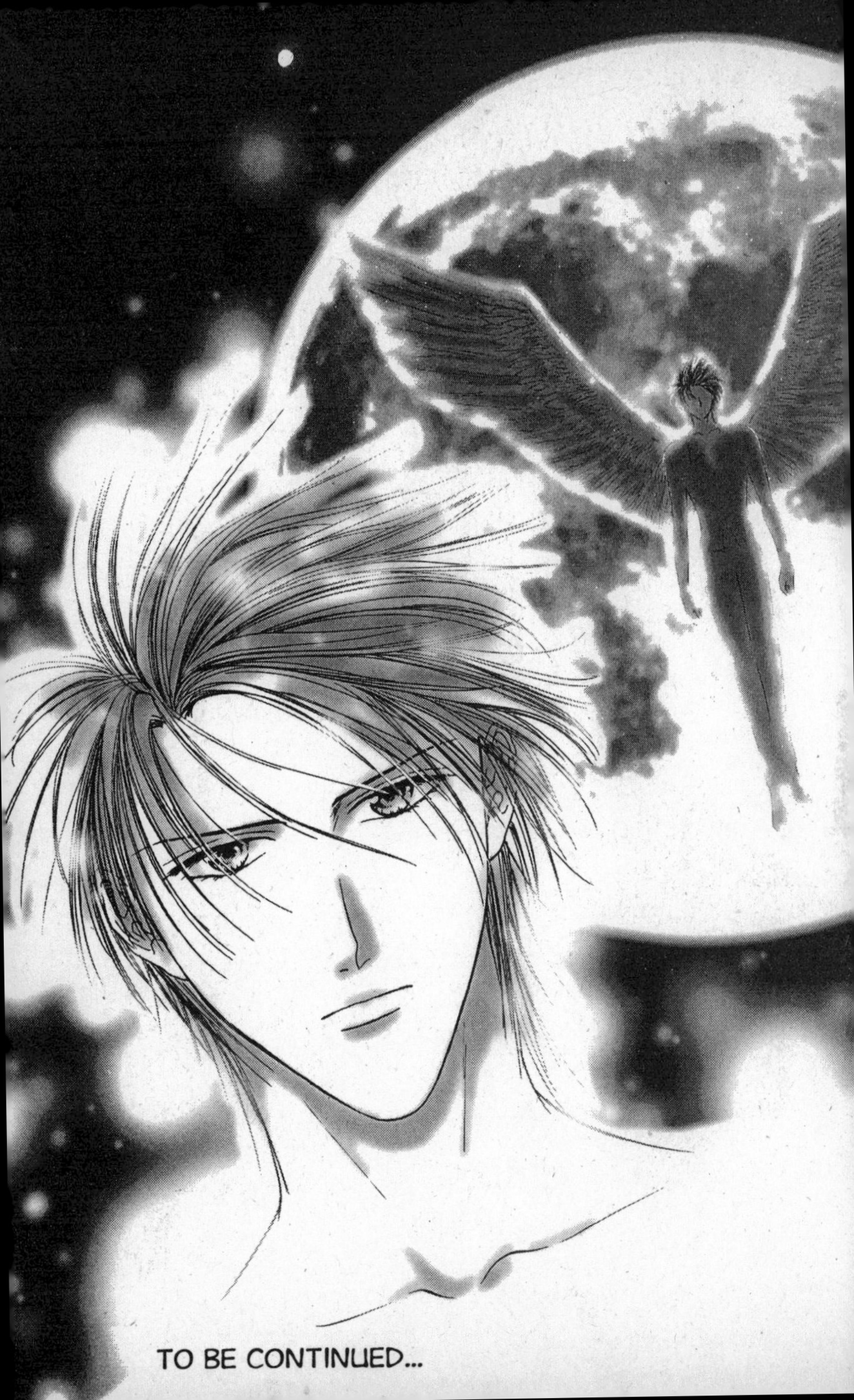
TO BE CONTINUED...

The CERES Guide to Sound Effects

We've left most of the sound effects in CERES as Yuu Watase originally created them—in Japanese. VIZ has created this glossary to help you decipher, page-by-page and panel-by-panel, what all those foreign words and background noises mean. Use this guide to impress your friends with your new Japanese vocabulary. The glossary lists the page number then panel. For example, 3.1 indicates page 3, panel 1.

38.1　FX: KA [tk]
41.4　FX: GU [yank]
42.2　FX: DOKA [wham]
42.3　FX: ZURU [slump]
43.2　FX: KAA [foom]
43.3　FX: KA [flash]
44.3　FX: GARI [scratch]
44.6　FX: BI [rrip]
47.4　FX: HA [aha!]
52.1　FX: PIKU [!]
54.1　FX: KA [glare]
54.3　FX: HA [aha!]
54.5　FX: DO [thunk]
55.4　FX: PAN [blam]
57.2　FX: FURA [wobble]
57.3　FX: ZURU [slump]
58.4　FX: ZURU [slip]
59.1　FX: SU [fwish]
59.2　FX: KA [tk]
64.3　FX: SUU [fft]
64.5　FX: ZA [sloosh]
65.1　FX: ZAAN [sloosh]
68.2　FX: BASHA [splash]
68.5　FX: DOSU [stab]
69.2　FX: GUI [tug]
70.3　FX: PASA [fwap]
71.1　FX: SU [fft]
71.3　FX: DOKIN [gasp]
75.1　FX: DOKIN [b-bmp]

10.2　FX: CHIRA [glance]
10.2　FX: JIRO [glare]
10.4　FX: SU [fft- fading]
11.2　FX: HA [aha!]
12.1　FX: KA [flash]
14.3　FX: BASHU [psht]
14.5　FX: ZURU [slump]
14.6　FX: BA [vash]
15.5　FX: FU [fft]
16.2　FX: DOSA [thud]
16.5　FX: KU [heh]
19.1　FX: HA [aha!]
20.2　FX: HA [aha!]
20.3　FX: GYU [clench]
22.1　FX: HA [aha!]
25.2　FX: NIKO [grin]
27.2　FX: GU [clench]
27.5　FX: GAKUN [slump]
27.6　FX: ZAWA ZAWA [murmur]
29.1　FX: GIRIRI [choke]
29.2　FX: PIKU [twitch]
30.3　FX: GICHI [chk]
31.4　FX: KURA [wobble]
32.1　FX: DO [thunk]
32.2　FX: BAN [slam]
32.3　FX: ZURU [slump]
33.1　FX: DOSA [thud]
37.1　FX: BAN [slam]
37.2　FX: GIRI [clench]

108.3 FX: BUHA [koff]
108.4 FX: BA [fwip]
113.1 FX: ZA [rustle]
113.2 FX: SUU [fft]
114.1 FX: ZAZA ZAZA [shfff]
116.1 FX: GATA [scoot]
116.2 FX: KURA [faint]
117.2 FX: PITA [pause]
117.4 FX: KA [tk]
119.1 FX: SUU [fft]
120.3 FX: YORO [stagger]
121.3 FX: SU [fsh]
124.1 FX: NIKO [grin]
124.2 FX: HA [!]
125.6 FX: FUWA [hug]
126.2 FX: SU [fwish]
130.4 FX: BA [leap]
131.1 FX: NYU [pop]
134.1 FX: KON KON [knock knock]
134.4 FX: KA KA KA KA [tk tk tk tk- steps]
135.4 FX: YORO [stagger]
136.1 FX: FU [fft]

77.2 FX: GA [whack]
78.3 FX: SU [fft]
79.2 FX: KA KA [tk tk]
79.4 FX: KA [tk]
80.3 FX: KA [flash]
81.3 FX: ZA [shk]
85.1 FX: PAN [slap]
88.4 FX: BASHI [slap]
89.1 FX: GA [whack]
89.2 FX: ZURU [slump]
90.3 FX: BA [slash]
97.2 FX: BAN [slam]
98.2 FX: PI [clik]
99.1 FX: KOKU [nod]
99.4 FX: FU [fft]
100.3 FX: GA [bash]
105.2 FX: ZURU [slump]
107.3 FX: KURA [faint]
107.4 FX: DON [bump]
107.4 FX: YORO [stagger]
108.1 FX: ZURU [slump]
108.2 FX: BURU BURU BURU [tremble tremble]

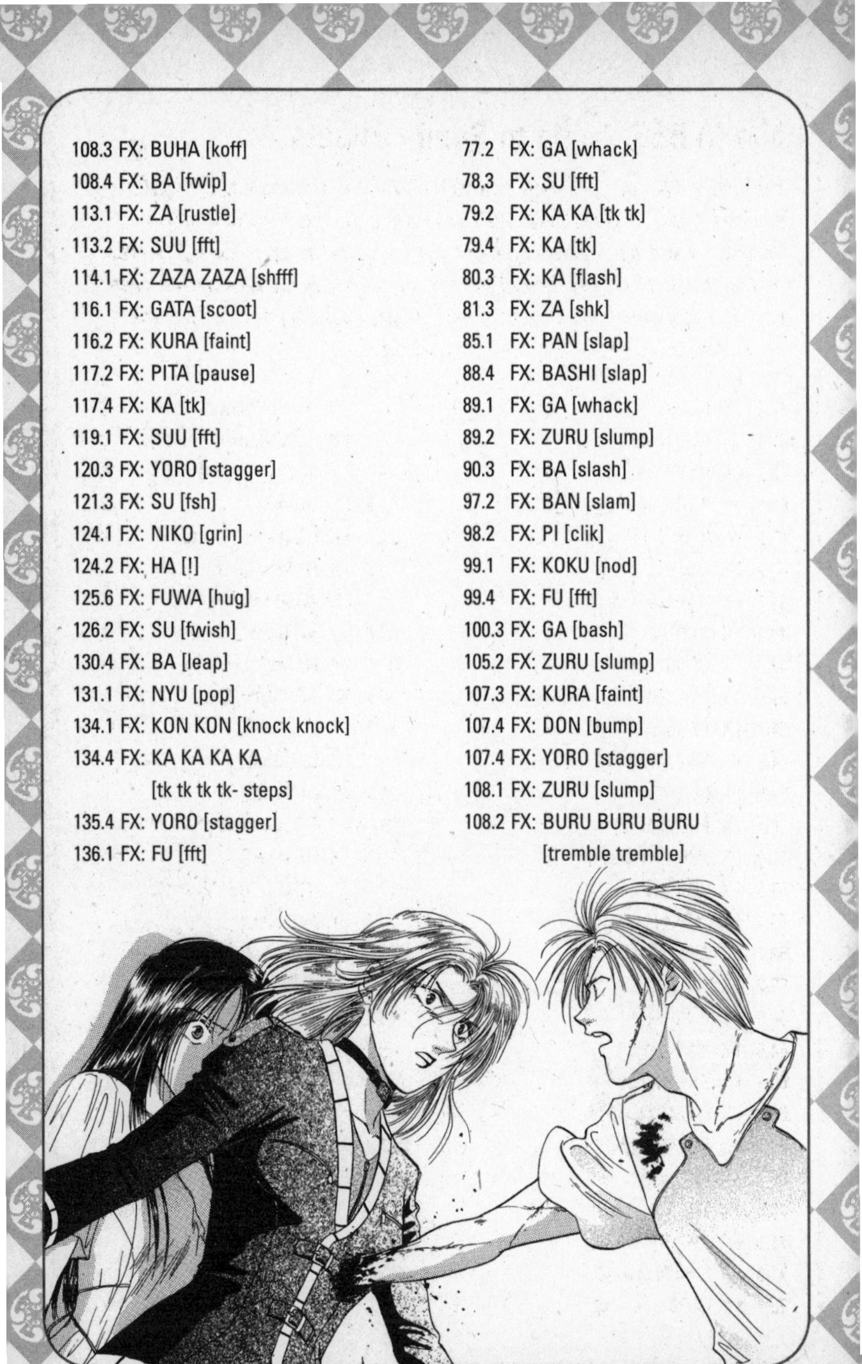

137.3 FX: FU [fft]
137.3 FX: DOKA [pow]
137.4 FX: KISHI [creak]
138.3 FX: KA KA [tk tk]
140.1 FX: WAA [raah]
141.2 FX: GYU [clutch]
142.2 FX: FURA [wobble]
145.1 FX: ZAWA [whoa!]
145.3 FX: ZAWA ZAWA ZAWA ZAWA [buzz buzz buzz buzz]
146.1 FX: SHIN [...]
146.6 FX: WAA [yeah!]
147.3 FX: SAA [hair flowing]
147.4 FX: HA [!]
149.3 FX: GATA GATA [shake shake]
149.4 FX: KATA KATA KATA GATA GATA [shake shake shudder shudder]
149.5 FX: GATA GATA GATA GATA GATA GATA [shudder shudder]
150.2 FX: ZA [zzt]
150.3 FX: PA [blip]
151.2 FX: ZUZUZU [rumble]
152.1 FX: PISHI [crack]
153.4 FX: GAKU [slump]
153.5 FX: SU [fft]
155.3 FX: ZUZUZU [rumble]
155.3 FX: PASHI [crack]
156.1 FX: BAN [smash]
156.3 FX: YORO [wobble]
156.4 FX: GAKU [slump]
156.5 FX: HA [!]
157.3 FX: FU [blink]
158.3 FX: SHIN [...]
158.4 FX: ZURU [slump]
159.2 FX: YORO [stagger]
161.3 FX: SUU [fft]
162.2 FX: YORO [wobble]
163.1 FX: DOKA DOKA [bash bash]
163.3 FX: KA KA [tk tk]
164.1 FX: KA KA [tk tk]
164.2 FX: KA KA [tk tk]

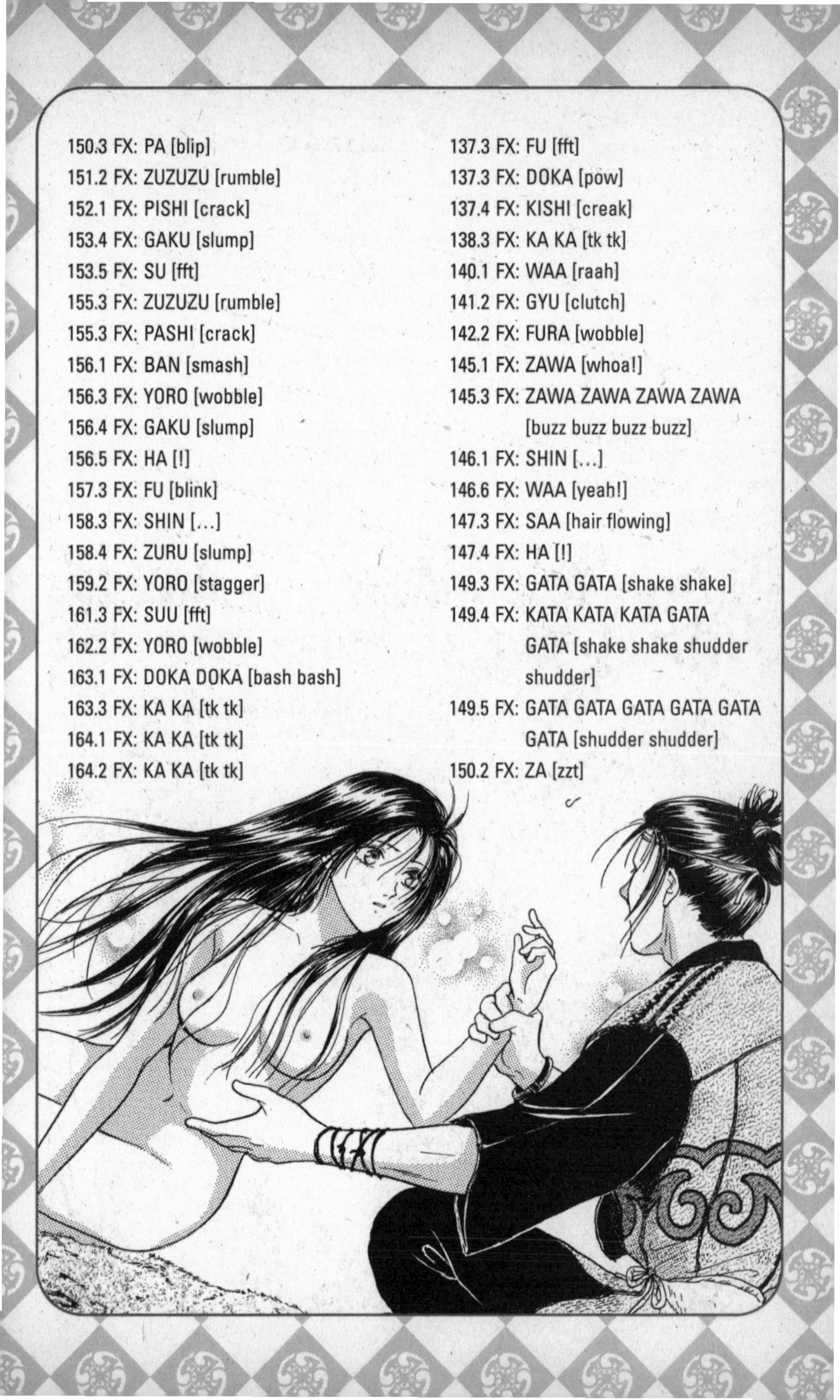

164.3 FX: KA [tk]
164.4 FX: KA [tk]
166.3 FX: BAN [slam]
168.2 FX: GU [clench]
172.1 FX: BA [slam]
172.3 FX: SHIN [...]
172.4 FX: GOSO [rustle]
173.2 FX: BAN [smash]
174.5 FX: GU [twist]
175.1 FX: CHA [chk]
175.2 FX: PATAN [chud]
175.3 FX: BAN [slam]
176.1 FX: BA [leap]
176.3 FX: BAN [blam]
177.1 FX: BARA BARA BARA [whud whud whud]
180.4 FX: BARA BARA BARA [whud whud whud]
181.3 FX: HA [!]
181.4 FX: CHA [chk]
182.3 FX: POSU [whump]
184.3 FX: ZAZAAN [sloosh]
186.1 FX: PISHI [crack]
186.2 FX: ZURU [slump]
188.4 FX: ZUZU [shoom]
191.5 FX: KA [flash]

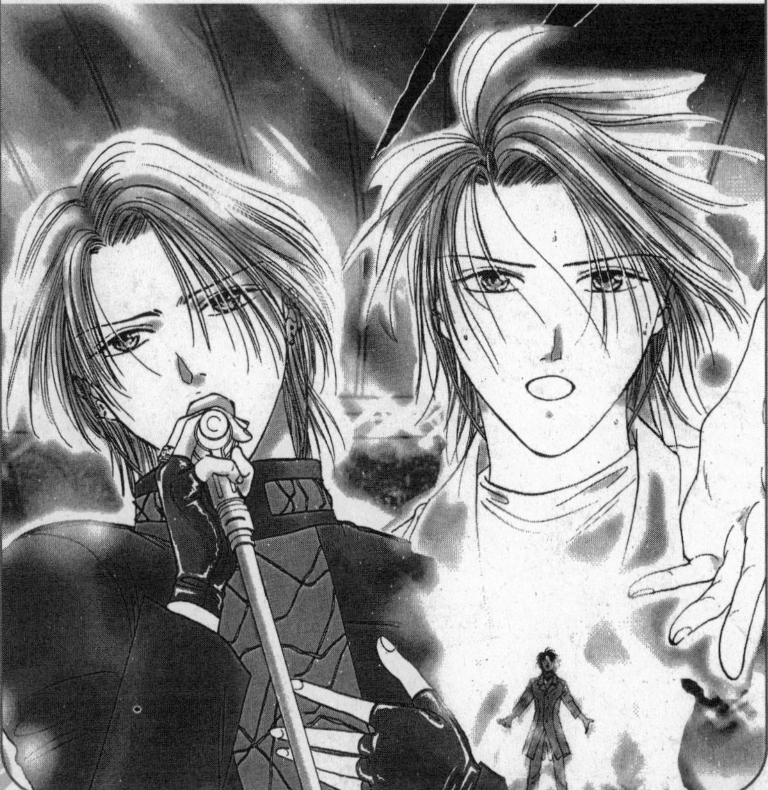

Yuu Watase was born on March 5 in a town
near Osaka, Japan, and was raised there
before moving to Tokyo to follow her dream
of creating manga. In the decade since her
debut short story, *Pajama De Ojama* ("An
Intrusion in Pajamas"), she has produced
more than 50 compiled volumes of short
stories and continuing series. Her latest
work, *Zettai Kareshi* ("Absolute Boyfriend"),
recently completed its run in Japan in the
anthology magazine *Shôjo Comic.* Watase's
other beloved series *Ceres: Celestial Legend,*
Fushigi Yûgi, Imadoki! (Nowadays), and *Alice
19th* are now available in North America in
English editions published by VIZ Media.

LOVE SHOJO? LET US KNOW!

☐ Please do NOT send me information about VIZ Media products, news and events, special offers, or other information.

☐ Please do NOT send me information from VIZ' trusted business partners.

Name: _____

Address: _____

City:_____ State:_____ Zip:_____

E-mail: _____

☐ Male ☐ Female   Date of Birth (mm/dd/yyyy): ___/___/_____ (Under 13? Parental)
consent required

What race/ethnicity do you consider yourself? (check all that apply)

☐ White/Caucasian   ☐ Black/African American   ☐ Hispanic/Latino

☐ Asian/Pacific Islander   ☐ Native American/Alaskan Native ☐ Other: _____

What VIZ shojo title(s) did you purchase? (indicate title(s) purchased)

_____

What other shojo titles from other publishers do you own? _____

_____

Reason for purchase: (check all that apply)

☐ Special offer   ☐ Favorite title / author / artist / genre

☐ Gift   ☐ Recommendation   ☐ Collection

☐ Read excerpt in VIZ manga sampler   ☐ Other _____

Where did you make your purchase? (please check one)

☐ Comic store   ☐ Bookstore   ☐ Mass/Grocery Store

☐ Newsstand   ☐ Video/Video Game Store

☐ Online (site:_____) ☐ Other _____

How many shojo titles have you purchased in the last year? How many were VIZ shojo titles?
(please check one from each column)

SHOJO MANGA

☐ None
☐ 1 – 4
☐ 5 – 10
☐ 11+

VIZ SHOJO MANGA

☐ None
☐ 1 – 4
☐ 5 – 10
☐ 11+

What do you like most about shojo graphic novels? (check all that apply)

☐ Romance
☐ Comedy
☐ Other _____

☐ Drama / conflict
☐ Real-life storylines

☐ Fantasy
☐ Relatable characters

Do you purchase every volume of your favorite shojo series?

☐ Yes! Gotta have 'em as my own
☐ No. Please explain: _____

Who are your favorite shojo authors / artists? _____

_____

What shojo titles would like you translated and sold in English? _____

_____

THANK YOU! Please send the completed form to:

NJW Research
ATTN: VIZ Media Shojo Survey
42 Catharine Street
Poughkeepsie, NY 12601